MW01484239

The Sun
Rising

The Sun Rising

King James I
and the Dawn of a
Global Britian, 1603–1625

ANNA WHITELOCK

VIKING

VIKING
An imprint of Penguin Random House LLC
1745 Broadway, New York, NY 10019
penguinrandomhouse.com

VIKING is a registered trademark of Penguin Random House LLC.

Maps by Michael Athanson, 2025.

Image credits may be found on p. 431.

LIBRARY OF CONGRESS CONTROL NUMBER: 2025039142
ISBN: 9780525429548 (hardcover)
ISBN: 9780698405752 (ebook)

First published in hardcover in Great Britain by Bloomsbury Publishing Plc, London, in 2025.

First United States edition published by Viking, 2025.

Printed in the United States of America
1st Printing

The authorized representative in the EU for product safety
and compliance is Penguin Random House Ireland, Morrison Chambers,
32 Nassau Street, Dublin D02 YH68, Ireland, https://eu-contact.penguin.ie.

For Rebecca Edwards Newman

It is not our conquest, but our commerce; it is not our
swords but our sails that first spread the English name
… over and about the world; it is the traffic of their
merchants, and the boundless desires of that nation to
eternise the English honour and name, that have induced
them to sail, and seek into all the corners of the earth.

Lewes Roberts, Treasure of Traffic[1]

Schools of the Prophets [were] newly adorned,
manufactures at home daily invented, Trading abroad
exceedingly multiplies, the Borders of Scotland peaceably
governed, the North of Ireland religiously planted,
the Navy Royal magnificently furnished, Virginia,
Newfoundland and New England peopled, the East India
well traded, Persia, China and the Mogor visited, lastly, all
the ports of Europe, Afrique, Asia and America to our red
crosses freed and opened. And they are all the Actions and
true born Children of King James his Peace.

Bishop Williams on King James VI/I,
Westminster Abbey, 7 May 1625[2]

CONTENTS

CONTENTS

AUTHOR'S NOTE

All dates have been modernised to reflect the new year changing in January rather than in March. All quotations are in modern English spelling for ease of reading. For monetary value in today's currency, rough estimates have been made using the Bank of England Inflation calculator.

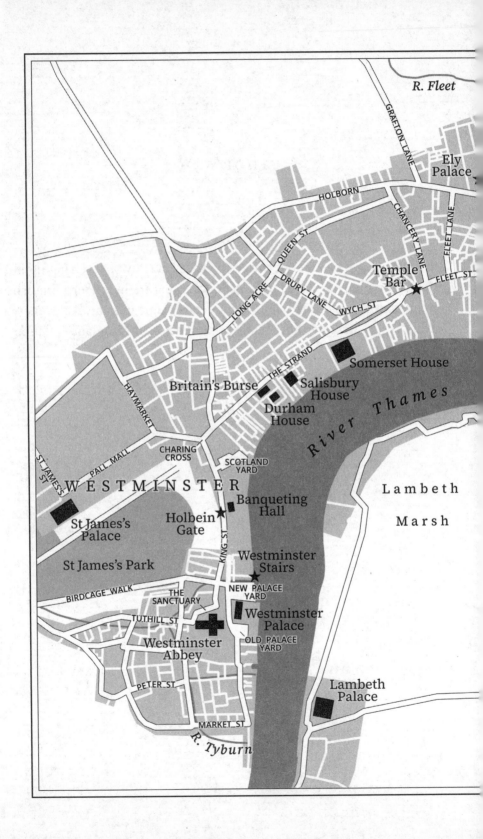

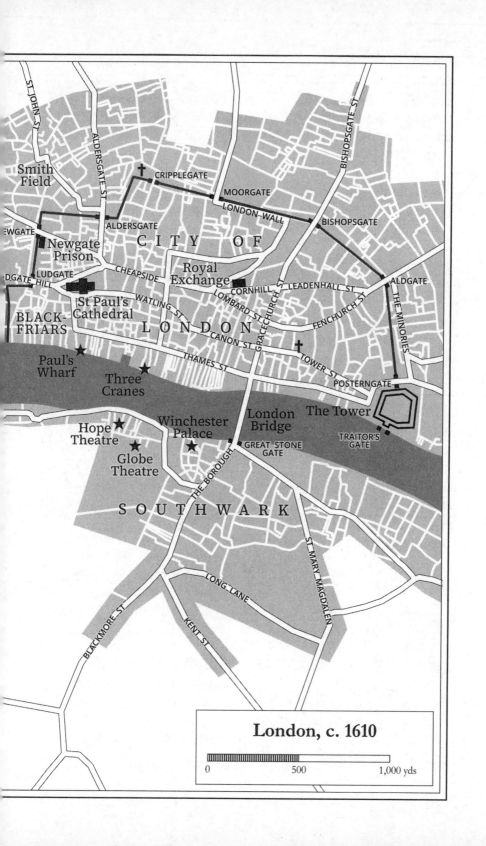

London, c. 1610

0   500   1,000 yds

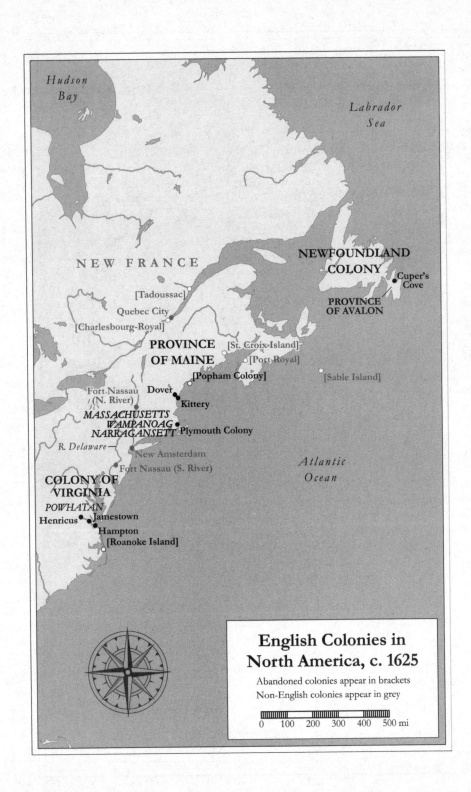

Hudson
Bay

Labrador
Sea

NEW FRANCE

NEWFOUNDLAND
COLONY
Cuper's
Cove

PROVINCE
OF AVALON

[Tadoussac]
Quebec City
[Charlesbourg-Royal]

PROVINCE
OF MAINE   [St. Croix Island]
            [Port Royal]
        [Popham Colony]

Fort Nassau   Dover
(N. River)
                Kittery
MASSACHUSETTS
WAMPANOAG
NARRAGANSETT   Plymouth Colony

R. Delaware—
            New Amsterdam
        Fort Nassau (S. River)
COLONY OF
VIRGINIA
POWHATAN
Henricus   Jamestown
            Hampton
        [Roanoke Island]

[Sable Island]

Atlantic
Ocean

English Colonies in
North America, c. 1625

Abandoned colonies appear in brackets
Non-English colonies appear in grey

0   100   200   300   400   500 mi

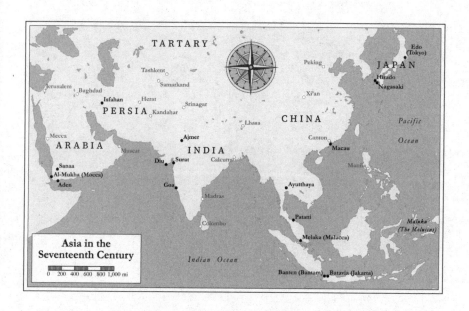

Asia in the Seventeenth Century

TARTARY

Tashkent
Samarkand
Jerusalem Baghdad
Isfahan Herat
PERSIA Kandahar Srinagar
Lhasa

Mecca
ARABIA Muscat
Ajmer
INDIA
Diu Surat Calcutta
Sanaa
Al-Mukha (Mocca)
Aden
Goa
Madras
Colombo

Peking
Xi'an
CHINA
Canton
Macau
JAPAN
Edo (Tokyo)
Hirado
Nagasaki
Pacific Ocean

Manila
Ayutthaya
Patani
Melaka (Malacca)
Maluku (The Moluccas)

Indian Ocean
Banten (Bantam) Batavia (Jakarta)

0 200 400 600 800 1,000 mi

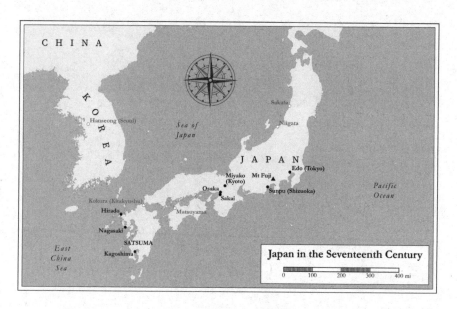

Japan in the Seventeenth Century

CHINA
KOREA
Hanseong (Seoul)
Sea of Japan
Sakata
Niigata
JAPAN
Miyako (Kyoto) Mt Fuji Edo (Tokyo)
Osaka Sunpu (Shizuoka)
Sakai
Kokura (Kitakyushu) Matsuyama
Hirado
Nagasaki
SATSUMA
Kagoshima
East China Sea
Pacific Ocean

0 100 200 300 400 mi

Introduction

In the summer of 1603, trading ships belonging to the London-based East India Company returned home after a successful maiden voyage to the East. After two and a half years away, they dropped anchor off the Kent coast fully laden with a valuable cargo of pepper, cloves, nutmeg and other much-prized spices.[1]

The fleet sailed under the command of experienced merchant and newly appointed East India Company director Captain James Lancaster, who had served under Sir Francis Drake against the Armada. Lancaster's flagship, the *Red Dragon*, had formerly been called the *Scourge of Malice*, a 700-foot privateering vessel with a crew of 200 which had harried Spanish ships in the West Indies. Six months after leaving Woolwich on 13 February 1601, the *Red Dragon*, and the *Hector, Susan, Ascension and Guest*, a small supply vessel, had reached the Cape of Good Hope and then sailed across the Indian Ocean to Aceh, a vibrant commercial port on the Indonesian island of Sumatra. Here the East India Company (or the Company of Merchants of London Trading into the East Indies, as it as it was then known) secured rights to trade. The *Ascension*, loaded with pepper and spices, returned to England, while Lancaster and the rest of his fleet made for the northwest coast of Java in Indonesia, and the port of Bantam – an important market, where Arab, Turkish, Indonesian, Indian, Chinese, Japanese and European merchants already traded. Two years later, these ships also returned home, carrying, besides a huge supply of pepper, silks, indigo and mace.

The death of Elizabeth I in 1603, signalling the end of the Tudor dynasty, was a denouement long feared by the English. The queen had failed to marry, produce an heir, or indeed acknowledge an heir or successor. The accession to the English throne of James VI of Scotland – a practised king, a 'foreigner' with a European wife, and children – heralded the arrival of a new dynasty, the Stuarts, and with it a new composite monarchy of England, Scotland, Ireland and the principality of Wales. It was the dawning of a new era.

James I's reign has long been overshadowed in the popular imagination by that of Queen Elizabeth I, and by the fatal nadir of the reign of Charles I – but James's monarchy was a time of huge significance, culturally and politically, and particularly in terms of travel and trade within and beyond his territories. The first decades of the seventeenth century were seminal in the making of modern Britain, with debates about nationhood and identity, about inherited fictions of Britain and Britishness, and a notion of Britain that served English interests. It saw the establishment of the principle of 'birthright citizenship', the creation of a common currency, and a British flag (the Union Jack), uniting the flags of England and Scotland (though not Ireland). For the first time ambassadors represented 'the King of Great Britain' to other nations; Britain began to establish colonies and forge relations and reputations abroad.

It was, however, an uneasy inheritance. The country had been living beyond its means for decades. The glory days of the Spanish Armada had long since faded; costly wars with Spain and in Ireland continued, as did demands for parliamentary subsidies, and forced loans. Years of conflict had also severely impacted trade, and this, together with harvest failures and unseasonal weather, had forced prices ever upwards, adding to the growing problems of poverty, vagrancy and social unrest in towns and countryside. The cost of the wars with Spain and in Ireland had brought the Exchequer close to bankruptcy. Elizabeth raised income through loans and by selling crown lands and monopolies, but this failed to match the rising cost of government. By the start of the new century there was little room for manoeuvre. With landowners reluctant to pay higher taxes, the Crown was becoming ever more dependent on taxes on trade – customs dues – and loans from City of London merchants and financiers. As Sir Robert Cecil, the queen's principal secretary, wrote in 1601: 'all the receipts are so short of the issue, as my hairs stand upright to think of it'.[2] At her death, Elizabeth would leave debts of close to £400,000, the equivalent of about a year's peacetime revenue.

England was also playing catch up internationally. Despite the efforts of Elizabethan adventurers such Sir Francis Drake, Sir Walter Ralegh and Richard Hakluyt, it had no colonial possessions, and had failed to discover sources of wealth, such as South American silver or Asian spices that swelled the coffers in Spain and Portugal and which latterly had sparked the rapid commercial growth of the Dutch. The English lagged behind the Spanish and Portuguese in the race to colonise what was referred to as the 'New World'. The queen had sponsored attempts to establish settlements at Baffin Island (off the coast of present-day Canada), Newfoundland, and most famously, Roanoke Island in North Carolina's Outer Banks, but all three ventures had been unsuccessful. Since the discovery of an ocean trading route to India around the Cape of Good Hope in 1498 by Portuguese explorer Vasco da Gama, the Portuguese had begun building what would be a long-lasting colonial empire in Asia and Africa. In 1580, King Philip II of Spain seized the Portuguese Crown and all its dominions, to form a powerful Iberian power. The Spanish Habsburg monarchy posed an ever-great threat to England, France and the newly independent Dutch Republic, officially named 'the United Provinces of the Netherlands' which had thrown off Spanish rule in 1579.

Trade between Asia and Europe became central to European commercial rivalries, as the demand for Eastern spices, silks and other luxuries continued to grow. For centuries goods from the East had been brought to Europe along overland trade routes – 'the silk road' – dominated by the Ottoman Empire. The opening of a sea route via the Cape of Good Hope allowed the Portuguese to establish direct access and a trading monopoly in Eastern markets. By the time of James I's accession, the Dutch and English were determined to access the profitable trade in the East for themselves.

London became the hub of 'Britain's' global ambition. The capital's merchants dominated England's overseas commerce, particularly through the development of London-based trading companies – not least the East India Company and Virginia Company, which had monopolies granted by the Crown. The trading companies located their dockyards and warehouses along the River Thames and conducted their business in the Royal Exchange – and later the New Exchange – in the heart of the City of London, and in the opulent homes of their richest members, the capital's emerging new elites. In return, the chartered companies could be tapped for loans, providing the king with a source of revenue without recourse to Parliament.

London also became, in playwright Ben Jonson's words, 'the Staple of News'. The main nave of St Paul's Cathedral known as Paul's Walk became a hub for the exchange of news and rumour. In the churchyard outside, at St Paul's Cross – 'the pulpit of the nation' – weekly sermons and royal proclamations were delivered and then disseminated in print.[3] James's reign saw the publication of the first newspapers – *corantos*, or broadsheets – reporting news from continental Europe, not least the war that centred on James's son-in-law, Frederick V of the Palatinate. Bookshops too proliferated around St Paul's Cross, and London theatres at the Globe and Blackfriars regularly staged plays reflecting the politics of the time.

London developed into a truly international port, with ships bound for the East Indies, colonies in North America, Russia, Persia (modern-day Iran), the Levant (far Eastern Mediterranean) and North Africa, and to bases from the Red Sea to India, China and Japan. Valuable cargoes of spices (nutmeg, cloves, cinnamon, pepper), perfumes, silks, and aromatic woods arrived in London to meet a growing consumer demand for luxury goods. With England's exports still dominated by heavy woollen cloth ('broad-cloth') which was largely unwanted in the East, ships would set sail from the Thames loaded with the silver bullion needed to buy Asian goods (the cost of which had to be covered by the cargo brought back to be resold in Europe for a profit). London warehouses held goods ready for merchants to ship to Russia, Antwerp, Italy and the Levant. The Crown, English trading companies, commerce and diplomacy, would steadily become more intertwined, with each impacting the other for good or for ill. As King James would later acknowledge: 'my customs are the best Part of My Revenue, and in Effect, the Substance of all I have to live on'.[4] In just a few decades, trade would change the nation's place in the world and help create a path for a new global Britain.

Following James's successful brokering of peace with Spain, men, and women too in increasing numbers, began to travel from Britain, and settle abroad. This growing engagement with the wider world was evidenced by the publication of travel accounts and journals and guides to foreign countries.[5] Indeed, English men and women, young and old, rich and poor, would prove more prepared to travel to America than other Europeans, while many Scottish and Irish settled on the continent. Some were fleeing persecution or poverty, others wanted to explore, to trade and build new lives. James's sub-jects were to become some of the most well-travelled people of the age, with their interests and religious loyalties ever more aligned with Protestants in Europe.

With the union of the English and Scottish crowns brought by James's accession, Britain could become one of the most powerful Protestant kingdoms in Europe, with the potential to counterbal-ance the Catholic kingdoms of Spain and France. For more than half a century, the European continent had been riven by religious con-flict and a struggle for dominance between France and the Habsburg powers in Spain and Austria, and between Spain and the northern provinces of the Netherlands. Though France and Spain had made peace in 1598, the war between the Dutch and Spanish continued, as did the Anglo–Spanish conflict which stretched back to the Armada. Europe seemed ready at any moment to be ignited in another conflict, given the papacy's claims to temporal supremacy.

By not responding to calls to intervene militarily in Europe to defend Protestantism and defeat 'the papal Antichrist', James I was derided as weak and feckless. Much too was made of the contrast between James and his 'war-hungry' eldest son Prince Henry. Yet there is evidence that James was using his son's image, deliberately pushing it centre stage. Through a mixture of polemic and posturing, and a reliance on companies of volunteer soldiers serving in the pay of foreign states, James sought to increase the kingdom's leverage in European politics whilst avoiding engaging directly in wars.

Maximilien de Béthune, the Duke of Sully, famously described King James I as the 'wisest fool in Christendom', referring to the king's intellect and seeming naivety in matters of great significance. However, James could be pragmatic, shrewd, and adept. A highly educated man with extensive views on issues ranging from theology and political philosophy to witchcraft, from tobacco use to silkworm-farming, he showed guile during his reign in England, balancing principle with a pragmatism that was driven primarily by the Crown's chronic need for money. From his early years in Scotland, James had learned to wield intellectual arguments as tools to persuade, reassure and deliberately mislead, and these he would finesse as the 'King of Great Britain'. French ambassador the Marquis de Tillières's early assessment of Queen Elizabeth's successor summed him up perfectly: 'This king of artifices who dissimilates above all the rest of the world'.[6]

James sought to secure his reputation abroad and grow and defend his new realm. In doing so he sowed the seeds of Britain's future wealth, national ambition and identity abroad. These early advances were not won by foreign wars, although there was bloodshed and oppression – including towards native populations in Ireland and in

North America. Instead, James sought prosperity and power through trade, diplomacy, realpolitik and the reunion of Christendom. He believed in a 'true Christian Church' achieved through the reconciliation of Christians of all faiths – English Protestants, Lutherans, Calvinists, Roman Catholics and Greek Orthodox – which would in turn, he proposed, prevent conflicts between states. Principle and pragmatism, given the Crown's limited finances, meant James had little option but to style himself as Europe's peacemaker, adopting the personal motto 'Rex Pacificus', meaning 'King of Peace'.

This book is neither a biography of King James I nor a comprehensive account of his reign. Rather it is a reframing, a 'provocation' which seeks to move beyond traditional accounts, to place James in a global context, as a 'politician' who defied expectations to be a 'warrior' king, and in doing so laid the foundations for the future development of Britain; its identity, ambition and place in the world.

Part One

Sorrows Joy

Elizabeths dead, – that rends my heart in twine:
and James proclaimed, – this makes me well again.
Whilst April showers do teach us how to weep
The sun betwixt two watery clouds doth peep.

*Sorrowes Joy. Or, A lamentation for our late deceased
soveraigne Elizabeth, with a triumph for the prosperous succession of
our gratious King, James, &c.* (1603)[1]

In March 1603, Queen Elizabeth I lay dying at Richmond Palace, Surrey. She was nearing seventy, growing weaker every day, and suffering from rheumatism, insomnia, and melancholy. Just weeks before, she had had to have her coronation ring cut off because it had grown into her flesh.[2] All around were stark reminders of her physical decay, and of a long life and reign now coming to an end.

There was a growing sense of a nation in peril, with no certainty as to what, or whom, would come next. It was a fact which had, in different ways, dominated the reign. Despite sustained pressure to wed, Elizabeth had remained unmarried, and childless, and had consistently refused to name an heir. Despair, stagnation and political paralysis had taken root. Everyone was waiting for the end to come. 'The people longed for change,' said the future Bishop Godfrey Goodman, 'being very generally weary of an old woman's government.'[3]

Four years earlier, in response to the many rumours of her death, the queen was said to have replied: '*Mortua sed non sepulta*' – Dead but not buried![4] She had become increasingly insecure in recent times, fearing that 'the people's affection towards her waxed more cold than had been accustomed'.[5] In 1581 Elizabeth's government had passed the 'Statute of Silence' (or the Act Against Seditious Words and Rumours), which introduced a series of gruesome punishments for anyone speaking or publishing anything that the queen did not wish to hear, including: 'Casting Nativities, or prophesying, &c. as to the Duration of the Queen's Life, or who shall succeed to the Crown, or wishing the Queen's Death, &c.'[6] Yet such laws could not stop rumour and speculation. The 'English succession' remained a hotly debated topic at home and abroad.[7]

In 1600 Thomas Wilson, an agent of Sir Robert Cecil, wrote a report 'on the state of England' outlining the claims of no less than twelve potential claimants. 'Thus, you see,' Wilson told his paymaster, the queen's principal secretary, 'this Crown in not like to fall to the ground for want of heads that claim to wear it, but upon whose head it will fall is by many doubted.'[8] There were growing fears that European countries would take advantage of the unsettled succession and invade, as they had in France following the death of Henry III. A disputed succession, and civil war on Elizabeth's death, seemed all but inevitable.

James VI of Scotland was Elizabeth's nearest royal relative – both were direct descendants of Henry VII – but in English law his claim was uncertain. His mother, the Catholic Mary Queen of Scots, had been executed in 1587 for plotting to assassinate her cousin, the Queen of England. The statute of 1581 insisted that if any claimants should conspire against Elizabeth, all their legal rights would be forfeited.[9] Moreover, as a Scotsman, James was regarded as a foreigner and since 1351, foreigners had been forbidden from inheriting English lands, and it was thought that this too might block James from inheriting the Crown. The will of Henry VIII had also sought to bar any claim by his Scottish relatives, the Stuarts, to the Crown of England through his eldest sister Margaret, who was married to James IV of Scotland. In the event that his children died without heirs, which they did, Henry VIII had identified the heirs of his younger sister Mary – the Grey family – as the rightful successors. This meant that by the terms of Henry VIII's will, Edward Seymour, Lord Beauchamp, eldest son of the Earl of Hertford and his wife Katherine Grey, would succeed upon Queen Elizabeth's death. Yet for many Catholics, their preferred candidate was Lady Arbella Stuart, a cousin of both James and Elizabeth, through their great-grandmother Margaret Tudor.

In 1603 James VI of Scotland was in the fourteenth year of a companionable marriage to Anna, sister of Christian IV the King of Denmark–Norway, who had close connections to a number of other royal and ducal houses in Europe through ancestral dynastic links and the marriages of her siblings. James had sailed to Denmark in 1589 to bring his young wife, then just fourteen years old, back to Scotland. Their first child, born on 19 February 1594, was christened Henry Frederick, after King Henry VII, James VI's great-great-grandfather, and founder of the Tudor dynasty; and after Anna's father, Frederick II. Amid several miscarriages and infant deaths, James and Anna went on to have a daughter, Elizabeth, in 1596, and another son, Charles, in 1600.

The birth of a male heir had dramatically improved James's standing, not only in Scotland but also as a candidate for the English throne. Ambassadors were sent to France, Denmark, the Low Countries, England and Germany, bearing invitations to the boy's baptism. The new prince's godfathers were two of the most powerful men in Europe: King Henri IV of France, who had converted to Catholicism the previous year to secure his accession, and the Protestant and Dutch leader Maurice of Nassau, stadtholder of the Dutch Republic. *A True Reportarie*, an account of the 'spectacular' baptism, was published in both Edinburgh and London and heralded James's providential purpose to effect a union between England and Scotland which Henry would then inherit.[10] The poem *'Principis*

Scoti-Britannorum natalia' similarly expressed hopes that Henry, 'a Prince born of a Scoto-Britannic king' would bring the nations 'into a single body of Scoto-Britannic people'. To what 'great heights', it asked, 'will Scoto-Britannic glory now rise. With no limits set by time and space? ... You press under your foot the triple crown of the papacy'.[11] Henry Frederick, the great hope of Protestants, would crush the papacy and bring glory to the British Isles. It was an image of his son and heir that James sought to encourage.

For the papacy, however, the contested English succession represented the possibility of returning England to the Roman Catholic Church. Although James VI had been baptised a Catholic and had never been excommunicated by Rome, he was widely regarded as a heretic. As the aged Queen of England's health declined, Pope Clement VII issued an edict calling on Catholics to defy the accession of 'any heretic or any person suspected of heresy, however much right of blood or succession'; and in England, Jesuit leader Henry Garnet urged English Catholics to act accordingly.[12] James VI was therefore at pains in these years to stress both his Protestant faith to English Privy Councillors, and to hint at a possible conversion in messages through unofficial agents and ambassadors to Catholic courts in Europe. And so, while ruling Scotland, James sought alliances with the Dutch Republic, Denmark–Norway and the German Protestant princes, while at the same time cultivating good relations with France, Spain and the papacy, and taking steps to win over significant figures in England.[13]

Meanwhile, Catholics in England and on the continent continued to try and find a candidate they could unite in support of.[14] In the end there was no one candidate whom all the Catholic states in Europe could support, and so the Habsburgs lost the opportunity to influence the English succession. Only in March 1603 did the King of Spain let it be known that he was willing to consider a non-Habsburg candidate, and by then it was too late.[15]

***

James VI had been doggedly laying the groundwork to succeed Elizabeth for years, networking and politicking with those south of the border to secure favour with the queen and the goodwill of those around her. In 1586 Elizabeth agreed to pay James VI an annual pension of £4,000 (the equivalent of over £1 million today), on the tacit understanding that he stayed Protestant and loyal to her. This raised for the first time the prospect of future acceptance of his right to the English throne. With his eyes firmly on the crown of England, James took steps to robustly defend his claim. He wrote and published a tract, *The Trew Law of Free Monarchies*, in which he argued for hereditary succession as ordained by God, and in his 'great oration' to the Scottish parliament of December 1597, he urged his allies abroad 'to stand his friends for this his urgent necessity to attain his right to the Crown of England.'[16] Funds were raised to pay for ambassadors to promote James's claim throughout Europe and to secure military support 'when the time came'.[17]

Taking nothing for granted, from the summer of 1594 – using ciphers to avoid detection – James began secret communications with Robert Devereux, the Earl of Essex, Privy Councillor and one of the queen's closest companions, to secure vital intelligence and support from the English court.[18] But by 1601, Essex was dead, executed by Elizabeth for plotting to seize control of government and force her to declare James VI her successor.

Next, James turned to the queen's principal secretary, Sir Robert Cecil. He continued the secret correspondence, reassuring James that the 'natural day shall come, wherein your feast may be lawfully proclaimed'.[19] Cecil and the Scottish king used numerical aliases – James was '30', Cecil was '10'. Sometimes they communicated directly, but mostly others wrote on their behalf, including Edward Bruce, Lord Kinloss, from Holyrood Palace in Edinburgh, and Lord Henry Howard from London. Cecil was only too aware of the dangers if the queen discovered his correspondence. In return James promised Cecil future favour and influence. '[I shall] rule all my actions for advancing of my lawful future hopes by your advice.'[20] Acknowledging Cecil's key role in securing the English throne, James would later write: 'My pen is not able to express how happy I think myself for having chanced upon so worthy, so wise and so provident a friend.'[21]

In the spring of 1601, James sent Kinloss and John Erskine, the Earl of Mar, to London as special ambassadors under the guise of congratulating Elizabeth on escaping Essex's plot, though in reality James sought to discover if he was implicated in it. The Scottish envoys were to remind Elizabeth that she had said, according to James: 'nothing shall be done by her, in her time, in prejudice of my future right', and to secure a written declaration that he was innocent of any plotting against her. James gave the envoys detailed instructions: to 'walk surely between these two precipices, of the Queen and the people', to discover the sentiments of the 'town of London', to make links with the Lieutenant of the Tower of London, to make certain of the fleet and sea ports, to secure the support of as many of the nobility and gentry as possible, to ascertain the arms of each county – and 'generally, to leave all things in such certainty and order, as the enemies be not able in the meantime to lay such bars in my way, as shall make things remediless when the time shall come'.[22] Finally, the envoys were to make clear to Cecil and the Scottish king's other allies, that they would face retribution if they tried to block his claim to the Crown. Increasingly confident of his position, James was forthright in asserting his expectations.

Yet the aged ailing queen made short shrift of the Scottish lords' congratulations. Despite a painfully arthritic hand, Elizabeth wrote direct to James making clear her displeasure. 'An upright demeanour bears ever more poise than all disguised shows of good can do,' she chastised her cousin. 'Remember that a bird of the air, if no other instrument to an honest king, shall stand instead of many feigned practices, to utter aught may any wise touch him.' She took exception to the request that she grant him 'English estates' to overcome legal objections to his succession on the grounds of his nationality, and signed off: 'We hope to hear no more of these matters.'[23]

***

As the merits of the candidates continued to be discussed and debated, the uncertainty of the succession weighed heavy on the population at large. Though treasonous to discuss the succession directly, narratives of dynastic civil wars and usurpations were depicted in masques and plays. Shakespeare's *Julius Caesar*, performed at the Globe in London from 1599, alluded to the threat of civil war, conspiracy and treason. England, like ancient Rome, was poised at a moment of impending political change, with questions of legitimacy, loyalty and the threat of treason in the air. *Hamlet*, performed around the same time, also reflected the pervasive succession anxiety and the terror of resistance, conspiracy and assassination.[24] While in *Hamlet*, legitimacy and order were restored without recourse to civil war, in *Julius Caesar* the assassination of Caesar leads to chaos in Rome. Shakespeare used these plays to posit versions of events after Elizabeth's death, which deliberately evoked national anxieties about the threat of the unsettled succession and the prospect of civil war.

As February gave way to March 1603, Elizabeth's condition deteriorated once more, and the Privy Council took steps to secure the capital. Watches were ordered across the city; 'rogues as might be apt to stir' were press-ganged into the army and sent abroad, and other 'suspected persons' jailed.[25] 'London is all in arms for fear of the Catholics,' reported the Venetian ambassador Giovanni Scaramelli; 'although they number forty thousand of them they have no leaders as yet.'[26] Extra guards were placed on key buildings and at 'every gate and street' in the capital.[27] All ports were closed; public meetings and assemblies were outlawed, and theatres in London, Middlesex and Surrey shut.[28] Over 4,000 armed infantrymen were deployed across London, and eight armed ships, each carrying 500 troops, positioned on the Thames, ready to ward off foreign invasion.[29]

As rumours of the queen's imminent death swept across London, gentry and nobles who lived in the suburbs brought their plate and jewels to safe houses in the City, where 'continual strong watches' were kept.[30] People began stockpiling armour, munitions and food, and the queen's Privy Council ordered that wheat be requisitioned and gathered in storehouses. Across England, local officials were issued with instructions to allay fear and panic. They should suppress 'all uncertain and evil rumours concerning the state of her Majesties health', and for the 'prevention and redress of all unlawful assemblies, actions, and disorderly attempts that such rumours may breed'. Above all they must take whatever steps were necessary to 'preserve both in public and private the peace [and] tranquillity' in all parts of the realm.[31]

This was easier said than done. The nervous energy in the capital was remembered by the poet and clergyman John Donne, who described citizens 'running up and down like ants, with their eggs bigger than themselves, every man with his bags, to seek where to hide them safely'.[32]

Meanwhile, Cecil, Howard and others, sent messages to James VI at Holyrood in Edinburgh, updating him as to the state of the queen's health, reassuring him that all was in hand, and that he was supported in his claim as Elizabeth's heir. Cecil sent James a draft of a proclamation he was preparing to announce the Scottish king's accession, when the time came.[33]

Still Elizabeth refused to name her heir.

On 19 March, Sir Robert Carey, a middle-aged military man and cousin of the queen, visited her and found that she was in 'melancholy humour'. The next morning Elizabeth attempted to attend chapel but was forced to hear the service lying on cushions on the floor of the Privy Chamber.[34] Carey, who had previously served as one of the queen's envoys in Edinburgh, wrote immediately to James VI in Scotland saying that the queen would be dead within three days, and electing that he would be 'the first man that should bring him news of it'.[35]

As rumours spread that Elizabeth was entering her last hours, the bells in the capital were silenced. Father William Weston, a Jesuit priest imprisoned in the Tower, noticed a strange hush descending on the city, 'as if it were under interdict and divine worship suspended.

Not a bell rang out. Not a bugle sounded – though ordinarily they were often heard.'[36] London was holding its breath. Finally, at about two o'clock on the morning of Thursday 24 March, Queen Elizabeth died in her sleep at Richmond Palace.

The moment of crisis, for so long feared, had arrived. After a reign spanning forty-four years and five months, the queen was dead. Few could remember life under another monarch. Those who surrounded her deathbed reported that, when she was no longer capable of speech, they asked her directly if it were indeed her will that James VI should succjeed, and that the dying queen had put her hand to her head making the gesture of a crown.[37] It was a convenient act, though not a verifiable truth. As treasury clerk John Clapham observed: 'These reports whether they were true indeed or give out of purpose by such as would have them so to be believed it is hard to say.'[38] Certainly within days, narratives emerged claiming that the queen had in the presence of Cecil among others, named, or gestured to acknowledge James VI of Scotland as her successor.[39]

***

Sir Robert Cecil immediately put in train carefully laid plans. As dawn broke, the councillors and nobility prepared to depart for Whitehall Palace. Around mid-morning, a procession of heralds, followed by the Privy Council, lords and courtiers, rode out to the front of Richmond Palace gates, where Cecil read out the proclamation which James had already approved:

> Forasmuch as it hath pleased Almighty God to call to his mercy out of this transitory life our Sovereign Ladie, the High and Mightie Prince, Elizabeth late Queen of England, France, and Ireland, by whose death and dissolution, the Imperial Crowne of these Realms aforesaid are now absolutely, wholly, and solely come to the High and Mightie Prince, James the sixth King of Scotland, who is lineally and lawfully descended from the body of Margaret, daughter to the High and Renowned Prince, Henrie

the seventh King of England, France, and Ireland, his great Grandfather.[40]

Local officials across the realm were reminded of their duty to prevent 'any disorderly assemblies' or any words of action 'in any way prejudicial' to the new king.[41] The crowds that had gathered in the English capital received the news calmly and quietly. One observer described how the proclamation was heard with 'great expectation and silent joy, but no great shouting', as a mark of respect for the late queen, although not doubting that Londoners' delight 'in the accession of so worthy a king'.[42] Another said that shouts of 'God save the King!' were uttered with little enthusiasm. 'There was evidently neither sorrow for the death of the Queen,' observed Giovanni Scaramelli, 'nor joy for the succession of the King.'[43]

By nightfall, celebratory bonfires were lit throughout the city and liquor drunk, in choreographed acts of celebration paid for by the civic authorities. London was once more filled with the sound of bells. Guards remained on the streets, yet all remained calm. Lawyer John Manningham described how: 'Every man went about his business as readily as peaceably, as securely as if there had been no change, nor any news ever heard of competitors.'[44] One court official wrote: 'Such is the condition of great princes more unhappy in this respect than their own subjects, in that, while they live, they are followed by all men, and at their death lamented of none.'[45]

Preachers gave thanks for the peaceful transfer of power, which few had expected. In the event, no other candidates appeared with armies, and James was not tested by foreign opposition. The French had become preoccupied with domestic concerns, the Spanish with the rebellion in the Netherlands. It was but a brief respite from European crisis.

***

Though the Privy Council had ordered the court gates at Richmond to be closed immediately after the queen's death, and no one allowed to leave or enter, Sir Robert Carey was determined to effect his plan to ingratiate himself with the new king and be the first to deliver the news of Elizabeth's death in person. Eluding the palace guards, he set out on an epic 400-mile ride from London to Edinburgh, outpacing the Privy Council's official delegation of Sir Charles Percy and Thomas Somerset. Carey had arranged for fresh horses to be waiting at points along the Great North Road that led up to Scotland, and rode at such breakneck speed that in the last hours of the journey he fell off his horse, causing himself a head injury.

Carey finally arrived at the palace of Holyrood on the night of Saturday 26 March. Despite the late hour, James readily received him in his bedchamber, whereupon Carey knelt before the Scottish king and saluted him as 'the King of England, Scotland, France, and Ireland'.[46] Next, he presented James with a blue sapphire ring – which James had previously sent south to Carey's sister, one of the late queen's women of the bedchamber, with instructions that it should one day be returned to him as evidence of Elizabeth's death.[47]

Without waiting for the arrival of the official Privy Council delegation, James immediately assumed his role as King of England. He ordered the mayor and aldermen of the garrison town of Berwick to maintain border security and wrote to the English Privy Council with instructions that the government there should continue as it was until he arrived in London.[48] He also wrote to Cecil, saying he was 'thankful for the news' that 'the whole state by the good advice and grave judgment of those that have voice in council had uniformly consented to proclaim us her lawful successor'. He added that the 'industry, care and devotion of councillors in the translation of a monarchy' would be rewarded. 'How happy I think myself by the conquest of so faithful and so wise a counsellor I reserve it to be expressed out of my own mouth unto you.'[49]

The king was quick to reward other allies and collaborators, including those who had taken up arms with the Earl of Essex years before to assert James's right to the throne. Before he departed Scotland, James received Essex's boy, twelve-year-old Robert Devereux, declaring him 'the son of the most noble knight that English land as ever begotten', and ordered that the late earl's friends, Sir Henry Neville and Henry Wriothesley (formerly the Earl of Southampton), who were imprisoned in the Tower of London, be released in order to join James on his royal progress.[50]

The king now readied himself for a journey for which he had been anticipating for most of his life. He had ordered five new horses and new clothes, including a purple velvet coat and breeches, and a splendid purple riding cloak trimmed with ermine.[51] Meanwhile, in London, extensive preparations were also underway for the king's 400-mile journey south with residences located to host the king and his retinue, entertainments prepared, and provisions supplied.

On Tuesday 5 April 1603, accompanied by a large retinue of Scotsmen, James set out on his journey to London. As he left Edinburgh, crowds called out both in sorrow and in celebration, glad that their king had won the English crown, yet lamenting that he was leaving them. Despite assurances that he would visit Scotland every three years, he would return just once (in 1617).

It was to be a truly unprecedented progress: a king of Scotland travelling south across the River Tweed to peacefully claim the crown of England after centuries of acrimonious rivalry and warfare between the two nations.

James entered his new kingdom at Berwick-upon-Tweed two days later – it was the first time he had been across the border – and was met by hundreds of people shouting, 'Welcome' and 'God Save King James!' For more than 400 years, Berwick, England's northernmost town, had been the focus of fierce battles between the Scottish and the English, and had several times changed hands. Now, as king of both 'auld enemies', James inspected the fortifications which Queen Elizabeth had spent over £15,000 each year maintaining. The cannons which had previously stood in place to defend the town against James's Scottish ancestors, were fired in celebration of his arrival.

The border area had shown its potential for disorder just days before. In the aftermath of Elizabeth's death – the 'Busy' or 'Ill

Week', as it became known – violent plundering, pillaging and raiding had taken place in the region amid the burning and spoiling of
land and property.[52] Over the months that followed James's accession, the old defences would be stood down. The king would describe
Berwick and the borderlands as 'the very h[e]art of the country', and
the borders 'no more the extremities, but the middle'.[53]

Confident that he had the support of the Privy Council and
control of the capital, James and his entourage adopted a lei-
surely approach as they progressed through England, hunting and
feasting as they went. It would take them over a month to reach
London. James was also keen that the queen's funeral take place
before he entered the capital, and was wary of the outbreak of the
plague there, which had spread from Spain and across the continent, the first cases having been recorded in the days leading up to
Elizabeth's death.

As James journeyed south, he was presented with numerous
petitions calling for change, some from Catholics and others from
Puritans, pointing to the economic and social effects of the long
war with Spain. As one petition described, 'Your subjects have
been of late years charged with many subsidies and tenths. And
without all doubt the commons are poor and indebted. They desire
some ease.'[54] It was to be a salutary warning for James as he made
his way to London. England was certainly wealthier than Scotland,
but it was significantly poorer compared to the main European
powers. Both France and Spain had stable revenues and permanent
standing armies. The new King of England had neither.

Yet for now, as Scottish courtier Roger Aston described, James
was 'like a poor man wandering about forty years in a wilderness
and barren soil, and now arrived at the land of promise'.[55] And he
behaved accordingly, liberally bestowing knighthoods, some 229, as
he progressed south. It was about the same number that Elizabeth
had created in the entirety of her 45-year reign. More would follow.
While it was widely believed that many paid for the honour – with
James's Scottish entourage being blamed for taking bribes – there

was also clear disapproval of all the expense. As one complainant wrote: 'It is said your Majesty giveth much,' yet 'your coffers are said not to be so full' that they should be emptied.[56]

One of those who received favour was James's distant kinsman, Sir John Harington, who was raised to the peerage as Baron Harington of Exton and appointed princess Elizabeth's guardian. On 23 April, James had dined at Harington's Rutland estate, Burley-on-the Hill, and enjoyed subsequent days of hunting and an entertainment. Lady Anne Harington and their eldest daughter, Lucy Russell, Countess of Bedford, were at the same time sent to Scotland to wait on James's 28-year-old pregnant wife Anna, who would follow once the necessary arrangements had been made.[57] The Countess of Bedford was appointed principal lady of the bedchamber.[58] It marked the beginning of an enduring relationship between the Haringtons and King James and his family.

Another Englishman, who had already proved indispensable to the new king, was Sir Robert Cecil. As James drew close to London, he stopped for several days at Theobalds, Robert Cecil's Hertfordshire mansion, to again express his gratitude to the man whom he would nickname his 'little beagle' on account of his energy and tenacity. Cecil was confirmed in post as Principal Secretary. Like his father William Cecil, earl of Salisbury before him, Sir Robert had been one of Elizabeth I's most influential ministers. Now, Cecil's role as kingmaker ensured his continued prominence in government. At Theobalds, on 3 May James held his first Privy Council meeting, swearing in five Scots – all long-time companions of the king – and agreeing the wording of a proclamation, issued four days later, promising redress of grievances. He wanted to 'make manifest to our people, how willing we are now, and will be ready hereafter, to be as forward in requiting their love, as they have been in expressing it'.[59]

Meanwhile, the last act of the previous reign took place. On Thursday 28 April, Londoners lined the streets to watch the funeral procession of the late Queen Elizabeth move from the palace of

Whitehall to her final resting place in Westminster Abbey. Elizabeth's coffin, carried on a hearse drawn by horses draped in black velvet, was topped with a wooden effigy of the late queen, a sceptre in her hand and a Crown on her head, clothed in her parliamentary robes. Above the coffin, covered in purple velvet, was a canopy supported by six knights, and surrounded by the Gentlemen Pensioners, the queen's ceremonial bodyguard. Behind the hearse was the long procession of her court, including Sir Robert Cecil, in his final service for the Tudors before he commenced work for the new Stuart king.[60]

2

The Wonderful Year

'Upon Thursday it was treason to cry God save King James, King
of England, and upon Friday treason not to cry so. In the morning
no voice heard but murmurs and lamentations, at noon nothing but
shouts of gladness & triumph.'

Thomas Dekker, *The Wonderful Year* (1603)[1]

During his royal progress south, King James was heralded as a
bringer of peace and unity to England and Scotland. A panegyric by Samuel Daniel was read to the king congratulating him on
his accession and celebrating the peaceful union:

What heretofore could never yet be wrought
By all the swords of pow'r, by blood, by fire
By ruin and destruction, here is brought
To pass with peace with love, with joy, desire.[2]

At Stamford Hill, a few miles north of the English capital, Sir
Richard Martin, a Middle Temple lawyer, delivered an oration, on
behalf of the Sheriffs of London and Middlesex, hailing the new king
as legitimate, peaceful and triumphant: 'the bright star of the North'
emerging out of the fear and darkness brought by Elizabeth's death.
Sir Richard's speech, vetted by Cecil, stressed that the English looked
to James both for 'admiral goodness' and for 'particular redress.'

The king had, as Martin observed, already demonstrated his 'prudence' in Scotland in 'reducing those things to order in Church and Commonwealth which the tumultuous times of your Majesty's infancy had there put out of square.' Now as king in England, James was called on to focus on areas where 'redress' was needed. Ireland would require James's justice after the 'miseries ... of Civil Wars', and in England, his 'temperance and moderation' would be looked for to address 'our true griefs', including 'unjust monopolies ... delay of justice', 'corruption' in the church and 'the exploitation of the poor by heavy taxation'.[3]

The 'deep and inward grief' for the loss of the queen had been 'turned into excessive joy' by the arrival of James, 'whose fame, like a new Sun rising, dispersed those clouds of fear'.[4] It would become a recurring image of a king of whom so much was expected. Two years into James I's reign, Ben Jonson, in his play *Masque of Blackness*, described a Britannia 'Rul'd by a Sun ... whose beams shine day, and night.'[5]

James's entry into London, however, was muted. Strict precautions had been put in place because of the plague, with road and river travel limited. The capital was in lockdown. Westminster was barred to ordinary citizens to prevent those infected from getting near the king as he entered the city. Many Londoners had tried to flee to the countryside, and hundreds died each week. Special prayers were read in the churches; the roads and markets were deserted. Thomas Dekker described a 'diseased city', with 'still and melancholy streets, the loud groans of raving sick men; the struggling pangs of souls departing ... [the] unmatchable torment of a worm-eaten generation'.[6]

After a few days in the royal apartments of the Tower of London, James and his entourage moved downriver to Greenwich, the old Tudor palace on the banks of the Thames, where he awaited the arrival of his family from Scotland.

***

James's accession was a moment rich in significance: a defining point in the history of the British Isles and the emergence of 'Great Britain'. England, Scotland, Wales and Ireland were now all ruled by a single monarch. Wales had been formally incorporated with England by Henry VIII, who had been declared King of Ireland in 1542. Until 1603, England and Scotland had remained two entirely independent kingdoms.

Within days of James's accession, politician and antiquarian Sir Robert Cotton declared that the king should 'revive' some 'ancient name' for his multiple monarchy, and that none 'ariseth any fitter than Britain'. Cotton had recently completed his *Discourse of his Majesty's Descent from the Saxon Kings*, likely written at the behest of Henry Howard, who was soon to be raised to the rank of earl by James for his loyalty. There had been a 'single kingdom some 2,000 years before' when 'great Constantine took ye title of Brittanicus, a glorious addition to the style Imperial'. Cotton argued that such a title was uniquely James's because he, unlike his predecessors, could trace his lineage back not just to William the Conqueror but also to the Saxon king, Alfred.[7] It was a name of supposedly ancient pedigree, first described in the twelfth century in Geoffrey of Monmouth's *Historia regum Britanniae* (*History of the Kings of Britain*), which stretched back to its foundation as a kingdom by Brutus. According to Monmouth, Brutus, a Trojan and great-grandson to Aeneas who took part in the establishment of Rome, founded London as a 'New Troy', and from this line descendants of British kings were born. It was a national myth – a story of England's past – which had been popularised by early Tudor publicists to herald the accession of Henry VII, a Welshman, to the English throne in 1485.

James's lineage from the Tudors gave him claim to this ancient mythological 'British' line. His genealogy had been traced and proclamations issued declaring him descended: 'By the divers direct loins to Brutus' and from him to 'Cadwalader, the last King of the British blood'. It was from them that James had his 'rightful title' to 'the Kingdom of Britain … [and] the Principalities of Northwales and

Southwales'.[8] Accordingly, when James commissioned an accession medal later that year, it named him: 'Emperor of the whole island of Britain.'[9]

***

At Greenwich, on 19 May 1603, James made his first official statement on the union. In a 'Proclamation for the Uniting of England and Scotland', he claimed that the union achieved by his accession was 'God's plan' and that he, James, had already united the two kingdoms which shared 'language, religion, and similitude of manners'. He described as having found in the hearts of subjects of both realms, 'a most earnest desire that "the said happy Union should be perfected"', and the 'inhabitants of both the Realms to be the Subjects of one Kingdom'. James pledged, 'with the advice of the Estates and Parliaments of both the Kingdoms', to make this happen as soon as possible.[10] He felt confident that a 'perfect union' could quickly and easily be achieved.

In the Scottish proclamation announcing his accession, James had ordered Scotsmen to acknowledge Englishmen 'as their dearest brethren and friends, and the inhabitants of both his realms to obliterate and remove out of their minds all and whatever quarrels ... with one universal unanimity of hearts'.[11] From London, James proudly proclaimed, 'I sit and govern ... with my pen, I write and it is done; and by a clerk of the Council I govern Scotland now.'[12] Policy was formulated by James in London, and then carried out by the Council in Scotland. The Scottish Privy Council's commission had been broadened to enable it to deal with the governance of the realm and maintenance of law and order. Over the next few months, a regular postal service evolved transporting correspondence between London and Edinburgh, a letter taking less than a week to pass between the two capitals.[13]

However, while England and Scotland now had a king in common, there was little else that the two countries shared, and huge obstacles to be overcome. The two realms were both Protestant, but their churches were divergent in practice, and there were no joint legislative, religious or legal institutions. For centuries the countries had been at war or in hostile alliances with other foreign powers. Scotland had long served as a backdoor to French ambitions against England, and rivalries, jealousies and cultural animosities continued to define the Anglo–Scottish relationship, despite the comparative peace of the last half-century.

While both countries formally acclaimed James's accession to the English throne, there were fears on both sides: the English that 'swarms of tawny Scots' would flock to England and take wealth and jobs; the Scottish, that their country would end up a vassal state.[14] In countless treaties and publications, the Scotsmen demanded that any further union be mutual and reciprocal, highlighting Scotland's greatness and proud heritage as an independent kingdom, and ignoring the economic disparities between the two.

Anti-Scottish feeling was latent south of the border. Over the previous months, Henry Percy, the Earl of Northumberland, had warned James that the 'name of Scots is harsh in the ears of the vulgar'. Although, he added, 'the vulgar will follow the example of their superiors'.[15]

But in the days and weeks that followed the king's accession, the 'vulgar' did speak. English nobleman Sir John Holles described how James had brought with him to London 'a crew of necessitous and hungry Scots', and 'filled every corner of the court with these beggarly blew caps'.[16] During his royal progress, five Scotsmen, friends and servants of the king, had been added to the existing Privy Council, 'much to the disgust of the lords of the Council who pretended that no one but Englishmen should hold honours and titles in England'.[17] The King's Bedchamber became an entirely Scottish domain, made up of James's most trusted companions. Antagonism only increased when a new Privy Chamber was created in mid-May 1603, comprised equally of twenty-four English and twenty-four Scottish gentleman. 'Every day, posts are taken from the English and given to the Scots,' observed Venetian ambassador Scaramelli.[18]

In many ways the arrival of a foreign king with a broad Scottish accent and large Scottish entourage at the English court, served only to increase traditional English antipathy towards Scotland and its people.

***

From Greenwich, James wrote to his brother-in-law Christian IV of Denmark–Norway, explaining that Anna would shortly be joining him, having travelled from Scotland with Henry, aged nine, and seven-year-old Elizabeth – 'our sweetest little daughter' – and that Christian would 'easily appreciate how much our enjoyment of this pleasure will be augmented'. James's youngest child, three-year-old Prince Charles, was regarded as too sickly to travel, and would, for now, remain in Scotland. James wrote too of his forthcoming coronation, at which Anna would be crowned queen, assuring Christian: 'We shall make your sister our choicest and most sweet wife share the crown and diadem.'[19]

Despite the plague's grip on the capital, preparations for the coronation at Westminster Abbey continued. James had hoped that all the nobility of the realm would attend his coronation, to confirm their acceptance of his legitimacy, but the plague forced drastic measures, including the postponement of the traditional coronation procession through the city. Just days before, the court had issued a proclamation stating that 'all show of State and Pomp accustomed by our Progenitors' would be deferred, including the pre-coronation entry. All those well-wishers who had intended to travel to the capital were ordered to stay at home and admission tickets were issued for the first time by the abbey to control numbers of attendees.[20] That said, an eyewitness account in German by Benjamin von Buwinckhausen, the ambassador who had been sent by Frederick, Duke of Württemberg, on James's accession, described how 'not only the Church (which is one of the largest and finest in Europe), but also all places and streets around it were so crowded with people, and the river are so full of boats, that one could not move for the multitude.'[21]

The coronation itself was to be a pared-down affair, retaining only those elements deemed essential, which meant only those ceremonies that took place within the confines of the abbey: the king's oath, his anointing and crowning, and the bishops' and peers' show of homage.

At ten o'clock on the morning of Monday 25 July, St James's Day, James and Anna were rowed the short distance from the palace of Whitehall to Westminster in a newly gilded barge, followed by an array of vessels carrying members of the court and royal household. The king and queen were met at the west door of Westminster Abbey by John Whitgift, the elderly Archbishop of Canterbury who, just weeks before, had prayed with the late Queen Elizabeth on her deathbed.

This was an occasion rich in significance: it was the first coronation to take place in England for almost half a century; the first of an adult male for nearly a century; the first that was completely Protestant, and the first to be conducted entirely in English rather than predominantly in Latin.[22] Anna would be the first crowned queen consort since Anne Boleyn.

Buwinckhausen noted that when in the ceremony the king was presented before the people in the four corners of the church and asked, 'whether they would acknowledge him for their King, and whether there was any present who would say to the contrary?' He went on, 'Whereupon all the people, with one clear, joyous shout cried out, "Yea" (*ja*, geschiren), held up their hands and hats, so that nothing could be heard or seen because of the noise and clamour of the trumpets and horns.'[23]

The coronation sermon delivered by Thomas Bilson, Bishop of Winchester, and likely vetted by James, was based on Romans 13.1: 'The powers that be are ordained by God'. It was addressed to a 'religious and learned king who both by pen and practise these many years hath witnessed to the world how well acquainted he is with Christian and godly government.' Bilson went on to warn that the king's subjects must obey him as God's viceregent on earth and ignore the pope.[24]

Then in front of the realm's lords, nobles and clergy, and the foreign ambassadors, James took the coronation oath promising to uphold the laws and customs of England, to keep the peace for church and people and to administer the law with justice and mercy. In his *Trew Law of Free Monarchies*, one of many political tracts written by James, the king had spoken of the importance of the coronation oath and the mutual obligations between subjects and their sovereign. James based his theory of monarchy on the Bible, particularly the Old Testament passages which referred to the duties of a king to administer justice, establish good laws, which are obeyed, and to secure peace. 'Kings are called Gods by the prophetical King David, because they sit upon God his Throne in the earth, and have the [ac]count of their administration to give unto him.'[25] The *Trew Law* stressed the sacredness of the coronation oath, by which a king undertakes: 'to maintain the Religion presently professed within their country, according to their laws, whereby it is established', and 'the ancient privileges and liberties of his subjects'. In return, people owed obedience to king as God's 'lieutenant on earth'.[26]

Trew Law had first been published in Edinburgh in 1598 and then reprinted in London in 1603. In fact, all of James's political writings as King of Scotland were reprinted when he came to the throne in England. He believed it was one of his chief duties to educate and enlighten his subjects. James had a thorough knowledge of the Bible, political and religious theory, the classics, poetics, mythology, and history. It was especially important for him to emphasise the breadth of his knowledge during his first few years in England, as he attempted to prove his intelligence and gentility in a country generally hostile to his native Scotland.

With the king enthroned, crowned and blessed, and communion received, the heralds proclaimed: 'The High and Mighty Prince James our Sovereign Lord, by the Grace of God, King of England, Scotland, France and Ireland, King, defender of the faith etc'.

On a medal struck to celebrate the occasion, James is shown as an emperor over several kingdoms as he kneels before an altar in his coronation robes. The inscription reads, 'James I, Caesar Augustus of Britain, Caesar the heir of the Caesars.'[27] The words are a reference to the traditions of the Holy Roman Emperors, who described themselves as Caesar. At the time of his coronation, James I had wanted to be proclaimed King of Great Britain, but this would require Parliament's consent. As a result, he was unable to refer to himself as 'King' of Britain, so instead used the title 'Caesar'.

The coronation medals, the first of their kind, were given to foreign ambassadors who had gathered in the abbey to witness the ceremonial affirmation of the new king. Some however had made their excuses and did not attend. Charles of Arenberg, the ambassador of the Archduke Albert of the Spanish Netherlands, explained his absence on the ground 'still used a crutch' on account of painful gout, but as Giovanni Carlo Scaramelli, Venetian Secretary, put it, 'the real reason, was that he had resolved never to attend a heretic ceremony.'[28]

3

The Eyes of All Men

'This succession drew towards it the eyes of all men ... the island of
Great Britain, divided from the rest of the world, was never before
united in itself under one King.'

Francis Bacon, *The Beginning of the History of Great Britain* (1623)[1]

A ged thirty-seven when he came to the English throne, having
survived multiple plots and violent traumas in Scotland, James
was already a wily and seasoned politician. As King of Scotland, he
had secured alliances throughout Europe and gained valuable supporters for his claim to succeed Elizabeth. In that campaign he had
managed and manipulated the fears and desires of foreign powers
for his own benefit.[2]

Such dissembling had left many hoping that James was a man who
had the potential to convert to Catholicism. At the same time, he had
underscored his Protestant credentials by proposing the formation
of a Protestant League against the growing power of the Catholic
Habsburg Empire. He acquired Danish and German allies after his
marriage to Anna, and the queen consort may well have played a
role in this politicking too. After their marriage and her arrival in
Scotland, it had been suggested that the Lutheran queen had secretly
converted to Catholicism. By 1603, James had raised his personal
profile on the European stage, enjoyed good relationships with all

the major European powers and had acquired a reputation as an effective mediator and peacemaker.

On becoming King of England, James inherited a war with Spain, and a commitment to support the United Provinces in its struggle to win independence from Spain. The United Provinces of the Netherlands, had been established as a republic over twenty years earlier, after seven Dutch provinces in the Spanish Netherlands revolted against Spanish rule and declared their independence. Philip II had handed over the south of the Netherlands to his daughter, the Infanta Isabella and her husband Albert, Archduke of Austria, who became Philip's governor-general in Brussels. James's accession to the English throne had come at a crucial point, as both the Dutch and Spanish struggled to make decisive gains that would define any final peace settlement.

England had been fighting in support of the Republic against the Spanish for almost two decades, and many Englishmen were loath to abandon their long-time Dutch allies and co-religionists. England had control of three strategically important 'Cautionary Towns' – Brill, Flushing and Rammekens – which had been captured by English and Scottish volunteers serving with the Dutch Protestants and ceded to the English in 1585 as surety for Elizabeth I's continued assistance.

As King of Scotland, James had been at peace with Spain and the Spanish Netherlands. The English Privy Council recognised that this might now change England's foreign policy, stating: 'Your Majesty hath in right of your Crown of Scotland, amity with Spain and the Archduke; but in the succession to the throne of England a descent cast upon you of confederacy with these provinces.'[3]

Indeed, such was James's equivocation that right up to Elizabeth's death he had been suggesting to Henri IV that the French king should counter any English overtures for peace with Spain by proposing a grand offensive alliance between England, France, Scotland and other Protestant states.[4] There was talk of a potential match for young Prince Henry with the Spanish infanta. When just days before the late queen's passing, the Habsburg rulers of the southern Netherlands sent an envoy to Edinburgh, James received him warmly and committed to allowing the recruitment of Scottish soldiers to be sent to Flanders. At the same time, in private, James told the Habsburg envoy that he in fact did not care for the Dutch and their cause – and that if he became King of England he would seek peace with Spain.[5] A report of the envoy's visit reached Archduke Albert in Brussels almost at the same time as news of James's accession, raising hopes that English support for the Dutch rebels would soon end.[6]

The European balance of power was at stake. James had spent the last few years promising anything to anyone while campaigning to win support for his claim to the English throne. Every party had come to believe that he would side with them. Now that James had been successful in his quest, no one quite knew what to expect, and all sought his favour. As the French envoy the Duke of Sully observed: 'It appeared as though all the princes of Europe considered gaining England in their interests to be of the utmost importance to them.'[7]

With James's accession, the new composite Protestant monarchy – Britain – became a significant player on the European stage. It was a time of fevered diplomatic activity, and tangible possibility, as Europe now looked to the court of King James I. As James later declared in a speech to Parliament: 'All foreign Kings that have sent their ambassadors to congratulate with me since my coming, have saluted me as Monarch of the whole Isle, and with much more respect of my greatness, then if I were King alone of one of these Realms.'[8]

As the news from England spread across the continent, ambassadors from across Europe – France, Spain, Flanders, the Dutch Republic, Savoy, Venice, Florence, the Count Palatine of the Rhine, Württemberg, Pfalz-Neuburg, Brunswick, Brandenburg, Lorraine, the Hanseatic towns, Denmark, and Poland – began flocking to London to offer their congratulations to the new king.[9] 'The eyes of all the world behold your majesty herein,' declared forty-nine-year-old Sir Walter Ralegh, 'and as your majesty shall deal like yourself, so shall your majesty be valued of all nations: if any persuade your majesty to pass it over slightly, he is ignorant, and understands it not.'[10] Ralegh, the late queen's captain of the guard was to quickly fall from royal favour after being accused of involvement in two treasonous plots against James. By the end of July, he was in the Tower where he remained for the next thirteen years.

Among the first to arrive in London, while James and his burgeoning entourage hunted and feasted across England, were Count Frederick-Henry of Nassau and Johan van Oldenbarnevelt, two of the most significant figures in the government of the United Provinces. With so much to lose from any possible Anglo–Spanish peace, they were keen to win the new monarch's favour and convince him to continue the support that Elizabeth had given them.

At their first meeting, on 17 May at Greenwich, the envoys tried to convince James to support a pan-European league against the Habsburgs. James was noncommittal in response. According to the resident French ambassador Christophe de Harlay, Count of Beaumont, Cecil told the envoys that James was waiting to receive the embassies of other princes before making up his mind about the United Provinces's proposal.[11] The arrival shortly afterwards of Prince-Count Charles of Arenberg, representative of the Archduke Albert in the Spanish Netherlands, underscored the delicate diplomatic balancing act required in these early weeks and the inevitable rivalry between ambassadors. Arenberg's mission to court the favour of the new king was hampered reportedly by an attack of gout, which forced him to delay his first audience, but thereafter he had been received favourably.[12]

A French delegation, led by Sully, Henri IV's most trusted adviser, arrived at Greenwich soon after Arenberg. The French sought to prevent an English rapprochement with Spain and to secure a new Anglo–French treaty of alliance. Ahead of his first audience with King James on 12 June, Sully reported a conversation he had had with the Venetian representative:

[the envoy] confirmed to me what I had before strongly suspected of the irresolution of James ... that his dissimulation, which his flatterers complimented in him as a virtue had always consisted in giving hopes to all, but accomplishing none; that it was not to be expected he would change his maxims, having frequently been heard to say, that it was to such an artful conduct alone he owed his security when King of Scotland; and therefore it was highly probable that he would again put those arts in practice, and pursue them more steadily than ever, at the beginning of a reign, and at the head of a great kingdom, whose people, affairs, and neighbours, he was utterly unacquainted with; all which were circumstances favourable to his maxim.[13]

It was an insightful summary of James's political strategy – and an approach to foreign affairs that would come to define his reign in England, as it had in Scotland. Equipped with the Venetian envoy's warning, Sully chose to ignore it.

On 30 July, James signed the Treaty of Hampton Court with the French to guarantee the security of the Dutch, as Sully reported to Henri IV, to resist 'the pernicious and ambitious designs of those [the Habsburgs] who aspire to the [Universal] Monarchy over Christendom, who have continually troubled [Europe] by wars and seditions.' James denounced Spanish ambition and duplicity and in conversations with Sully, shared his suspicions of Spanish declarations of friendship. Sully believed his mission had been a success and Henri IV declared: 'That which contents me the most is that the King of England has assured me again by his ambassador that he will make no contract with Spain prejudicial to our alliance or the estates of the Low Countries; that being the case the Spaniards will be unable to do any mischief.'[14]

The following year, however, England refused to contribute to the Dutch war effort, despite having agreed to do so. Appalled by James's deception, Henri IV concluded: 'We must distrust his intentions, his inconsideration and natural weakness and to the contrary hope for more from his inconstancy, timidity and bad conduct than from his prudence and the sincerity of his affections.'[15]

In fact, through his dissembling, James had achieved a highly favourable outcome. The Dutch, supported by the French, would continue to tie up Spain's military forces, leaving James able to negotiate a peace treaty without risking England's own security.

The only significant foreign representative James had yet to meet over the summer of 1603 was the Spanish envoy, Juan de Tassis, Count of Villamediana. He eventually arrived at Dover on Sunday 21 August 1603 – his delay raising suspicions as to Philip III of Spain's intentions, with rumours spreading at court of a planned Spanish invasion.[16] In fact Villamediana had been instructed to wait in Flanders to observe the progress of Ambassador Arenberg before crossing the Channel.

In early September, Villamediana had an audience with James at Greenwich. He was the first ambassador of a Spanish king to be presented at an English court in almost twenty years. Villamediana was at pains to insist on Philip III's good faith and desire for peace, but it quickly became apparent that neither he, nor Arenberg, had yet to be granted full powers to conclude a peace.[17] 'He had no particular commission for his master to treat with his Majesty,' Cecil told Sir James Elphinstone; 'and therefore till sufficient authority came out of Spain, we held it not fit to proceed any further.'[18]

With the arrival of Villamediana and his entourage, representatives from most of the great continental powers – including France, Spain, Venice, Florence, Savoy and the Netherlands – were now all at the new king's court, which had been moving between a series of royal residences, including Windsor, Greenwich, Hampton Court, and Woodstock in Oxfordshire, on account of the plague. Rivalry, suspicion and intrigue marked the relationships between the dignitaries. Before long, tensions became so acute between the French and Spanish envoys that they could not be present at the same court functions, for fear of a situation whereby one might be forced or tricked into giving precedence to the other.

Towards the end of the year, with the plague showing little sign of abating, the court moved to the splendid redbrick palace of Hampton Court, twenty miles up the Thames from Greenwich. It was the perfect place to mark the transition from the rule of the Tudors to the Stuarts. The stained-glass windows of the Great Hall, where plays were staged and feasts enjoyed, depicted Henry VIII's lineage from Edward III, as well as the union of the two houses of York and Lancaster. A series of spectacular banquets and balls, masques and plays was planned for the ambassadors' entertainment and to signal James's ambition for 'Britain' in the world.[19] Among those due to be performing were the King's Men, the company of William Shakespeare, who was now the king's official playwright with royal licence to put on plays for King James and his subjects. Productions would be rehearsed at the Globe and then brought to court for special performances. It seems likely that *Hamlet*, written little more than a year before, and *A Midsummer Night's Dream*, were put on for the dignitaries.

Tensions and disputes between diplomats continued, with all ambassadors demanding to be treated with commensurate respect. Matters came to a head in the run-up to two masques – *The Masque of the Knights of India and China*, sponsored by the Duke of Lennox, and Queen Anna's masque, *The Vision of the Twelve Goddesses*. The queen's masque was clearly the most prestigious. According to English diplomat Dudley Carleton, it created 'brabbles amongst our ambassadors'. So strong was the 'competition for a place and precedence' between the envoys of Savoy and Florence that a decision was made to invite neither in order to keep the peace. 'It was thought best to let both alone,' said Carleton.[20]

Relations between the French and the Spanish caused the greatest difficulties. Villamediana was the (unofficial) guest of honour at the queen's masque, much to the chagrin of the French envoy, Beaumont, who failed to secure an invitation. The queen was known to favour an Anglo–Spanish entente, and her masque was intended to celebrate the 'glory of peace' and signal a new era of amity between

England and Spain. In light of Beaumont's displeasure, it was suggested that the masque be cancelled, but James refused, saying, 'the will of the Queen was her own', and that she could have the masque 'whenever she might like to'.[21] It was decided that the French envoy should be invited to the lesser masque (Lennox's), scheduled for New Year's Day. This decision then caused such a furore that the queen's masque, originally scheduled for Twelfth Night, had to be put back by two days.[22] Beaumont was so affronted that he wrote to Henri IV, threatening 'at the hazard of my life to kill the Spaniard ... at the feet of the king'.[23]

It was the Stuarts' first Christmas in England and the first New Year celebrations of King James at a court apparently full of well-wishers. But amidst the feasts, plays and entertainments, the fractures and fault lines between the continent's ambassadors were clear for all to see. James's desire to reset England's relations with Europe and restore peace would be no easy task

4

The Reunion of Christendom

'I could wish from my heart, that it would please God to make me one of the members of such a general Christian union in Religion, as laying wilfulness aside on both hands, we might meet in the middest, which is the Centre and perfection of all things.'

King James I speech to the English Parliament (1604)[1]

Writing from Rome shortly after James's accession, the Somerset-born Jesuit leader Robert Persons described how unnamed Italians recognised the extraordinary scale of the Scottish king's triumph. They talked of James's 'lucky entrance into England with more facility than ever was expected', and of the king's future prospects. 'His first great fortune' now was that he was 'an enemy to no prince or State (for neither has he broken hitherto with the pope, nor king of Spain but, rather, has held friendly treatises with them both as is said)'. The English Jesuit leader concluded: 'He will hold this indifference towards all.'[2]

Persons' analysis was echoed by Ambassador Scaramelli who predicted that James would 'seek to gratify the emperor' and look for alliance with Spain, and also 'remain bound to the Protestant princes by his religion'. He would 'secure the friendship of France' as well as 'the respect of the whole world'.[3] Indeed King James was then held in such high regard that Persons wrote of one 'very great man' in Rome who said that if 'this king' refrained from committing 'great

43

errors', and that if the election of the next Holy Roman Emperor 'should go out of Germany', then the new King of England was 'the likeliest man to be had in consideration'.[4]

***

Both James's accession and the intentionally mixed messages he had given to secure the English throne, had consistently raised the hopes of both Catholics and Protestants for religious change and toleration. James had scarcely left Edinburgh on route to London before he was presented with the 'Millenary Petition', said to have been signed by a thousand Puritan clergy, calling for further reform of the English Church, the eradication of the last vestiges of Roman Catholicism and 'a conference among the learned' to resolve outstanding issues'.[5]

Days later, at Theobalds, the Earl of Northumberland had presented James with a petition on behalf of the Catholics, which assured the king of their 'devoted' allegiance, reminded him of their sufferings on behalf of his mother Mary Queen of Scots and called on him to make good the promises of toleration he was reported to have made before his accession.[6] It was one of a number of petitions on the subject the king received during his progress south. James made clear that the treatment of Catholic recusants was to be one of the first issues he would address in England. In a letter from Newcastle dated 10 April, James ordered the Privy Council, pending his arrival in London, to investigate the recent actions that had been taken against Catholics.[7]

Within hours of James's English accession, the London presses had begun printing thousands of copies of his *Basilikon Doron* ('Royal Gift'). A treatise on kingship originally written in letter form, four years earlier for his son and heir Prince Henry, now became James's manifesto as 'King of Britain'.[8] It quickly became a bestseller across Europe, feeding interest and curiosity about the intentions of the new king. It was estimated that between 13,000 and 16,000 copies sold in London in the late spring of 1603 alone, and numerous translations, including in Dutch, German, Swedish and Hungarian, were printed and circulated across the continent.[9] The English edition carried a new preface, titled 'To the Reader', in which James sought to clarify that which might otherwise alienate his new subjects. He refuted suggestions that he had made a 'vindictive resolution against England' after the execution of his mother, and stressed his desire to strike a balance between those of the Catholic and Protestant faiths – for, 'I do equally love and honour the learned and grave men of either of these opinions.'[10]

***

James's concern for moderation and church unity had been forged during his time as King of Scotland, where he witnessed the horrific effects of religious conflict, including the deposition of his mother, and the murder of several regents. He himself had been the focus of power struggles between Catholics and Protestants fighting for control of the Scottish Crown and Kirk (church). At age sixteen he had been kidnapped and imprisoned in the so-called Ruthven Raid, which sought to remove him from Catholic influences. His mother, Mary Queen of Scots, had spent most of her life and his childhood abroad, in France, having been placed there initially for her safety as an infant, and then during her brief time as queen consort to the French king, François II.

During this period, Scotland underwent the beginning of the Protestant Reformation. In the Edinburgh parliament in the summer of 1560, the mass and papal power were both abolished in the country and a new confession of faith introduced. When the widowed Queen Mary returned to Scotland in 1561, she was a Catholic monarch ruling an officially Protestant realm. While she did not attempt a Catholic restoration, her marriage in 1565 to a Catholic – her cousin Henry, Lord Darnley – and the birth of their son James on 19 June the following year, seemed to threaten the future of the Protestant church in Scotland.

Yet from the outset, James's birth was also heralded for its opportunities for peace-making, religious reconciliation and a 'British' union. Poems written in Latin to mark the occasion celebrated how, 'the author of all things is turning war, burning in civil strife, into peace', with Mary having given birth to a 'great hero' to 'unite the world'.[11] Scottish minister Patrick Adamson and the renowned Calvinist scholar George Buchanan both heralded the boy's birth as the 'promise of a golden age and the end of warfare'.[12] Adamson and Buchanan saw in James the potential of peace and union for 'Britannia', who now needed to 'bind [her] brows with the leaves of the peaceful olive', and 'chosen by the British kingdoms, cherish both Scot and Englishman with no distinction'.[13]

Nonetheless, James's homeland remained engulfed in violent feuding and civil war. After failing to quash a rebellion of Protestant nobles, Mary Queen of Scots was imprisoned in Loch Leven Castle in 1567 and in July of that year was forced to abdicate, leaving one-year-old James to be crowned king.

James VI grew up under the supervision and protection of the Earl and Countess of Mar at Stirling Castle, surviving countless plots to kill or kidnap him. As James's tutor, the aged George Buchanan would take every opportunity to remind the boy-king that he was the son of a 'wicked papist'. James would form a much closer relationship with his other Calvinist tutor, Peter Young. As a young man James developed a supreme confidence in his own intellect and opinions. In addition to his native tongue, 'Middle Scots', he could read Greek, Spanish and Italian; was fluent in French and Latin; and was able to recite long sections of the Bible. At the age of eight, he was described as 'the sweetest sight in Europe', a young prince with 'extraordinary gifts of ingenuity, judgement, memory and language'.[14] He was also rigidly schooled in Buchanan's Calvinist views on the obligations of a king towards his subjects and the right to depose a monarch if he failed to rule justly.[15]

Having come of age, James VI worked hard to establish royal control in Scotland and improve relations with the nobility and the

Scottish church – ultimately confirming all the Kirk's liberties, privileges and freedoms, but with royal and parliamentary control over it. Accepting that Presbyterianism was entrenched in Scotland, James sought to conciliate and moderate the extremes – winning round previously opposed ministers, reintroducing bishops in a reformed Kirk, and welcoming Catholics at court. Such conciliation also improved the Crown's relations with the nobility and the aristocracy. James avoided alienating nobles unnecessarily and took time to reconcile major disputes. By this means, the Crown in Scotland grew steadily in reputation as a symbol of unity and of authority, a rare example in post-Reformation continental Europe, where many fires were still blazing.

Reflecting in *Basilikon Doron* on the Reformation in Scotland, James wrote that he had no doubt it had been the pride, ambition and avarice of the Old Church which had brought about its own downfall, but also that 'many things were inordinately done by a popular tumult and rebellion' which lacked a 'Prince's order'.[16] He warned his son Henry to avoid the two extremes in the church: 'the one, to believe with the Papists, the Church's authority, better than your own knowledge; the other, to lean with the Anabaptists, to your own conceits and dreamed revelations'.[17] Just as the princes should be wary of the 'vain Puritan', so they should be wary so not to suffer 'proud papal bishops'.[18]

Drawing on these experiences, James explained in his *Trew Law* that his intention was to correct the 'many endless calamities, miseries and confusions' of 'our so long disordered, and distracted Commonwealth'. He argued that any rebellion was unlawful because 'kings are called Gods' and 'sit upon God's Throne on the earth'.[19]

Having sought to moderate the extremes in the Kirk, in 1589, James VI proposed an alliance of Scotland, Denmark–Norway and the German princes, who would seek to mediate between the warring countries of Spain, France and England, and negotiate a 'common peace of Christendom' to prevent the further 'effusion of Christian blood' and to 'avert the common danger that threatens all the

Christian world'.²⁰ The 'common danger' was the Ottoman Turk, but during these years James VI was primarily interested in establishing his claim to the English throne, to which Spain represented the main challenge. In his ambition to unify Christendom, James was reviving an earlier notion of a Christian league, plans for which were frequently laid, but never actually implemented.²¹ More than half a century before, Henry VIII, following the earlier example of Cardinal Wolsey, had urged 'a universal peace in all Christendom' so that common action might be taken against the Ottoman Empire.²²

***

In his early conversations with ambassadors and diplomats after his arrival in England as king, James had stressed his commitment to religious reconciliation and his plan to achieve it through a European general council of all Christian churches, chaired by the pope.²³ In one of their first audiences at Greenwich in July 1603, James spoke to the Count of Beaumont in some detail of his plans, which he hoped the French king would support. There were, he observed, ceremonies and 'other indifferent things that have been introduced in the Church either by the excessive zeal of the people or the ambition and avarice of ecclesiastics' that were matters of dispute among Christians including Roman Catholics, Lutherans, Calvinists, English Protestants and Greek Orthodox, as well as disagreements about matters of faith. He believed these questions should now be discussed and decided by a general council 'legitimately assembled in a neutral place'.²⁴

Without such a resolution, James argued, the 'diversity of religious opinions' which had 'spread across all nations' would continue to be a justification of wars fomented by ambitious princes and sometimes by the popes themselves 'in order to better establish their own grandeur.'²⁵ According to James, the 'laziness, negligence, ambition and division of Christian princes' after the Reformation had allowed Rome's power to grow, and the pope to dominate them, impede their freedom to rule, and 'authorising their subjects to rise against them and usurping a kind of absolute empire over crowns'.²⁶

Many on both sides of the religious divide, Catholic and Protestant, sought reconciliation and peace and accepted the idea of a church council with supremacy over the pope to secure this. When he talked about reconciling Western Christendom, James was envisaging the main religious conflict in Europe as a battle not simply between Protestants and Catholics, but between those who defended the pope's claims for supremacy and the actions of their 'firebrand' Jesuit agents against the freedom of national churches, and those who asserted the right of secular rulers to act free from the threat of papal interference. If differences and conflicts continued within the church, James saw no prospect that peace in Christendom 'would ever be firm and assured'.²⁷

In his audience with the king, Beaumont assured James that if he would only return to the Old Church from which he 'had been snatched away from his youth', then his master, Henri IV, who had converted to Catholicism to secure his hold on the French throne and end the religious wars, would support James with advice and influence to achieve 'the Union and the reformation of the said Church in Christendom'. He knew, he said, that one of James's 'greatest ambitions' was 'to promote the peace, and the union of the Church'. Henri IV agreed, writing to Beaumont that he too believed Christendom could never be 'firm and assured' whilst there was such 'discord in religion'.²⁸

***

On New Year's Eve 1603 – in the midst of the spat between the French and Spanish envoys at Hampton Court – Henri IV's counsellor and president of the Parlement of Paris, Jacques-Auguste de Thou, wrote to King James on a higher matter. After offering congratulations on his accession, he asked the new king to promote 'the concord of the Church with common consent'. At Henri IV's request, de Thou enclosed a book inscribed to James, the first volume of *Histoira sui temporis*, in which de Thou traced the efforts of political and religious leaders to end religious conflict.²⁹ Using specific examples, the book endeavoured to show that princes who 'preferred sweetness to the force of arms for terminating wars of religion, even on disadvantageous terms, have acted prudently and in conformity with the maxims of the ancient Church.'[30] The dispatch of Thou's letter and book to James signified his reputation as an ambitious and influential king who shared a commitment to the task of religious reconciliation.

James regarded Ottoman Turkey and the 'Grand Turk', Sultan Ahmed I, as the chief enemy of Christendom and as the Venetian ambassador Nicolò Molin reported, 'wishes that the Christian Powers, instead of fighting among themselves, would unite to drive him out.' As Molin added, 'the idea is so fixed in his mind that he frequently expresses it in terms of great derision, declaring that he would always take the lead if other princes would do their part.'[31] Through proclamations and in speeches to the English Parliament, James insisted that there was no prince more eager than he to assist with a truly general council, 'not only out of a particular disposition to live peaceably with all states and princes of Christendom', but also 'to resist the common enemy ["the Turk"].'[32]

***

First, James sought to achieve a united church in England that would include all Christian faiths and might then become the blueprint for a universal Christian church and the reunion of Christendom. In his 'Proclamation Concerning Such as Seditiously Seek Reformation in Church Matters' of 24 October 1603, James explained that, while the 'constitution and doctrine' of the Church of England were 'agreeable to God's word and near to the condition of the Primitive Church', some 'things used in this church were scandalous'. He therefore proposed his own 'general council' – a conference comprising both conservative bishops and radical reformists – to be held in London in early January 1604, to identify those 'things' that needed reform.[33]

After the Christmas and New Year festivities finally came to an end, amid bitter January weather, four moderate Puritans led by Dr John Reynolds, Master of Corpus Christi College Oxford, together with Richard Bancroft, Bishop of London, and three other bishops dressed in the robes the Puritans so loathed, gathered at Hampton Court on Saturday 14 January for a three-day conference which, it was hoped, might reconcile differences within the English church.[34] As James made clear in his opening address, while he did not intend to make 'innovation', he would, like a good physician, 'examine and try the complaints'. He wanted both moderate Catholics, who rejected the papacy's claims to secular authority, and Puritans to find a place in the church.

While reaffirming his commitment to order and hierarchy, and making clear that 'Popish remnants' would remain in the church, James announced that reforms would be made in private baptism, excommunication, the disciplinary role of the bishops, and to the Book of Common Prayer. Much to the Puritans' disappointment, *all* would be expected to conform, to achieve uniformity and unity throughout England.[35]

The most significant outcome of the Hampton Court conference, however, would be James's commissioning of a new translation of the Bible which had been proposed by John Reynolds. It was to be 'consonant to the original Greek and Hebrew' with no marginal notes and was designed to strengthen unity under James's divine authority. 'His Highness wishes that some especial pains should be taken in that behalf for one uniform translation,' it was announced. This was to be performed 'by the best learned of both the universities ... to be reviewed by the bishops and chief learned of the church', then presented to the Privy Council, and ratified by James so that his 'whole church to be bound unto it, and none other'.[36]

'You will scarcely conceive how earnest his Majestie is to have this work begun,' wrote Bishop Bancroft, who James had appointed 'chief overseer' of the project, in his letter to officials at Cambridge University in July 1604, just six months after James had announced he was commissioning a new Bible.[37] James was personally involved in the selection of fifty-four translators from London and Cambridge and Oxford universities.

Over the next seven years, the scholars and theologians would work to translate the different books of the Bible: the Old Testament from Hebrew; the New Testament from Greek; and the Apocrypha from Greek and Latin. The translators were divided into six committees called 'companies', each assigned to translate a different section of the Bible. Bancroft, presumably under the direction of James, had drafted a document providing detailed rules to be used to ensure uniformity and as unbiased a translation as possible.[38] By design, the new Bible was more a revision of previous bibles than a new translation. The Bishops' Bible, which had been translated by English bishops and published in 1568, was the core text, and forty unbound copies were distributed among the translators. Working from this as their base, the translators examined the other bibles (including the Hebrew Bible; the 1565 edition of the Greek New Testament by Theodore Beza; all of the English Bible versions, from the Tyndale Bible of 1526, the Coverdale Bible of 1525 through to the Geneva Bible first printed in 1560; and the 1582 Catholic translation known as the 'Rheims New Testament'), and selected what they felt were the most accurate words for every verse. Committees of nine men, each under a 'director', reviewed each other's work, before an editorial board checked the final text.

By 1608 the first stage was ready, and the drafts were gathered for review, debate and amendment. They aimed to capture both the Catholic emphasis on mystery and the Puritan commitment to the clarity and accessibility of the written word. In 1610, the translation was formally submitted for printing, and in 1611 the first edition of the King James Bible (Old and New Testaments as well as the Apocrypha) was published. A decorative title page was affixed that contained the inscription: '*THE HOLY BIBLE, Containing the Old Testament, and the New. Newly translated out of the original tongues: & with the former Translations diligently compared and revised, by his Majesties special Commandment. Appointed to be read in Churches...*' A three-page dedication to King James followed, which alluded to the 'thick and palpable clouds of darkness' that 'overshadowed the land' on the death of Queen Elizabeth I, and how 'the appearance of your Majesty, as of the sun in his strength, instantly dispelled those ... mists'.[39]

James hoped the new translation would unify his kingdom and build a national identity in which he, the Bible, and the church stood together. A single Bible translation equalled a unified church, and a unified church was the first step to a unified country. James intentionally wanted his authorised Bible to be free of the sort of marginal notes of the Geneva Bible that allowed the laity to interpret the text for themselves. The new translation would reinforce the role of the church and of the state, by making the interpretation of the word of God the work of the clergy and bishops alone. The King James Bible was created with politics, as much as theology, in mind.

The King James Bible should also be regarded as the first of the ambitious new king's acts of union. It became the standard authorised work of English Protestantism. Over time, it was adopted by almost all sects of Christianity in English-speaking nations: a contribution to his vision for the reunion of Christendom. The Bible's dedication praised James I's 'zeal' towards the 'house of God' which was 'manifesting itself abroad in the furtherest parts of Christendom by writing in defence of the Truth'. James had become the most important Protestant ruler in Europe. Indeed, the translators added, James 'may be the wonder of the world in this latter age'.[40]

5

King of Great Britain

Britannia, which the triple world admires,
This isle hath now recovered her name...
With that great name, Britannia, this blest isle
Hath won her ancient dignity, and style
A world divided from the world: and tried
The abstract of it, in his general pride ...

Ben Jonson, *The Masque of Blackness* (1605)[1]

In the spring of 1604, after a delay of a year, and with the plague sufficiently abated to allow crowds to gather, the traditional pre-coronation three-mile procession finally took place through London.[2]

The 'royal entry' was designed to show off to audiences far and wide the new monarch, and the splendour, riches and ambition of his kingdoms. Colourful descriptions of the day were written, printed and distributed to ensure the event could be 'witnessed' both at home and abroad. The accounts of the Spanish and Venetian ambassadors, Villamediana and Molin, attest to the political and diplomatic significance of James's royal entry. They concluded that it was the finest and most extravagant England had ever seen.[3] And not since Elizabeth I's coronation entry forty-five years earlier had the country witnessed a royal event on this scale.

The procession set out from the Tower at eleven o'clock on the morning of Monday 15 March and moved westwards through the City of London, from Fenchurch Street to Cornhill and Cheapside, past St Paul's Cathedral and via Fleet Street to Temple Bar, and finally to Whitehall. Erected at key points along the route, and spanning the width of the streets, were seven magnificent triumphal arches, paid for and commissioned by the civic authorities and also by Italian and Dutch merchants. It was the City's official welcome to the new monarch, a means to pledge allegiance and signal hopes and expectations of the new reign. The vast Roman-inspired, painted and gilded structures – specially designed by London joiner and architect Stephen Harrison and his team of craftsmen – towered up to one hundred feet (30 metres) above the heads of the royal family. Some of the arches had stages and galleries built into them and held actors and musicians. Although the structures were only temporary, and were removed after the procession, we know precisely what they looked like and what they represented as they had their own commemorative, illustrated book: *Arches of Triumph*.

At the head of the procession rode King James's messengers, on horseback, then the magistrates of the City, followed by servants of the royal households and court functionaries, the clergy, bishops and archbishops, earls, marquises, barons and knights. One of those in the king's retinue was William Shakespeare, now a courtier as well as a playwright, who walked with eight of the King's Men.

Next came ten-year-old Prince Henry on horseback. Eyewitness Gilbert Dugdale wrote that the 'young hopeful Henry Frederick', acknowledging the crowds' cheers, smiled 'as over-joyed to the people's external comfort'.[4] Ten paces behind rode King James on a small white horse, with a saddle of purple velvet, embroidered with pearls, and under a canopy of yellow tissue-cloth – 'glittering, as late washed in a golden rain' – adorned with gold silk fringes, ribbons and ten large plumes, and held aloft by eight 'splendidly dressed' Scottish and English gentlemen of the Privy Chamber.[5]

The Danish queen, dressed in white, followed twenty paces behind, in a chariot drawn by two white mules. Dugdale described her as: 'Our gracious Queen Ann[a], mild and courteous ... Of exceeding beauty, did all the way with so humbly and with mildness, salute her subjects,' so 'that women and men in my sight wept with joy'.[67] Princess Elizabeth was deemed too young to attend. A year earlier, she had been placed in the guardianship of Lord and Lady Harington at Coombe Abbey, Warwickshire, and there she remained. Charles, younger still, was with his guardians in Scotland.

For the first time in decades, the English could celebrate having a royal family, and a flurry of poems, tracts, family trees and ballads were published in praise of the fact. As one pamphleteer put it: 'We have a King, and this same King an heir/A toward Prince (if fame be true) or rather/A virtuous son sprung from a virtuous father.'[8] After more than a half century of uncertainty about the succession, the English Crown now seemed secure.

Prince Henry had spent his early years separated from his mother, as was the Scottish practice, in the charge of John Erskine, the Earl of Mar, and his mother, the dowager countess. Queen Anna had found the arrangement distressing, and this had contributed to a deterioration in relations between the royal couple. After James left Scotland to begin his progress south, Anna had insisted on taking charge of Henry so that he might be brought to England with her. Anna eventually successfully wrested control of Prince Henry from the Mars, but there had been a bitter stand-off with James, played out through couriered messages. The dispute had been so traumatic, it was claimed, that it had led to Anna miscarrying and losing a pregnancy.

Princess Elizabeth had spent the first six and a half years of her life in the care of Lord Livingston and his Catholic wife at Linlithgow Castle. This was an arrangement that suited Queen Anna far better, as Lady Livingston was attached to the queen's household and Anna could see her daughter whenever she wished.[9] Over time – and particularly when it was rumoured that Anna had converted to Catholicism – the Kirk began to oppose Princess Elizabeth being brought up in what it saw as a Catholic household. The Church of Scotland's general assembly blamed 'the education of their Majesties' children in the company of professed, avowed and obstinate Papists, such as Lady Livingston, etc.', for what they saw as a 'great defection being sensibly entered in this Kirk, from the purity, zeal and practice of religion'. The Kirk maintained that James and Anna, through the choice of those entrusted with the care of their young daughter, were undermining the 'true religion'. While initially James held firm, in the end the Kirk got its wish. When the royal family moved to England in the summer of 1603, Lady Livingston did not go with them.

Prince Henry and Princess Elizabeth spent their initial months in England together, first at Windsor Castle, and then at Oatlands palace in Surrey, where they set up a court together with a joint household. At the end of the year, however, the siblings were separated: Elizabeth sent to live with the Haringtons in Warwickshire and Henry's household established at Nonsuch Palace, built by Henry VIII adjacent to Hampton Court.

The ceremonial route through London had been railed off 'to keep back the violent pressing of the multitudes', and crowds of spectators crammed every vantage point, watching from scaffolds and windows that had had their glass removed, eager to catch a fleeting glimpse of their new king.[10] At each of the seven arches, flanked by City officials and the guilds dressed in their ceremonial liveries, the king and his retinue stopped for speeches and pageants performed by actors perched up high on platforms, and written for the occasion by Ben Jonson and Thomas Dekker.[11] Jonson, Dekker, and Stephen Harrison, the designer of the arches, had been patronised by James I, and their designs and artistry doubtless reflected the iconography and ambition James wished to convey to audiences at home and abroad. However, such was the size of the crowd and the king's impatience, the royal entry proved a rather chaotic affair, and not all the planned speeches or performances could be completed.

The pageant at the first of the seven arches, written by Ben Jonson, and at the East End of Fenchurch Street, celebrated London as a Roman City 'Londinium' and the king as the new 'Emperor of Great Britain'.[12] Across the top in place of a pediment was a spectacularly carved fifty-five foot (17 metres) wide panorama of the City of London. Seated at the central stage was 'Monarchia Britannica', a woman dressed in 'cloth of gold and tissue', and beneath her the Crowns of England and Scotland. She held a sceptre in her hand and on her lap was a small globe inscribed in Latin with the words: 'The world of Britain, divided from the world.'[13] As Jonson described, the arch was covered with a curtain of silk 'painted like a thick cloud', which was drawn aside when the king drew near.[14] The 'clouds' were gathered 'upon the face of the City, through their long want of his most wished sight: but now, as at the rising of the Sun, all mists were dispersed and fled'.[15] James's entry into the City – and the realm – was depicted as a new dawn, with the king as the sun, whose accession had dispersed the clouds of uncertainty and chaos that had darkened the last years of Gloriana's reign.

A pageant followed in which one of the great actors of the age, Edward Alleyn, played 'The Genius of the City'. Dressed in a mantle, he held a goblet in one hand and a 'branch full of little twigs, to signify increase and indulgence' in the other. A boy actor playing 'The River Thames' welcomed James to his 'Empire's Seat' with the words: 'Never came man, more long'd for, more desired', and gave thanks for the arrival of a British monarch who descended from Brutus, 'the first king of Britain'.[16]

Prince Henry was celebrated as the 'springing glory of thy godlike race; His country's wonder, hope, love, joy and pride'.[17] The Stuart monarchy was described as a 'broad spreading tree/under whose shade may Britain ever be!' Genius then addressed Queen Anna, praising her birth and virtues: 'Daughter, Sister, Wife of several kings: daughter to Frederick II, King of Denmark–Norway, sister to Christian IV, King of Denmark–Norway, and wife to James VI/I.'[18]

The second arch, at Gracechurch Street, had been paid for by London's Italian merchants, and was filled with art works and carved figures. In the centre over the archway, there was a painting of James on horseback, styled as a Roman emperor, receiving the sceptre from Henry VII and beneath it the royal arms which now incorporated those of Scotland – a lion rampant – and Ireland – a gold harp. To the king-emperor's right, an actress representing 'Peace' stood holding an olive branch; to the left a woman held a shield with a motto proclaiming James as the 'Surest hope of all things.'[19]

The next arch was vast – around eighty-five feet (26 metres) high – and had been commissioned by the Dutch merchants and erected in front of the Royal Exchange. Two large fish curled in baroque scrolls framed the central gable to symbolise the importance of fishing to the Dutch community. An actress representing 'Divine Providence' stood on a stage at the top of the arch, her finger pointing up to heaven. Beneath was a picture of James seated on a throne, dressed in imperial robes and a crown, and holding a sceptre and sword. The allegorical figures 'Religion' and 'Piety' stood on either side of him, and then the larger figures of 'Justice' and 'Fortitude'. As the king approached the arch, seventeen young women performers appeared representing the provinces of the Dutch Republic. The dedication on this arch described James as the: 'Restorer of the world, securer of peace, defender of the faith, our Lord King James ... father of the country.'[20] It cast the king as a European ally and called on him to uphold the political-religious and economic interests of both England and the Republic.

As the royal party moved on, they passed a scaffold positioned with nine trumpets and a kettle drum which, much to the Queen Anna's delight, played a Danish march, her own country's music. The fourth arch in Cheapside was entitled *Nova Felix Arabia* ('New Happy Arabia') – a play on 'Arabia Felix', the legendary land of peace and home of the phoenix, the bird of virtue. James was cast as a new phoenix, risen from the embers of Elizabeth's reign to create a new *Arabia Britannica* – a land flourishing due to the presence of the new king. As James approached the arch, a woman signifying Fame stepped forward to proclaim his descent from Henry VII and from Brutus of ancient Troy, who landed in England more than a thousand years before. A chorister from St Paul's Cathedral sang that James was: 'Great Monarch of the West, whose glorious stem/Doth now support a triple Diadem/Weighing more than that of thy grand Grandsire Brute' whose reign heralds a 'new Spring.'[21]

At the Cross in Cheapside by St Paul's, City officials stepped forward with the Recorder of the City, Sir Henry Montague. The Recorder gave a speech of welcome and presented gold cups to the king, queen and young prince. Over the 'Little Conduit' (the medieval water fountain) at Cheapside an arch had been placed and decorated with fruit and flowers, representing the Garden of Plenty and anticipating a time of peace, prosperity and abundance for the country. An actor representing Sylvanus, Messenger of Peace, observed that Peace and Plenty had, 'languished many heavy months' for the king's presence.[22]

Hoisted up on the next arch, standing 100 feet (almost thirty metres) above the conduit on Fleet Street, was a large rotating orb depicting the new united kingdom – or 'the New World' as this pageant was titled. A speaker explained that the orb of England had been unsteady after Elizabeth's death, but it was now, with James's arrival, rotating correctly once more: 'Our Globe is drawn in a right line again'. And the four kingdoms under James – England, Scotland, Ireland and France – were 'all again united and made one'.[23]

The final arch, at Temple Bar, was devised by Ben Jonson as a representation of the Temple of Janus – a fusion of London and ancient Rome, designed to celebrate a return of 'golden times' when: 'Peace was with us so advanced, Rest received, Liberty restored, Safety assured.'

The pageant ended in grand style, with the conduit at Temple Bar running not with water, but with claret wine.[24]

James's entry through the main streets of the City of London highlighted its rising importance as a centre of commerce and its special relationship with the Crown. The City of London Corporation had commissioned five of the seven pageants, and these emphasised James's English lineage, his reunification of Britain and his new style as 'King of Great Britain'. There was also a truly international dimension here too: the patronage and involvement of Italian, Dutch and Belgian merchants and the presence of foreign ambassadors, allowed James's vision of monarchy and nationality to be broadcast abroad. Throughout all the entertainments 'Peace' was continually invoked and James was seen as bringing light, unity and hope where before there had been darkness and despair. A sun rising to bring a new dawn.

Whilst the published accounts of the day describe the royal entry in all its finery and exaltation, a key event had not gone to plan. At one point along the route, two players on horseback, one dressed as Saint George, the other as Saint Andrew, were to trot forward and unite, just as King James reached them. However, such was the press of the crowds that the two riders were unable to reach each other, and the royal procession passed by none the wiser. An unfortunate omen maybe, as shortly James would be meeting with Parliament to propose a formal union of Scotland and England.

***

Four days after the royal entry, the first Parliament of the reign, delayed because of the plague, met at Westminster. In his opening speech, James first stressed his lineage and rightful claim to the throne. He recalled how, twelve months earlier on his arrival in England, 'the people of all sorts rid and ran, nay, rather flew, to meet me; their eyes flaming nothing but sparkles of affection; their mouths and tongues uttering nothing but sounds of joy'.[25]

Peace and union, which had defined the pageant earlier that week, were the underlying themes of his speech.[26] James compared Henry VII's union of the warring houses of York and Lancaster with the peace he himself had brought through the union of two 'ancient and famous kingdoms'. He believed the formal union of England and Scotland would be popular and unopposed – other than by those 'either blinded with Ignorance, or else transported with Malice'. It was, said James, both 'the greatest and least question that ever came in Parliament'. It was God's plan and the fulfilment of British history: 'Hath he not made us all in One island, compassed with One Sea?' – England and Scotland being separated, 'neither by Sea, nor by any great River, Mountain, nor other strength of Nature, but only by little small Brooks, or demolished little Walls; so as rather they were divided in apprehension, than in effect'. And, he continued, 'in the end and Fulness of Time, United the Right and Title of both in my Person alike'.[27]

James now looked to Parliament to formalise that union. 'What God hath conjoined then, let no Man separate. I am the Husband, and all the whole Isle is My lawful Wife. I am the Head, and it is My Body. I am the Shepherd, and it is My Flock,' he told them. 'I hope therefore, no Man will be so unreasonable, as to think that I, that am a Christian king under the Gospel, should be a Polygamist, and Husband to Two Wives.' It was his wish to leave on his death, 'one worship to God: one kingdom, entirely governed: one uniformity in laws'. He sought to eradicate the names 'Scotland' and 'England' and instead insist both peoples 'shall pass under the common name of Britons', and all part of one kingdom 'Great Britain'.[28]

But how? Given the complexity of the issue, both Houses had to agree on what aspects to discuss first. The politician and philosopher Sir Francis Bacon, a keen advocate of union, headed a committee selected to agree an agenda. Upon his first meeting with the king in the spring of 1603, Bacon had cautioned him against moving 'faster perhaps than policy will bear'.[29] Now, the House of Lords suggested that a collective name be chosen for the kingdoms before the thornier issues of common laws and government, but the Commons did not agree, and resolved that there should be no union of name before discussion of a union of government. Bacon would soon emerge as the leading spokesman for the union in the Commons and urged that attention should focus on four areas: 'Union in Name, Union in Language, Union in Laws and Union in Employments.'[30] Union in laws, in particular the Scottish and English legal systems, would, he believed, be most difficult to attain, and moderation and time would be needed, noting: 'nothing amongst people breeds so much pertinency in holding their customs as sudden and violent offer to remove them'.[31] This would be something James would take time to comprehend.

Parliamentary opposition to James's proposals was vociferous, however, and would be long-lasting – with fears for the economy, for trade and for the loss of jobs after an influx of Scotsmen. Moreover, the English believed a change of name to 'Great Britain' would cause unnecessary confusion and invalidate laws, oaths and treaties made in the name of 'England'. Sir Edwin Sandys led the Commons opposition against the union, and stressed the gravity of a decision to change England's name. This, he said, was 'the weightiest cause, that ever came' before the Commons, and so they ought to 'proceed with a leaden foot'. He argued that by taking away the name of England, 'the maxims of the law' would also be taken away and the English Parliament could not 'make any Laws to bind Britannia'.[32] Indeed, they claimed, having already made James 'King of England', Parliament could not undo its own work by making him 'King of Britain'. A change of name would therefore necessitate a complete union, otherwise treaties in the name of England and Scotland would be affected, as would the status of ambassadors abroad and the king himself.[33]

There was much discussion of English precedence, with some arguing that Scotsmen should yield and 'just accept' the superior name of England and that English law superseded Scottish law. Moreover, Sandys added, though the king's subjects could take a new oath of allegiance to replace the one that expired with the old title, James would be free forever from the coronation oath guaranteeing his subjects' liberties, 'unless there were a new coronation'. In other words, a change of name by royal authority would seem to give James the status of conqueror. Sandys proposed that the most perfect union achievable was, in effect, annexation, which would see Scotland incorporated – like Wales before it – into a 'Greater England'. But this, as Sandys well knew, would be much too much for the king, let alone his Scottish subjects, to stomach. Sandys did however concede the necessity of a commercial union, but believed it was possible to have a single market without common laws or political institutions.[34]

On 21 April 1604, the king once again addressed the Commons, this time seeking to emphasise his open-mindedness, stating: 'I am so far from being wedded to any opinions of mine.' He then asked that Parliament appoint a commission to examine the best way to unite the realm. However, in advance of that, he wanted the Speaker to offer a loyal address, petitioning him 'to acknowledge yourself king of the whole united realm of Britain'.[35] This request was refused. Following consideration by the judges of the legal case for union, Cecil, on the judges' behalf, announced that if Parliament gave the king the name of Great Britain, immediately thereafter there would be 'utter extinction of all the laws now in force.'[36] Such a change would amount to conquest. 'Neither of the Parliament[s] of England and Scotland can do this of a sudden,' the Lords argued, 'and therefore that by the authority of both, there may be appointed of the nobility, clergy and Commons, selected commissioners to see what laws are to be taken away, what to be new made, [and] what else to be done for the perfecting of the Union.'[37]

Sir Francis Bacon continued his work as the king's agent, researching the king's case for formal union. He argued in the Commons that the names 'Britain' and 'British' were historic and honourable and such a unified style would help bury antagonisms inherent in the names 'England' and 'Scotland'.[38] While Bacon repeatedly defended the project, he admitted 'the more we wade, the more we doubt'.[39] Nevertheless, he believed the union of Crowns would bring a balance of power in Europe, and so 'disposing of the affairs of Europe thereby to a more sure and universal peace and concord'.[40]

Others, however, saw the union of two 'mighty and warlike' peoples on the same island, as a means by which European Protestantism might go on the offensive. The anonymous Scottish author of *A Treatise about the Union of England and Scotland* wrote that: 'The fear of our unified forces [would] deter the foreign enemy from invasion' by providing a Protestant counterbalance to the large, Catholic multiple kingdoms of Spain and France, and might indeed even lead to an offensive against the papal Antichrist.[41] Scotsman John Gordon declared that James should use the valour of his two kingdoms 'for the delivery of his church, from the barbarous tyranny wherewith she hath been long oppressed by Popes'.[42] Several other tracts about the union argued that James was placed on earth by God to 'not only unite Britain in true religion but also to purify all Christendom of its idolatry'.[43]

In his opening speech to parliament, James repeated his desire to be part of a general council to reconcile Christendom. 'I could wish from my heart,' he declared, 'that it would please God to make me one of the members of such a general Christian union in Religion, as laying wilfulness aside on both hands, we might meet in the middest, which is the centre and perfection of all things.'[44] Yet he also allowed his son and heir Prince Henry to be looked upon as a future British king who would lead the charge of Protestantism in Europe.

***

Throughout the summer and autumn of 1604, the idea of union was promoted and debated in tracts, pamphlets and letters carried from London north across the border and across the Channel too.[45] Parliament was prorogued at the end of October, and the work of the union commissioners began.

Meanwhile, James proceeded to take matters into his own hands, using the royal prerogative to pursue his vision of Britain. Despite Parliament withholding permission for a change of name, for which James blamed 'the curiosity of a few giddy heads', he pushed on regardless and issued two major royal proclamations.[46] The first announced the change of royal style, the second a new coinage.[47]

James declared his title to be 'King of Great Britain'. The two kingdoms, he observed, shared an island which 'within it self hath almost none but imaginary bounds of separation ... making the whole a little world within it self'. Its inhabitants shared: 'a community of Language, the principal means of Civil society, a unity of Religion, the chiefest band of hearty Union, and the surest knot of lasting Peace'. Even the ancient laws of the two kingdoms were marked by 'a greater affinity and concurrence' than existed between those 'of any other two Nations'. James emphasised that rather than union, it was reunion: he was 'reuniting' the ancient kingdoms of England and Scotland 'under one Imperial Crown'. This had been brought about not be conquest and bloodshed but by his succession and descent from the ancient royal lines of both kingdoms.[48]

As the king's proclamation explained, 'Great Britain' was 'the true and ancient name which God and time have imposed upon this isle, extant and received in histories, in all maps and cartes [charts] wherein this Isle is described, and in ordinary letters to ourselves from divers foreign princes'. It was 'warranted also by authentic charters, exemplifications under seals, and other records of great antiquity giving us precedent for our doing, not borrowed out of foreign nations but from the acts of our progenitors, Kings of this Realm of England, both before and since the conquest'.[49] Here was an appeal to a new national mythology.

The king's new title was to be used on all proclamations, treaties and other official government literature, and on all coins. However, it would not apply 'to any legal proceedings, instrument or assurance until further order be taken in that behalf'.[50] In justifying the change in style, James I argued that he was not assuming 'any new affected name devised at our pleasure', but rather 'out of undoubted knowledge do use the true and ancient name which God and time have imposed upon this isle'.[51]

***

On 20 October 1604, the day that James proclaimed himself King of Great Britain, the 'Commission for Union' assembled in the Painted Chamber at Whitehall. This was a carefully selected group of nobles, gentry, lawyers, statesmen, clerics and merchants. James had instructed that the Scottish and English commissioners be matched 'with persons of like quality and rank'.[52] On 29 October, things got going with rapid progress being made over the next six weeks. In December, the commissioners reported back. Compromise had been reached, though the agenda had been a limited one and confined to three areas: the abolition of hostile laws, trade, and the naturalisation of subjects. More contentious issues such as religion, and legal and parliamentary union, were set aside for the time being.

In mid-November, new coinage was issued, including a new gold coin called 'The Unite', valued at twenty shillings. which would be valid and of equal value both sides of the border. The coins were emblazoned with the Scottish crowned thistle and English crowned double rose. On the reverse of the sovereign coin was a portrait of James and his new title: 'King of Great Britain, France and Ireland'. For the reverse, James had chosen a Latin inscription from the Old Testament Book of Ezekiel, 37.22: *'Faciam eos in genem unam'*: 'I will make them one nation.'

Yet this attempt to make 'one nation' would disregard centuries of parliamentary tradition, England's ingrained sense of superiority and national mythology. James's assumption of the persona of a British monarch, with trappings of national flag, name and nascent British identity – all without parliamentary approval – threatened English sensibilities. While the Scottish Parliament accepted and adopted the name of Great Britain, albeit reluctantly, Parliament in England did not.[53]

6

Rex Pacificus (King of Peace)

'Come they not hither, as to the fountain from whence peace springs?
Here sits Solomon and hither come the tribes for judgement. O happy
moderator, blessed Father, not father of thy country alone, but Father
of all thy neighbour countries about thee.'

Thomas Middleton, *The Peace-Maker, or
Great Brittaines Blessing* (1618)[1]

When James first entered London, his 'Empire's Seat', he did
so, said Scaramelli, 'without a sword at his side, on purpose'.
This was a statement that he had come to his kingdom in peace,
and that 'he will preserve it in peace for himself and his subjects'.[2]
Within days James had ordered an end to all privateering raids and
reprisals against Spanish shipping, the first steps towards coming to
terms with Spain and ending the long-running war that had blighted
England's finances and prospects for trade.

In his maiden speech to Parliament, he proclaimed that the most
prominent advantage of his policy of peace would be the enrich-
ment of commerce. 'At My coming here,' he said, 'I found the State
embarked in a great and tedious War; and only by Mine Arrival here,
and by the Peace of My Person, is now Amity kept.' Peace 'abroad
with their Neighbours', he asserted, would allow the towns to flourish, the merchants to become rich, trade to increase, and 'the People
of all Sorts of the Land to enjoy free Liberty to exercise themselves
in their several Vocations, without Peril, or Disturbance'.[3]

A series of wars with Spain over eighteen years had put a severe strain both on the English economy and government finances. Many merchants, not least those exporting woollen cloth, the dominant staple of the economy, had been adversely affected. With the demise of the Antwerp market, sacked by the Spanish, and the markets closed in France, Spain and Portugal, the Company of Merchant Adventurers of London, who controlled the export of woollen cloth, longed for peace and stability.

But some had profited from war. It had allowed the English privateers to raid Iberian merchant ships returning to Europe from the East and West Indies, and Spanish silver fleets in the Caribbean.[4] Through the 'necessity' of war, the English had begun to look beyond Europe to opportunities on a global stage. Faced with a hostile Catholic Europe, England had forged new commercial relations with the Muslim East – Turkey, Morocco and Persia – giving English merchants in the Levant Company (first chartered in 1582) the opportunity to trade directly in the Eastern Mediterranean and along the Barbary coast of North Africa.

Now people looked forward with eager anticipation to the riches and expansion of trade that the end of the war would bring. 'The ports and havens of these kingdoms, which have long been barred, shall now open the mouths of their rivers, and arms of their seas, to the gentle amity and just traffic of all nations,' declared Richard Martin, Middle Temple lawyer on James's arrival into the city. Domestic and foreign trade would nourish the new nation, 'desiring (by the exchange of Home bred commodities with foreign) into the veins of the land that wholesome blood and well-got treasure, which shall strengthen the sinews of your Majesty's kingdoms'.[5]

***

In late 1602, Captain James Lancaster, who was in command of the East India Company's first voyage, established England's first 'factory' (trading post) in the East. It was the foothold English merchants had long sought. In 1600, 'the Company of Merchants of

London Trading into the East Indies' (to become known as the East India Company) had been granted a charter conferring a fifteen-year monopoly on English trade between the Cape of Good Hope and the Strait of Magellan. To support its trading, the Crown allowed the company to carry out of England up to £30,000 of gold bullion or silver coins annually, to supplement sales of English exports and with which to buy Asian goods. Such trading privileges provoked resentment in England from the moment they were granted. The export of the country's bullion became a focus of great debate and with it the merits, or otherwise, of East Indian trade to the English economy. Was the import of luxury goods not a corrupting influence on morality and the export of bullion damaging to the nation's economic prosperity?

In 1602 the Dutch East India Company (Verenigde Oostindische Compagnie [VOC]) was established by the States-General of the United Provinces, marking the beginning of an intense rivalry between the companies that would test the peaceful alliance of the two countries in Europe. Both produced many of the same goods for export – above all textiles – but with superior sea power, the Dutch were able to steal a march on the English in the race to access the East Indies spice markets. Denied trade with France and Spain because of the war, the VOC aggressively sought new markets in Italy, Russia, Turkey, the East Indies and the Orient. The Dutch had already established a factory to trade in nutmeg, mace and cloves at Bantam. Indeed, it was the success of the Dutch in their first voyage to the Indies that stirred up London merchants to seek their own charter to trade there.

From the outset, the VOC enjoyed the steadfast support and capital of the States-General, the assembly of the seven United Provinces of the Netherlands, and this quickly made it a force to be reckoned with. Within just a few years, the Dutch had become the dominant European trading power in the Indonesian archipelago, displacing the Portuguese, who had held a monopoly for much of the sixteenth century.

Led by its founding governor Sir Thomas Smythe, the East India Company lagged well behind the VOC in terms of finance and government support. Smythe was an experienced and successful governor of early trading companies, most notably the Muscovy and Levant companies, which had procured luxury goods from the Middle East for European markets for some twenty years. After a short time imprisoned in the Tower for his association with the disgraced Earl of Essex, Smythe was now enjoying a rehabilitation under James, receiving his knighthood in May 1603.

Smythe was one of the most prolific merchant-adventurers and commercial promoters of the age. He would remain governor of the East India Company almost without interruption until 1621. His house in Philpot Lane near Fenchurch Street in London was the centre of company activities. General assemblies were held in the great hall, complete with an 'Inuit canoe' hanging from the ceiling, reflecting the great hope of Smythe and the company of finding a northern sea passage to the East. Merchants and sailors crowded the halls looking for employment. Through his many roles, contacts and general networking, Smythe would do much to advance London's global trade and James's colonisation projects in the Americas.

By September 1603, when the *Hector* and the *Red Dragon*, the last of the company's maiden's fleet to return home, dropped anchor in the Downs, much had changed. Lancaster and his crew were returning not to the queen who had granted their charter, but to a new monarch. James greeted the fleet warmly and knighted Lancaster a month later in acknowledgement of the success of the voyage. Recognising the profit that might be made, James immediately purchased a huge amount of the ships' cargo of pepper and threatened to block the company from selling theirs, until the Crown had sold its supply. Thomas Sackville, the Lord Treasurer, proposed instead that the merchants buy back the king's pepper or market it on his behalf with their own; they respectfully declined.[6] The incident marked the beginning of a fluctuating relationship between the East India Company and the king. The company would be regarded with favour by James, but often as a means to an end, and when it suited him. Crown and company were united by the shared purpose of profit, but the company's profit might always potentially be claimed by the Crown.

With preparations beginning in earnest for peace negotiations with Spain, the East India Company was determined to protect its interests and future prospects. Thomas Alabaster, the company's accountant, repeatedly told Cecil that the essential concessions of a peace treaty must include the ability to trade freely in the New World and the East. Restoring pre-war commercial relations was not sufficient; trade to Italy and Spain was 'no longer trade of importance'. Rather, it was long-distance trade with America and Asia that represented England's commercial future. The East India Company's petition, addressed to those commissioners who would be negotiating the treaty with Spain, demanded nothing must be done to hinder their trade, 'out of which there maybe grow so great a benefit & strength to his Majesties dominions & the common Wealth of this kingdom'.[7] As Alabaster starkly put it, if this wasn't one of the concessions of peace, Spain 'shall effect by this Peace which they could not do by wars'.[8]

***

Overtures for a settlement had been made by both Spain and England in the months before Elizabeth's death. But with the accession of James, who as king of Scotland had not been at war with Spain, the prospects for the conclusion of a peace treaty greatly improved.

From the earliest weeks of his reign, detailed preparations had been set in motion to enable negotiations to begin. James met with the ambassadors and went over some of the key issues – such as whether the Dutch would be included in the treaty and, if not, whether the English would continue to support them in any way, including allowing subjects to volunteer to fight against Spain. He even discussed the arrangements for the talks themselves, and made it clear that he wished to be consulted on everything and to remain closely involved with the negotiations. The Habsburgs would be sending two delegations: one to represent the King of Spain, the other the rulers of the Spanish Netherlands, and James suggested the number of commissioners he expected each of the groups to comprise.

On 1 October 1603, Philip III named Juan Fernández de Velasco, 5th Duke of Frías and Constable of Castile, Spain's most pre-eminent nobleman, as his ambassador extraordinary for the negotiations. The Constable set out from Valladolid three weeks later, and by the end of the year was in Brussels, writing to Villamediana of his safe arrival 'with all the powers and funds necessary for the peace'. He suggested, however, that Flanders was a 'more appropriate' setting than London for the negotiations, due to 'the decorum of His Majesty', and that 'a Neutral country' be more desirable 'for the sake of precedence.' The Constable warned the King of Spain and Portugal that by going to England, it would 'appear that we were showing too much desire to agree', and this would lead to a 'damage of reputation', as would the prospect of 'returning in favour' if the peace talks failed.[9]

Villamediana relayed the Constable's request that the talks be held in Flanders, saying that Juan Fernández de Velasco was tired and in poor health and would need time to recover before he could even consider crossing the Channel to England.[10] But James would not give way. At Richmond Palace, a delegation headed by Cecil, explained to the Spanish ambassador that the king wished the matter to be resolved as soon as possible, that the talks were to be held in England, and that James expected to be consulted on everything and would stay involved in directing events.[11] The discussions reached an impasse, with the Constable and his 200-strong entourage remaining on the other side of the Channel.

Villamediana complained bitterly in his dispatch to Philip: 'This King and Kingdom and the Council are exceedingly vain, and so much that they think and they give themselves to understand that [the choice between] Peace or the universal discord of the world will be in their hand and power.'[12] To move the situation on, James reassured Velasco of his personal commitment, adding such was his desire for a peace, that it would be 'very firm and last many centuries'.[13] In February 1604, after many months' delay, the Constable agreed that he would cross the Channel, but only once the peace negotiations had reached a conclusion, maintaining that an attack of gout prevented him from leaving his lodgings on the Flemish coast.[14]

Finally, on Sunday 20 May, the formal peace negotiations began. Over the next three months English, Spanish and Flemish delegates met at Somerset House on the Strand in London (shortly to be renamed Denmark House in honour of Queen Anna). In the Constable's absence, Villamediana was accompanied by the Senator of Milan. Alongside the Spanish commissioners representing the governor of the Spanish Netherlands (Archduke Albert, and his wife Isabella, Philip III's sister), sat three of the most powerful men at the court in Brussels: Prince-Count of Arenberg, Jean Richardot, and Lodewijk Verreycken. The five English commissioners were the leading members of James's court and Privy Council: Sir Robert Cecil; Thomas Sackville, Earl of Dorset (the Lord Treasurer); Charles Howard, Earl of Nottingham; Charles Blount, Earl of Devonshire (Lord Lieutenant of Ireland); and Henry Howard, Earl of Northampton.

While the question of support for the Dutch rebels in the United Provinces and actions of the Spanish Inquisition against English travellers and traders were key areas of discussion, the most intense parts of the negotiations related to the 'intercourse' of trade – particularly free trade for the English with the East and West Indies, which the Spanish strongly resisted. When the issue had first been raised, the Spanish commissioners ended the session but when talks resumed on 4 July, Henry Howard, earl of Northampton delivered a belligerent speech based on careful notes he had prepared in which he asserted that the law of nature and previous trading agreements precluded the right of the Spanish to prohibit English trade in any part of the world. He added 'if any may bar us from trading into those parts, the right of exclusion belongs properly to those Indian princes themselves'.[15]

Having made the case, and presented the demands of the English merchants, Northampton was content for the negotiations to proceed and a compromise reached.

On 16 August 1604, after eighteen sessions around the conference table, the representatives of 'James, King of Great Britain, France and Ireland, and Defender of the Faith' and Philip III King of Spain and Portugal, the archdukes of Austria, and dukes of Burgundy signed the Treaty of London, thus ending years of Anglo–Spanish conflict stretching back to the Armada. It was the first major peace treaty between a Protestant and a Catholic power in the post-Reformation era, and it was one that would endure until shortly after James's death.

By the final terms of the treaty, the English appeared to have won significant concessions: free commerce was to be established and maintained between the King of Spain and the King of Great Britain, 'as well by Land as by Sea and fresh Water, in all and singular the Kingdoms, Dominions and Islands'.[16] There was, however, a significant caveat: freedom to trade would only be permitted to those territories where the English had traded before the 'breaking out of the War'.[17] Moreover, the treaty was ambiguous in two key places: Japan and the Mughal Empire; the English concluded that they had the right of access, the Iberians thought they did not.

The peace treaty (the 'Articles of peace, intercourse, and commerce'), was announced at the court gate at Whitehall, and then at locations throughout the City.[18] While Villamediana observed that James's subjects received the proclamation with great joy, the French envoy Beaumont reported the opposite, writing that there were no bonfires or cannon salutes at the Tower, and the announcement was 'received in sullen silence' punctured with the occasional exclamation of 'God preserve our good neighbours in Holland and Zealand.'[19] Venetian ambassador Molin noted: 'There is a general disaffection towards this peace, for no one can bear to see the Dutch abandoned.'[20] Indeed, many of the London churches offered prayers for the success of the Dutch as they continued their struggle against Spain.[21]

Expressions of disaffection did not die down. A year later, James was forced to issue a proclamation ordering the English to desist from hostility towards the Habsburg powers and to follow his Majesty's own example: to 'embrace and cherish' a 'perfect amity and friendship' towards their 'good brethren' of Spain and Austria. The English commissioners had rejected Spanish demands to include clauses giving freedom of conscience to Catholics, and a number of preachers had spoken out against peace with a country they regarded as being in league with the Antichrist.[22] The lack of significant concessions to Catholicism would seed resentment among certain Catholics in England, who had looked to Spain for protection, and who would, before long, take matters into their own hands.

With the treaty now agreed, the Constable of Castile and his entourage finally made the crossing to England. Having landed at the Downs due to contrary winds, they were ferried to Dover, where on 15 August they were met with a grand ceremonial welcome and gun salute. After taking a day to rest, the Spaniards began their journey towards London with great crowds lining the route. Finally reaching Greenwich, the Constable was rowed upriver to Somerset House.

James was not in London to greet the Constable. Frustrated by what he saw as Velasco's uncooperative behaviour, James deliberately did not return from his progress in the Midlands until towards the end of the month, at which point the treaty formalities and celebrations commenced. On Sunday 29 August, placing his hands on a Latin Bible, James swore to uphold the peace. Those gathered around cried out: 'Peace, peace, peace! Long live the King! Long live the King! Long live the King!' The rest of the day was given over to feasting and entertainments all over the capital, with the king hosting an elaborate banquet at Whitehall Palace. It was, said James, a particularly happy day, not just because of the peace but because it was Princess Elizabeth's birthday and 'therefore he hoped that through her name there might be means of preserving the kingdoms of Spain and England in friendship and union, unlike that other hostile Elizabeth who had caused so much damage'.[23] The Constable responded by raising a toast to James's children. It was an acknowledgement of the potential for a future marriage between the two countries, to seal the new alliance.

***

The following March, a vast embassy, estimated to have included between 650 and 900 people, led by Charles Howard, Earl of Nottingham – the Lord High Admiral who had led the English fleet against the Armada twenty years before – set sail for Spain to witness Philip III ratify the treaty. This was a deliberately British entourage, with many of the leading families of Scotland and England forming Nottingham's embassy. From Coruña, the group made the two-week trip to Valladolid, where the Spanish court was in residence. Three weeks of entertainments and celebrations ensued, outdoing the celebrations in London the year before.

On the party's departure, Sir Charles Cornwallis remained as resident ambassador, the first for two decades. He was tasked with setting up an English embassy first in Valladolid and then the following year in Madrid. During Cornwallis's first summer, discussions were held at the Spanish court about James's proposal for a general council of all Christian churches. Writing to Cecil, Cornwallis said that he had been told that 'if the King [of England] hath a will, there will at his Desire be granted a general Council and that in the most free and unrestrained manner'.[24] A fortnight later Cornwallis added: 'the Pope's Nuncio is daily here expected and that this Pope' – the recently elected Paul V – 'is said to be very affectionate to the king my master'.[25] It appears that some Spanish officials were prepared to back James's proposal for a council, not for the broader aim of religious reconciliation, but as a condition that James end English aid for the Dutch rebels – a matter which had failed to be addressed in the Treaty of London negotiations.

But, in late November, as Cornwallis prepared to send his secretary, Walter Hawkesworth, to London with more details of the Spanish 'overtures', he was astonished to receive news 'of the happy Discovery of [a] horrible treason'.[26]

7

The Powder Plot and Paper War

'No Man can aggravate the Powder Treason: To tell it,
and know it, is enough.'

Attorney-General Sir Edward Coke, 1606[1]

On 11 November 1605, James wrote to Christian IV, King of
Denmark–Norway, 'of the most horrid and detestable of all
treasons undertaken anywhere in the world'. A plot had been discovered to blow up the Houses of Parliament and kill James and
his government as they gathered for the state opening. It was, as
James continued, 'all the more atrocious since it was to be undertaken by men professing themselves to be adherents and avengers
of the Roman and papist religion (or a more impure superstition)'.[2]
Robert Catesby, a Northamptonshire gentleman, together with a
small group of other young Catholic gentlemen from the Midlands
who felt betrayed by James's inaction as king, had determined to
take decisive action. As Catesby put it: 'All foreign Princes [and]
their Ambassadors had been here, and had done nothing for
Catholics, neither did he hope of good from any of them. And therefore he had resolved of that Course.'[3] The seven main conspirators
were Catesby, brothers John and Christopher Wright, Robert and
Thomas Wintour, Guy Fawkes, and Thomas Percy, the latter a member of 'the band of gentlemen pensioners', the king's bodyguard.
Save for Percy, all had experience of fighting for the Spanish in the

Netherlands. All were known to the authorities, except Fawkes, who had spent considerable time abroad.

Catesby's original plan was that the conspirators would tunnel into the basement of the House of Lords from a building that Percy rented next door. However, when the cellar beneath the Lords in the Palace of Westminster came up for rent, Percy took the lease. The gunpowder was to be stored there, ready to be ignited when Parliament was sitting. It was intended that the explosion would kill the king, Queen Anna, Prince Henry and the entire ruling elite. Afterwards the plotters would lead an uprising of Catholic gentry in the Midlands. They aimed to kidnap nine-year-old Princess Elizabeth from her guardians at Coombe Abbey, place her on the throne as a puppet queen, and through her rule the country and restore the rights of Catholics.[4] Prince Charles, who had been moved to England the previous year, was closely guarded in London and had not been identified as an immediate target.

On Saturday 26 October an anonymous letter was sent to William Parker, Lord Monteagle, warning him to stay away from the opening of Parliament on 5 November because those who attended would 'receive a terrible blow'.[5] Monteagle passed the letter to Cecil, who passed it to the king. The Palace of Westminster was searched and on the evening of the 4th, Guy Fawkes was discovered in the cellar with thirty-six barrels of gunpowder. He was arrested and taken to the Tower to be interrogated, as the king instructed, with torture if necessary.

When the plotters heard news of Fawkes's arrest the following morning, they fled northwards to pursue the second part of the plan. An arrest warrant was issued for Thomas Percy. His patron and distant cousin, Henry Percy, Earl of Northumberland, who had petitioned the king before and after his accession for some form of Catholic toleration, was sent to the Tower of London where he would remain for sixteen years.

On 6 November Cecil received word from Lord Harington, Princess Elizabeth's guardian, informing him that the stables at Warwick Castle had been broken into and all the 'great horses taken'. Sensing 'some great rebellion',[6] Harington sought Cecil's 'opinion and the king's pleasure', as he feared that the rebels might seek to kidnap the princess. Without waiting for a reply, Harington moved Elizabeth from his estate to 'a place of far more safety both in respect of the strength of the city, and also for the loyal affection which I know to be in the citizens'.[7] Sir John reported that when the princess was told of the plot, she replied: 'What a Queen should I have been by this means? I had rather have been with my royal father in the parliament house, than wear his crown on such condition.'[8]

A royal proclamation promptly circulated on 7 November curated the official narrative of events. It claimed that the rebels had been 'seduced' by the 'superstition of the Romish Religion', and that religion was actually a 'cloak for their true intention' which was 'the Subversion of the State' and widespread anarchy. The proclamation made clear that James knew the difference and could distinguish between traitors and otherwise loyal Catholics, and he regarded those subjects who did not profess the 'true religion' to be good subjects nevertheless. Most significantly, the proclamation declared that, despite contrary rumours, James did not believe foreign princes or states were involved. He therefore wanted to correct those 'busy persons' who might try to 'scandalise the Amity where we stand with all Christian princes and States' by starting rumours of foreign involvement with the conspiracy.[9]

The rebels got as far as Holbeche House in Staffordshire where, on the morning of 8 November, Richard Walsh, the Sheriff of Worcestershire and a company of men put the house under siege. In the shoot-out that followed, Catesby and Percy were reportedly killed by single shots. Wintour was hit in the shoulder while crossing the courtyard; John Wright was shot and injured, as were his brother and another man, Ambrose Rookwood. These surviving conspirators were captured and brought to London for interrogation. They were tried, found guilty of treason and hanged. After their bodies had been castrated, eviscerated, and cut into pieces, their heads were placed on spikes along London Bridge and their quarters on gates in the City.

***

On Saturday 9 November, James addressed Parliament. This time he went out of his way to attribute the plot not merely to the personal resentments of a handful of embittered men, but to ideas directly promoted by the Roman Catholic Church. In his opening speech he emphasised that 'merely and only religion' was the sole motive of the conspirators. It was only Roman Catholics who claimed, 'by the grounds of their religion', that it was 'lawful' or 'meritorious to murder princes'. However, the king was also at pains to stress that the plot was the work of a few 'fanatics' – 'the treason of a few' – rather than the wider Catholic community at home or abroad. He also emphasised that those foreign rulers who were rumoured to be connected to the plot were innocent, as he believed none would 'abase himself so much'.[10]

Within a matter of weeks, the King's Printer had published the speech in English and in Latin. *The King's Book – or, His Majesties Speech ... concerning the Gunpowder Plot ... together with the Discourse of the manner of the discovery of this late intended treason* – promoted the official line that no foreign power had been involved in the plot, and was intended to feed public demand for news at home and reach a wider European audience abroad.[11] It was vital to reassure Europe that England remained committed to safeguarding the lives of all its 'well-affected' Catholic subjects.

The *King's Book* was just one of a number of texts printed after the plot, at the King's Printing House, based at Northumberland House in St Martin's Lane, Aldersgate, as the king and his government sought to counter 'divers uncertain, untrue and incoherent reports'.[12] It was also a means of projecting far and wide James's image as a champion of Protestantism, of challenging the pope's authority to depose kings and spreading the word that leading Jesuits (priests and clerics of the Catholic missionary order the Society of Jesus) had helped plan the conspiracy.[13] Henry Garnet, England's most senior Jesuit priest, was tried in the London's Guildhall in March 1606. According to Attorney-General Sir Edward Coke, Garnet was bent on 'devilish treason', the 'Deposing of Princes, Disposing of Kingdoms, Dauting and deterring of subjects, and Destruction'.[14] He was found guilty and hanged, drawn and quartered on 3 May in St Paul's Churchyard. A Latin summary of evidence against Garnet was compiled and published for a European audience.[15]

Outside government circles, anti-Catholic polemic also appeared in print calling on King James to lead Britain in the protection of Protestantism at home and abroad, and in defeating 'the Antichrist' (the pope). In his polemic poem *The Double PP*, Thomas Dekker described the Powder Plot as the most recent of countless Jesuit conspiracies sponsored by the pope to undermine Protestant monarchies and murder Protestants.[16] Whilst drawing attention to papal abominations, polemists called for Protestants across Europe of all stripes to come together. The *Devill of the Vault*, a pamphlet published under the pseudonym 'J. H.', called for Protestants to put aside their doctrinal differences and profess one faith. The author prayed God to 'inspire the hearts of Christian Kings, t'unite the force in one: And drag that triple-Crowned Beast, from out his monstrous throne.'[17]

James did nothing to discourage the publication of such texts. Indeed, in his own writings as James VI of Scotland, he had identified the pope as the Antichrist. Since his accession to the English throne, he had commissioned or supported anti-papal polemics, including those by Robert Abbot, Bishop of Salisbury, and the royal chaplain and later Bishop of Derry, George Downame.[18]

Whilst James did not give up his vision for a united church at home and abroad, after the Powder Plot, he grew more vociferous in challenging the pope's claims to temporal power. In doing so, he was drawn into a great European conflict, not of the sword but of the pen.

***

On 22 June 1606, an Oath of Allegiance requiring Catholics to pledge loyalty to the king became law. Every subject was to accept King James and his heirs as the 'lawful and rightful' rulers of Britain and acknowledge that the pope lacked the 'power or authority to depose the King ... or to authorise any foreign prince to invade or annoy him or his countries, or to discharge any of his subjects of their allegiance and obedience to his Majesty'. In addition, Catholics had to swear that they 'abhorred, detested and abjured' as 'impious and heretical' the 'damnable doctrine' that princes, excommunicated or deprived by the Pope' may be 'lawfully deposed or murdered.'[19]

According to James, the oath was designed to distinguish loyal Catholics – 'who though blinded through the superstition of Popery yet carried a dutiful heart towards our obedience' – from disloyal ones, who saw difference in religion as a 'safe pretext for all kind of treasons and rebellions against their sovereign'.[20] The oath carefully distinguished between purely spiritual matters and the pope's claims to authority in secular matters.

When news of the oath reached Rome, the newly elected Pope Paul V wrote expressly forbidding Catholics in England to 'bind' themselves by the oath, which 'must evidently appear unto you by the words themselves, that such an Oath cannot be taken without the hurting of the Catholic Faith and the Salvation of your Souls'.[21] However, the head of the Roman Catholic community in England, Archpriest George Blackwell, who had been horrified by the 'Powder Treason', chose not to distribute the pope's letter. Apprehended and questioned by Archbishop Bancroft in June 1607, he said he approved of the Oath of Allegiance but had 'divulged his judgment and direction for the lawfulness of the taking of that oath,' only verbally and not in writing.[22] Under arrest in the Gatehouse in Westminster, Blackwell was ordered to send a letter to priests making clear that it would not be lawful or just for the pope to excommunicate King James, and that if that were to happen, the king's subjects 'would still be bound in the same way as now to maintain their loyalty' to the Crown. Blackwell urged Catholics to take the oath, as he himself had done, 'so shall we shake off the false and grievous implication of treason'.[23] On 23 August 1607, Pope Paul addressed another letter to English Catholics, making clear that, despite Blackwell's reservations about the oath, it should not be taken under any circumstances.[24] Weeks later, the Jesuit theologian Cardinal Bellarmine wrote to Blackwell condemning his 'slip and fall' in not refusing an unlawful oath. The oath, Bellarmine argued, in professing temporal allegiance to the king, required Catholics in England to 'deny the Primacy of the Apostolic See.'[25] Blackwell countered immediately. In a letter to Bellarmine, he claimed that the writings of the church fathers had never subscribed to the view that 'the most holy successor of S[t]. Peter]' had 'an Imperial and Civil power' to 'depose a king'. And in a letter directly to English Catholics written on 20 January 1607 from the Clink prison, and subsequently printed by the King's Printer, he made clear that whilst the pope was 'head of the Catholic Church' and that all rulers were 'subject in some cases unto his spiritual censures', he had no right to depose them or claim temporal power and English subjects could rightly owe allegiance to their king.[26] Two days later, the pope deprived Blackwell of his position as archpriest.

Frustrated in his belief that the oath was being wilfully misunderstood in Rome and that his sovereign authority was being undermined in the pope's letters to English Catholics, James composed a 112-page treatise: *An Apologie for the Oath of Allegiance*. The tract was published anonymously in English by the King's Printer ('and by royal authority') in February 1608. Included with the tract were the two letters the pope had sent to English Catholics and a letter from the Jesuit theologian Cardinal Bellarmine to Blackwell condemning the archpriest's actions. James's authorship of the tract was an open secret, and it was quickly translated and published in Latin and French. Indeed, some ambassadors who received copies were told it was the king's work.

In his *Apologie* James was at pains once again to distinguish between those subjects who whilst 'Popishly affected' maintained a 'natural duty' to their king, and those who would use their faith as 'a safe pretext for all kind of Treasons, and rebellions against their Sovereign'.[27] Those swearing the oath were not required to disavow the pope's power to excommunicate anyone, but rather his power to depose kings; nothing in the oath was contrary to Christian faith and practice, nor did it challenge the pope's spiritual authority. James cited numerous examples to challenge Cardinal Ballarmine's claim that no pope had ever 'either commanded to be killed, or allowed the slaughter of any Prince, whatsoever, whether he were a Heretic, Ethnic, or Persecutor'. James noted that Bellarmine had focused on 'murdering' whilst failing to mention 'deposing, degrading, stirring up of Arms, or Rebelling against' kings. Nevertheless, there was countless evidence for 'the Popes allowing the killing of Kings' despite there being no justification in the scriptures.[28] Having set out his case, James was to leave it to his readers to judge 'wisely and unpartially' the merits of his argument.[29]

The publication of the *Apologie*, which included texts of the pope and cardinal's letters and the Oath of Allegiance, sparked a European-wide controversy. This was played out through published pamphlets and letters by many of the continent's most prolific theologians, including Bellarmine, who at the pope's request, wrote a reply to the *Apologie* which he published as *Responsio* in the name of his chaplain, Matteo Torti.[30]

'Good Lord, what a stir we had,' wrote Bishop James Montagu, Dean of the Chapel Royal and one of James's closest confidants; 'what roaring of the wild bulls of Bas[h]an what a commotion in every country.[31] There is scarce a people,' the bishop continued, 'language or nation in Christendom, out of which his Majesty hath not received some answer or other; either by refuting or at least by railing.'[32] The King of Great Britain was fast becoming a cause célèbre across the continent for his aggressive rhetorical attacks on the pope's assumed secular authority.

***

Yet, when the opportunity came to take more direct action, James chose to dissemble and delay.

In April 1606, Pope Paul V had placed the Venetian Republic under an interdict and excommunicated the whole state. This was part of an ongoing dispute about how the Republic exerted control over its Catholic clergy. For a time, Venice and the papacy, supported by Spain, appeared ready to go to war. Both sides started to raise troops. James expressed strong support for Venice. Through Sir Henry Wotton, his ambassador in Venice, James made clear that the pope's actions amounted to no less 'than the laying of the axe unto the root and the hewing down of the glorious tree of sovereignty', and as something 'precious to all princes and states', he would never be found 'cold or backward' in taking action.[33] Wotton was ordered to 'use all the speeches' he could to 'animate them [the Venetians] upon the confidence of his Majesty's resolution'.[34]

The French ambassador in London, Antoine Lefèvre de la Boderie, was less easily convinced. In his dispatch to Henri IV, he astutely observed that the words of 'le Roi de la Grande Bretagne' were more 'full of animosity against the Pope than of any desire or will to incur risks', adding: 'although his ambassador gave large assurances to the Republic ... to lend them aid and assistance in the present quarrel with his Holiness, we do not think that English arms will pass the Alps'.[35]

And so it proved. When the Venetians asked James to follow through on his promises to help them and recruit additional allies in Germany and Denmark–Norway, James was evasive. Cecil told Wotton that his Majesty viewed their request as a 'somewhat untimely motion', and 'very improper', seeing 'as yet the pope had not proceeded to open action of hostility'.[36] James gave assurances of support, but ultimately did not commit to action. In part, this was because he did not have the money to match words with deeds, and he knew Parliament was unlikely to grant subsidies or the City more loans. In March 1608, Boderie reported that Cecil had been overheard complaining that 'their necessity is extreme and that this last loan is almost entirely eaten up, since they were constrained to send most of it to Ireland'.[37]

Perhaps the strength of James's challenge to the papacy, as expressed in the *Apologie*, revealed his true attitude which, if he had had the means, he might have sought to assert through military action. Indeed, it was exactly the attitude expressed by his eldest son. Prince Henry was increasingly styled as Britain's future warrior king, representing the old martial values after which many militant Protestants still hankered. In a letter to Wotton read out in the Venetian Senate in May 1607, thirteen-year-old Prince Henry declared that, if 'he were of age he would come in person to serve the Republic'.[38] In making such statements, and in his warrior-like styling in portraits and engravings, Henry, and through him James, demonstrated the commitment of Britain to an 'offensive against the Antichrist', if not to be realised now, in the future. In the dedication to Prince Henry in his *The Triumphs of King James*, writer George Marcelline stressed that father and son were as one, Henry 'shall be the arm and strength': the king 'the head and counsel'; 'Yours the Action, but he the Agent: You for him, & he for you, and you and he jointly together, shall win an immortal glory.'[39]

Around this time, James commissioned for himself an ornate gilt brass table alarm clock from Scottish horologer David Ramsay (whom he would later appoint King's Watchmaker and to his Privy Chamber). On the clock's bottom plate – the underside that would sit on a mantel, or table – was engraved a shocking scene. It depicted a Catholic cardinal and three friars watching in horror as James and the young princes Henry and Charles held the pope's nose to a grindstone which was being turned by pair of archbishops.[40] It was a sardonic symbol of James's increasingly hostile public posturing against the papacy.

***

In 1609 James put his name to a reissued *Apologie*, publishing with it a new, longer and more inflammatory treatise. His *Premonition to all most Mighty Monarchies* directly appealed to the secular rulers of Christendom, urging them to reject the papacy's pernicious doctrines and destructive efforts to meddle in secular affairs, which, he said, posed a threat to their peace and security.[41] Specially commissioned and ornately bound copies of both the *Apologie* and *Premonition*, clearly identifying the author as the 'King of Great Britain, France and Ireland', were produced in English, Latin and French as gifts for English ambassadors to present to leaders throughout Europe. On the pope's instruction, many Catholic rulers, including the King of Spain and archdukes in Brussels, refused to accept copies. Henri IV of France passed his to a committee of Catholic theologians who concluded that, although the work 'contained errors', it was 'full of wisdom and modest as well as good intentions and conceptions, all tending to defend and conserve his royal and sovereign authority, rather than offending anyone'.[42]

Once again James publicly called for a general council to deal with the ills and disorders of Christendom – and his view, shared by the militant Protestants, that the pope was the Antichrist. Whilst he made clear this was just his own 'conjecture', he refused to withdraw the claim until the pope renounced any further 'meddling against Kings.'[43]

In the end, the king's aggressive polemic did not need to be backed up by direct engagement in war: the French mediated a settlement between Venice and the papacy, and military intervention to support Venice was not needed. James had been let off the hook.

8

The Monarchs Meeting

Two Kings in England have been rarely seen,
Two Kings for singularity renowned:
The like before hath hardly ever been,
for never were two with more honour crowned.

England with Denmark, Denmark eke with us,
Are firmly now in league, conjoined in one ...
We thus applaud the monarchs happy meeting.

John Ford, *The Monarchs Meeting; or,*
The King of Denmark's Welcome into England (1606)[1]

In the summer of 1606, an impressive flotilla of eight ships crossed the North Sea to the Kent coast. On board the flagship was the twenty-nine-year-old King of Denmark–Norway, the most powerful ruler in northern Europe, on a journey to see his brother-in-law, James, King of Great Britain, his sister Queen Anna and, for the first time, his niece and nephews.

Such a state visit was highly unusual. European rulers rarely set foot in each other's kingdoms because of potential threats to them. The last monarch to visit England had been Emperor Charles V during the reign of Henry VIII, more than eighty years before.[2] Poems and pamphlets produced to commemorate the visit recognised its rarity and significance: 'It is no common thing seen every day,' said one, 'It is no common honour, that is done', 'Two Kings in England have rarely been seen.'[3] The risk of travel, and 'the adventure of fears and enemies', was seen as the proof of the 'true instance of ... fast undoubted love' that Christian had for his brother-in-law.[4] Parliament, nobles and the mercantile guilds and companies gave significant sums towards the planned festivities to celebrate the king's visit, and huge crowds were anticipated in the capital. Christian's visit, was it seems, to shore up the alliance between the Stuart and Oldenberg dynasties, particularly now that James had acceded to the English throne and as Denmark– Norway faced the continued threat of Swedish expansion.

James and Christian had met once before, when the King of Scots sailed to Oslo to bring back his young bride Anna in 1589. Christian was only ten years old then and had been king for a year. Seventeen years later, James was king of a new composite monarchy, and a significant player on the European stage, whether this might be through future war, as many militant Protestants hoped, or diplomacy, as he had championed so far.

Like James, Christian ruled over multiple territories: Denmark; the majority of Norway (a Danish province after 1536); Iceland (a Norwegian vassal state); Greenland; the Faroes; and the 'Sound' provinces of Skåne, Blekinge and Halland on the southern tip of the Scandinavian peninsula. As a member of the House of Oldenberg, he was also Duke of Holstein and Schleswig. Denmark–Norway was a key power bloc, not least because much of British–European trade was directed towards the North Sea, with the Baltic regions the principal source of grain, and raw materials – timber, tar, pitch, hemp and flax – all being essential to sustain seaborne trading nations. Danish officials would collect tolls from vessels passing through the Øresund, the narrow channel between the Danish islands and the Scandinavian peninsula which formed the only entrance to and exit from the Baltic Sea. Anyone who wanted to trade with Russia via Archangel, not least the merchants of London's Muscovy Company, based at Seething Lane, had to pass through Danish–Norwegian waters and pay tolls for the privilege.

The English continually questioned the right of the Danish government to restrict or penalise navigation in those open waters, through which ships sailed without seeing land on either side. Indeed, English voyages around the North Cape to the White Sea, access to the fisheries controlled by the Danish king off the coasts of Norway and Iceland, English attacks on Danish shipping and tolls on the Sound had all been regular areas of dispute between the Danes and the English. While the Danes claimed English merchants were not reporting the true value of their cargo to avoid paying the full dues, the English claimed the Danes were overcharging them and being inconsistent in their assessment and collection of dues. Just prior to her death in 1603, Queen Elizabeth had forbidden Danish–Norwegian ships, en route to Spain and carrying timber for shipbuilding, from using the English Channel because of the ongoing Anglo–Spanish War. The Danes had responded by letting it be known that they and their Polish allies intended to block the Sound and seize English ships until the ban was lifted. This served only to further provoke the English and London merchants, who began supplying the Turks – then at war with Poland – with gunpowder and ammunition. Ambassadors from Denmark pleaded again and again with the queen, for the sake of good Christian relations between the two countries, to put an end to this policy of 'piracy'.[5] The English government met the complaints by continually asserting its right to seize any goods which would help its enemies, and claimed that it was the duty of the Danish king to see that his subjects did not assist those who threatened his English ally.

Since becoming King of England, James had tried to ease the underlying tensions. Writing to Christian about the trade situation, he suggested 'past disputes' could 'easily be put to rest and thoroughly removed owing to our mutual friendship', and maintained that their 'fraternal intimacy' would do much to settle the 'many controversies [that] have existed between the subjects of this Anglican kingdom of ours and your subjects'.[6] James also replaced English diplomats in favour of trusted Scottish envoys, who would now represent his monarchy as 'British' ambassadors. In August 1603, English diplomats Roger Manners and Robert Naughton were withdrawn as direct English representatives in Denmark–Norway and replaced with Sir Andrew Sinclair of Ravenscraig, Scottish ambassador in Denmark–Norway since 1590, who was now to mediate on behalf of England as well.[7]

Yet, despite James's efforts, he often found himself engaged in disputes with his brother-in-law, due to a series of specifically English–Danish trade conflicts which tested the familial and political alliance between the two monarchs. The fisheries claimed by Christian IV, especially those around Greenland, proved to be a recurring thorn in the side of Stuart–Oldenburg relations. James argued that English ships had been in the region since 1553 while searching for a northeast passage to Cathay (China), and that the region was a 'legitimately acquired possession of our English Crown'. While James would yield to Christian with respect to Iceland, the Faeroes and Spitzbergen, he remained determined to press the British claim to Greenland.

***

Christian arrived on 17 July 1606, his fleet dropping anchor at Gravesend. The following morning James and Prince Henry were welcomed on board the mighty Danish flagship the *Tre Kroner*, which had been 'gilded and covered with flags' for the occasion.[8] Given James's ambition to secure the formal union of his three kingdoms, the ship's name doubtless drew his attention. *Tre Kroner* or 'Three Crowns' represented an ongoing source of tension between the Danes and the Swedes, who had originally claimed this as their exclusive national symbol and feared that Denmark–Norway, in appropriating it as a part of its royal coat of arms and in naming a flagship, was aggressively signalling its imperial aspirations towards Sweden.[9] That afternoon Prince Henry, the two kings and their entourages, were taken by barge upriver to Greenwich Palace, passing ships in Blackwall docks, the *Susan Constant*, the *Godspeed* and the pinnace *Discover*, which were preparing for voyages to the Americas.

At Greenwich, Christian was reunited with his sister, whom he had not seen since she left Denmark with James following their marriage. Queen Anna had just lost a baby daughter, Sophie, who had been laid to rest in Westminster Abbey. She was the fourth child Anna and James were to lose in infancy, the second since they had been in England.

The publications celebrating Christian's visit hailed it as underlining the new era of British foreign relations, moving the nation beyond the relatively isolationist years of Elizabeth's reign. Foreign policy decisions were no longer dominated by relations with Spain and France. The alliance with Denmark–Norway, after James's union with Anna, had become 'central' to Britain's relations abroad. John Davies, poet and Prince Henry's writing master, declared: 'The Danes, and ours made one united Might.' The poet John Ford described the union of the two powers as a force 'all the world could scarce ... withstand'.[10] The friendship between the two kings was presented as the cornerstone of a Protestant union, with Britain, according to *The King of Denmarkes Welcome*, now 'both in the eyes & ears of all domestic and foreign people'.[11]

On 24 July, the royal parties headed twelve miles north of London to Theobalds, the estate of Sir Robert Cecil, now Earl of Salisbury. The kings and their retinues spent five days there, enjoying hunting, feasting, and entertainments at Cecil's expense (totalling approximately £1,180 or £300,000 today).[12] Such was James's love of Theobalds that the following year he appropriated it for himself, giving Cecil the old Bishop's Palace at Hatfield in exchange.

***

There is an account of the entertainments at Theobalds in a letter from Sir John Harington to his friend William Barlow, Bishop of Lincoln. Sir John, a cousin of Princess Elizabeth's guardian of the same name, was a writer, the late Queen Elizabeth's godson, and the inventor of the flushing toilet. The letter describes James and

Christian enjoying a riotous night at Cecil's home from where Harington composed his letter.

'The fright is got out of all our heads,' wrote Sir John, 'and we are going on, hereabouts, as if the devil was contriving every man should blow up himself, by wild riot, excess, and devastation of time and temperance.'[13] Such were the levels of drunkenness, that many of the performers, he said, could barely stand up or remember their lines. The women in the roles of Faith and Hope in *Solomon and the Queen of Sheba* were found 'sick and spewing in the lower hall', with Peace bludgeoning anyone who got in her way with her olive branch. The woman chosen to play the main role of the Queen of Sheba was so drunk that when the moment came to present the Danish king with rich offerings, she fell onto his lap, spilling her gifts. Then when Christian attempted to stand, he toppled over and needed to be 'carried to an inner chamber and laid on a bed of state'.[14]

By this, Harington concluded: 'The Danes have again conquered the Britons, for I see no man, or woman either, that can now command himself or herself.' They had corrupted the court, having 'strangely wrought in our good English Nobles, for those whom I never could get to taste good liquor now follow the fashion, and wallow in beastly delights'.[15]

Harington now feared for the future of the nation, given 'how folly doth grow'. He worried that there would be 'future mischiefs of those our posterity, who shall learn the good lessons and examples held forth in these days'.[16] Domestic matters had been forsaken for international ones, such as the celebrations of the Anglo–Danish alliance, and 'good lessons' should have been learned in the wake of the Powder Plot.[17]

Sir John's account struck a surprisingly critical note, and there may have been antipathy and bias behind it. Despite his efforts to win the new king's favour, in 1603 Harington had found himself in a debtor's prison for a year. His efforts thereafter to gain office had been unsuccessful, with the king rejecting his requests for the posts of Archbishop of Dublin and Lord Chancellor of Ireland.

Other accounts of King Christian's visit hailed it positively – as representing a new phase in Anglo–Danish relations and the possibility of a pan-European Protestant alliance. According to the *King of Denmarkes Welcome*, James gave his subjects 'joyful and not formerly unheard-of hours of most unspeakable happiness'.[18] Harington, by contrast, saw the carousing at Theobalds as proof of the corruption of the court under James, something he said would never have happened under his late godmother, Queen Elizabeth: 'I have much marvelled at these strange Pageantries, and they do bring to my remembrance what passed of this sort in our Queen's days ... I never did see such lack of good order, discretion, and sobriety as I have now done.'[19]

***

By the end of July, James and Christian were back in London to attend celebrations. The kings and Prince Henry sailed by royal barge to Tower Wharf, where they were greeted by the Lord Mayor, Sir Leonard Holliday. The royal party then processed through the City streets, which had been railed off to keep back the crowds and decorated with Danish blue cloth emblazoned with the royal arms. Members of London's livery companies, dressed in gowns and hoods, lined the route. The two kings, both wearing 'plain suits ... but rich in jewels', rode side by side, and were surrounded by the Danish guard and King James's guard amid a huge procession of knights, barons, earls, nobles, clergy and senior figures of both the Privy Council and Christian's Danish council.[20]

Henry Roberts, a poet and writer attached to the court who was renowned for his stirring tributes to Elizabethan adventurers such as Sir Francis Drake, wrote a pamphlet commemorating the day. *The Most Royall and Honourable Entertainment*, was sold at William Barley's booksellers in Gracious Street, and was dedicated to the *primus motor* of Britain's global trade, Sir Thomas Smythe.[21] Roberts's account stressed the importance of James's peace treaty with Spain – which has given 'our merchants sure and safe traffic to all nations, and they to our land, where they trade at their pleasures'.[22]

The Recorder of London welcomed the two kings on behalf of the City of London at Cheapside, where a triumphal arch had been erected covered with marine scenes. This then became the stage for a pageant, set in an ocean full of sea monsters and sea gods. Above the ocean 'stood Great Britain', depicted on a map and guarded by Neptune, mounted on a seahorse, and an armed Vulcan, the God of Fire, riding on a dragon. Above the map sat 'Peace Enthroned', supported by Justice and Policy, and 'the old Giants of this island' bearing shields 'wherein are drawn the foreign marriages of the Kings of this realm, and especially his Majesty's most happy match with Denmark.'[23]

The pageant celebrated the union of the ruling houses of England and Scotland with Denmark and Norway, and with it the peace and prosperity that such an alliance could bring. As the kings approached, Peace descended to 'the lowest skirt of the map of Britain', signifying that as long as Peace governed the island, no foreign king could 'at any time enter in a hostile manner'. When a king approached 'with peaceable and friendly' intentions, 'the island gave way to entertain him'. Then the map of Britain was drawn aside to reveal London, attended by 'Commerce' and 'the Arts and many other honours of a City'. Speeches of praise for the two monarchs were delivered in Latin, and loud music hailed their 'most joyful acclamation'.[24]

At Fleet Street a 'fine artificial summer bower' had been erected, inside of which a shepherd courted a 'coy shepherdess'. She would not love him, she said, until she 'could behold two Suns at one time of equal brightness: when there were two Majesties of like splendour, or two Kings in one state'.[25] With James and Christian's arrival at the arbour, the conditions had now been met, a point made by the shepherd. After speeches and songs of farewell, the kings rode on to Temple Bar.

Festivities and tours of the capital continued apace over the next few days. Christian and his nephew Henry visited St Paul's Cathedral, where they climbed to the top of the steeple to survey the city. They then rode to the Royal Exchange in Cornhill to see, in the words of Roberts, 'the riches of the inhabitants, the Goldsmiths, Mercers, and other wealthy trades, all the way setting their commodities to sale: a sight which may delight any Prince in the world to behold'.[26] Christian had heard from the merchants how they 'make great exchanges of their merchandise, make their traffic to foreign nations'.[27] At the Tower of London they were met by James, who showed Christian the offices of the Jewel House, the Wardrobe, the Ordnance and Munitions, and the Royal Menagerie, home to various exotic animals including lions, leopards, pumas and an elephant.

The royal sightseeing tour continued the following day. Led by Prince Henry, the party headed to Westminster Abbey where on display was a collection of life-size wood, wax and plaster effigies of seven of England's greatest kings, including Edward III, Henry V and Henry VII, and their queens. During the run-up to Christian's visit, James had instructed that the effigies be removed from the abbey stores, refurbished and presented to show the English succession and royal lineage to which James belonged. Mannequins, each with painted faces, and dressed in wigs and robes, had been lined up in a 'press' (a special case), so that they could be seen standing in order, in a macabre pageant of English monarchs.

In Henry Tudor's Lady Chapel, the royal party inspected a newly erected monument to Queen Elizabeth. Earlier that year, perhaps influenced by the unsettling experience of the Powder Plot and concerns for his place in posterity, James had ordered that Elizabeth I be exhumed from her original resting place in the Tudor family vault – where she had been buried in April 1603, alongside her grandparents, Henry VII and Elizabeth of York – and reburied on top of the remains of her predecessor and half-sister Mary I. An elaborate eight-column monument was erected by James over their remains, complete with a life-size marble effigy of Elizabeth, created by Maximilian Colt and Nicholas Hilliard. At the same time, James commissioned a tomb for his mother in Westminster Abbey. By burying the late queen together with Mary I on the north aisle of the chapel, James sought to sideline both, restore the reputation of his mother, Mary Queen of Scots, and underscore his hereditary claim to the English throne.

It would take a few more years for his mother's tomb to be finished, but on its completion, Mary's body was removed from the south choir aisle at Peterborough Cathedral, where it had lain for twenty-five years, and brought to London. In a letter to the dean of the cathedral, James explained: 'It appertains to the duty we owe to our dearest mother that like honour should be done to her body and like monument be extant of her as to others her and our progenitors have been used to be done.'[28] Since James then had his mother buried in Westminster Abbey's Lady Chapel – which had been constructed on the orders of Henry VII and in which Henry himself was buried – it is likely that Henry VII was one of the progenitors James had in mind. As James's hereditary claim was based on his descent from Henry VII and Elizabeth of York, burying his mother so close to them emphasised these familial connections. By moving the bodies of both Elizabeth I and Mary Queen of Scots, he had usurped the burial place of Elizabeth, the monarch who had ordered his mother's execution, and reaffirmed Stuart legitimacy.

***

During Christian's almost month-long visit, he and James attended sermons and communion together. Before them at Hampton Court Palace on 5 August 1606, on the sixth anniversary of the Gowrie conspiracy, a sermon was delivered by the Bishop of Winchester, Lancelot Andrewes. He took as his text Psalm 144, Verse 10: 'It is He that giveth salvation unto kings, who delivereth his servant David from the perilous or malignant sword' and sees 'that it fits both to our purpose and to the time'. Andrewes spoke of 'the threat the previous November', saying it 'had been visceral'. If the Powder Treason had succeeded, it 'would have made it rain blood, so many baskets of heads, so many pieces'. He raged at the 'monster-like' Jesuits, the 'traitors to kings' who are committed 'to the overthrow of kingdoms, in what state forever they get footing'.[29] It was as much a message for the two kings before him as for the international audience that the sermon, published in Latin, was intended to reach. It echoed too James's letter sent to his brother-in-law in the aftermath of the Powder Plot, in which he warned that 'among all kings, we two have now been left as the ones against whom the counsels and attempts of the papists are chiefly directed.'[30]

Prince Henry's tutor John Davies also raised the spectre of Catholic plots in a published poem, 'Bien venu Great Britaines welcome to hir greate friendes, and deere brethren the Danes', which directly referred to the attempted 'powd[e]ring [of the] Prince, and Peers'.[31] The poem decried those who used religion to attack rightful rulers – 'Using thy [zeal's] name to pull Kings from their Thrones' – and argued that James and Christian's alliance must defend their faith and prevail against such foul deeds as making 'the SACRED bleed'. For, as Davies continued, nations allied to each other are indomitable, and "Gainst other force invincible become.'[32]

Looking back at his brother-in-law's visit that summer, James alluded to the time the two kings had discussed the injustices of the pope's temporal power, which posed, he had told Christian, so 'much danger' that it threatened 'all Christian princes'. They had concluded that forming a Protestant union was the obvious way to counter papal power, although they acknowledged that differences between the Protestant states could make it impracticable. James stressed the importance of making it work and assured Christian that he would help 'most eagerly to conform the minds of all of them'.[33]

James wrote that he wanted the Protestant alliance to be 'a spiritual or celestial relationship', and to be long-lasting – operating 'also by the law of progeny and relationship or affinity' such that 'our descendants' would 'have the same relationships and affinities'.[34] He had no doubt that the Danish king would be best placed to lead such an endeavour, given his influence in Europe and particularly with the Protestant princes of Germany. The Venetian ambassador Zorzi Giustinian also noted to the Doge that James was seeking 'to work up' the Danish king in support of Venice against the papacy, 'to such a heat that should matters come to an extreme pitch we will not have to pipe for long to that sovereign, for he will dance of his own accord without the need of our music'.[35]

***

On Saturday 9 August 1606, after days of hunting, feasting and jousting at Greenwich, King Christian together with James, Anna and Prince Henry were rowed down river for the final days of Christian's visit. At the royal dockyard at Chatham on the River Medway, the royal party enjoyed an 'aquatic banquet' on board one of the English ships. Christian had requested that Royal Navy sailors and vessels be presented and the King's Master Shipwright, Phineas Pett, put two of the navy's most impressive fighting ships from the days of the Armada, the *Ark Royal* and the *Victory*, into dry dock for inspection. Both ships had recently been gifted to Prince Henry by his father.

At Gravesend, Christian hosted the royal family at a farewell banquet on board the *Tre Koner*. Giustinian recorded in his dispatch to the Doge: 'The King of Denmark assured the King of England that he would always preserve the accord between their respective kingdoms.'[36] Newsletter-writer John Pory similarly discribed how Christian 'gave himself and his heart to the King, as long as he lived, all friendly offices both in word and deed. Whereto the King answered: "That never man was to him so welcome as the King of Denmark; nor ever should any – till he came again."'[37] The visit had sought to emphasise the religious solidarity between the two monarchs and the strength of the Stuart–Oldenberg alliance.

The state visit would leave a deep impression on Prince Henry. He had inherited his Danish family's affinity for the sea, demonstrating an interest in fighting ships from an early age. King James had given the Lord High Admiral, the Earl of Nottingham, apartments at the royal palace of Nonsuch in Surrey, from where he could counsel and mentor the young prince. Henry would endlessly question Nottingham on the building and equipping of ships; on how he had won naval battles, such as those against the Armada; and how the navy could be used to defend merchant ships against attack. Henry was also schooled in how he might mount expeditions to discover new lands and claim them for England and himself and enrich his subjects. Nottingham ordered Phineas Pett to build a 25-foot [c.8 metre] long model ship for the prince, and Pett was instructed to sail it up to Limehouse and drop anchor 'right outside the king's lodgings' ready to surprise the young boy. Henry named this, his first ship, the *Disdain*.[38]

His second was given to him by King Christian. As a parting gift, Christian gave his nephew his most modern warship, the *Vice-Admiral*, one of the squadron of eight ships he had brought with him to England.[39] After his uncle's visit Henry resolved that the Royal Navy, which had been in steady decline for years, should be overhauled to become more like the Danish fleet. He proceeded to swear Master Shipwright Pett into his service and commissioned him to build a new Royal Navy three-decker 55-gun warship, named the *Prince Royal*. It was a spectacular statement of intent by a young prince with an all-conquering ambition.

9

Union Jack

'It is already a perfect Union in me, the Head. If you wanted a Head,
that is me, your King over you all; or if you were of yourselves no
Body; then you had Reason to say, it were unperfect; but it is now
perfect in my Title and Descent, though it be not an accomplish[ed]
and full union.'

King James I, *speech in Parliament*, 2 May 1607[1]

As the English Parliament continued to debate and delay the
king's proposals for formal union between England and
Scotland, James used the royal prerogative to pre-emptively celebrate what he called the 'happy marriage' by creating a 'British flag'.

The new union flag combined the red and white cross of Saint
George with the blue and white saltire of Saint Andrew. In a royal
proclamation of 10 April 1606, addressed to 'all the subjects of this
isle and kingdom of Great Britain', James ordered that all royal and
British merchant shipping should fly the new flag from atop the main
mast.[2] The union flag was intended to amplify the King of Great
Britain's authority at home and abroad, and spread the image of a
united 'Britain' around the world.

Designing a new flag had proved to be no easy task. Of the initial six proposed red, white and blue designs, none were immediately
approved. All floundered on the question of how to combine the two
kingdoms whilst giving both equal status. The design eventually

chosen had both crosses occupying the same space on the flag, but with the English cross of Saint George superimposed on the Scottish cross of Saint Andrew. James's Scottish subjects immediately protested, and an unofficial Scottish version with the cross of Saint Andrew dominant, began to be flown on Scottish ships. The Union Flag or Union Jack, Jack being a shortening of Jacobus, the Latin version of James, was slow to be adopted by either nation. Despite the king's 1606 proclamation, 'South Britons' (the English) flew either the cross of Saint George or the Union Jack (because of the prominence given to the cross of Saint George); and 'North Britons' (the Scots), flew the cross of Saint Andrew, or the unauthorised form of the Union Flag with the Saint George cross under that of Saint Andrew.[3]

When Parliament met for its third session of James I's reign, the agenda was dominated by one thing: the union – 'the greatest and weightest matter of all', as the king described it. Since the last session, two years before, the appointed commissioners – English and Scots MPs – had been researching and deliberating on the best path to achieve the union. Their 'Instrument of Union' was now to have its formal reading in the Commons and in his opening speech, lasting more than an hour and a half, James sought to frame the debate that would follow. First, he addressed the objections made by 'men of humorous or malicious minds'. It 'was not his purpose to deprive England of its Laws, nor of Goods, nor of Lands; but to lay Scotland subject to the laws'. Scotland and England were to him, as 'two brothers' that had 'equal parts of his Affections' and should be subject to 'one Rule and to one Law'. The union would not, he assured the house, favour Scotland at England's expense, and 'he wished himself no longer alive, but dead, if his desires were not directed to the commonwealth of both kingdoms'. If his union 'proposition' was 'disappointed of its due success', it would greatly damage his reputation abroad, he warned – it 'being known, as it was, so publicly to so many Nations, and the Eye of all the World in Expectation of the Event'. If it failed, it would be 'imputed either to his Folly to propose it, or to the Obstinacy of his People, not to approve it'.[4]

Erudite and articulate, James weighed his words carefully with colourful imagery designed to cajole, reassure and persuade. He wanted to be perceived as 'England's Solomon' – a scholarly, wise, pious and loving king. As Bishop Williams would later reflect, the king's eloquence was 'rare and excellent in the highest degree ... Those Speeches of his in the Parliament,' he said, 'do prove him to be the most powerful Speaker that ever swayed the Sceptre of this Kingdom.'⁵

Two days later, on 21 November, the 'Instrument of Union' drawn up by the commissioners was introduced for its formal reading in the Commons. It stopped short of the 'perfect' union James had envisaged but made three specific proposals: free trade – that is, 'a single market' – between England and Scotland; the abolition of 'hostile' laws between the two countries; and mutual naturalisation, in other words 'common citizenship'.

Naturalisation was the question that had most passionately engaged the union commissioners. It was accepted by all that the post-nati – those born after the day of James I's succession – were by law natural subjects of either kingdom, and this was confirmed by the commission. The controversy lay over the future state of the ante-nati – those born before 24 March 1603. A number of Scotsmen had already been naturalised, including the Duke of Lennox and his brother Lord D'Aubigny; the Earl of Mar; Lord Kinloss; and Sir George Hume (the Lord Treasurer of Scotland) – all of whom were subsequently appointed to offices of state. This served only to heighten English hostility to a general naturalisation and confirm suspicions that this would lead to a 'massive influx of Scots'. The commission took the view that a general naturalisation would be a step too far and agreed that the ante-nati would require substantial legislation to become subjects in England, as well as a royal commitment to ensure that their access to English offices was limited.

For the Instrument of Union to become law, it would need to be passed by both the English and Scottish parliaments. The debate in London proved to be far more vociferous than James had imagined.

While the prospect of abolishing 'hostile' laws was broadly supported, mutual naturalisation and free trade between the two nations proved more contentious. Fears were raised that the balance of trade might favour Scotland, given their merchants' low trading costs, and that they might undercut the English in domestic and continental markets. Even though the propositions were comparatively modest – given James's initial ambition to create a formal union with one parliament and one set of laws – by the end of 1606 the only concrete achievement after several years of work was the abolition of laws governing the border region that were hostile to the Scots.

***

The festivities at court for Christmas and into the new year reflected James's ongoing desire for 'perfect union'. On 26 December 1606, the King's Men performed *King Lear*, which focused on the foolishness of division and disunity, and spoke directly to Parliament's opposition to ending the separation of the kingdoms of England and Scotland.

On Twelfth Night, to underscore his idealised vision of union as a 'marriage', James hosted the wedding of English heiress Honora Denny to Scotsman and gentleman of the King's Bedchamber, Lord James Hay, 1st Earl of Carlyle. The wedding was turned into a national and political event. The spectacular *Lord Hay's Masque*, staged by Thomas Campion and performed after the nuptials, praised James as the architect of union, which was now mirrored in the union of Denny and Hay.[6] James played an active role in the wedding preparations, applauding such Anglo–Scottish unions as a means of nation-building at court, and creating a new 'British' aristocracy.

When Parliament reconvened on 10 February 1607, attention turned to the naturalisation question. The commissioners who had drawn up the Instrument of Union recommended that both ante-nati and post-nati Scotsmen and Englishmen should become 'British' citizens (rather than either English or Scottish). The proposal met with fierce opposition, being described by the anonymous author of the *Paper Booke* as 'the weightest case that ever came into the parliament'.[7] The author feared a flood of 'hasty and giddy-headed' Scottish people into England. Christopher Piggott, MP for Buckinghamshire, was vitriolic in his condemnation of 'the Scots' as 'murderers' and 'thieves'.[8] King James immediately ordered that Piggott be expelled from the House and sent to the Tower. Piggott sent a plaintive letter to Cecil, explaining that he did not often speak in the House and that he had got carried away in the moment. He was released from the Tower some ten days later, pleading sickness, but was stripped of his seat.

Nevertheless, many in the Commons agreed with what Piggott had said and defended his right to free speech. Others expressed themselves more corporeally. Amid the debate, Henry Ludlow, MP for Andover, audibly broke wind. Robert Bowyer noted the incident in his diary, adding that it was not done in disgrace, since Ludlow's father, Sir Edward, had also farted during a committee meeting: 'So this seemeth Infirmity Natural, not Malice.'[9] Nevertheless, this outburst was immortalised in *The Parliament Fart*, which became one of the most popular comic political poems of the early Stuart era. While essentially an extended fart joke, the couplets also refer to events in James's first Parliament, not least the union and more generally freedom of speech and parliamentary liberties. As one couplet read: 'Be advised quoth another look to the lot / If you fart at the union remember Piggott.'[10]

As Henry Ludlow's fart came to symbolise, the union was determinedly resisted by the Commons. When Nichols Fuller MP opened the debate, he set out to 'prove that this union is dangerous to both nations.' He spoke of the 'notorious poverty and quarrelsomeness' of the Scottish people and his fears that many would come to England looking for work, crowding cities, and that Scottish merchants would undercut their English rivals. He also emphasised constitutional principle and maintained that union could only be achieved by 'assent of Parliament'. Any other way would be 'injurious'.[11] And so, the debate continued.

Diplomat, prolific letter-writer and former Oxford don, Dudley Carleton, who witnessed the exchanges, recounted to his friend John Chamberlain some of the more outrageous anti-Scottish jibes. One MP gave a 'long declamation' against the 'Britons' – 'that they were first an idolatrous nation and worshippers of the devil'; while another spoke out bitterly against England's neighbours, 'calling them beggarly Scots'. Yet there were some who were prepared to defend the king's position and, like Francis Bacon, made the case for naturalisation – claiming the 'inconveniences' had been exaggerated. England was far from being 'peopled to the full' and a growing population could only add to the country's stature and its security. 'I think a man may speak it soberly and without bravery,' wrote Bacon, 'that this kingdom of England, having Scotland united, Ireland reduced, the sea provinces of the Low Countries contracted, and shipping maintained, is one of the greatest monarchies, in forces truly esteemed, that hath been in the world.' Bacon also praised the Scottish subjects as 'a people ingenious, in labour industrious, in courage valiant, in body hard, active and comely'.[12]

The Scottish parliament had its own concerns. That year, alarmed at the way its English counterpart appeared bent on promoting an incorporating union, the Privy Council of Scotland wrote to King James expressing their grave concern that: 'Your Majesty's ancient and native kingdom should not be so disordered and made confused by turning of it, in place of a true and friendly Union, into a conquered and slavish province to be governed by a Viceroy or Deputy, like such of the King of Spain's provinces.'[13]

The debates and discussions ran on into the end of March 1607, when James again addressed Parliament. This time, he finally acknowledged that he had underestimated the task of achieving union – 'the error was my mistaking, I knew mine own end, but not others fears'. He had hoped and believed it would be welcomed unreservedly. He bemoaned the 'many crossings, long disputations, strange questions, and nothing done'. How much longer, he asked, did Parliament intend to drag 'leaden feet' over an issue that was clearly indisputable? He was now determined that they find 'a middle way' between 'foolish rashness' and 'extreme length'. He stated again his reasons for wanting union and proceeded to address the objections that had been made, rejecting fears of a 'flood' of impoverished Scotsmen, and emphasising the benefits of union for peace and security.[14]

James also made clear to Parliament that England would have precedence and be the 'greater part' of the new kingdom – 'the husband to Scotland's wife', as he put it. Gradually, by mutual consent, English law would 'conquer' Scotland, and a united parliament would make Scottish law conform to English statute. As king, he said, he found it impossible to rule over two kingdoms when 'the One the greater, the other a less, a richer and a poorer'. He reiterated that he wanted: 'a perfect Union of laws and Persons and such a Naturalizing as may make One Body of both Kingdoms under me your king.' He told the MPs that the union would be as one achieved through conquest, but 'cemented by love'. James asked the English Parliament to 'make a good Conclusion, avoid all delays, cut off all vain questions, that ... [he] may have his lawful desire, and be not disgraced in his just ends'.[15]

Once more James stressed that failure to agree union would be damaging: 'What will the neighbouring judge, whose eyes are fixed upon the conclusion of this action but that the king is refused in his desire ... and the king disgraced?' All foreign kings, he said, 'that have sent their ambassadors to congratulate me since my coming, have saluted me as Monarch of the whole Isle, and with much more respect of my greatness, than if I were king alone of one of my realms'.[16] Giustinian, the Venetian ambassador, noted the underlying motivation. The king was 'now forced to desire the union, not only because it is useful, but also for his own reputation's sake'.[17]

Despite James's rhetoric, the Commons remained defiant. In the debate that followed, Sir Edwin Sandys argued that the king's proposal would mean a radical alteration to England's common law, her 'ancient constitution'. Sandys denied that no precedent for a perfect union existed, and doubtless as a means to delay, urged that another commission investigate how a 'perfect' union of parliaments, laws and institutions might be achieved. Only the repeal of 'hostile laws' between England and Scotland was agreed. The Commons refused to accept that the king's Scottish subjects, even those born since James ascended the throne of England, were native-born 'English'.[18]

The session ended abruptly on 2 May 1607, when James prorogued Parliament with unvarnished fury. 'I am your king,' he railed. 'I am placed to govern you; and shall answer for your Errors; I am a man of Flesh and Blood and have my Passions and Affections as other men: I pray you, do not too far move me to do that which my Power may tempt me unto ... make not all you have done, frustrate.' He warned them to 'tempt not the patience of your prince' but instead 'proceed swath as much as can be done at this time and make not all you have done frustrate'. The Commons was infertile ground, 'barren by preconceived opinions'.[19]

The following year, determined to establish a common citizenship, James turned to the courts and a test case. In June 1608, the case of a Scottish child, Robert Calvin (also known as Colville), who had been denied two estates in England, was brought before twelve judges in the Exchequer Chamber. It was to be one of the most important legal judgements of the king's reign, with Sir Francis Bacon leading the team presenting the case on behalf of Calvin, and prominent opponent of naturalisation, Sir Edwin Sandys, among those lawyers for the defence.[20]

The outcome of what became known as 'Calvin's case' was of little surprise. The judges decided that, with respect to his privileges and freedoms, Robert Calvin was both Scottish and English: the post-nati were declared citizens, entitled to recourse to English law.[21] It was a landmark ruling, enshrining a principle of birthright citizenship.

Calvin's case formally set out in English law the boundaries of English subjecthood, defining who could and would be considered English. Everyone born within the dominions of the King of

England was under the protection of English common law, owed allegiance to the king, was both subject to all duties, and entitled to enjoy all the rights and liberties 'of an Englishman'. James had secured naturalisation but without Parliament's consent.

***

While James had failed in his attempts to achieve a more 'perfect' union of laws and institutions, there was a growing identification of 'Britain' in print culture. In 1606, a new history of 'Great Britain' was written, which framed the story of the island as a united people who had been invaded by the Romans, Danes, and, finally, the Normans. In 1611 John Speed told the story of 'Great Britain' and its 'British peoples'.[22] The following year, his *Theatre of ... Great Britain* – the first atlas to contain maps of England, Scotland and Ireland, and dedicated to King James – used the term 'Empire of Great Britain' to denote all of James's dominions: England and Scotland ('Britain') together with Ireland and the Isle of Man.[23]

Viewed from abroad, James's vision of a British kingdom also seemed to take hold, not least because England and Scotland had a common foreign policy and diplomatic corps. Foreign courts increasingly referred to ambassadors as representing 'Great Britain'. All diplomatic treaties and instructions after 1604 were issued in the names of the 'King of Great Britain and Ireland', and James's ambassadors typically described themselves as 'British'.[24] Yet, there was also confusion as to what exactly Great Britain was, and in a number of foreign official documents, James was described as the 'King of Great Britain, France, Scotland and Ireland.'

A British identity also emerged more indirectly, in the responses to events abroad, particularly in relation to continental Protestantism. A desire was expressed to see 'Britain' as a new Protestant power in Europe. In this vision, Prince Henry – 'he upon whom the nation's eyes were bent' – was the focus of hopes for future victories against the 'papal Antichrist'.[25]

Prince Henry and the Grand Tour

'Travel, in the younger sort, is a part of education;
in the elder a part of experience.'

Sir Francis Bacon, *Of Travel* (1625)[1]

Despite the diplomatic tensions created by the new Oath of
Allegiance, the Powder Plot and James's pronouncements
about the pope, the Anglo–Spanish peace had initiated a new phase
in British relations with the continent.

Before the peace, travel from England was generally limited to
Protestant areas of Europe. Licences to travel, which were issued by
the Crown, precluded visits to Rome, while travel to the Kingdom
of Naples, the Duchy of Milan and the territories of the King of
Spain were regarded as hazardous. Now, as embassies reopened, and
with Europe a safer destination, Britain's merchants, diplomats and,
increasingly, private individuals, began to trade and travel more
freely across the continent. 'The people of Great Britain,' wrote Sir
Thomas Palmer in *How to Make our Travailes into Forraine Countries
the More Profitable and Honourable*, dedicated to Prince Henry, 'of
all other famous and glorious nations separated from the main continent of the world are by so much the more interested to become
Travellers.'[2]

Just a few years before, it had all been very different. As the Swiss
traveller Thomas Platter noted, in the last years of Queen Elizabeth's

reign the English had passed their time: 'learning at the play what is happening abroad: indeed, men and womenfolk visit such places [theatres] without scruple, since the English for the most part do not travel much'.[3] Now, after a long period of cultural isolation, something of a 'grand tour' was developing. Before commencing their studies in Oxford, Cambridge or the Inns of Court, it became fashionable for young English and Scottish gentlemen to head to France, Italy and Spain, as well as Germany, Switzerland and the Low Countries, seeking education, pleasure and culture, and to acquire books and artworks to build their own libraries and collections back home. In his essay *On Travel*, Sir Francis Bacon advised travellers to keep a daily diary and be accompanied by a 'tutor or grave servant' to direct young men's attention to the main sights, control expenses and to limit drinking, 'whoring' and 'dangerous contacts' with English (Catholic) religious exiles.[4]

Yet the growth of travel purely for pleasure was viewed with alarm by some writers. Sir Thomas Palmer acknowledged that: 'Italy moveth most of our Travellers to go and visit it, of any other State in the World.' He agreed that it might be visited for practical reasons, such as health, study and learning about political systems, but dismissed the viewing of 'special galleries of monuments and old aged memorials of histories' as being 'a fantastical attracter, and a glutton feeder of the appetite, rather than of necessary knowledge'. And he sternly abjured the idea of any kind of stay in Rome – 'the Forge of the very policy that setteth Princes at odds ... the temper of subjects to civil dissensions and the seller of all wickedness and heathenish impieties, or ... of evil policies and practices'.[5]

Joseph Hall, future Bishop of Norwich, felt much the same when he published *Quo Vadis?* ('Where are you going?').[6] Hall deplored both 'casual' travel and educational travel which, he argued, prudent parents should forbid for their young, immature sons. He believed travel should be undertaken only for the state, or for trade. Hall's main concern was the risk of conversion to Catholicism and much of his book focusses on the 'sorcery' of the Jesuits. He believed the gentry should be happy at home and that King James should enforce restrictions on travel.

From his post in Venice, Sir Henry Wotton became something of a supervisor of gentlemen travellers to Italy. This was in response to James's concern that many Englishmen, 'under pretence of travel for their experience ... not contenting themselves to remain in Lombardy or Tuscany, to gain the language there, do daily flock to Rome, out of vanity and curiosity to see the Antiquities of that City'. Here they were in grave danger of being corrupted by Jesuit doctrine and returning 'again into their Countries, both averse to Religion, and ill-affected to Our State and Government'.[7] Although Florence was beyond his remit, Ambassador Wotton informed Cecil of 'the danger that I foresee of corrupting many in that Court', drawn 'by the beauty and security of the place, and purity of the language. For there is in that town at the present a certain knot of bastard Catholics, partly banished and partly voluntary recusants who with pleasantness of conversation, and with force of example, do much harm, and are likely to do more.' Florence, he concluded, was a place in which one may 'speak well' and 'do ill'.[8]

***

Travel between England and the continent was two-way – and not least in these years to and from the household of the young Prince Henry. His father took care in the appointments to Henry's house-hold (at the palaces of Oatlands, Nonsuch, and then St James's) to ensure the inclusion of both English and Scottish appointments. Anglo–Scottish marriage lay at the heart of the prince's house-hold. Henry's English governor and then chamberlain, Sir Thomas Chaloner, and Scottish cofferer, Sir David Foulis, both married sis-ters of Prince Henry's Receiver General, Sir William Fleetwood. Henry's Latin tutor and secretary, Scotsman Adam Newton, also married an Englishwoman.[9]

Henry's household was established by James as a 'courtly college or collegiate court' – a place of learning to inculcate the young prince in values and knowledge the king believed were important to create a suitable heir to his throne.[10] In his *Hero-paideia*, John Cleland, who was in the prince's household at this time, described this 'Académie of our Noble Prince' as 'the true Pantheon of Great Britain', where 'young Nobles may learn the first elements to be a Privy Counseller, a General of an Armie, to rule in peace & to command in war'.[11]

Henry's court attracted foreign visitors including European princes, ambassadors, military commanders, artists, craftsmen, musicians and engineers. On a trip to England, soldier and art patron Don Giovanni de' Medici visited Nonsuch where he watched the eleven-year-old prince dance and ride. He later wrote to his half-brother Ferdinand I, Grand Duke of Tuscany, that Henry had performed everything 'with incredible talent' – 'con incredibile disposizione'.[12] The following year, Marchese Vincenzo Giustinian visited Henry and observed that when the boy wasn't riding, he was studying and learning Spanish.[13]

Besides his daily study, the prince spent a great deal of time exercising. As James had outlined in his guide to kingship, *Basilikon Doran*, Henry must exercise his body; be a horseman; study scripture, law, history and the military arts.[14] When in April 1606, King Henri IV appointed Boderie as his ambassador to England, he had given him specific instructions to pay particular respect to his godson, Prince Henry. The French king sent the prince six horses and a French riding master, Monsieur de St Antoine, to hone his equestrian skills.

Boderie noted that, as far as he could discern, 'his Highness's inclination was entirely toward France', adding: 'It would be a great fault to neglect a prince who promised such great things'. He suggested to Henri that four or five members of Prince Henry's court receive pensions, as they had great influence with the boy. Indeed, Boderie advised that he thought it 'highly proper to cultivate' the prince's friendship, 'and to manage it early by all means suitable to his age and condition'. Boderie suggested suitable gifts for Henry including 'a suit of armour, well gilt and enamelled, together with pistols and a sword', and 'a couple of horses, one of which goes well, and the other a Barb (Arab)'. All for a prince 'whose friendship, cannot but one day be of advantage to France'.[15]

In the early summer of 1607, Henry received more approaches from the French with the arrival of nobleman Claude de Lorraine, Prince de Joinville. His visit was 'to cultivate that young plant' which 'is promised to produce fruits much more favourable to France, than that stock from which it was raised' (meaning James I). Writing from London on 2 August, Boderie emphasised the prince's 'great accomplishments and courage': he would 'soon make himself talked of and possibly give jealousy to his father, and apprehensions to those, who had the greatest ascendant at court'.[16]

Sir George Carew, English ambassador at the court of France, meanwhile wrote to Cecil that King Henri 'ever speaketh with great show of passionate affection towards my lord the prince; and at this time, he accounted of his as of his own son, as he hoped his good brother of Great Britain would do the like of the Dauphin'.[17] Joinville presented Henry with an exquisite suit of armour, as Boderie had suggested – an ostentatious and extravagant gift, particularly given that the thirteen-year-old would soon outgrow it. The prince asked to have his own envoy to France, so that he could communicate directly with the French king.

***

While the young prince was not allowed to go on his own grand tour, he drew into his household young men such as John Harington (son of Lord John Harington, his sister's guardian) and Viscount William Cranborne (son of Sir Robert Cecil), who acted as his eyes and ears on the continent. Young Harington would become one of Prince Henry's closest aristocratic companions.

A portrait *In the Hunting Field*, by leading court painter Robert Peake, commissioned a few years earlier by Sir John Harington, shows a close relationship between Henry and young John. Aged nine and eleven, the boys are depicted having just killed a deer.

The prince is sheathing his sword, fresh from cutting the creature's neck, while Harington is holding its antlers. Hung on the tree are the shields of the two families. Prince Henry stands in the centre of the picture while John kneels in a subservient manner as he looks up at his friend.

In the summer of 1608, sixteen-year-old John embarked on a tour of the continent accompanied by his tutor John Tovey and a retinue of gentlemen and servants. It was a tearful departure. Accounts describe Prince Henry welling up as the pair travelled to Whitehall to get Harington's 'passport'.

Henry and John had planned the eighteen-month itinerary together. John would effectively act as Henry's ambassador and represent the prince at the courts of Europe. He took with him a miniature portrait of Prince Henry, which he kept with him at all times.

The two immediately established a regular correspondence. Indeed, Cecil asked his son, Cranborne, during his own continental tour to write more regularly, saying: 'I find every week in the prince's hand a letter from young John full of news of the place where he is, and the countries as he passeth, and all occurrents.'[18] In addition, John sent Prince Henry gifts and souvenirs of his travels, including a printed version of the entertainments performed at the marriage of Grand Duke Cosimo of Tuscany; copies of verses delivered at a tournament at Verona; and an oil painting taken from the council chamber at Venice (it depicted Pope Alexander III with his foot on the neck of the Emperor Frederick Barbarossa). John also kept a diary of his travels, to show the prince on his return.

Brussels was the first stop on John's itinerary, where he was presented to the Habsburg Archduke. He then visited the universities of Heidelberg and Basle and attended lectures and met with professors. By the autumn of 1608, he had travelled to Florence and by Christmas he was in Venice, which had just broken off relations with the papacy. At the court of the Doge he was introduced to the Senate by Ambassador Wotton, who announced young John as 'the right eye of the Prince of Wales who will one day govern the kingdom'.[19] After writing to Prince Henry that he did not wish to be a tourist but to gain a grounding in 'statecraft', 'the better to serve his sovereign', John stayed in Italy for a further six months.[20]

Much of young John's correspondence was deliberately guarded: he was aware that 'a wall of paper is too feeble to guarantee any secret of importance'.[21] He regularly referred to, however, the criticisms of Rome that had been circulating within Venice since the papal interdict of 1606. Attending the church of San Lorenzo, John reported that 'every day during Lent a Brother Fulgenzio of the Servite Order has preached the word of God purely and without intermixture'.[22] Were it not for the risk of interception, John informed Henry's secretary Adam Newton, he would have sent 'a wad of my crude observations on the trifles and trickeries of the false religion'.[23] In a letter clearly sent by a courier he trusted, John told the prince: 'If I write to Your Highness of the superstitions, false miracles and relics which are displayed in this time of Lent, there would be not one letter but another *Legenda Aurea*.' [The *Golden Legend*, a huge medieval collection of stories about the lives of saints.][24]

From Venice, John headed for Rome at the invitation of the Catholic exile and former Elizabethan spy 'Pompeo Pellegrini', Sir Anthony Standen. However, such a visit at the height of the Oath of Allegiance controversy was risky, and John diverted to Venice via Urbino, probably arriving by sea shortly before Christmas 1608.[25] This itinerary avoided the overland route via Bologna, where the Inquisition was systematically arresting Protestant tutors such as Tovey.[26] From the imperial court in Prague, John sent Henry an overview of German politics.[27]

John's homeward journey was delayed by illness, and with the Lower Rhine closed by the threat of war over the succession to the duchy of Jülich-Cleves, he probably took a circuitous route back to Paris, where he arrived on 8 October 1609. He stayed there for a few months, possibly at Prince Henry's behest, as the French were rumoured to be considering a match between the dauphin and Princess Elizabeth, before returning to England in early 1610.

The significance of his travels should not be underestimated. The tour ensured Prince Henry had a steady supply of diplomatic intelligence from a trusted source, from which he could develop his own opinions on European affairs. The Venetian ambassador in London was probably not the only diplomat who advised his master that 'any show of regard for them [the Haringtons] will be very well invested'.[28] Certainly, even before his formal coming of age as Prince of Wales, Henry had acquired a reputation and status in Europe. Viscount Cranborne talked of how knowledge of the young prince's virtues 'shines abroad', having been spread by several gentlemen who have frequented the prince's court.[29]

Part Two

11

Jamestown, Virginia

'Britons you stay too long, quickly aboard bestow you ... to get the Pearl and Gold, and ours to hold, Virginia, Earth's only Paradise.'

Michael Drayton, *To the Virginian Voyage* (1606)[1]

On 19 December 1606, a fleet of three ships, *Godspeed*, *Discovery* and *Susan Constant*, under the command of Captain Christopher Newport, set sail from London for Virginia. Newport was an experienced mariner who had led numerous privateering raids against the Spanish under Queen Elizabeth. He had recently returned from a trading expedition to the West Indies, and had presented James with two young crocodiles and a wild boar.[2]

Newport's latest commission was to lead the first voyage of the Virginia Company of London, chartered not simply to trade, but to establish a permanent colony on the east coast of America. Eight months earlier, a group of merchants and courtiers had petitioned James for a 'Licence, to make Habitation, Plantation, and to deduce a colony of sundry of our People into that part of America commonly called VIRGINIA'. On 10 April, the king granted the 'First Charter of Virginia.'[3] It established two separate enterprises: the 'First Colony' under the Virginia Company of London, and the 'Second Colony', under the Virginia Company of Plymouth. Each company was awarded settlement rights on the Atlantic coast of North America and up to a hundred miles inland. The Plymouth

Company, made up of merchants and financiers from Bristol, Exeter, Plymouth and smaller West Country ports, had permission to settle an area stretching from the Chesapeake Bay to the coast (now known as Maine). The London Company, comprising City merchants and investors, was licenced to found settlements in an area between what is present-day North Carolina and New York. (The Plymouth Company would collapse after just two years, after its settlement at the mouth of the Kennebec River lasted just one dismal winter.)

His Majesty's Council of Virginia, consisting of thirteen men, appointed by the king and sworn to his service would oversee the colonisation from London. Among those appointed were Sir Thomas Smythe; Sir William Wade, lieutenant of the Tower of London; Sir Walter Cope, member of parliament for Westminster and adventurer in a variety of overseas enterprises. A governing council was then to be established in each of the two colonies – to 'govern and order all Matters and Causes' according to 'such Laws, Ordinances, and Instructions' as shall be 'given and signed' by the king. Each of the two councils was to have a royal seal, with the king's arms on one side and his portrait on the other bearing the words: '*Sigillum Regis Magnæ Britanniæ, Franciæ, and Hiberniæ*' – King of Great Britain, France, and Ireland.[4]

The charter began by framing the enterprise. It would be for 'the propagating of Christian religion to such people, as yet live in darkness and miserable ignorance of the true knowledge and worship of God, and may in time bring the infidels and savages, living in those parts, to human civility, and to a settled and quiet government'.[5]

The primary motivation, however, as the charter made clear, was 'to take order, to dig, mine, and search for all manner of mines of gold, silver, and copper' – which the king could then tax. James, together with his 'heirs and successors' would receive 'the fifth part … of all the same gold and silver, and the fifteenth part of all the same copper'.[6] In granting the charter, James was supporting a venture that would, it was hoped, secure new sources of revenue, not least the precious metals of the New World that poured into Spanish coffers, funding their expansionist designs.

The establishment of a permanent settlement in America had long been the ambition of English explorers and merchant-adventurers, both to find gold mines and as a gateway via a northwest passage to the so-called South Sea – the Pacific Ocean – and the riches of the East. Elizabethan adventurers such as Ralegh and Sir Humphrey Gilbert had embarked on a number of ventures, in search of rumoured wealthy indigenous cities and to establish settlements. Ralegh sponsored three expeditions to Roanoke Island, off the coast of what is now North Carolina, and attempted to establish a settlement there, which he named Virginia in honour of Queen Elizabeth, 'the Virgin Queen'. He lobbied for state funding but with no success. Elizabeth would not sponsor high-risk ventures, she would only offer royal assent, and so Elizabethan attempts at colonisation relied on private investors and the actions of individual adventurers. Insufficient food, conflict with native peoples and repeated supply failures meant that none of the settlements lasted longer than a year.[7]

English colonial exploration and ambition had been powerfully articulated by Richard Hakluyt in his *Discourse Concerning Western Planting*, and in his *Principal Navigations, Voyages, Traffiques and Discoveries of the English Nation* (1598–1600). Hakluyt argued the importance of colonisation for the 'enlargement of the gospel of Christ'; for commodities which were supplied by Europe, Africa and Asia; the 'employment of many thousands of our idle people', and as a challenge to the wealth and power of the Spanish in Europe and in the Indies.[8]

In 1606 Hakluyt was one of the chief petitioners to James I for permission to colonise Virginia. The departure of the first fleet of the Virginia Company signalled the beginning of a new era of colonial endeavour in which companies were chartered under the direct control of the Crown. Cecil was a key part of this shift. His experience of the last years of Elizabeth's reign had taught him that rather than being subject to the ambivalent support of the monarch, colonial enterprise needed to be grounded in the state. Under James I it would acquire a legitimacy and governance which would both strengthen the British state and provide new sources of revenue for the Crown.

***

In the early hours of Sunday 29 April 1607, 104 English men and boys – among them gentlemen, labourers and carpenters – arrived on the southern shore of Chesapeake Bay, which they immediately named Cape Henry in honour of the king's son and heir. Prince Henry was a great enthusiast for the venture and had sent Robert Tindall, who described himself as the Prince's 'gunner', to keep a journal of the voyage and initial months in Virginia on his behalf.[9] The settlers next planted a cross and took possession of the territory in the name of King James. With its abundant natural resources and its location a safe distance from Spanish America, it was seen as an ideal place for settlement. They named it 'James City'; to become known as Jamestown, sited on the banks of the 'James River'.[10]

The settlers opened sealed instructions with the names of those appointed by London to serve on the colony's first council. Edward Maria Wingfield, captain of the *Susan Constant* and founding member of the Virginia Company, was elected as the first president of the Virginia colony. Wingfield and the council members were then required to swear an oath of allegiance to the king promising to govern according to his wishes. Newport was to lead 40 settlers on an exploration of 'such ports and rivers as can be found in that county', and which may flow to the East India Sea, and to 'try if they can [to] find any mineral'. Having loaded two of their ships with 'all such principal commodities and merchandise that can be found', Newport was to return to England for resupply, 'bringing with him full relation [...] of all that is done.'[11]

Over the next few weeks, following their instructions from London, the settlers began to build a fort, while Newport and a party of men went in search of silver and gold. Returning empty-handed, Newport found the settlement reeling from an attack by some two hundred Native Americans, who had only been repelled when Wingfield ordered the cannons of the ships to be fired on them. Three settlers, two men and a boy, had been killed. The land chosen by the English for their Jamestown settlement was inhabited by Powhatans, part of a powerful confederation of at least thirty Algonquian-speaking Native American tribes living in an area of over 6,000 square miles, and ruled over by the 'chief of chiefs', Wahunsonacock. The Powhatans inhabited the areas around the waterways of the Powhatan River ('James River'), in settlements made up of longhouses; and grew corn, beans and squash; fished and hunted for deer, turkey and other game; and gathered fruits and nuts from the surrounding woods.

On 22 June 1607, Captain Newport sailed for England with letters from the colonists, a map of the settlement, the journal of Robert Tindall for Prince Henry and mineral samples, which, it was hoped, would indicate the presence of gold in Virginia. The colony's leaders requested that the Virginia Company send a second expedition as soon as possible, to prevent the Spanish from laying their 'ravenous hands upon these gold showing mountains'.[12] As one of the settlers William Brewster put it in a letter to Cecil: 'Now is the King's Majesty offered the most stately, rich kingdom in the world,' and predicting: 'You yet may live to see England, more rich and renowned than any kingdom in all Europe.'[13]

Such early enthusiasm was soon to fade. The gold samples brought back on the *Susan Constant* turned out to be nothing of the sort (and were likely nuggets of pyrite). The company drew up a letter for Newport to take back to the settlers, criticising them for having failed to find gold and ordering them to stay in Virginia until they had found gold or a sea passage to the Pacific. According to John Smith, who was to become a governor of the colony and wrote a history of its first years, the colonists thereafter became 'slaves' to the aspirations of gold: 'there was no talk, no hope, no work, but dig gold, wash gold, refine gold, load gold ... all necessary business neglected'.[14]

When Newport arrived back in Jamestown on 2 January 1608 with his ship – the *John and Francis* – laden with supplies and a hundred new colonists (including two goldsmiths, two metal refiners and a jeweller), he found just 38 of the 104 original settlers alive.[15] A combination of bad water from the river, disease-bearing mosquitoes and dwindling food supplies had created a wave of dysentery and fevers, with 66 colonists losing their lives.

Newport had also brought with him from King James a copper crown and a red woollen robe to be used in a ceremony to make Wahunsonacock the chieftain of the mighty Powhatan confederacy, a vassal of King James, thereby securing his 'submission and recognition' that he and his people were subjects of the British Crown under the 'overlordship of James I, King of Great Britain, France, and Ireland, and Virginia'. According to Smith who accompanied Newport to the chieftain's base at Werowocomoco for the ceremony, Wahunsonacock initially refused to bend his knee to receive the crown, 'he neither knowing the majesty nor meaning of a crown', and so 'after many persuasions, examples and instructions, as tired them all', the colonists 'leaning hard on his shoulders' put the crown on his head.[16] However much the Virginia Company might later claim that the Powhatan chief had willingly accepted the crown, with a full acknowledgement of duty to their king, he had clearly been coerced. Wahunsonacock had seen the ceremony for what it was and made clear to Smith and Newport, 'I also am a king, and this is my land'.[17]

Over time, as they failed to plant enough corn to make the colony self-sufficient – instead spending their time tirelessly probing for gold – the English settlers grew more and more dependent on food traded by the Powhatan tribes. When drought hit, and the tribe had less food to trade, the colonists took what they wanted by force. The Powhatan retaliated, killing the settlers' livestock, and burning their crops.

***

Reports of setbacks and difficulties in the colony began to percolate back to London. Realising a new approach was needed if they were going to attract continued investment and new settlers, in February 1609, the Virginia Company commissioned a promotional booklet. *Nova Britannia – Offering Most Excellent Fruites by Planting in Virginia*, was written anonymously by 'R. J.' (likely Robert Johnson, son-in-law of Sir Thomas Smythe of Philpot Lane). It emphasised that Virginia was a national project to create a 'New Britain'.[18] The colony would glorify God, and the king, spread Christianity among the native peoples, challenge the wealth of the Spanish and secure the riches of the New World. 'How strange a thing is this,' it asked, 'that all the States of Europe have been asleep so long? That for a hundred years and more, the wealth and riches of the East and West should run no current but into one coffer.' Despite coming late to such endeavour, it continued, the English would 'make good the common speed', for they are 'best at imitation and so do soon excel their teachers'.[19]

The 'most excellent fruits' on offer in Virginia included a range of resources and the many industries that might flourish, including silkworms and mulberry trees 'for making Silk, comparable to that of Persia, Turkey, or any other'. There was also hemp for cordage, essential for shipping; flax for linen cloth; and wood which 'can hardly now be obtained from any other part of the world'. Moreover, the cultivation of land in a North America would allow new markets to be found for English woollen cloth exports. 'This little Northern corner of the world' would in a 'short time, be the richest Store-house and Staple for Merchandise in all Europe'. Reflecting on the enhanced role of the state in supporting such colonial enterprises and the opportunities presented, it concluded: 'the honour of our nation is now very great by his Majesty's means ... if we sit still and let slip occasions, we shall gather rust, and so unfeather our own wings'.[20]

Soon after *Nova Britannia*'s publication, the Spanish ambassador to London, Don Pedro de Zuñiga, wrote to Phillip III enclosing a copy: 'They [the Virginia Company] have printed a book ... in which they call that [country] Great Britain, which, for the exaltation of their religion and its extension throughout the world, all should come to support with their persons and their property.'[21] It was the latest in a series of letters sent to the Spanish king reporting the establishment of the company, the dispatch of their first fleet and the great hopes that King James had for the colony.

The Spanish ambassador had, he said, repeatedly asked James about English plans in Virginia. Philip III saw the English settlement as a direct and hostile threat to the Spanish Indies, and to their determination that Protestantism be wholly excluded from the 'New World'. In response, James feigned ignorance and said he had not been fully informed as to what was going on, and that he had never known of the Spanish claim, as it 'was not stated in the peace treaties with him and with France that his subjects could not go [where they pleased] except the Indies'.[22] Not wishing to antagonise the Spanish or jeopardise the Treaty of London, he lied and dissembled, maintaining that the colony was a private enterprise, which he neither directed or encouraged.

Indeed, the Virginia Company had deliberated over whether to publish *Nova Britannia*, unsure as to how James would represent the company's actions. 'It is more than probable,' company members warned, that the Spanish king's ambassador 'will forthwith expostulate with his Majesty about this writing, and then it is not conceived how far his Majesty will be pleased to avow it [the Virginia Company] which may intimate disavowing.'[23] On balance, the company believed it was worth the risk. They were determined to launch a new campaign to promote the colony and knew that the king's involvement – or at least close association – would provide it with a legitimacy the project had not previously had. *Nova Britannia* concluded: 'this plantation hath been formerly miscarried, yet it is now going on in better way... Spearheaded by a 'mighty Prince (such as ours)', and with the involvement of the 'whole State'.[24]

The Venetian ambassador in London requested further clarification. Marc'Antonio Correr asked whether James's continued assurances to the Spanish envoy, 'that the undertaking is a private one, and that he [his Majesty] cannot interfere', remained the case.[25]

The truth was, as English minister William Crashaw later celebrated, both King James and Prince Henry were avid supporters of the Virginia venture, 'Where was there ever a voyage that had such a King and such a Prince to be the Patrons and Protectors of it?' asked Crashaw.

The one to begin, the other to second it. What voyage ever was there which had so many honourable undertakers, and of so many sorts and callings, both of the clergy and laity, nobility, gentry and commonalty, city and country, merchants and tradesmen, private persons and corporations? As though ever kind and calling of men desired to have their hands in so happy a work.

In making themselves 'fathers and founders of this plantation', said Crashaw, they thereby show themselves to be a 'new Constantine or Charles the Great; for by the attempt and achieving of this great work of the heathens conversion, let their highnesses be assured, the ages to come will style them by the glorious names of James the Great, and Great Henry'.[26]

For Prince Henry, and for the imprisoned Ralegh, with whom the young prince had struck up a friendship, and for those who wished to retain the spirit of Elizabethan adventurers, colonial expansion represented a direct challenge to Spanish domination in the New World.[27] As the Venetian ambassador noted: 'To the ears of the Prince, who is keen for glory, come suggestions of conquests far greater than any made by the kings of Spain.'[28]

***

On 23 May 1609, James granted a second charter to the Virginia Company.[29] In order to attract a wider range of investors, it became a joint stock trading company, offering stock at a sale price of £12 and 10 shillings (approximately £3,000 today) per share. Every investor was promised land in Virginia and monetary return when the stock was divided in 1616. The company also won the right of self-government in Virginia. The Council of Virginia in London, with members appointed by the king, was replaced by a council elected by investors, and with a treasurer at its head. In the colony, the president and council were now to have a governor, who would select members for their council.

The company membership grew from the typical small number of wealthy and well-connected men to include hundreds of men predominantly from London and southern England. The charter listed 650 investors by name, including Sir Robert Cecil; Henry Wriothesley, Earl of Southampton; Sir Edwin Sandys; Sir Dudley Digges; Sir Humphrey Weld (Lord Mayor of London), and as corporate subscribers, fifty London companies and guilds (including those of the goldsmiths, vintners, masons and plumbers). Sir Thomas Smythe was elected treasurer. Conspicuous among the new investors was Prince Henry. As Venetian ambassador Correr reported: 'I hear that not only are [there] many great personages in the scheme – Lord Salisbury [Cecil] sending a number of stallions and other animals on his own account – but the prince has put some money in it, so that that he may, some day, when he comes to the Crown, have a claim over the Colony.'[30]

The second charter, issued in the king's name, clearly spelled out the project's spiritual purpose. The 'Conversion and Reduction of the People in those Parts unto the true Worship of God and Christian Religion' was the mission's highest possible goal, and carried the further explicit royal instruction, that the company prevent 'the Superstitions of the Church of Rome and Catholic nations from establishing further footholds in the Americas'.[31]

With the issuing of the new charter, the Virginia Company renewed its fundraising and propaganda campaign, printing pamphlets and commissioning sermons which urged people of all walks of life to emigrate to the New World. At St Paul's Cross and at Whitechapel, Jacobean churchmen like Crashaw, William Symonds and Robert Gray preached James's vision of imperium as a monarchical project that would 'efface savagery'.[32] Sermons dedicated to the Virginia Company were both delivered and then printed at St Paul's Churchyard.

These ministers framed support for the Virginia colony as a Christian moral imperative, tied both to the propagation of the Church of England and as a collective national undertaking. In *A Good Speed to Virginia*, Robert Gray maintained that England had a right to settle there by virtue of the fact that the natives 'misused their territory'. As Gray continued, 'The Lord hath given the earth to the children of men', yet 'the greater part of it [is] possessed and wrongfully usurped by wild beasts, and unreasonable creatures, or by brutish savages, which by reason of their godless ignorance, and blasphemous Idolatry, are worse than those beasts which are of most wild and savage nature.' Gray advocated conversion by any means necessary, including force: 'A Christian king may lawfully make war upon barbarous and Savage people, and such that live under no lawful or warrantable government', and by doing so 'make conquest of them.'[33] The colony represented an opportunity 'whereby the glory of God may be advanced, the territories of our kingdom enlarged, our people both preferred and employed abroad, our wants supplied at home, his Majesty's customs wonderfully augmented, and the honour and renown of our nation spread and propagated to the ends of the world'.[34] Or, in the words of Protestant minister Richard Crankthorpe, in a sermon delivered at St Paul's Cross, they set out to create 'a new BRITAIN in another world'.[35]

Yet in these years, the settlers who moved to the colony were mostly 'South Britons'. In the early seventeenth century, few Scottish people had the means to become promoters of overseas colonisation, and the vast majority of those who did wish to move settled in Ireland, whilst Irish and Scottish Catholics frequently decamped to Catholic countries in Europe such as France and Spain. James sought to ensure the Virginia colony was a 'British' society and on October 1607, the Spanish ambassador reported that English settlers bound for Virginia 'are complaining' of 'the King's urging the Scots to go there and that he favours them more than these'.[36] Nevertheless, the settlers who moved to the colony in these years remained almost exclusively English.

***

On 2 June 1609, Sir Thomas Gates – who had served with Sir Francis Drake against the Spanish in the Caribbean and with the Earl of Essex at Cadiz – set sail from England for Jamestown as the colony's new deputy governor on the Virginia Company's new flagship, *Sea Venture*. It was part of a large fleet of nine ships, commanded by former Elizabethan privateer Sir George Somers, carrying approximately 600 new settlers, plus enough livestock and provisions to last a year.

More than a month into the voyage, in late July, the fleet was caught in a hurricane and scattered. *Sea Venture* was driven onto a reef near the uninhabited coast of Bermuda, allowing Gates, Somers and around 150 crew and settlers to get to shore on the largest of the islands (which was later named Smith's Island, in honour of company-man Smythe). Here they remained for the next ten months. The surviving ships sailed on to Virginia.

Two castaway survivors, William Strachey and Silvester Jourdain, narrated accounts of the shipwreck. Their memoirs describe the passengers and crew stumbling ashore and discovering an island that had an abundance of food and fauna – wild hogs, game birds, huge tortoises, and fish – a semitropical climate, countless tobacco plants and 'bountiful soil'.[37] With materials salvaged from the *Sea Venture* and wood cut from Bermuda cedars, the group of castaways built two small vessels, the *Deliverance* and the *Patience* and in May 1610 left Bermuda for Jamestown.

The survivors' accounts were amplified by William Shakespeare in his new play *The Tempest* which celebrated the miraculous salvation of those previously assumed to have been lost at sea, and was first performed by the King's Men in 1611 at the Banqueting House in Whitehall.

The castaways' survival was duly interpreted as evidence of Britain's divinely ordained purpose in the New World and of Bermuda as an earthly Paradise.[38] 'They now fix their eyes upon the colony in Bermuda,' wrote the Spanish ambassador in London, 'partly because of its fertility and being unoccupied (by savages) so they will meet with no opposition.'[39]

***

While the castaways had been exploring subtropical virgin lands, skirmishes and tensions had escalated between the settlers and indigenous peoples in and around Jamestown. From late 1609, local tribes laid siege to the English fort, 'James Fort', trapping around 300 people inside for months. The settlers were eventually driven to eat snakes, rats, and dogs, and even to dig up corpses of the dead and boil them into stews with salt and herbs. During the winter of 1609–10, later referred to as 'the starving time', the population of Jamestown colony plummeted from 500 to a mere 60.[40]

In June 1610, the *Patience* and *Deliverance*, carrying the ship-wrecked settlers, finally made landfall in Virginia. Shocked by the conditions that confronted them – colonists looking like skeletons, buildings wrecked, and streets deserted – Deputy Governor Gates resolved they abandon the colony and return to England. As they sailed down the James River, however, they were met by company supply ships carrying the colony's new governor, Thomas West, Lord De La Warr, plus around 300 new settlers, and men and munitions. The first nobleman to govern in the English colony and with instructions to impose martial law, much was expected of him. Lord De La Warr demanded that the settlers return to Jamestown and vowed to rebuild it.

A week later, De La Warr ordered Somers, together with his nephew Matthew, back to Bermuda to hunt and fish for urgent food supplies. Somers died on the island on 9 November, apparently of exhaustion. His nephew Matthew buried his heart and entrails there before returning the rest of his body to England for burial. With great ceremony, Somers was buried at Whitchurch Canonicorum in Dorset. In tribute to Somers, Bermuda thereafter became known by the English as the Somers Isles, and in November 1612, the Somers Island Company (or Bermuda Company) was established to run the colony.

Meanwhile in Jamestown, De La Warr's arrival had had an immediate impact. Through his royal commission as captain-general and as governor, he was authorised to attack the colony's enemies, and he did so more vigorously than any of his predecessors. He sent orders to the Powhatan chief to return all captives and stolen weapons, and insisted that Wahunsonacock recognise the homage he owed King James following his coronation as an English vassal. According to William Strachey, the Powhatan chief responded with his own ultimatum, telling the colonists to either 'depart his country or confine [themselves] to James Town only', else 'he would give in command to his people to kill us'.[41]

The English retaliated with force. In August, George Percy, captain of the Jamestown fort, and a company of seventy men, launched an attack, ravaging settlements, decimating crops and indiscriminately killing Powhatan men, women and children. The first 'Anglo–Powhatan war' had begun.

12

The Plantation of Ulster

'I had rather labour with my hands in the plantation of Ulster, than
dance or play in that of Virginia'

Sir Arthur Chichester to King James, 1610[1]

As part of his vision of a unified 'Britain', James was determined
to extend royal authority and religious conformity across the
island of Ireland. The Virginia colony provided some inspiration; as
Lord Deputy Sir Arthur Chichester wrote in 1608, Ireland should be
treated similarly to 'America, from which it doth not greatly differ'.[2]

James's reign in Ireland had begun auspiciously. Six days after
Elizabeth's death but unaware of the queen's passing, the rebel leader
Hugh O'Neill, Earl of Tyrone, had surrendered to the English government thereby ending the Nine Years' War in Ireland. It had been
the latest conflict between the Tudors and the Gaelic Irish since
Henry VIII was declared King of Ireland in 1542. Indeed Thomas
Radcliffe, Earl of Sussex, Elizabeth's first Lord Deputy in Ireland,
remarked candidly that he had often wished Ireland 'to be sunk in
the sea'. English withdrawal was unthinkable, both for reasons of
prestige, and because of the danger that the kingdom might be used
as a springboard and rallying point for an invasion of England. Yet
the cost of the war had been enormous. The queen had resorted to
selling Crown lands and imposing loans, and when these proved

insufficient, was forced to draw increasingly large sums from the Exchequer. It brought England close to bankruptcy.

Tyrone's submission shortly before James I's accession presented a timely opportunity for the decisive assertion of English royal authority. Yet much to the outrage of many Englishmen, James pardoned Tyrone. In return for promising to 'abjure all dependency on foreign potentates and to assist the abolition of all barbarous customs contrary to the laws', he allowed Tyrone, and the other Ulster lord, Rory O'Donnell, Lord of Tyrconnell, to retain their titles and most of their lands. It was a similar approach to that which James had taken in the Scottish Highlands. At Tyrone's behest, no Lord President of Ulster was appointed. On 11 March 1605, the Irish Council issued a proclamation affirming that all inhabitants of Ireland were free, natural and immediate subjects of King James I, and not subject to any local lord or chief. All offences committed before the day of James's accession, 24 March 1603, were to be pardoned on condition of taking an oath of loyalty.[3]

However, in the wake of the Powder Plot the mood changed. In 1606 James's Lord Deputy in Ireland, Sir Arthur Chichester, together with Attorney-General for Ireland, Sir John Davies, launched a new wave of intense persecution against Catholics, marked by the surrender of territory, beatings, deaths and imprisonment, and the execution of priests who were hanged, drawn and quartered. In September 1607, the earls of Tyrone, Tyrconnell, their families and almost a hundred of their followers fled Ulster and boarded a ship at Lough Swilly bound for Rome and exile. It marked the start of an Irish Catholic diaspora on the European continent, the effective collapse of an independent Gaelic Ulster, and prepared the way for a more radical policy intended to fully conquer Ireland. 'There was never a fairer opportunity offered to any of His Highnesses predecessors,' Chichester wrote to James in 1607, 'to plant and reform that rude and irreligious corner of the North than by flight of the traitorous Earls.'[4] The lands of the earls, together with the confiscation of the property of the lesser Gaelic lords, left the Crown with the land of six of the province's counties – Armagh, Cavan, Coleraine, Donegal, Fermanagh and Tyrone – and so open to 'plantation', settlement to control, anglicise and 'civilise' Gaelic Ireland.

From the beginning this was envisaged as a 'British' effort. Land-hungry English and Scots 'planters' would cross the Irish Sea and establish new landholdings in what would be referred to as the 'Ulster Plantation'. Given the geographical proximity and perceived similarities in language and culture between Scotland and Ireland, James optimistically believed that he had a better understanding of his new Irish kingdom than his Tudor predecessors.

Plantation was an approach James had tried, albeit with little success, in the Scottish Isles. He had written of these experiences in *Basilikon Doron*: 'For those that are utterly barbarous, follow forth the course that I have intended, in planting Colonies among them,' and so, 'within short time may reform and civilise the best inclined among them; rooting out of transporting the barbarous and stubborn sort, and planting civility in their rooms.'[5]

James believed that those people who dwelled 'in our main land [the mainland], that are barbarous for the most part, and yet mixed with some shew of civility', differed from those 'that dwelleth in the Isles' and that all are 'utterly barbarous, without any sort or show of civility'.[6] While the former might be adequately subjugated by the nobility, for the others 'planting' colonies was the most effective approach, bringing the unruly to heel and securing their submission to the authority of the English Crown.

The official scheme for plantation began in 1609. That summer, surveys of each county were conducted by Lord Deputy Sir Arthur Chichester, who employed surveyors to identify the acreage of land available in each county. A plan was then submitted to the king the following year. Each county would be divided into precincts, or 'baronies', which would then be organised into estates of three sizes – 1,000, 1,500 and 2,000 acres. These would be granted to three main groups of settlers ('planters' or 'British tenants') who would control, 'civilise' and anglicise Ulster, which hitherto had been the region most resistant to English rule. Of the three groups of settlers, the 'undertakers' were English and Scottish landowners; the 'servitors' were mostly career soldiers who had fought in Ireland during the Nine Years' War (including Sir Arthur Chichester); and the Irish 'grantees' (also known as the 'deserving Irish') were those who had remained loyal to the Crown during the Nine Years' War.

Each grant came with strict conditions. Each undertaker would 'undertake' to erect a stronghold – a stone house, castle or 'bawn' (fortified courtyard) – on his estate, remove the existing tenants and import settlers at the rate of 24 men per 1,000 acres. These were men over the age of eighteen and to be either English or inland Protestant Scots – in other words not the 'barbarous sort' who lived in the isles. Undertakers could keep arms and were not allowed to lease their land to Irish tenants. All were expected to take possession of their grant by September 1610 and to have fulfilled all the conditions of their grant within five years, when it was anticipated that the new arrivals would be established enough to begin paying rent to the Crown. Conditions for the servitors were similar, although they were allowed Irish tenants on their land, and had only two years rent-free. The 'deserving Irish', meanwhile, would have rent due after the first year and at a higher rate. Some alterations were made to these conditions in the years to follow, most notably, time periods were extended, and undertakers were allowed to have Irish tenants on their estates.

The establishment of twenty-five new towns – intended to be a focus of government authority, trade and industry and the Protestant religion – was to be a key objective of the plantation. Generous land grants were also given to the Church of Ireland, Trinity College Dublin, and for the creation of six new royal schools at Raphoe, Cavan, Armagh, Dungannon, Newry and Enniskillen.

Attorney-General Davies optimistically predicted that the settlement of Ulster would be 'a mixed plantation of British and Irish, that they might grow up together in one nation' and 'with the blessing of God'. The plantation 'will secure the peace of Ireland, assure it to the Crown of England forever and finally make it a civil, and rich, a mighty and a flourishing kingdom'.[7] James believed the planting of the North of Ireland would create a new British society, where colonists as 'New Britons' would work together as equal partners, their ethnic differences melded and subsumed into one nation.[8]

***

The cost of developing the Ulster Plantation meant that additional investment would be needed. The Crown turned to the wealthy City of London to supply some much-needed capital and expertise. In January 1610, articles of agreement were signed under which the twelve principal London livery companies agreed to undertake plantation in the new County of Derry (formally County Coleraine and parts of County Tyrone). A new body called the 'Society of the Governor and Assistants, London, of the New Plantation in Ulster' (generally known as the Honourable Irish Society) was created to oversee the plantation. Each of the companies received an estate in the county, and these were allocated by lottery in December 1613. The companies to receive grants were: the Drapers, the Vintners, the Salters, the Ironmongers, the Clothworkers, the Merchant Tailors, the Haberdashers, the Fishmongers, the Grocers, the Goldsmiths, the Skinners and the Mercers.

In their appeal to London's merchant companies, the government drew attention to the natural advantages of Ulster: beef, pork, fish, and game in abundance; timber for shipping; butter, cheese; hides and tallow; ports ready for mercantile traffic with England, Scotland, Spain and Newfoundland. For an initial payment of £20,000 (around £4.7 million today), the Honourable Irish Society was granted over half a million acres and other inducements, including all customs income from the plantation for ninety-nine years, and the rights to fish in the rivers and off the coasts in perpetuity.[9]

Yet the City companies were extremely reticent about becoming involved, though they could not realistically oppose the Crown. Having reluctantly agreed to spearhead a plantation in the newly established County of Londonderry, the companies were required to follow an extremely restrictive set of guidelines that included removing all Irish tenants, building twenty-five new towns, expanding the urban ports of Coleraine and Derry (the latter renamed Londonderry) and establishing new settlements.

For the native Irish, the policy of plantation was devastating. 'The Irish,' wrote an English settler in 1610, 'are the most discontented people in Christendom.'[10] They had lost their homes, their lands, their leaders and were being forced to live under foreign customs. A poem in 1610 by Lochlainn Ó Dálaigh describes Ireland through the eyes of the dispossessed. 'Where have the Gaels gone?' they ask. 'We have in their stead an arrogant, impure crowd, of foreigners' blood.'[11] While many young Irish escaped abroad – the men often recruited into continental Catholic armies – other displaced Irish remained as outlaws, waiting for a chance to regain their lands. As the authorities feared there was unrest, leading to small skirmishes in 1615. These gathered little support, as many Irish people still believed that their situation would improve, and that they would be looked after in the new society.

Indeed, one of the original conditions of the grants to the planters – the removal of existing Irish tenants – was not carried out. It became clear early on that the Irish were needed on these estates. A later critic described 'a world of Irish' continuing to live on the estates as tenants.[12] Moreover, despite Protestant church ministers migrating to Ulster to convert the native Irish to the Protestant faith, and a national convocation of the church issuing new articles against Catholics, the Catholic Church in Ireland continued to grow in strength.

In June 1613, Ferdinand de Boischot, the ambassador of the Archdukes Albert and Isabella of the Spanish Netherlands, noted that James I had spoken of enforcing religious conformity in Ireland by armed force. But since he lacked money and feared provoking Catholics into taking 'extreme measures', such as seeking support from foreign princes, it seemed unlikely that he would follow through.[13] William Trumbull, James's ambassador in Brussels, reported that Irish exiles in the Spanish Netherlands were planning a new armed rebellion.[14] In an effort to ease tensions, in January 1614 Sir Charles Cornwallis was sent to Dublin with instructions to 'compose the controversies and alterations', and negotiate a settlement which would allow for Catholic mass to be held in private.[15] There was to be no wholesale attempt to enforce even nominal conformity to Protestantism in the province.

Upon his appointment as Lord Chief Justice in Ireland in June 1617, Sir Francis Bacon airily declared Ireland to be 'the last ... of the daughters of Europe, which hath come in and been reclaimed from desolation and desert (in many parts) to population and plantation, and from savage and barbarous custom to humanity and civility'. Though work was 'not yet conducted unto perfection', it was 'in fair advance'.[16] Sir John Davies, the Attorney-General in Ireland and now a significant plantation owner in his own right, went further: the English policy was notable for its benevolence. Whereas the Irish, 'in former times, were left under the tyranny of their lords and Chieftains', they are now under the protection of the Crown. The 'common people' despite being 'rude and barbarous', nevertheless 'quickly apprehended the difference between the Tyranny and Oppression under which they lived before, and the just Government and Protection which we promised under them for the time to come.' He continued: 'The common people were taught by the Justices of the Assize that they were free Subjects to the Kings of England, and not Slaves and Vassals to their pretended Lords.' The kingdom had been cleared of 'Thieves, and other Capital Offenders'; and 'these Civil Assemblies at Assizes and Sessions' had 'reclaimed the Irish from their Wildness, caused them to cut their Glibs and long Hair; to convert their Mantles into Cloaks; to conform themselves to the manner of England in all their behaviour and outward forms' and to learn the English language. Thus, Davies concluded, whereas the 'neglect of the Law' had once 'made the English degenerate and become Irish, now the execution of the Law, doth make the Irish grow civil, and become English'.[17] By 1620, it was with some relief that colonist and judge, Luke Gernon, expressed his belief that the Irish were now exhibiting all 'the symptoms of a conquered nation'.[18] The planting of Ulster, undertaken by the English, Scots, Welsh and loyal Irish to whom James referred to as 'the British undertakers and servitors' had, according to his officials, began to realise James' vision for a new 'British' society.[19]

Whilst Sir Francis Bacon and John Davies undoubtedly painted a deceptively rosy picture of success in Ireland, society slowly seemed to be becoming less lawless. However, the lingering grievances of many sectors of the population would come violently to a head in decades to come, leaving thousands dead on both sides. As plantations developed along the eastern coast of America, Ireland came to be viewed more as part of the Atlantic than as part of a unified Britain. The province of Munster, wrote cartographer John Speed, was 'open southward to the Virginian Sea', and in 1617 Fynes Moryson described Ireland as 'this famous Island in the Virginian Sea'.[20]

Meanwhile, around 2,000 nautical miles west of Ireland, in Newfoundland, another 'British' colony, the only in fact to be chartered in the name of James as 'king of Great Britain' rather than of 'England and Scotland', was also being planted.[21] In the summer of 1610, John Guy, a Bristol merchant, attempted to establish a settlement at Cuper's Cove (now known as Cupids), thereby becoming the colony's first governor. Guy had been placed in charge of the venture by the forty-eight – all English – founding members of the Newfoundland company which had received its charter on 2 May 1610.

The colony at Cuper's Cove hoped to profit from agricultural, forest and mineral resources. When the expected rewards failed to materialise, the Company began selling land to Irish, Welsh and Scots promoters, among them Welshman Sir William Vaughan, who established a short-lived colony at Renews, the Scotsman, William Alexander, later earl of Stirling, and Englishman Sir George Calvert, later Lord Baltimore, who established the Colony of Avalon at Ferryland in 1621 which became a haven of religious toleration. Through their collective efforts, men such as Vaughan, Alexander, and Calvert built a British colony which was to endure for several centuries.

13

Britain's Bourse

'The thrifty Citizen ... seeing the golden age returned into the world again, resolves to worship no Saint but money. Trades that lay dead & rotten ... started out of their trance.'

Thomas Dekker, *The wonderful yeare* (1603)[1]

Back in early seventeenth London, trade was changing the look and feel of the city. From wharves along the River Thames, ships were loaded and unloaded with timber, oil, pepper, nutmeg, cinnamon, cloves, currants, fabrics, textiles, lace, porcelain, and much more besides, all destined for consumers at home or for re-export to Europe. In his *Chronicles of England*, John Stow observed that London well deserved 'to bear the name the choicest storehouse in the world', as it is 'a city filled more abundantly with all sorts of silks, fine linen, oils, wines & spices, perfection of arts, and all costly ornaments and curious workmanship, then any other province'.[2]

To encourage trade and prosperity, James I had early in his reign repealed all the English sumptuary laws, which controlled purchasing, including who could buy luxury goods. Such laws, which had been introduced throughout late medieval Europe, required people to dress according to their social status, regulated what was seen as the consumption of 'immoral' luxury and ensured that the import of expensive goods such as silk did not lead to an outflow of a country's wealth. Rulers across Europe sought to protect their domestic industries; if these industries suffered, so too did income into the Exchequer. Now, with a growing and affluent middle class emerging across Europe, monarchs like James were persuaded that it was inappropriate for the Crown to dictate on personal matters such as clothing or spending.

Given the boom in demand for luxury goods, London needed a new commercial space in which to display and sell the fruits of global trade. In 1570 Sir Thomas Gresham had built the Royal Exchange at Cornhill and Threadneedle Street in the heart of the City. Modelled on the Bourse (or 'Exchange') in Antwerp, London's Royal Exchange was primarily a place for merchants to meet and discuss trade and finance, rather than to sell commodities, although some retail units were later added upstairs. In 1608, Cecil, a powerful advocate for the East India Company, decided to spearhead and fund a project to build a new exchange, one that would surpass Gresham's in terms of grandeur and function, where the well-heeled could browse, inspect and buy the fine new luxury goods arriving at London's docks. A new exchange would be a fitting monument to London's status as a centre of commerce and a means of developing a fashionable shopping area west of the City, where Cecil had recently completed the building of his new London residence, Salisbury House. The site chosen for the new centre was on the south side of the Strand where the old stables of Durham House were demolished for Cecil's new venture in the heart of the newly aristocratic West End.

The New Exchange took just ten months to construct and was suitably admired. The Venetian ambassador Marc'Antonio Correr, noted that it was indeed superior to the old Royal Exchange and that Cecil had 'fitted up one of the shops very beautifully', and added, 'over it ran the motto: "All other places give for money, here all is given for love."'[3] The New Exchange comprised a colonnaded 200-foot-long arcade, arranged over two floors, each divided into an inner and an outer walkway, and containing over a hundred luxury boutiques. The upper storey had five huge stained-glass windows emblazoned with the arms of King James, Queen Anna and Prince Henry, and the Cecil heraldic insignia.

Intended both as a place to purchase a range of imported luxury goods and the place to be seen, it would open from 6 a.m. to 8 p.m. in the summer, and from 7 a.m. to 7 p.m. in the winter. Haberdashers, stocking sellers, drapers, seamsters; goldsmiths, jewellers, milliners, perfumers, silk mercers; stationers, booksellers, confectioners; and sellers of china, of pictures, maps and prints – all would be welcome to offer their wares to the fashionable elite of the capital and beyond. The fact that most of the goods showcased came from the East was deliberate. All those who gathered for the opening ceremony recognised that anything acquired in the mysterious Eastern world was the ultimate in luxury and refinement.

Cecil oversaw preparations for the Exchange's opening in April 1609, making sure the shelves were fully stocked, using pieces of porcelain from his own collection to fill gaps in displays and persuading members of the East India Company, who were heavily invested in the success of the Exchange, to do the same. Sir Thomas Smythe, the company's governor, donated items from its warehouses for the event, including pepper, fans, inks and dishes.

In 1609, the East India Company was ten years into its fifteen-year monopoly and had undertaken five voyages using a fleet of fourteen ships. Eight vessels had reached Aceh in Sumatra and the port city of Bantam in Java, where factories had been established; five ships had made it through the straits of Sunda into the Spice Islands (Moluccas). The company had become increasingly dependent on Cecil's support, as can be seen in the commissions of their voyages in the period 1607–9, which included the note: 'remember to do your best to bring for the Lord of Salisbury some parrots, monkeys, marmosets, or other strange beasts and fowls that you esteem rare and delightful'.[4]

The grand opening ceremony took place on 11 April 1609, with the king, queen and all three royal children in attendance. James named the New Exchange 'Britain's Bourse', deliberately conceiving of it as a British initiative. Cecil had commissioned a celebratory masque by Ben Jonson for the occasion before the king, queen, Princes Henry and Charles, Princess Elizabeth together with ambassadors and members of London's mercantile and political elite. *The Key-keeper, or Entertainment at Britain's Bourse*, was performed by players contracted from the King's Men, with Jonson's protégé, Nathan Field, in the lead role.

Greeting the king, queen and Prince Henry, the Key Keeper explains that visiting the New Exchange is like travelling to a distant country: 'You may seem upon some land discovery of a new region here, to which I am your compass.' The Shop Boy and his Master – a merchant – then appear, and the boy reels off the names of the goods: 'What do you lack? What is't you buy? Very fine China stuffs of all kinds of qualities? China chains, China bracelets, China scarves, China fans, China girdles ... caskets, umbrellas, sundials, hourglasses, looking-glasses, burning glasses, concave glasses, triangular glasses.'[5] The Master announces at one point that he is 'going shortly for Virginia [...] and so overland to China' – thereby invoking the quest for a northern sea passage to the East.[6]

Since the discovery of a sea passage from Europe to Asia around the Cape of Good Hope in 1498, European traders had enjoyed direct access to the markets of the East. But the route became dominated by the Spanish and Portuguese, exposing merchantmen to attacks by Iberian warships. The discovery of a shorter, northern sea passage to Asia across the top of the globe, northwest or northeast, promised huge rewards: it would allow merchants to avoid the long, dangerous southern route, and would in turn lead to greater profits. As explorer Sir Humphrey Gilbert put it, English merchants would thereby purchase spices 'far better cheap' than the Portuguese, enabling Englishmen to seize the continental market and acquire 'great abundance of gold and silver'.[7]

***

The *Entertainment at Britain's Burse* had praised the opulence and abundance on display, all made possible by the boldness and ambition of England's trading companies. While most in the audience would have basked in this celebration of global commerce, others may have noticed a satirical vein, mocking the growing appetite for luxury. Though luxury was a marker of nobility, it could also be seen as a surrender of reason to sensual and indulgent pleasures. Jonson's entertainment, whilst seemingly wholly in praise of such trade, reflected too contemporary moral concerns about a growing obsession with luxury goods among the increasingly affluent merchant and gentry classes.

To purchase the luxury goods and spices so in demand, the East India Company relied heavily on the export of bullion. With the total value of British imports increasing by a staggering 40 per cent between 1600–20, the Crown had to address an imbalance of trade. The main English export, woollen broadcloth, did not achieve significant sales in the East. And so, to address concerns over the adverse balance of trade and the drain of national wealth, and to provide employment opportunities for the poor, James sought to engage national interest in a project to promote domestic industry and the national economy. In doing so, he was directly replicating the plans of the esteemed king of France, Henri IV. In both countries, the drive to create domestic silk production would become national endeavours. In Britain, James began to urge his subjects to plant mulberry trees and raise silkworms to supply the new industry.

Small quantities of silk to make 'narrow wares' such as ribbons and broads, had been woven in England for centuries from raw silk brought from China and Persia, along the silk road to eastern Mediterranean trading centres such as Venice and Aleppo. But as demand for silk clothing, fabric, ribbons and threads grew, more raw silk was needed for the domestic manufacture of such finished goods.

In May 1607, James promoted Nicholas Geffe's translation of *The Perfect Use of Silk Worms and their Benefits* by Olivier de Serre, which explained all aspects of sericulture and silk production – how to care for silkworms, harvest raw silk from the cocoons, how to spin the silk.[8] This edition included poems by Elizabethan favourite Michael Drayton which celebrated the peace brought by James I and imagined foreign envy. The silkworm was a creature which from 'small beginnings' could be 'the strength and maintenance of Kings'. He anticipated a future in which Britain overtook the European producers of silk: 'Naples, Granada, Portugal, and France/All to sit idle, wondering at our trade.'[9]

Geffe argued that private desires for luxury promoted the public good, and that the production of silk at home 'will cloth our backs sumptuously and fill our purses royally … our private profits and public benefit are deeply interested therein'. Reflecting on England's historic dependence on wool production, he mourned the 'mass of money … which strangers fleece from us', and urged, 'we may as well be silk-masters as sheep-masters'.[10] Geffe emphasised that there would be benefits for all, in what would be a national project. While the nobility and gentry would make 'thousands of crowns' and 'keep their hands from the … tradesman's book' (by buying on credit), silk production could provide employment for the poor.[11]

The starting point, according to Geffe, was to 'plentifully plant' marginal lands with mulberry trees. But the country had no mulberry trees and so all would need to be imported. King James appointed William Stallenge, a sixty-year-old former customs officer from Plymouth, to oversee the project, who in turn enlisted the help of French horticulturist François de Verton (alias 'Monsieur de la Foret [Forest]'). In 1606 Stallenge and de Verton were granted a royal patent to bring mulberry trees into England, with a price cap of one penny apiece, and an expectation that one million would be imported per year.[12] James then wrote to all the 'Lord Lieutenants of the Shires of England' ordering them to oversee the purchase and distribution of 10,000 mulberry plants per county. The scheme did not extend to Scotland, Ireland or Wales, likely on account of the climate which also made cultivation in England very challenging.

Mulberry saplings were offered at a discounted rate with more affordable packets of mulberry seeds available for the less well off. The project would see thousands of mulberry trees planted across the country.

De Verton travelled up and down the country, monitoring progress, reporting back to Cecil that most of the lord lieutenants had implemented the scheme.[13] The French horticulturalist estimated that he had covered 1,100 miles and distributed 100,000 trees to the English gentry, though he went no further north than Lancashire.[14] Cecil arranged for 500 mulberry trees to be planted in the grounds of the newly built Hatfield House in Hertfordshire, which were laid out by gardener John Tradescant. In London, Stallenge created an impressive four-acre Mulberry Garden 'for His Majesty's use, near to his palace of Westminster' – in what is now the grounds of Buckingham Palace. Thousands of mulberry trees were planted, silkworms purchased, and labourers hired. Within a couple of years, the king's Westminster plantation had yielded modest results, generating around 9 lbs of silk, enough to make about nine silk robes. It was a start.

In 1609, Stallenge, now Keeper of the King's Mulberry Gardens, published *The Instructions for the Increasing of Mulberry Trees and the Breeding of Silk Worm, for the making of Silke in this Kingdome* which included the king's letter sent to the Lord Lieutenants in which he cited Henri IV as the project's inspiration: 'Our brother the French king, hath, since his coming to that crown, both began and brought to perfection the making of silks in his country.' The rewards, James added, benefitted everyone: 'He hath won to himself honour, and to his subjects a marvellous increase in wealth.'[15]

***

Weeks after the opening of the New Exchange, the king granted the East India Company a fresh charter which confirmed their monopoly indefinitely over 'the whole entire and only trade and traffic to the East Indies'.[16] The company commissioned a new state-of-the-art vessel to replace their ageing flagship *Red Dragon*, which had returned to Plymouth in September 1609 laden with spices, but with a leak.

As he had after their first voyage returned in 1603, James informed the company that he wished 'to buy all the pepper now brought home', and 'at such rate and price as any other would give the same'. The company's shareholders were dismayed, believing that 'the merchant that beareth the dangers of the sea and land should have the gain happening by a rising market'.[17] Reluctantly the company agreed to accept the king's offer, but vowed to 'appoint some fit man to make the Lord Treasurer [Cecil] acquainted with the Company's frustration' and the 'inconvenience that may happen both to his Majesty and the Company' by setting a price before the pepper has been 'first seen and known'.[18] Cecil mediated and a reassured Smythe reported back to the board on 6 October 1609 that the Lord Treasurer intended 'to use all possible means for encouragement of the company in this their trade both honourable and profitable for this kingdom'.[19] Cecil also may have persuaded James to think again, as he was subsequently able to tell the company: 'his Majesty was not now so inclined to deal with the pepper or any part thereof' and that 'he was altogether unwilling to do that which might be distasteful unto them'.[20] The following month, the company successfully petitioned the king to restrict the sale of Dutch imported pepper. The company, it seemed, was now in high favour at the palace of Whitehall.

When the company's new flagship was ready to be launched on the Thames at Deptford, the king, queen and Prince Henry all attended the celebrations. On New Year's Eve 1609, the royal family enjoyed a lavish banquet on board the ship, the interior of which had been draped with silks and tapestries. Court gossip John Chamberlain reported that the king presented Sir Thomas Smythe with 'a chain, in manner of a collar, worth better than £200, with his [Majesty's] picture hanging in it and put it about his neck with his own hands'.[21] James named the new flagship, then the largest merchant ship ever to have been built in

England, the *Trades Increase*. It was both a statement of the company's ambition and a bold affirmation of Britain's growing presence in the East. Prince Henry named a smaller ship, a pinnace, the *Peppercorn*, after the company's main import. Yet as the ship launched, it became stuck, being too broad to float out of its dock.

The ship finally set sail later in January 1610 but failed to make it back to England. A leaky vessel prone to running aground, it was set ablaze by arsonists in Java four years later (apparently at the instigation of a renegade Spaniard 'turned moor') and became a cindered wreck. The East India Company's most expensive ship to date had proved too badly damaged to repair and was left abandoned.[22]

When the news eventually reached England of the loss of *Trades Increase*, an anonymous pamphlet of the same name appeared in a bookshop in St Paul's.[23] (The author's identity was quickly exposed as one Robert Kayll.) It directly referred to the ship and highlighted the cost of such fruitless voyages. The pamphlet claimed that monopolistic trade, such as that enjoyed by the East India Company – whereby no other English subjects could trade from the Cape of Good Hope to the Straits of Magellan – was an abuse of the nation's resources. Rather than helping to enrich Britain, the company was impoverishing the state by importing luxury goods which drained national resources and bullion. 'How much more we, murmuring at this iniquity,' the author asked, 'may affirm that we are all Britons, all subjects to one royal king, all combined together in one natural league, and therefore not to be barred from trading in all places?' Unrestricted access to trade would, he argued, increase customs revenues, promote shipbuilding, create new employment, and benefit the country as a whole. Whereas free trade advocates attacked the East India Company as a 'boundary to the expansion of commerce', the company's supporters argued that monopoly rights were necessary to make long-distance trade with Asia both possible and profitable.[24]

Smythe was furious when he saw the pamphlet, and asked diplomat and company member Sir Dudley Digges to publish a riposte.

The Defence of Trade refuted the accusations point by point. East India Company merchants were like 'busy bees', said Digges, bringing honey to 'the Commonwealth'. What was more, the company would soon turn London into 'a staple of commerce for the world', leading to 'much life and quickening to the navigation and affairs of this whole island'.[25] Digges believed the Crown could and should encourage private action for public benefit, for: 'We are the bodies of our king, and of our country.'[26]

14

The Way of the North

'I can greatly commend those valiant minds that do attempt
such desperate voyages, and the rather when they do it for
knowledge sake, and profit their Country, and not altogether for
private gain and lucre [money]'

Thomas Blundeville, *M. Blundeuile his exercises* ... (1613)[1]

In May 1607, English navigator and explorer Henry Hudson
had sailed out from Gravesend in the three-masted barque, the
Hopewell, with a crew of ten men. They then headed north, beyond
the furthermost reaches of the Britain Isles, and towards the Arctic
Circle. This was the latest in a series of attempts by European explorers to find the northern sea passage to the East.

According to the writings of merchant-adventurer Richard
Hakluyt, in his *Principal Navigations*, published in full at the turn of
the century, the northern passage seemed preordained as England's
own. Hakluyt wrote: 'God doth yet still reserve this great enterprise
for some great Prince of England to discover this voyage of Cathay
[China] by this way, which for the bringing of the spiceries from
India to Europe were the most easy and shortest of all ways hitherto
found out.' Rather than having to purchase spices through middle-
men in the Levant, a direct route from India could carry such commodities straight back to Europe. Hakluyt continued: 'And surely,
this enterprise would be the most glorious, and of most importance

than all other, that can be imagined, to make his name great, and fame immortal, to all ages to come.'[2] Cleric Samuel Purchas meanwhile called upon all intrepid and adventurous men to set sail in search of a passage towards the 'spiceries, which would shorten every step they took towards the Pole.'[3]

Since the reign of Henry VII, many men and expeditions had tried and failed to search for a navigable northern route, first over the North Pole, then by the northeast and latterly by the northwest. Whilst all had failed, albeit discovering Russia in doing so, the charter of the Muscovy Company ('the Company of Merchant Adventurers to New Lands') granted it both the rights to the northern route to Russia but also monopoly rights to explore the north and northwest as well. By 1607 the company was preparing for another such voyage. On Hakluyt's recommendation, the Muscovy Company commissioned experienced sea captain, Henry Hudson, whose family had shares in the company. Included in the *Hopewell*'s crew was Hudson's son John.

The voyage proved slow and stormy, taking more than a month to reach the Arctic Circle, and then six weeks, through ice-packed waters, to sight the east coast of Greenland. The *Hopewell* continued northwards, finally reaching Spitsbergen in the Svalbard archipelago, before impenetrable masses of ice barred further progress north and the expedition was forced to turn back and head home.

Hudson had failed to find the northern route across the Pole to China, but in the waters around Spitsbergen he had discovered great numbers of whales, walruses and seals. With opportunities to source profitable whale fat to make goods such as lamp oil and soap, the Muscovy Company would send regular whaling ventures to the region and in 1613 received a new charter giving it exclusive rights to fishing there. The arrival of the newly chartered Dutch Noordsche Compagnie (Northern Company) in 1614 and expeditions commissioned by King Christian IV, sparked fierce competition. First, the Muscovy Company, on behalf of James, and then Danish traders, on behalf of Christian IV, claimed the 'no-man's land' for themselves.[4]

The Dutch steadfastly refused to recognise the claims of either monarch. Competition between Dutch and English ships and crews frequently sparked into open conflict. Dutch and English diplomats discussed, but never resolved, the conflicting claims of the Northern and Muscovy companies. Nevertheless, whaling became a valuable boost to the English economy and Spitsbergen ceremoniously named by the Muscovy Company, 'King James his New Land.'

Though his first attempt to find a northeast passage had failed, Hudson began to prepare for a further expedition just weeks after returning to England. In April 1608, he set sail once more on behalf of the Muscovy Company in the *Hopewell*, with a fourteen-man crew. This time he went looking for a passage through the Arctic waters north of Russia, exploring the coast of Siberia, further east than the company had ever ventured before. Once more, however, after passing along the Norwegian coastline into the Barents Sea and reaching Novaya Zemlya, an island off the north coast of Russia, his voyage was thwarted by ice-laden waters. Hudson wanted to steer a course for North America, but his crew threatened to mutiny, and he was forced to return home.

Hudson's failure to make any significant discoveries or progress led to the Muscovy Company losing interest in further explorations of the north. Next, Hudson turned to the Dutch East India Company (VOC), which was as eager as its English rival to find a trade route to the East. The Dutch company assigned him the *Halve Maen* (*Half Moon*), a half-ton ship and a crew of eighteen. In the spring of 1609, Hudson sailed out of Amsterdam and up the coast of Norway. At North Cape, where he would turn east, he wrote in his logbook that progress was difficult. It may well have been that, given his experience of previous voyages to find the passage, Hudson knew that the attempt would prove futile. Acting, it would seem, in defiance of VOC instructions, he now headed west, for the coast of North America.

On 12 June, the *Halve Maen* reached what is now Nova Scotia, and sailed south along the American coast. It entered Chesapeake

Bay and 'Poutaxat' (Delaware Bay), and in early September, 'Lenapehoking' (New York Bay). Hudson then sailed about 140 miles along what was subsequently named the Hudson River, to present-day Albany. Hudson found the river too shallow to proceed. The ship's log recorded the indigenous name for the large island in the lower reach of the river as 'Manna-Hata'. Shortly after Hudson's return, the Dutch sent settlers and established New Amsterdam at the mouth of the river, creating the beginnings of the future New York City.

On his return to England in November 1609, Hudson was commanded to appear before the king, who forbade him from continuing to voyage 'to the detriment of his country'.[5] Whilst being contracted to sail by another friendly country was accepted practice for a navigator as experienced as Hudson, sailing under the flag of the Dutch, one of Britain's key primary trading competitors, was another matter. A guard was placed on Hudson's house to prevent him leaving the country. Before long, however, James was persuaded to release him.

***

In 1610 Sir Dudley Digges, a shareholder in both the Virginia Company and East India Company, Sir John Wolstenholme a Yorkshire landowner and collector of customs for the port of London; and Sir Thomas Smythe, governor of the East India Company, came together with twenty others, including the Prince of Wales, to sponsor another voyage in search of the northwest passage. Hudson was the obvious choice to lead the expedition and so was released from house arrest and given command of the syndicate's fifty-five-ton ship the *Discovery*, part of the original fleet to the Virginia colony.

As the ship prepared to depart, Prince Henry, Smythe, Wolstenholme and Digges raised a toast to Captain Hudson in his cabin before joining the assembled crowd on the dock, among them Richard Hakluyt, to watch the ship sail. That year Edward Wright had dedicated his enlarged edition of *Certain Errors in Navigation* to

Henry. The prince, now sixteen, was known for his keen interest in the search for the northern passage and in 'the discovery of strange and foreign lands and nations yet unknown'.[6] Digges also dedicated to Prince Henry a presentation copy of explorer John Davis's earlier work, *The Worlde's Hydrographical Description*. This volume apparently included a handwritten folio sheet entitled 'Motives Inducing a Project for the Discoverie of the North Pole Terrestrial.'[7]

The 'Motives' presented the advantages of commerce, especially for island kingdoms such as Britain, and argued that since the profits of English merchants trading with neighbouring kingdoms had sunk so low, it was now necessary to open trade relations with countries more remote. This made the discovery of a northern passage to China, Japan and other countries in what was then called the South Sea all the more urgent. The handwritten piece suggested that the king should create an order of knighthood for those financing such voyages, and that these 'Adventurers' should be incorporated into a company with a view to discovering and 'Planting' the northwest passage. They should be men either of noble birth or high position who, in return for their investment, should then receive land wherever the 'Plantation' shall be located, and other benefits at the discretion of Prince Henry. All other things, the document concluded, would be communicated to the prince by word of mouth. To enable the prince better to understand the project, the writer explained that he had left with 'Edward Wright of the Prince's Household' a small terrestrial globe for Henry in the royal library at St James's.[8]

***

Shortly after dawn on 17 April 1610, the *Discovery* set sail from St Katherine's Pool, below the Tower of London, with a crew of twenty-three men led by Hudson and including once more his son John. By early June, they had reached the coast of Greenland, before moving south and crossing Davis Strait. A month later they rounded Resolution Island and entered the 'Furious Overfall', what would become known as Hudson Strait, which carried them into what

Abacuck Prickett, the *Discovery*'s navigator described as 'a great and whirling sea', what is now Hudson Bay. Sailing west under the Union Flag, Hudson named the islands as they passed them: 'Prince Henry's Foreland', 'King James his Cape', 'Queen Anna's Cape' and 'Mount Charles'.[9]

That winter the ship was forced south to Monsonis (now James Bay) where large chunks of ice blocked them from going further or returning home. After six months, and with supplies running low, discontent spread among the crew; there were frequent quarrels, not helped by Hudson's own volatile character. In late spring, as Hudson readied the ship to sail, and push north once more, there was a mutiny led by two of the crew, Robert Juet and Henry Greene. Refusing to change plans, Hudson, his son and seven others were put in a shallop and set adrift. The *Discovery* returned to England, under the command of the mutineers, many of whom died on route. Neither Hudson nor any of the abandoned crew were seen again.

The voyage's sponsors in London launched an investigation into the venture's failure. It focused as much on progress and discoveries made as on the fate of Hudson and half the ship's crew. In their depositions, the *Discovery*'s remaining crew members described a 'great flood' or easterly tide they had experienced in the bay. This was interpreted by the company as clear evidence of a northwest passage to the 'South Sea'.[10]

With the firm belief that Hudson had discovered the northwest passage, the syndicate quickly organised a new expedition. Captain Thomas Button, a Welsh Royal Navy officer then in the service of Prince Henry, was given command of the *Discovery* and the *Resolution*, to follow up on Hudson's discoveries and explore what lay on the western side of Hudson Bay.

Before his departure, the king issued Button with a letter of credence and 'certain orders and instructions' which had been dictated by Prince Henry, demonstrating the importance placed on the mission, and its royal endorsement. The letter was to be shown to the ruler of any country Button 'discovered', or to any prince, king or emperor he encountered, as the mission sailed beyond the South Sea. The king addressed his letter to the 'Right high, Right Excellent and Right mighty Prince', and explained how 'divers of our subjects, delighting in navigation and finding out of unknown countries and peoples, having heard of the fame of you and of your people, have made a voyage' to see your countries, and to trade. The king recommended Button and his crew to the prince's 'favour and protection'.[11]

Henry's instructions reveal his confidence in the voyage. 'We assure ourself by God's Grace you will not return, without either the good news of a passage, or sufficient assurance of an impossibility,' wrote Henry. Further, as soon as the passage was found and Button had entered the South Sea, a pinnace would be dispatched to bring the news back to England.[12] To avoid disasters, such as the mutiny that had ended the *Discovery*'s last expedition, Prince Henry ordered that the crew undertake daily religious devotion, that there should be 'no quarrelling or profane speeches', and that 'no drunkenness or lewd behaviour' should go unpunished. Button was to keep accurate and full journals; follow a certain course on his outward voyage; and spend no time searching for anything other than the passage. With crews totalling some 160 men, the *Discovery* and *Resolution* left England on 14 April 1612.

Captain Button's fleet passed through Hudson's Strait into Hudson's Bay, where he sailed to the western shore, which he named New Wales. He also named the point where he landed: 'Hope Checked', to signify the disappointment felt when he had realised that he had not reached the South Sea. Instead, he sailed southwards entering Port Nelson on 15 August where the ships wintered. When the ice melted the following spring, it crushed the *Resolution* which had to be abandoned. The *Discovery* proceeded to search the whole western side of the bay for a way through, and when this proved impossible, they returned south-eastward and explored the western end of the Hudson Strait to investigate the 'great flood' or tide which the survivors of the Hudson voyage had described. With the autumn approaching, the *Discovery* prepared to returned home. The expedition had reached uncharted areas of Hudson Bay but had failed to find the fabled passage.

Three months later, James granted a charter for the establishment of the 'Company of London Merchants Discoverers of the Northwest Passage'. Sir Thomas Smythe was appointed its governor and Prince Henry its patron. The company's members included Privy Councillors, court officials, nobles and merchants of the City of London. These individuals were confidently described as 'the first adventurers and discovers of the North-west Passage'.[13]

With Hudson's voyage having 'found a straight or narrow sea', the Northwest Passage Company now sought to 'advance a trade to the great kingdoms of Tartaria [Central Asia], China, Japan, Solomons Island, Chilli, the Philippines and other countries in or upon the said sea'.[14] The charter explained that, as this was an 'enterprise tending to so worthy an end', the king wanted 'some extraordinary means to grace and honour the same'. He resolved that his 'dear and well beloved' eldest son and heir would be the 'Supreme Protector of the said Discovery of the Company'.[15] The chartering of the company had been exactly what the 'Motives', written and presented to Henry two years before, had suggested. Now all the company's discoveries would be celebrated in his name.[16]

New voyages would be sent out in 1614, 1615 and 1616, but finding their progress blocked by ice-choked waters, all were forced to return home. The failure to find a northern passage and the unforgiving conditions for ships and men, brought a halt to the search, at least in England, for several generations. Other countries, including Denmark–Norway, continued the quest.

For now, Prince Henry remained committed to overseas exploration, adopting as his own the Northwest Passage Company's motto: 'Goes into the deep'. It captured both his desire to explore and his love of the sea.

15

A Thirst for Glory

'The eyes, and hearts, and hopes of all the Protestant world, be fixed upon your Highness, all expecting your Gracious faithfulness, & readiness in the extirpation of that man of sin [the Pope].'

Daniel Price, *The Defence of Truth* (1610)[1]

While many of Britain's new mercantile elite looked towards the prince as 'Supreme Protector' of their expansionist plans, Henry was also seen as the great military hope of many Protestant Britons.[2] In *Basilikon Doron*, written a decade earlier in Scotland, James had warned his young son to avoid the extremes of the church. But for fervent Protestants – both English and Scottish – Prince Henry had come to represent the fulfilment of their belief that a British monarch would lead them against the Antichrist, in the great final struggle that scripture prophesied. Clement Edmondes, a Scottish colonel in the Low Countries, had compared the prince at a young age to the Black Prince, claiming that Henry's name 'begins already to be spread through the whole world'.[3] While James championed peace at home and abroad, the king also encouraged the image of Prince Henry as a martial figure, to mollify those who urged a Protestant crusade against Rome and to consolidate Britain's position in Europe.

Sampson Lennard, a soldier who had fought in defence of the United Provinces, wrote in 1611 that the king's 'pen hath made way for your sword, and his peace, if God give long life, may farther your wars'. Dedicating to Prince Henry his translation of Du Mornay's anti-papal *Mysterie of Iniquitie*, Lennard wrote in 1611 that he longed for the day when Henry might 'live to march over the Alps', and 'trail a pike before the walls of Rome, under your Highness' standard'.[4] Lennard's book proved so popular with militant Protestants in Britain that it went to three editions.[5] But now, as Henry's investiture as Prince of Wales approached in the summer of 1610, an evolving political crisis in Europe placed the king and Prince Henry's respective roles in sharp relief.

***

The ongoing conflict over the right of succession to the north German state of Jülich-Cleves, which had ignited in June 1609, threatened to draw Catholic and Protestant states in Europe into all-out war.

James had been urged to commit a military force alongside Henri IV of France and Christian IV of Denmark–Norway. While expressing his willingness to help, James had prevaricated and sought to justify a more limited military response. Via Sir Ralph Winwood, the English ambassador in the United Provinces, Cecil relayed the king's stance: that contribution ought to be 'always parallel'd to the present Estate of the party assisting', and that as Britain 'lay much further from the disputed territories', it would not be able to make as large a contribution as the French.[6] James was at pains to stress, seven years after Elizabeth I's death, that he was still saddled with her war debts, that: 'At our coming to the Crown we found not only this Kingdom exhausted but wrapt into great Arrear of Debts, by reason of a continual war that hung upon it; and since our coming have been put to many several occasions of Expense which necessarily could not be avoided.'[7]

Cecil added that there were additional complications, such as the time and cost of levying and transporting men to a place 'more remote from us than the others', the 'Incommodities and Incertainties of

Wind and Weather', together with 'Considerations of State', 'where we shall have cause to charge and burden our People many ways'.[8] The latter was a reference to the upcoming session of Parliament, which would open on 9 February 1610, in which Cecil sought to secure, on James's behalf, a regular parliamentary tax for the Crown in exchange for the surrender of its remaining feudal privileges. Winwood was to make clear to the States-General that unless those Scots and Englishmen already fighting in the Low Countries could be redeployed, then that 'aid which we do give may be rather accepted in Money, than in other kinds'.[9]

As talk of war engulfed the court, and Henri IV declared his intention to lead the French army in person, James sought to justify his policy through curated discourse and debate, once again using his eldest son as a foil. He commissioned scholar and antiquarian Sir Robert Cotton to write *An Answer to Certain Military Men Regarding Foreign War*.[10] Whilst framed as a response to specific 'arguments' presented to Prince Henry, *An Answer* was more likely a response to the ongoing debate, at court and beyond, as to the value of peace over war.[11]

Having first set out the apparent arguments made for engaging in war, Cotton went on to dismiss them one by one, arguing that history has shown that war is damaging to the country as a whole. Rather than building discipline and virtue, military experience accustomed common soldiers to loose-living and violence. The 'civil troubles of this state' had generally been stirred up by men with military experience, who, having enjoyed 'command' in war, had forgotten how to 'obey' in peace. Moreover, foreign wars were ruinously expensive.[12]

Given all this, the safest and most honourable course for Britain was 'to remain, by a neutrality, Arbiter of Europe'. France and Spain in particular were so closely matched that it would only require 'a little weight' to 'sway ... the balance'. Britain was therefore well placed to adjudicate: 'princes by their orators shall resort unto us as to the Common Consistory of Judgment in their debates'. In this way, as Cotton continued, 'shall we gain the seat of honour, riches and safety, and in all other but endless expense, trouble, and danger'.[13] It was a perfect summation of James I's diplomatic strategy.

With the rejection of Cecil's Great Contract by both James and Parliament, it became virtually guaranteed that the British Crown would remain too poor to commit to a major war. Yet failing to act would, Winwood observed, risk damaging King James's honour and reputation by demonstrating his reluctance to support a cause 'not only of state but of religion'.[14]

In spring 1610, James finally agreed to a temporary defensive alliance with the Protestant Union of German Princes, contributing 4,000 English and Scottish soldiers in a British expeditionary force. These were soldiers already serving in the Dutch army whom James would pay while they were in Germany.[15] The Dutch and French would together muster 23,000 men and the Protestant Union a total of 10,000 men. James's allies had again agreed to shoulder most of the burden, but he had at least consented to spend some money in their support. Despite James finally promising military aid, Boderie, the French ambassador in London, was certainly not convinced of the king's commitment. Whilst acknowledging that the British had played an active role in negotiating an alliance to support Protestant claimants, and were now contributing troops to their defence, it was 'principally' he said, 'to make it appear to the whole world that they are parties to this cause and that they want to run the same lance in it as his majesty [Henri IV]'.[16] The French king agreed, adding: 'I am quite suspicious of the constancy and firmness of their faith.'[17]

Yet James had played a canny hand. He would provide a British military force but by using men already serving in the United Provinces, and at much less cost for the Crown. Moreover, he made clear that the soldiers, under the command of Sir Edward Cecil, nephew of Sir Robert, be seen as being directly in the pay of the 'King of Great Britain'.[18] For the first time, a British expeditionary force would fly the Union Flag.

As allied forces readied in May 1610 for an invasion of Jülich-Cleves, all came to a halt when news spread of the murder of

Henri IV. The French king had been stabbed to death on 14 May by a Catholic zealot in Paris. Horror at Henri's loss spread across Europe and was felt keenly in England. Rumours abounded that the assassination was part of a wider Catholic plot. James issued a royal proclamation describing the 'evil' behaviour, 'manifested first by the Priests Treason [an early conspiracy against James I] immediately after Our entry into this Kingdom, and next, at the horrible Powder Treason the unnatural cruelty whereof is never to be forgotten'. These, James declared, were 'joined to this horrible and lamentable accident abroad (we mean the devilish and most unnatural murder of the late French king our dearest Brother)'.[19]

Despite fears for the royal family's safety, and Prince Henry's profound shock and grief at the loss of the French king, his godfather, it was determined that his investiture as Prince of Wales would go ahead.

***

On 4 June 1610, the first formal creation of a prince of Wales for more than a century took place in London. The last had been that of Prince Henry (future Henry VIII), after the death of his brother Arthur. Now, supported by the earls of Nottingham and Northampton, and preceded by twenty-four newly installed Knights . of the Bath and a host of noblemen, Henry walked in procession to the Palace of Westminster where the ceremony would take place. Standing in front of his father who sat on his throne, Henry declared his obedience three times and then knelt to listen to the words of the investiture, read by Cecil. James then robed his son in a mantle of purple velvet, and placed a coronet on his head, a ring on his finger and a golden wand in his hand. Finally, his father ceremonially kissed him on the hand and on the head.[20]

The queen, Elizabeth and Charles looked on, together with the Lords and Commons, the lord mayor and aldermen of London, and an array of ambassadors representing courts across Europe, who had gathered for the ceremony and days of festivities. James was only able to stage the elaborate investiture programme because the City of London had lent him money and bore part of the cost. Such a golden opportunity to present Britain and its heir to the world could not be missed. It was an event of huge significance for Britain and the continent: the much-celebrated Protestant prince had come of age just weeks after the loss of Henri IV. In a tract dedicated to the new Prince of Wales, French Huguenot Jean Louiseau de Tourval, who was in London at the time, urged the prince to head 'our Christian army', take on his namesake's mantle, embrace the role of general of the Protestant forces in Europe and avenge the king's murder. The tract was a rallying cry for a holy war, a crusade against the Jesuits and Spain, who so many believed were behind the assassination.[21]

Henri's widow Marie de Medici, regent for their young son King Louis XIII, now reduced the French contribution to the Protestant forces preparing to lay siege to the town of Jülich to a token force of infantry and cavalry. Henry, Prince of Wales, requested that Sir Edward Cecil, commander of the 4,000-strong British contingent serving under Prince Christian of Anhalt, send him full reports of the battle and drawings and diagrams on the fortification and the progress of the siege.[22] On 21 August, just as the assault of Jülich was to begin, the governor of the town surrendered. Jülich was to be handed over to the Count Palatine of Pfalz-Neuburg and the Elector of Brandenburg.

The fears of French weakness with the long minority of Louis XI and the regency of his mother Catherine de Medici, and then, on 19 September the death of the Elector Palatine, made the Protestant Union look again to James I. Prince Christian of Anhalt came to England to lobby personally on behalf of the German princes for James to assume the leadership of the union. Fearful as to the military commitment that might entail, James sought to draw into the union the Dutch (who joined in 1613), and unsuccessfully France, Sweden and Denmark.[23] Nevertheless, Batta Boisschot, the archdukes' ambassador in London, observed James was energetically promoting this alliance because it appealed to his vanity by making it appear as though he had become the leader of the Protestants throughout Europe.[24]

In April 1612, a defensive alliance was concluded between King James and the Protestant Union of German Princes. As the capstone to this agreement, James and Anna's daughter, fifteen-year-old Princess Elizabeth, was to be betrothed to fifteen-year-old Frederick V, the new Elector Palatine.

***

Sir Robert Cecil was, as ever, central to these negotiations. But amid celebrations of the marriage alliance, his health began to rapidly deteriorate. The previous August he had been diagnosed by the king's physician as having two large abdominal tumours, and had since then suffered with shortness of breath, rheumatism in his right arm, fevers and melancholy. Overworked and reportedly in great pain and mental anguish, he visited the hot springs in Bath, before setting off back to London. He got as far as Wiltshire, dying at the former priory of St Margaret in Marlborough, on 24 May 1612, at the age of forty-eight. He was buried with little fuss, as he would have wished it, in the parish church in Hatfield, a fortnight later.

Though his reputation had been damaged by the Great Contract negotiations in parliament, and his relationship with the king had suffered because of it, he remained Principal Secretary, Lord Treasurer – and James's greatest advocate. The loss of Cecil removed a pivotal figure at the heart of James's government. Having been kingmaker in the period leading up to 24 March 1603, he had remained loyal to James, a tireless workhorse attending to matters from the union, to brokering peace with Spain, to attempts to reform royal finances, and to negotiating wine contracts for the king – his last appearance in Parliament. He had proved to be an invaluable sponsor of trade and commerce, with networks across the City of London, and agents and contacts stretched across the continent. An enthusiastic supporter of Prince Henry and his household, latterly Cecil's diplomatic efforts had focused on securing marriage alliances for James's children, to ensure Stuart Britain's future place in Europe.

***

Following James's formal acceptance of Frederick's marriage proposal, the young Elector Palatine and Princess Elizabeth began exchanging letters – in French and using suitably formal language. 'I give you most humble grace for the assurances you have given me of your love,' Elizabeth wrote in one letter, 'which I will cherish the more affectionately because I am commanded to do so by the king, whose paternal wishes I regard as inviolable as law.'[25]

The Prince of Wales was a keen supporter of the match, which he imagined would be the prelude to active military intervention against Catholic states on the continent. As plans progressed for the Protestant marriage of his sister, so too did talks for a Catholic marriage for Henry to the Princess of Savoy, a Catholic state strategically located between France and the Spanish territory of Milan.

Writing to his father on 5 October 1612, the prince made it clear that if he had to have a Catholic bride, he preferred to marry one who would 'give the greatest contentment and satisfaction to the general body of the Protestants abroad', adding hopefully: 'I am of the opinion you will sooner incline to France than to Savoy' referring to his preference for a marriage with the daughter of Henri IV.[26] Several of the Prince of Wales's friends were more vociferous in their opposition to the Savoy match. Sir John Holles, comptroller in the prince's household, spoke of the religious difficulties presented by this pairing, arguing that a Catholic queen would encourage others to convert and warning that 'one mass at court begets 1,000 in the country'.[27] From the Tower of London, Ralegh wrote that Savoy was too attached to Spain, that closer relations with Savoy would alienate Geneva and other Protestant princes, and that the match would embolden English Catholics. He believed Henry's marriage should not be rushed: 'While his majesty is yet unmarried, all the eyes of Christendom are upon him.'[28]

As preparations for the Palatinate marriage intensified, Prince Henry, who was heavily involved in all the arrangements, began to show troubling signs of ill health. In early October he was described as being pale and thin, with constant headaches and increasing lethargy. After spending three days in bed after two 'small fits of an ague', he struggled to make the journey from Richmond to London for the arrival on 18 October of Elector Frederick, whose train included powerful noblemen from Protestant Europe, including Count Henry of Nassau and Prince Maurice of the Netherlands, gentlemen whom Henry greatly respected for their history of fighting the Spanish.[29]

After seeking to continue to entertain the Protestant princes and prepare for his sister's wedding, on Sunday 25 October, the Prince of Wales was forced to take to his bed. For the next twelve days he grew steadily weaker. Physicians tried to restore his health by letting blood from his arm and shoulder, and having shaved his head, applied 'warm cocks and pigeons newly killed, but with no success'.[30] At Queen Anna's behest, Ralegh sent from the Tower a small vial of 'Balsam of Guinea', a concoction of herbs, roots and bark collected during his travels. Elizabeth tried in vain to visit her brother, even donning a disguise, but was refused entry for fear his condition was contagious. Finally, just before eight on the evening of Friday 6 November, eighteen-year-old Henry died. 'Thus,' wrote Sir Charles Cornwallis, the prince's treasurer, 'lost we the delight of mankind, the expectation of Nations, the strength of his Father, the glory of his Mother, Religion's second hope.'[31]

James wrote to Christian IV of his devastation. 'The grief which we can scarcely express out loud, but on behalf of our greatest trust and love we must nevertheless report the death of our dearest first-born, which happened yesterday.' We cannot, he continued, 'fully express our immense grief in a longer letter, so let this suffice for you; we are still so confused by the distress and sorrow from this most serious and unexpected misfortune that we could scarcely collect our thoughts.'[32]

Anna's heart was broken, Ambassador Foscarini told the Doge, writing many weeks after the loss of her son: 'The Queen's life has been in the greatest danger owing to her grief. She will receive no visits nor allow anyone in her room, from which she does not stir, nor does she cease crying.'[33] Henry was the fifth child she had lost. In the aftermath of her brother's death, Elizabeth cried constantly and refused food for two days.[34] For the twelve-year-old Prince Charles, who had, just days before, pressed his brother's favourite little bronze horse into his hand imploring him to recover so they might ride together again, all was now to change. Charles, who for a time was thought unlikely to survive infancy, was now the king's heir. Reflecting on Henry's relationship with his family, Francis Bacon wrote: 'He was a wonderfully obedient son to the King his father, very attentive also to the Queen, kind to his brother; but his sister he especially loved.'[35] According to courtier Sir Arthur Gorges it was – for the country, the king's family and the Protestant cause in Europe – an 'Olympian Catastrophe'.[36]

Within twenty-four hours of the Prince of Wales's death, the first of a torrent of elegies, epitaphs, poems, and compositions – more than for any English or Scottish monarch to date – poured from pen and press, mourning the loss of the chivalric and militant Protestant ideal that Henry had come to represent.[37] Phineas Pett wrote of how 'our royal and most loving master, departed his life, not only to the loss and utter undoing of his poor servants, but to the general loss of all Christendom of the Protestant religion'.[38] Reports from France described the devastation of the Huguenots, who had 'built their hopes on the Prince and had already chosen him as their chief support and head'.[39] Dispatches from Cologne, Dusseldorf, Heidelberg, Stuttgart and Zeeland express similar sentiments. From Stuttgart a German named Daniel Buwinckhausen wrote to William Trumbull in Brussels: 'The news of the death of the Prince of Wales has stunned us all. It is a very great loss to us Germans also.'[40] On 17 November 1612, Foscarini told the Doge that the death of 'Henry, Prince of Great Britain', will certainly cause 'great changes in the course of the world', adding: 'The foes of this kingdom are freed from a grave apprehension, the friends are deprived of a high hope.'[41]

A week later, Foscarini reflected further on Henry. His was 'a thirst for glory if ever any prince was ... many predictions centred round his person, and he seemed marked out for great events ... His whole talk was of arms and war' and he was 'obeyed and lauded by the military party'. He 'protected the colony of Virginia' and 'begun to put the navy in order'.[42]

He was, the elegies all said, 'Britain's' great hope. Henry had represented a future where the pope's claims of secular authority might be vanquished, and he had served as an important figurehead for the militant Protestantism that was beginning to define an evolving British identity.

Not everyone felt a sense of profound loss, however. From Madrid Ambassador Digby observed that the Spanish could not have grieved less. Much of the reason, he noted, was Henry's ambitious and expansionary plans, and his fervour for finding the Northwest Passage. Digby reported that the Spanish hoped 'business of that nature' would grow much colder 'since the death of the late Prince'.[43]

In Virginia, Deputy Governor Sir Thomas Dale lamented the demise of his principal patron, saying it would be both his own undoing and cause the unravelling of the entire colony. 'My glorious master is gone,' he wrote. 'He was the great Captain of our Israel, the hope to have builded up this heavenly new Jerusalem' with his death 'the whole frame of this business fell into his grave' and 'Virginia stands in desperate hazard.'[44]

Suddenly the future of the Stuart dynasty seemed to hang in the balance. Now all eyes turned to twelve-year-old Charles. The prince's early years had been punctuated by ill health and developmental difficulties. His speech and walking were both delayed, the latter by weak ankle joints, possibly caused by rickets. He had overcome some of these hurdles, though retained a stutter, and was still regarded as being weak. He appears 'so slight and so gentle', wrote Foscarini, and 'those who wish well to the Crown would fain to see him stronger'.[45] There were fears that Charles would not reach adulthood, let alone marry and go on to produce an heir to the throne.

There were implications also for Elizabeth's future. There are 'doubt in many minds', the Venetian ambassador reported, 'whether it is expedient to allow the Princess to leave England, now that there is only the Duke of York remaining'.[46] Chamberlain told Dudley Carleton that after Henry's death, 'the Scots take not so great joy in this match' and he had heard suggestions that she instead be married to 'their Marquis Hamilton'.[47] This was a rather fanciful proposal, not least as the second Marquess of Hamilton was already married.

James considered postponing Elizabeth's wedding until the following May to allow for a full period of mourning. Foscarini reported that the Privy Council questioned whether 'in view of the prince's death, the marriage of the Princess should take place at all'. There was also the issue of the expense. 'The nuptials will be celebrated at great cost,' he added. 'They are delayed for that very purpose.'[48] But to prevent any further opposition, James resolved to bring the wedding date forward.[49] An amended marriage contract was signed stipulating that Elizabeth and Frederick would now exchange vows on 6 January 1613, with the public solemnisation of the wedding taking place thereafter.

16

Union of Thames and Rhine

Come forth, come forth, and as one glorious flame
Meeting another grows the same,
So meet thy Frederick, and so
To an inseparable union go

...

John Donne, *'An Epithalamion, or, Marriage Song'* (1612)[1]

At ten o'clock on the morning of 6 January 1613, Princess Elizabeth and the Count Palatine, head of the Protestant Union of German princes, exchanged vows at the Banqueting House, Whitehall, Frederick having learned sufficient English to do so:

I, Frederick, Elector of the Holy Roman Empire, Count Palatine of the Rhine, Duke of both Bavarias, take you Madame Elizabeth, daughter of the most powerful, high and glorious King of Great Britain, for rich or poor, for well or ill, to be my wife while life me lasts.[2]

Frederick wore purple velvet 'richly laced with Gold lace, and a cloak lined with cloth of gold', and as Sir Isaac Wake wrote to Sir Dudley Carleton, to: 'make an even mixture of joy and mourning', Elizabeth 'wore black satin with a little silver lace, and a plume of white feathers in her hair'.[3]

The marriage contract was read out and the couple repeated their vows before George Abbot, the Archbishop of Canterbury, gave his blessing.[4] One absentee was Queen Anna, still in mourning for her son, and who, it seems, disapproved of Frederick, believing he was not worthy of her daughter. Wake noted her absence as being due to 'some sharp fits of the Gout that have lately vexed her'. Chamberlain saw this an excuse at the time, but by mid-February reported that 'the Queen grows every day more favourable and there is hope she will grace it [the wedding] with her presence'.[5]

As Elector Palatine and one of seven imperial electors, Frederick did have influence over the Holy Roman Empire, but only in terms of deciding the imperial succession. By the seventeenth century, this succession had become dominated by the Austrian Habsburgs, making the imperial Crown was effectively hereditary, although a series of childless emperors in the late sixteenth and early seventeenth centuries complicated matters. Protestants were outnumbered in the electoral college: there were three Protestant electors, as opposed to four Catholic ones. Frederick's powers within the imperial hierarchy were therefore limited, and he was constitutionally subject to the emperor. However, he ruled in the Upper and Lower Palatinate by hereditary right and decided on most of the laws and – crucially – the faith to be followed in his dominions.

This was the first royal wedding to take place in England since the marriage of Mary Tudor and Philip II of Spain in 1554, which had then celebrated the alliance of the two Catholic countries. Now, decades later, this event would celebrate a Protestant union of 'Thames and Rhine'. For James it was the first step towards the fulfilment of his vision to achieve peace in Europe though the marriages of his children. For some, however, this alliance presented the opportunity to refashion British national identity as militantly Protestant, in staunch defence of the Protestant cause in central and northern Europe. In his 'Marriage Song', John Donne described how the marriage fuelled hope for the nation: 'Be thou a new start, that to us portends End of much wonder.'[6]

It was a union of considerable European significance and took place against a backdrop of mounting confessional tension between the radical states of the empire, led by the Palatinate, against the Austrian Habsburgs whose counter-Reformation fervour and close ties with Spain were regarded with deep suspicion. The Prince of Wales's death had intensified the symbolism of Elizabeth and Frederick's marriage, which now embodied the hopes of Protestants across Europe and expectations for Britain's new interventionist role. Leadership of the envisioned pan-Protestant crusade now fell on the shoulders of the young couple. Chamberlain told Carleton (now Sir Dudley) that extensive security arrangements had been set up in the City of London in the lead-up to the wedding as there was 'intelligence' of 'some intended treachery'.[7] Rumours circulated of 'a Spanish Armada which is gathering; some say it is for Virginia, some for England, some for Ireland'.[8]

Three days before the wedding, as part of the festivities, the royal family and thousands of spectators watched a mock sea battle on the River Thames involving three dozen 'Christian ships' and 'Turkish galleys'. It was a naval display that the late Prince of Wales had helped plan and design. A castle representing the Moorish castles of Tunis or Algiers in north Africa had been constructed on the riverbank and filled with fireworks and gunpowder, and was to be detonated in the explosive finale.[9] According to onlooker John Taylor, 'the Water Poet', the sea battle recalled 'the manner of the happy and famous battle of Lepanto' in Cyprus, fought between the Christians and Ottoman Turks in 1571. The defeat of the Ottoman navy, hailed as a decisive battle in the conflict between the Christian West and the Muslim East, had been heralded by James VI in his poem 'His Maiesties Lepanto' and then reprinted and translated into several languages on his English accession. The poem celebrated the victory, but it reflected too the long-recognised belief that the rise of the Ottoman Empire had been facilitated by divisions within Christendom. For James, his daughter's wedding to the Elector Palatine was a step towards healing these divisions. It was also for this reason that James sought a reunion of the Christian church in Europe. Negotiations were already underway for a Catholic match for twelve-year-old Prince Charles.

The mock sea battle ended with the surrender of both the castle and galleys to the 'English admiral, who fired many of the said galleys, sacked the Castle and took prisoner the Turks' Admiral', pashas and 'other Turks'. The captives were then rowed along the Thames to the King's Privy Stairs at Whitehall, which caused 'delight' to the royal family and 'all there present'.[10]

Such was the official line. John Chamberlain, who watched the display, described a rather different outcome. 'The king and indeed all the company took so little delight to see no other activity but shooting and putting off guns' that the event was called off before it was finished. The subsequent dismantling of the gunpowder-filled castle proved catastrophic, leaving many men injured, 'one lost both his eyes, another both his hands, another one hand, with divers other maimed and hurt'.[11]

***

On Sunday 14 February, Valentine's Day, the public solemnisation of the marriage took place. It was an event both anticipated and celebrated in equal measure. In the words of writer Anthony Nixon: '*England* hath put a face of gladness on; young and old alike celebrate This Nuptial day, wherein we all enjoy/Such perfect comfort throughout *Brutes* new *Troy* [London].'[12]

Westminster Abbey had originally been planned as the location for the wedding, but it was now considered inappropriate so soon after the Prince of Wales's funeral and would have required the bride to walk past her brother's tomb. It was therefore decided to relocate the ceremony to the Chapel Royal in Whitehall Palace. Thousands of people crowded outside to witness the procession which began with Frederick dressed in a 'white satin suit, richly beset with pearl and gold', and accompanied by the Earl of Lennox, one of James's most trusted Scotsmen, and Charles Howard, Earl of Nottingham, one of England's most senior nobles, and a number of young English, Scottish and German courtiers.[13]

Princess Elizabeth followed behind, led by Prince Charles and Henry Howard, Earl of Northampton. She was dressed in a white satin gown, 'upon her head a crown of refined gold, made imperial by the pearls and diamonds, thereupon placed which were so thick beset that they stood like shining pinnacles upon her amber coloured hair'.[14] Accompanying her were her guardians Lord and Lady Harington, the latter leading many ladies dressed in white who carried Elizabeth's enormous veil. Finally – after a procession of heralds at arms, earls, lords and barons, Privy Councillors, and four bishops – came Thomas Howard, Earl of Arundel, bearing the king's sword in front of the king and queen. James wore 'a sumptuous black suit with a Diamond in his hat of a wonderful great value' and Anna was dressed 'in white Satin, beautified with much embroidery, and many Diamonds'.[15] Chamberlain thought James 'somewhat strangely attired', on account of the 'cap and a feather, with a Spanish cape and a long stocking'.[16] A sign from the king perhaps that the next marriage alliance he sought was for Prince Charles with Catholic Spain.[17]

Inside the chapel, a stage had been erected: to the right sat the king, the Earl of Arundel bearing the king's sword, and Frederick and Prince Charles, who sat on stools. To the left sat the bride and her mother. After an anthem by the chapel's choir, the Bishop of Bath and Wells James Montagu delivered a sermon based on the account of Jesus's wedding miracle at Cana in Galilee. Having retired to the vestry to don 'rich copes' [long cloaks worn by bishops], Montagu and the Archbishop of Canterbury returned to the stage to conduct the wedding ceremony, which would, for the first time, follow the service in the Book of Common Prayer. After an exchange of vows, the couple knelt before the communion table whilst the Garter Principal of Arms made the official announcement of their titles, followed by shouts of congratulations from all lords present. Thereafter, the news was declared across the capital with bells rung and fires lit.

The wedding and entertainments – James's showcasing of his vision for Britain – stretched over ten days and cost a total of £93,293 (c.£20 million today).[18] Courtier Roger Wilbraham described 'the court abounding in jewels and embroidery beyond custom or reason: God grant money to pay debts.'[19] John Chamberlain concluded that 'this extreme of cost and riches makes us all poor'.[20]

On the evening of the wedding, guests gathered for Thomas Campion's *Lords' Masque* at the Banqueting House, its walls hung with huge tapestries depicting the defeat of the Spanish Armada in 1588, the great English Protestant triumph over Catholic Spain.[21] All of Europe's ambassadors now sat beneath them, apart from the Spanish envoys; neither Ambassador Velasco nor the Spanish Netherlands envoy Boischot attended the wedding celebrations, unwilling to participate in an official event at which the destruction of the 'Great and Most Fortunate Fleet' was being flaunted in such a prominent way.[22]

Campion's masque, commissioned by James, presented his vision for the marriage. In the words of the prophet Sibylla, Frederick and Elizabeth would produce an heir who would be the first of a new line of kings and emperors which will add 'to Germany British strength' and be means to 'unite both nations, faith and the worship of God.'[23]

The following evening George Chapman's *Memorable Masque of the ... Middle Temple and Lincoln's Inn* took centre stage.[24] Unusually, the entertainment began with a pre-masque on the torch-lit city streets, near the Inns of Court with a triumphal procession described by Chapman as a 'show at all parts so novel, conceitful and glorious; as hath not in this land...been ever before beheld.'[25] The total cost to the two Inns for the whole performance was £2,255. 8s. 11d. [c.£495,000 today], an amount 'so great', as the Venetian ambassador noted, 'that, in spite of their being very rich, they will feel it for some time.'[26]

But such excess was exactly the point. This was a spectacle intended to celebrate the new establishment, the interweaving of mercantile, governmental, church, and court elites, the Inns of Court, and the capital's guilds and trading companies.[27] Lawyers from the Inns of Court had been involved in the drafting of the Virginia Company's charters. Many of the company's most prominent members were former Inns of Court men whose interest in colonisation was underpinned by the view that the law was the means to enforce conformity and godly order, and that 'uninhabited' lands could be justly conquered through the maxim of *terra nullius* (no man's land).

In financing and taking part in Chapman's *Memorable Masque*, the Inns were demonstrating their support for the colonial enterprise at a time when the failure to find gold brought accusations that the Virginia Company was offering empty promises to potential investors. Prince Henry, as patron of the Virginia plantation, had also had a hand in planning the entertainments, and the dramatist Chapman was a member of his household.

The procession from Chancery Lane to Whitehall was designed as propaganda for the Virginia Company and for the colony on the grandest scale, with students from the Inns dressed up in elaborate clothing, their skin stained brown and feathers in their hair. As narrated by Chapman, the mock-Virginians were paraded before huge crowds of Londoners, not as slaves or prisoners brandishing 'cane dart' weapons, but rather they arrived in state having been converted and 'civilised' by the English, their darts now ceremonial staffs made from the 'finest gold' – symbols of New World wealth.[28]

After the procession to the tiltyard at Whitehall, the main masque began in Banqueting House before, as Chapman describes, 'the King, Bride, and Bridegroom, with all the Lords of the most honour[e]d Privy Council, and our chief Nobility'.[29] The musicians were dressed, as 'Virginian priests' with 'strange hoods of feathers and scallops about their necks' and 'turbans, stuck with several-coloured feathers'.[30] The principal masquers were styled as caricatures of Native Americans, 'Princes of Virginia' and 'Sun priests' dressed in 'cloth of silver embroidered with gold', with olive-coloured masks. The central device of the masque was the conversion of the sun-worshipping Virginians to a veneration of James, the 'sun king'.

The masque suggested that the colonial venture would see gold mines 'opening' to Britain, and that a new golden age would issue forth from the riches of the colony, as it would from the marriage of Elizabeth and Frederick, the union of Thames and Rhine.[31]

***

In April 1613, Elizabeth, Frederick and a large entourage of relatives and servants left London to make their way to Heidelberg, the capital of the Lower (Rhenish) Palatinate. The king and queen accompanied the wedding party as far as Rochester and said their farewells, and Prince Charles rode on as far as Canterbury.

At Margate, Elizabeth and Frederick prepared to sail for the continent on the *Prince Royal*, the spectacular warship built by Phineas Pett for Prince Henry. Less than two years before, Elizabeth and her family had congregated at Woolwich for its launch. But, as had happened with *Trade's Increase*, the ship got stuck in the dock gates; the naming ceremony became a solitary affair with Henry returning at high tide the following day to see it float free from its moorings. For the young prince, the launch of the *Prince Royal* had heralded what he hoped would be the start of a rebuilding of the Royal Navy.[32] As it was, Henry's ambitious plans for reform died with him.

From the Kent coast on 26 April, Elizabeth wrote to her father:

Sire, It is at this time that I feel the disagreeable effects of the separation and distance from Your Majesty, my heart, which was oppressed with grief and dismayed at my parting now gives me leave to my eyes to weep at being deprived of the view of the most precious object that they have ever knowingly contemplated in this world. I shall possibly never, as long as I live, again see the flower of princes, the King of fathers, the best and most gracious father under the sun. But the most humble respect and devotion, with which I shall unceasingly honour Your Majesty will never wipe from the memory of the one who waits here for a favourable wind, and who would wish to return once more to kiss the hands of Your Majesty if the state of affairs, or her circumstances could allow it, to demonstrate to Your Majesty with what burning affection she is and will be till death.[33]

Writing from Brussels three weeks later, William Trumbull reported the royal couple's safe arrival in Heidelberg on 7 June. The wedding festivities had continued, with the new Electress of the Palatinate and her husband having been feted in towns in the Netherlands and all along the Rhine. The ambassador's letter carried the welcome news that: 'her Highness's Physicians do report that in all appearance she should be with Child'.[34] Sibylla's prophecy in Campion's masque was perhaps to come true.

17

A Russian Proposition

'Sir, that God will see this through to the end for His honour and
His glory, to the confusion of the enemies of His truth, to the great
contentment of Your Majesty and to the joy of all the faithful, and
for the incredible profit that would come from seeing such a vast
country being humbled by the true knowledge of God and obedient
to Your Majesty.'

Captain Jacques Margeret to James I, spring 1613[1]

For the celebrations of Frederick and Elizabeth's marriage in
February 1613, the royal family and wedding guests were
treated to a performance of one of Shakespeare's most recent plays,
The Winter's Tale. Like the assembled audience, the play's charac-
ters hailed from all over Europe: Polixenes is the King of Bohemia;
Leontes is King of Sicily, and his wife, Hermione, is the daugh-
ter of the Emperor of Russia. When Hermione says of her father,
'O, that he were alive and here beholding/His daughter's trial',
Shakespeare's likely inspiration was Ivan IV, also known as Ivan the
Terrible, the recently deceased first tsar of Russia.[2]

As he watched the performance, James was perhaps thinking of a
proposal presented to him just months earlier by John Merrick, chief
agent of the Muscovy Company, that he, the King of Great Britain,
establish a protectorate over northern Russia and take the place of

the Russian emperor. It was a spectacularly audacious offer – which James would shortly put before the Privy Council.

***

England had had a significant presence in Russia since the days of Ivan the Terrible, when the tsar granted English explorer Richard Chancellor favourable trading rights in the White Sea, which in turn led to the creation of the Muscovy Company in 1555. In the north of the country, hitherto uncharted territory, English merchants established profitable trading posts (factories) in Arkhangelsk, Kolmogory, Vologda and Yaroslav, as well as having an English 'house' and trading post in Moscow: the Old English Court, one of the oldest surviving buildings in the city and regularly visited by ambassadors. Russia provided markets for English woollen cloth, munitions, lead and copper, and luxury goods produced in the Mediterranean, in exchange for furs, leather, wax, and was increasingly important for supplying materials for ship-building such as timber, tar, cordage, flax and hemp. Whilst in other regions of the world, the Dutch had arrived ahead of the English, in Russia, England arrived first and secured customs-free trade there. The Dutch began to trade with Russia via the White Sea route in the 1590s, and the region would become yet another theatre for escalating Anglo–Dutch competition.

The tsar had welcomed trade with English merchants at a time when Russia was isolated and effectively surrounded by Poland and Sweden, who were endeavouring to keep it segregated from contacts with the West. But all changed in 1584 when Ivan IV suffered a fatal stroke, apparently while playing chess. The throne passed to Fyodor I, his middle son, and when he died in 1598, the 700-year old Rurik dynasty came to an end. A series of national crises ensued. When James I came to the throne in England, Russia was in the midst of power struggles, civil wars and famine that threatened its very existence.

In 1604, when Fyodor I's brother-in-law Boris Godunov became tsar, James sent a diplomatic mission to Moscow, to both congratulate the new emperor and secure confirmation of the Muscovy Company's trading monopoly there. The man chosen was Sir Thomas Smythe, then governor of the Muscovy Company, the East India and Levant companies. He was recommended as the 'likeliest to respect both his Majesty's honour and the good of your trade.'[3] As Smythe was preparing to return home in April 1605, after just under a year in Russia, his mission both well-received and partly successful, Tsar Boris died after a lengthy illness. His sixteen-year-old son Feodor II succeeded him but ruled for less than a month before being challenged by the first of the 'False Dmitris', imposters who claimed to be long-lost sons or half-brothers of Ivan the Terrible. Following Feodor's murder in June, a Polish-supported 'False Dmitry I' assumed the throne, who was in turn replaced by Vasily Shuysky, a powerful Russian nobleman, after a *coup d'état* by the Russian boyars (nobles). Taking advantage of Russia's protracted 'time of troubles', as the period came to be referred to, armies from Poland and Sweden invaded and occupied huge swathes of Russian territory, including Moscow and the northern provinces.

In 1609 Sigismund III of Poland, who had been deposed from the Swedish throne ten years earlier following his attempts to unify the two countries as a Catholic kingdom, responded to Sweden's intervention by leading a large army into Russia and seemed on the point of seizing the Russian throne for himself. Despite Sigismund's zealous Catholicism, James's relations with the Polish Crown since his accession had been generally good, not least because Poland was a significant market for English cloth and a major supplier of basic raw materials like flax and hemp which were of particular importance to the navy. Indeed, for a time a marriage alliance was discussed between Princess Elizabeth and Sigismund's son Ladislaus (in Polish, Władysław) as part of James's vision to use his children's marriages to bring rapprochement and reconciliation across Europe.

However, when Sigismund wrote to James notifying him that the English would now be required to pay all the normal customs dues from which they had been hitherto exempt, and with the threat of further Catholic expansion, the marriage plans between Britain and Poland were hastily abandoned. The Polish advance had to be checked: James was called to act. Again, he resisted any definite military commitment but supported British mercenaries – English, Scots and Irish – joining the Russian resistance against the Poles.

Meanwhile, in the spring of 1610, Sweden, Poland's implacable enemy, anxious about the threat to its borders and with its own trading interests in Russia, sent a delegation to London to petition James for a military alliance. Again, finance precluded any such commitment and instead James offered to ease the pressure on Sweden by mediating in its growing dispute with Denmark.[4]

***

In the summer of 1610, Thomas Chamberlayne, a prominent English mercenary soldier, wrote from Smolensk to Cecil with news that the Russians were 'content to make' Sigismund III of Poland their tsar, and also for his son to succeed him, provided that they did not introduce 'papistry'.[5] By autumn the following year, the situation had reversed, with Scottish mercenary James Hill reporting to Cecil from Moscow that the cruelty of the Poles made the Muscovites so 'half-headed' that they would now be glad of *any* other prince. In fact, aside from Christian IV of Denmark, it was thought that none could do it better than James himself, with Hill adding: Russia 'would be a thousand times more profitable than Virginia'.[6]

In the autumn of 1612, John Merrick returned to England with further details of this extraordinary proposal. 'Divers principal and eminent persons' in Russia, he said, would be willing to place themselves under James's care if there was any hope of him agreeing to rule them.[7] Weeks later James received a formal written proposal – a 'Proposition by the Muscovites [Russians] to render them subjects to the King of England' – which seems to have been authored by Chamberlayne but actively encouraged by the Muscovy Company.[8]

The 'proposition', now in the king possession, described how the Russians in the 'Northern parts of that Empire' were yet 'entire and free from any touch of war', but feared the 'hostility of Poland' and the 'unfaithfulness of Sweden', but 'without a head and in great confusion', look through necessity 'to cast themselves into the arms of some prince that will protect them, and to subject themselves to the government of a stranger'. As the proposal continued, having had 'long commerce' with England 'to the mutual benefit of both' and given the 'fame of His Majesty's great wisdom and goodness', they 'do much desire to cast themselves into his hands than any other'.[9]

The document went on to explain that the offer of 'sovereignty' of this part of Russia – an area between Archangel and the Volga River, and the tract along the Volga to the Caspian Sea – would safeguard access to Russian markets, which were increasingly threatened by the Dutch, and the supply of essential Russian goods. It would also allow trade to be extended to Persia (Iran) and to the East via the Volga. Access to the East via the overland route across Russia would be much easier and cheaper than the current means of acquiring goods – by way of Turkey, through 'many hands', and at great expense. It was hoped that this new 'colony' would extend all the way down the Volga River to the Russian border with Persia.[10] Besides supplying the British market, goods could then be sold into 'France, Germany, the Low Countries and Denmark to the great employment of our shipping and the notable increase of his Majesty's customs'. The proposition concluded that this would be the 'happiest overture that ever was made to any King of this realm, since Columbus offered King Henry VII the discovery of the West Indies'.[11]

Russian documents have ever been found to identify who these 'principal and eminent' Russians were, nor indeed whether the Russians made the proposal in the first place or that they wanted an English protectorate. It is possible that this all may have been a ruse by the Muscovy Company and British mercenaries to encourage James to intervene in Russian affairs.

James, however, enthusiastically embraced the idea of being Protector of north Russia, and in April 1613, submitted the proposition before the Privy Council.[12] Writing from London to Sir Dudley Carleton in Venice, John Chamberlain reported how the 'council have been busied of late about certain projects in Muscovy [Russia]' that had been made to John Merrick by some of the Russian nobility to 'put themselves and their country under the King's protection'. He said that James supported the proposal: 'He saith he never affected anything much and seriously but it came to good pass, and he never affected anything more than this so that he doth not doubt of success.' Chamberlain was a little more sceptical, 'these I doubt are but discourses in the air'. He surmised that the Russians would have expected Prince Charles to be 'their emperor' but now, with Henry dead, and Charles the only heir, that would not be possible.[13]

A memo of 14 April 1613 written by Chancellor of the Exchequer Sir Julius Caesar noted details of the discussions and his concerns about the proposal's feasibility and costs, including the expense of transporting and maintaining a garrison force of an estimated 10,000 men to secure the crucial northern port of Archangel, and the need for a governor or deputy to rule there.[14]

Yet despite such reservations, politics and commerce here overlapped. Eighteen of the twenty-three members of the Privy Council were investors in the English trading companies and saw the opportunities that a colony in northern Russia could bring. For the king, too, there were considerable potential rewards, including increased customs revenues and an extension of his dominions. Further, by establishing a protectorate, Britain could push back the attempts of Catholic powers to advance into Russia, as threatened by the 'Jesuit king' Sigismund of Poland. This was encouraged by those in the council, such as Sir Dudley Digges, Henry Neville and George Abbot, Archbishop of Canterbury, who had long been advocating a more aggressively Protestant foreign policy and who now, following the death of Cecil, held greater sway. For James it provided a means to act but not at his cost: all expenses were to be paid by the Muscovy Company and by taxing the Russians.

By May 1613, James had appointed Merrick and his associate William Russell as ambassadors to Russia to commence negotiations. A letter of credence was drawn up, addressed to 'the right noble and excellent Lords, the right reverend Fathers and our most worthy friends and allies', and two royal commissions.[15] Since the situation on the ground remained turbulent, and the Russians had approached Merrick more than a year earlier, care needed to be taken in case circumstances had changed and an English protectorate was no longer wanted. Drawing up two commissions was an unusual but not uncommon practice and allowed the ambassadors to surrender to Russian officials that which was most appropriate to avoid jeopardising English interests. One commission contained no mention of the English protectorate and expressed only the king's concern for Russia's plight, his desire to maintain the friendship between the two countries, and his wish to protect the trade of the Muscovy Company. The second commission, however, directly addressed the Russian proposal. It ordered Merrick and Russell to discuss 'the propositions or overtures afore mentioned, or any other' as 'pertaining to the defence and protection of that country' and demonstrated that the English government fully intended the ambassadors to negotiate for an English protectorate over northern Russia.[16]

Meanwhile, during the spring of 1613, James received an undated and unsigned letter informing him that a national liberation movement had ousted the Poles from Moscow and on 21 February had elected the sixteen-year-old Michael Romanov to the Russian throne. The letter's author, who can be identified as a French Protestant mercenary soldier, Captain Jacques Margeret, urged James to proceed with the plan for establishing a protectorate or sovereignty in northern Russia regardless. Margeret believed the young tsar would not be able to pacify his country and rule effectively, which would likely lead to a further Polish military offensive later that year. He was convinced that English military intervention would be successful and that, in checking Catholic Poland's eastward expansion, King James would be performing a great service not only for the Russians but also for the entire Protestant world. The letter is undated, so it is unclear whether Margeret's argument was decisive in encouraging James to send envoys to Moscow to pursue the idea or if it made him aware that Merrick's commission would be dead on arrival.

***

At Archangel on 8 June 1613, Merrick and Russell, on being told the news of Michael Romanov's election, realised that the idea of an English protectorate was redundant. Merrick promptly dispatched Muscovy Company agent Fabian Smith to Moscow with a new message congratulating the young tsar on his accession and with one of the credence letters James had penned in May, 'signifying that they were sent from the King's Majesty of England about the settling of a peaceable trade for his Subjects in those countries and procuring some privileges for the better managing of their affairs'.[17]

Tsar Michael responded positively, writing to Merrick on 2 July, that he accepted the explanation that, because his election had not been known in England when the envoys departed, the documents were not addressed to him. The tsar was keen to maintain close relations – 'finding the hearty love and princely affection which we entirely desire of our most dear brother your great sovereign lord king James' – and acknowledged the English ambassador's previous service in Russia, 'done to these Lords and Kings in anything they have commanded'. He concluded by promising to continue the Muscovy Company's trading rights, but made clear that this would be dependent on England assisting Russia 'against our enemies and the supporters of them'. In return for such an alliance the tsar would 'hold you and your nation, not as strangers but as our own native-born subjects' and the former privileges would then be 'written in our princely name; and in all our dominions of Russia you shall trade more freely than ever heretofore'.[18]

With Poland and Sweden still occupying sizeable parts of Russia, and neither country having withdrawn its claim to the throne, the threat of further conflicts was still very real. For decades both the Muscovy Company and the English government had sought to maintain trade with Russia, while avoiding political and military involvement in Russia's wars. Now Tsar Michael needed both England's friendship and military aid but, as his letter made clear, the right to trade was conditional. He advised that he would shortly be sending ambassadors to London, and if Merrick was not going to return with them, then he should send letters to the Muscovy Company that they should 'further our affairs' with the king.[19]

***

On 26 October 1613, the new tsar's ambassadors, Aleksei Ivanovich Ziuzin and Aleksei Vitovtov, disembarked at London's Tower Wharf.[20] The delegation was welcomed ashore with a deafening gun salute from a Royal Navy ship – larger and louder, it was said, than any in living memory for a foreign ambassador. This was the first Russian embassy to England for fifteen years, since the onset of the 'Time of Troubles'. Representatives of the government and the Muscovy Company stood ready to greet them accompanied, as Chamberlain reported in a letter to Sir Dudley Carleton, by '100 citizens on horseback in velvet coats and chains of gold and most of the aldermen in scarlet, with about twenty coaches furnished with courtiers and gallants'.[21]

Ziuzin and Vitovtov had their first audience with James on 7 November in the Banqueting House. The Russians' letter of credence did not elaborate on the precise goals of their mission. It stated only that they would announce the accession of Michael as tsar and discuss other important but unspecified topics.[22] In their initial meeting with James, and in subsequent talks with representatives of government and members of the Muscovy Company, Ziuzin revealed that his main task was to acquire the king's help; Poland and Sweden continued to occupy Russian territory and had not withdrawn their claims to the Russian throne. Ziuzin reminded James of 'the most injurious dealings of the kings of Poland and Sweden, whose unjust and cruel practices' threatened the stability of the new regime and asked for 'monies and other provisions of war' to aid Russia against its enemies.[23]

Besides wanting England's military and financial support, Tsar Michael also looked to James to broker agreements with Poland and with Sweden which would see the peaceful withdrawal of their armies from Russian soil. James had played a decisive role in negotiating the peace between his brother-in-law Christian IV of Denmark–Norway and Charles IX of Sweden which led to the Treaty of Knäred earlier that year. The event was widely celebrated and had reinforced James's reputation as an 'honest broker and mediator'. Michael hoped that he might now do the same for Russia.[24]

The king welcomed the re-engagement. He hoped the tsar might want to join a northern Protestant alliance against Sigismund III and his allies – the Catholic league of German princes led by Maximilian, Duke of Bavaria – and help prevent the domination of Europe by Catholic forces. But he was wary of getting involved in Russia's territorial disputes. When James offered no definitive commitment of military support, the Muscovy Company made clear its concerns. They feared that the king's indecisive stance might lose them trading privileges and allow 'the Hollander' to take over, with the Dutch ambassador undoubtedly making 'large offers to obtain privileges, to expel us, and make England and all Christendom beholden to them for materials for shipping'.[25]

The ambassadors remained in London until late spring 1614. Despite petitions from the Muscovy Company and concerns among Privy Councillors, many of whom were investors in the company, about the consequences of refusing Russia direct support, James procrastinated. The truth was, even if he had been minded to, he simply did not have means to offer financial aid or an army to the tsar. In the so-called Addled Parliament which opened on 5 April,

James petitioned Parliament to grant him new sources of revenue. He had opened it with the wish that it would come to be known as the 'Parliament of Love', and that it would prove possible, as he told the Commons in his opening address, to 'take away the misunderstanding between you and me which was in the last Parliament'.[26] But in the face of their continued resistance to grant funds, it was angrily dissolved by the king less than eight weeks later.

The talks with the Russian envoys concluded with no progress beyond the offer of a diplomatic rather than a military alliance. With the promise that an English ambassador would soon be dispatched to Moscow to commence peace negotiations between Tsar Mikhail and the King of Sweden, and the vague suggestion that a loan would be granted in due course, Ziuzin and Vitovtov prepared to leave London. Whilst the ambassadors had secured no commitment of military aid, they did return to Tsar Michael with gifts, including 'three small pieces of ordnance [artillery]... one sacare and two mynions'.[27] It was a token gesture, reflective of James's familiar strategy: make the very smallest military commitment whilst at the same time offering to seek a resolution through diplomacy.

**

Accompanying Ziuzin and Vitovtov back to Russia was Sir John Merrick, Britain's new ambassador to Moscow.[28] Before his departure, Merrick had been rewarded by the king for his previous good service with a knighthood and the honorary title 'Gentleman of the Privy Chamber'.[29]

Merrick was to represent both the king and the Muscovy Company, and each issued him with a set of instructions. He was also tasked with satisfying the political expectations of the tsar: 'to intercede betwixt' Russia and Sweden, and, as James directed, 'to conclude such a peace betwixt them as may bind up all their former dissensions in amity and love', whilst also confirming the trading privileges of the company.[30] Sir John's task, of balancing politics and trade, would be made all the more difficult by the threat posed by the

Dutch, as the Muscovy Company directors had predicted. They too had offered to mediate in the peace talks between Russia and Sweden in the hope of securing a monopoly over Russian trade, and they continued to make their presence felt. Meanwhile Merrick was told to dissemble over the 'loan', suggest that it was only temporarily delayed, and that the English Parliament would in time accede to the tsar's requests.[31]

At his first audience with the Tsar Michael in January 1615, Merrick asked for confirmation that the trading rights of the Muscovy Company would be preserved. This was granted. However, the tsar would not agree to a licence for its merchants to travel via the Volga River to Persia, nor any other requests to expand the company's activities in Russia.[32] This would be considered, Michael promised, once peace with Sweden had been settled. Merrick prevaricated when questioned as to whether the English would provide military aid if peace could not be secured. While expressing his personal belief that James would help Russia, Sir John explained that when he left England, Parliament had not yet decided on the matter of funds, and so he could not guarantee when the final decision would be taken.[33] In fact Merrick had received a letter from Sir Ralph Winwood, Secretary of State, dated 5 October 1615, that made clear that James would support Tsar Michael's peace initiative in every way short of war, for, laying the blame on parliament, he said he could not bear the cost of going to war for him if that peace failed.[34]

Over the next two years and after many false starts, Sir John would work tirelessly to conclude a peace between Russia and Sweden. The Swedes were reluctant to end their siege of the Russian city of Pskov, or to accept Merrick as mediator, not least because of his long history with the Muscovy Company and the fact that he was James's ambassador in Moscow. Negotiations had only formally opened in December 1615 after many delays, and there were ongoing tensions between Merrick and the Dutch, who Sweden insisted also acted as mediators. In June 1616, the Dutch withdrew, having become convinced that a peace settlement would prove impossible, leaving Sir John as sole negotiator. Finally on 27 February 1617, at Stolbovo, a peace treaty was signed by representatives from both countries and by Sir John on King James's behalf.[35] Its provisions called for Sweden to return Novgorod and its other acquisitions in northern Russia to the Russian government but allowed Sweden to retain Karelia and Ingria, between Estonia and Finland, thus cutting off Russia's access to the Baltic Sea.

Merrick had played a central role in the negotiations, and won the praise of both the tsar and the Swedish king Gustavus Adolphus. James wrote to Tsar Michael praising the English ambassador's role, and adding pointedly: 'And we for our part will be ever ready to cherish this peace wherein *our mediation* hath so happily prevailed.'[36] This was an opportunity to burnish his reputation as a peacemaker and mediator which James was not going to miss.[37]

In late July 1617, Sir John was given a grand send-off by Tsar Michael. A triumphal procession, comprising 3,000 people, accompanied the Englishman through Moscow culminating at the Kremlin, where the tsar hosted entertainments and a dinner in the ambassador's name. Merrick was then rewarded with the rare privilege of being invited to the royal hunt, and given lavish gifts including furs, silk robes, a goblet set with precious stones, and a gold chain holding a picture of the young tsar – a mark of special favour. The boyars toasted his accomplishments, with no mention of King James, saying Merrick would be remembered for centuries.[38] It was not quite what James had intended.

18

Eastern Fantasy

'If the trade of the Chinese could be drawn to Japan, it would prove
the best factory in the world.'

Martin Pring, East India Company captain, 19 October 1621[1]

O n 18 April 1611, the year that James celebrated the production of the first silk from his Mulberry Garden near the Palace
of Westminster, and as efforts to raise silkworms continued across
the country as part of the king's initiative to encourage domestic
industries and address the trade balance, Captain John Saris set sail
aboard the East Indiaman the *Clove*. The ship was loaded with the
East India Company's stock-in-trade – English woollen cloth – and,
£6,500 in bullion 'in case' sales of cloth were not sufficient to purchase goods (which they invariably weren't). The *Clove*, together
with the *Hector* and *Thomas* were to undertake an extensive voyage
which it was hoped would secure trade at Surat in India or, failing
that, procure pepper at Bantam in Java and spices from 'the Spice
Islands' in the eastern Indonesian archipelago. Then, if circumstances allowed, Saris was authorised, as the company's instructions
outlined, to go for the first time to Giapan (Japan) and explore the
prospects of selling: 'Cloth & lead, Iron & other of yo[u]r Native
Commodities as by your observation you shall find more vendible
there'. If the market looked promising, he was to consider whether
to establish a factory there.[2]

Saris carried with him letters in four formats prepared in the king's name: one to 'the Great Mogul of Surat and Cambay' (the Mughal emperor); one to the 'king of Achin' (the Sultan of Aceh); and another for 'the High and Mightie Prince the Emperor of Japan &c'. The addressee of the fourth was left blank in case they encountered rulers unknown, whose name and title could be added as required. Each of the king's letters opened with: 'There is nothing which increaseth more the glory and dignity of sovereign princes upon earth then to extend their renown unto far distant nations', and requested 'friendship and amity' and the 'interchange of such commodities of each other's countries as may be most of use the one to the other'.[3]

John Saris had previously travelled to Asia on the East India Company's second voyage, where between 1605–9 he had worked as a factor and then as chief merchant at Bantam. During his time there and drawing on information gleaned from Chinese and other merchants, Saris produced a memorandum, 'Observations on Eastern Trade', for the company's directors in London in which he listed a range of other products that were popular in Japan. These included decorative table-carpets, pictures of 'lascivious stories of wars by sea and land', copper, lead, iron, tin, thread, tapestries, India cloth, satin, drinking glasses, bottles, Spanish leather, wax for candles, pepper and 'elephants' teeth'. Saris also confidently cited 'broad cloth of all sorts' which could be used by 'the better sort in vest, covering for their saddles and cases for their Cattans [swords]'.[4] England's chief export looked to have a new market.

Whilst no English ship had reached Japan before, there was an Englishman who was already in the country. Helmsman William Adams, from Gillingham in Kent, had been among the few surviving crew members of the Dutch East India company's ship *De Liefde* ('The Love'), which had been wrecked off Kuroshima in 1600, and now lived in Edo (now Tokyo). Adams's arrival in Japan had coincided with the island nation's emergence, after a century of civil war, as an increasingly strong and united country. In 1603, the great military leader Tokugawa Ieyasu had established peace and assumed the title of *shogun* – supreme ruler. Although he officially abdicated two years later in order to ensure the peaceful succession of his son Hidetada, Ieyasu effectively remained Japan's ruler until his death in 1616. The Tokugawa family would rule the country for the next 264 years (fifteen shoguns in all) and established the city of Edo as the centre of government. William Adams found favour with Shogun Tokugawa Ieyasu, married a Japanese woman, and never returned to England nor to his English wife and children.

On 23 October 1611, after learning of the presence of East India Company merchants at Bantam, Adams wrote a letter addressed to 'unknown friends and countrymen'. He outlined who he was and how he came to be living in Japan, his relationship with Tokugawa Ieyasu, the honours he had received, and claimed that the emperor refused to let him leave in order to take advantage of his ship-building expertise. He asked that news of his survival be sent to his wife and family in Kent. Adams wrote of the arrival of the Dutch two years before and how they had found an 'Indies of money', as 'in Japan there is much silver and gold'.[5] It was the currency that the company so desperately desired. Selling goods in Japan for silver would reduce the quantities of bullion that had to be exported from Europe to buy Asian goods.

Adams's long letter assured the English merchants that he would use his favour with Tokugawa Ieyasu to make them 'so welcome and free in comparison as in the river of London'. However, drawing on his experience of Japanese trade, Adams feared 'there will be no profit' for the 'commodities of our country', as woollen cloth was already sold by the Dutch traders (who had been there since 1609), and Iberian merchants (since the sixteenth century). Instead, Adams encouraged the company to use Japan as a base to access trade with China and other Asian territories, including Siam (Thailand). There, raw silk, damask, satin and velvet and other Chinese commodities might be obtained to be traded for silver in Japan. 'Then shall our country make great profit here, and your worshipful [East]

Indian Company of London shall not have need to send money out of England, for,' he continued, 'in Japan is gold and silver in abundance'. In conclusion he added: 'There has not been, nor shall not be, a nation more welcome' than the English.[6]

***

On the afternoon of 11 June 1613, the *Clove* dropped anchor off the coast of Hirado – or Firando as the English and Dutch called it – a port town on the northwest coast of Kyushu, the southernmost of the four main Japanese islands. Saris ordered the crew to fire cannon-shot in greeting, 'it being the custom, as I am informed by the naturals [natives], so to do', he noted in his journal, and immediately sent word of his arrival to William Adams in Edo.[7]

Shortly afterwards, the *Clove* was met by a flotilla carrying Matsuura Takanobu – the twenty-year-old daimyo ('king') of Hirado – and his seventy-two-year-old grandfather Matsuura Shigenobu, the former daimyo. Both Matsuuras were welcomed on board and feasted and entertained with 'a good consort of Music, which much delighted them'. They received 'with great Joy' news that at King James sought permission for the East India Company to establish a factory in the country, and thus to trade with Japan. Takanobu was seeking to establish Hirado as a global trading hub, and keen to welcome another group of foreign traders in addition to the Dutch.[8] Over the next month, as Saris waited in Hirado for the arrival of Adams, Takanobu set out to flatter the English, assuring Saris and the other company merchants that he respected them, their king and their country. When on 25 July, the English merchants celebrated James's accession day by ordering shots to be fired from ordnance on their ships, Saris noted that the king of Hirado commended 'our order in remembering our duty.' When Saris went to visit Takanobu at his court that afternoon, the Matsuuras raised a toast – 'an admirable strong wine' as Saris described it – to 'his Majesty of England.'[9]

Finally, in early August, with William Adams having arrived in Hirado, Saris, Adams and an entourage of seventeen others, including Englishmen and Japanese, set off on the 700-mile journey to Sunpu for an audience with Tokugawa Ieyasu, the former shogun, and now the power behind his son's throne. On their arrival a month later, Saris handed Ieyasu the letter from King James formally requesting trade with Japan, and presented him with a spectacular gift designed to intrigue and impress: a silver gilt telescope sent by the East India Company in the name of the king.[10] Only patented in 1608, this was the first telescope of its kind to leave Europe and the first made specifically as a presentation item.[11] It was a gift designed to convey an image of Britain as superior to other European trading partners, an advanced nation of learning and knowledge that would appeal to the Japanese.

In return, Ieyasu presented ten spectacularly painted gold-leaf folding screens as gifts for James, and a letter addressed to 'the King of Great Britain'. In it he wrote that he was 'not a little glad to hear of your great wisdom and power, as having three plentiful and mighty kingdoms under your powerful command'. He thanked James for the present 'of many rare things such as my land affordeth not, neither have I ever before seen', and desiring 'the continuance of friendship with your highness', gave licence for James to send 'your subjects to any part or port of my dominions, where they shall be most heartily welcome'.[12] A short time after, he granted a *shuinjo* – a document stamped with a vermillion seal – which gave the English merchants permission to live and trade freely throughout Japan.

A week later, Saris and Adams travelled to the shogunal capital Edo, where Saris exchanged gifts with Tokugawa Hidetada. Saris presented him with a sumptuous Turkish carpet, and Hidetada gave him gifts for his king: two beautifully crafted suits of samurai armour decorated with dragons and swirling clouds with 'pumpkin-shaped' helmets (one of the suits of armour is now displayed in the Tower of London).

With diplomatic gifts exchanged and trading privileges granted, it was decided that Hirado would be chosen as the location for the company's new trading post, on the basis that the Dutch were already there and apparently doing well. Adams had suggested Edo as a more suitable place, because of its proximity to the shogun's court on the main island of Honshu, but Saris disagreed, believing Adams was merely trying to get the English trading centre established near his own estate which was located next to the harbour of Uraga, the traditional point of entry to Edo Bay. Relations between the two Englishmen did not improve when Adams, having inspected the *Clove*'s cargo of trading goods, dismissed them as being not 'very vendible', warning that he 'did not see any ways in this land to requit the great charges thereof'. As Adams had clearly explained in his letter to English merchants at Bantam, the market was already flooded with broadcloth. There was also, he pointed out, little demand for the pepper and spices that Saris had also brought to sell.[13]

In an attempt to address the broadcloth issue, Saris suggested to the head of the Dutch factory, Hendrick Brouwer, that both companies fix a price for the sale of cloth to 'advance our Native commodities', but Brouwer demurred. The Dutch promptly reduced their prices to sell the large supply of cloth that they had. The prospects for the sale of English cloth were not helped by the fact that much of it had become worm-eaten during the voyage. It quickly become clear that it was silk rather than broadcloth that was in demand in the shogunate and it was here that significant profits could be made.

On 5 December 1613, as Saris prepared to depart after a stay of some six months, he confirmed the East India Company's appointment of Richard Cocks as captain and chief merchant of the new factory, and the names of the six factors to remain with him. Cocks was a wool merchant of many years' experience, who had once worked as an 'intelligencer' for Cecil, living among the Catholics in Bayonne, southern France. It may well have been Cecil who persuaded Sir Thomas Smythe to appoint Cocks as chief factor in Japan the previous year. Cocks would now be in charge of the company's operations in Japan. Saris left him with the instructions he had been issued with in London more than two years before.

Besides exploring the opportunities for trade in Japan's principal cities, Edo, Osaka and Heian-kyō (now known as Kyoto) and to go to Tsushima to see what commerce might be had with the people of Korea, the English merchants were to purchase and fit out a local sailing vessel, a junk, and fill it with 'broadcloth, Cambray cloth, [and] elephant's teeth' and send it to Siam. It was hoped that the inter-country trade in Southeast Asia would allow the merchants to sell their remaining broadcloth in return for silk which could then be exchanged for silver in Japan.[14]

After Saris's departure, little time was wasted in taking steps to carry out London's instructions. Merchants William Eaton and Richard Wickham were sent to Osaka and Edo, and Edmund Sayers to Tsushima, with cargoes of goods. Tempest Peacock and Walter Carwarden meanwhile sailed for the port of Faifo (now Hoi An) in Cochin-China (Vietnam) with a junk laden with ivory, broadcloth, Indian piece-goods (textiles) and silver. The latter proved to be an ill-fated voyage from which neither man returned. It was later established that after reaching the court of the king of Cochin-China, Peacock was murdered. Carwarden apparently escaped, only to then be shipwrecked. This failed venture alone lost 13 per cent of the initial stock of the Japan factory.

In 1615, Adams and two other English traders sailed with a local crew of fifty-eight men for Ayutthaya in Siam (Thailand) on a 200-ton junk at Nagasaki, which they refitted and renamed the *Sea Adventure*. The previous year they had had a false start when the junk proved unseaworthy, but this time reached Ayutthaya on 18 January 1616, where they bought large quantities of sappanwood (used for dyeing fabric and food) and deer skins. This, the third voyage was an unqualified success – as was the fourth, which reached Siam on 19 January 1617 – returning to Hirado for the first time with a cargo that included raw silk. More success was to follow. On 3 May, Sayers and another English factor named Nelson made it to Cochin-China on an East India Company junk named the *Gift of God*, and presented its ruler Lord Nguyễn Phúc Nguyên with a letter from King James (one of those he'd left blank) and gifts of looking-glasses, amber and samples of broadcloth. Lord Nguyễn, who was looking for allies to strengthen Cochin-China's military and economic power, granted the English an 'unlimited' trading licence and unrestricted access to its markets.[15]

***

Meanwhile, on 24 September 1614, a letter arrived at Philpot Lane, London, addressed to Sir Thomas Smythe in his capacity as governor of the East India Company. It was from Saris, who was heading home after more than three years away. Saris wrote again a week later confirming what the company already knew: that the *Clove* had arrived back and was anchored at Plymouth.[16] Smythe organised for Saris to appear before a company committee meeting as soon as he arrived in London.

But Saris stayed put in Plymouth. When he blamed storms 'more tempestuous ... and our lives more endangered than during the whole voyage' for delaying his onward journey, rumours circulated that he had high-value Japanese items hidden in the hold of the *Clove* which he intended to sell for himself. Having been tipped off that he was falling under suspicion, Saris wrote again to Smythe explaining that he had indeed brought back some Japanese goods, but they were not 'for private trade' but for company sale, and suggesting that they should be displayed at London's New Exchange.[17]

The company directors asked Saris to compile a detailed account describing the setting up of the factory at Hirado and the prospects for trade in the shogunate. The resulting memorandum, 'Concerning requestible commodities vendible in Japan', was read out by Smythe at the committee meeting on 25 October.[18] It included a range of goods strikingly similar to those Saris had detailed in his earlier 'Observations on Eastern Trade', written before he had had direct experience of the Japanese market, including 'Broadcloth', despite the fact that very little had been sold during the six months he was at Hirado. Yet Saris' Observations suggested that English cloth sales would grow in Japan, just as those to the continent were plummeting.

Various initiatives had been introduced that year in an attempt to boost the production and sale of English cloth. Over half of domestic cloth exports consisted of 'white' unfinished broadcloth, produced in Kent, Essex, Suffolk, Worcester and Somerset, which was exported to the Low Countries to be dyed and dressed by local workmen, and then exported onwards at greatly enhanced prices. William Cockayne, a wealthy London merchant and alderman, proposed that it was time for this to change. If English cloth was 'fully manufactured' at home – in other words dyed and dressed in England before being woven, and only finished cloth goods exported – the value of textile exports would rise, employment could be provided for thousands of workers in the cloth industry, and the king would enjoy increased customs revenue through the import of 'dyestuffs'. It would open up the cloth trade beyond the 'Merchant Adventurers of London', the company dating from the early fifteenth century that controlled the export of undyed English cloth.

Seeing an opportunity to gain much-needed revenue, not least after the failure of the Addled Parliament of that year, and to boost domestic industry, James readily supported Cockayne's proposal, dismissing the reticence of some of his Privy Councillors. In July 1614, a royal proclamation not only permitted the export of finished cloth to the continent but banned its export in an unfinished state – thereby ending, in Cockayne's words, the 'deceitful dressing practices of the Dutch'.[19] The States General immediately retaliated, threatening a trade embargo on finished English cloth and encouraging its own cloth-weaving industry.

Finally, on 12 November, Saris appeared before the East India Company's committee. When he was asked 'of the hopes for trade with Japan', he maintained that it was a good market for broadcloth and other European goods, and that participation in the junk trade between the islands could secure sufficient silk to exchange for Japanese silver. Even though the Dutch had by that stage reduced the price of cloth and swamped the market, Saris assured them that 'Mr [Richard] Cocks and the Fleming [Brouwer] are agreed and have advanced the price again.' He told the merchants and investors gathered at Smythe's home in Philpot Lane: 'Japan will prove by the next return more profitable to you than it may be you expect' and that the court of directors should act on his advice, 'for it is true'. It was concluded that 'the place was very hopeful'.[20]

Saris's report on the prospects for trade in Japan seemed to have come at just the right time, but much of it was inaccurate and misleading. Given the cloud of suspicion that surrounded Saris since his arrival at Plymouth, he may well have simply told the company what they wanted to hear, perhaps to distract from his own illegal activities. He had no grounds to claim there had been any agreement with the Dutch, and while broadcloth had some market in Japan, it was never in great demand and would never supply the quantity of silver which the company required. The other marketable commodities listed by Saris were also, for the most part, a fiction.

The English merchants at Hirado regularly wrote to London, informing the company of the state of their sales and the markets, and complained in virtually every letter that company ships were arriving with 'invendible' goods. They told them that expectations of the trading post were unrealistic, and how the charges in Japan were much greater than elsewhere in the East Indies. Yet to no avail. The company was desperate to believe that Japan would provide the silver to fund their Eastern trade. As Richard Wickham, Cocks's deputy in Hirado, wrote with considerable frustration: 'The honourable company in England had been much abused by wrong information given them of this country, making them believe that Japan would yield present money for any commodity for our country.'[21] Ship after ship continued to be sent to the region – the *Hosiander* in 1615, followed by the *Advice* the year after, and the *Thomas* after that – all loaded with goods that Saris insisted were 'vendible' in Japan: English broadcloth and Indian fabrics, Russian hides, knives, spectacles, gallipots, guns and paintings. Besides their general unsuitability, many of the items arrived in poor condition, the guns rusty, the cloth stained with damp or spoiled by insects, sacks of pepper filled with sticks and stones and, as Cocks complained, the pictures 'wrapped together face to face &, as it seemeth, were not dry. So that in opening of them one spoil'd another.' While he'd managed to salvage some of them for sale, 'it costest much to make them clean'. Cocks reiterated his demand that the company send 'greater quantity and better commodities than yet we have had out of England or from Bantam'. His anger was clear and directed: he called on the company's directors to explain who had 'spoke so largely of this silver country', and knowing the answer, asked, exactly how many chests of silver Saris had in fact returned with.[22]

Wickham too blamed London: 'If we were learned alchemists, we could not so soon turn metals into silver as the Honourable Company, being deluded, are boldly confident that we can turn these idle commodities into money.'[23] Ultimately, the English lacked the goods that the Japanese favoured most: if the trading post in Hirado was to continue, its factors had to acquire silk. Without it the prospect of Japanese silver was little more than a mirage. Yet the factory's early attempts to involve itself in the 'junk trade' to procure silk had met with little success. Cocks resolved that the only hope now for trading success in Japan and Southeast Asia lay in China – China trade being the one 'we all sweat for'.[24]

***

China, or Cathay as it was called then, was regarded as 'the most noble and rich realm of the world'.[25] Since the late thirteenth-century voyages of the Venetian explorer Marco Polo, it had been the primary target of European merchants, idealised as an almost utopian kingdom of craftsmanship and opulence, abundant in gold, silks, spices and precious stones. Trade with China had long been the ambition of English traders: the chance to acquire silk and other luxury goods in plentiful supply to exchange for Japanese silver. It was, in the words of the governors of the Muscovy Company: 'the country that we chiefly desire to discover'.[26] Despite a lack of commercial contact between England and China, the turn of the century

Portrait of James VI/I by an unknown artist, c. 1619

Anna of Denmark, whose own dynastic links played an important part in strengthening the Stuart dynasty

Henry Frederick, Prince of Wales, on horseback

Portrait of Charles as
Prince of Wales, c. 1623

Princess Elizabeth, who
later married Frederick
V, Elector Palatine, and
drew her father into
the Thirty Years War

A portrait commemorating the Treaty of London negotiated between English and Spanish commissioners at Somerset House, 1604

The Gunpowder Plot conspirators, 1605

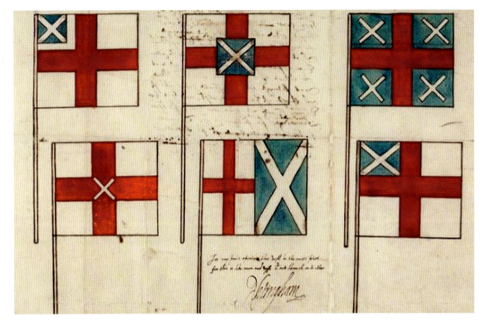

Designs for the Union Flag, which sought to equally depict the English cross of St George and the Scottish saltire, c. 1604

The gold 'Unite' coin picturing James, 'King of Great Britain'

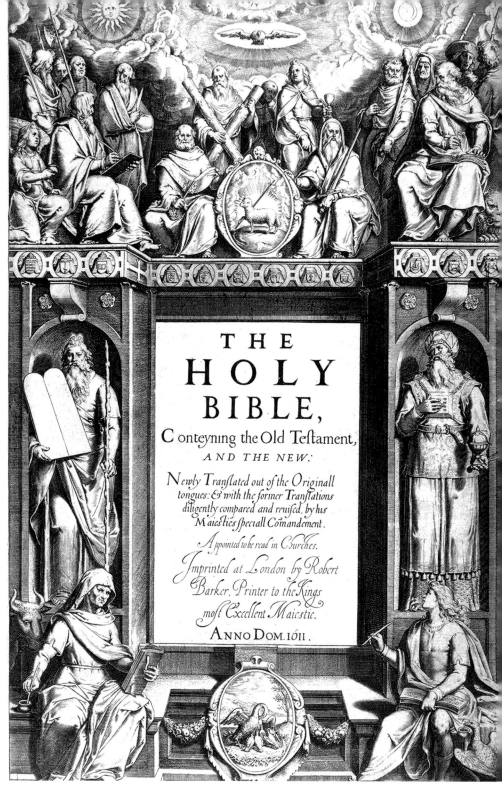

THE
HOLY
BIBLE,

Conteyning the Old Testament,

AND THE NEW.

Newly Translated out of the Originall
tongues: & with the former Translations
diligently compared and reuised, by his
Maiesties speciall Comandement.

Appointed to be read in Churches.

Imprinted at London by Robert
Barker, Printer to the Kings
most Excellent Maiestie.

ANNO DOM. 1611.

The King James Version of the Bible published in 1611 was one of the enduring achievements of
the reign

Christian IV of Denmark–Norway, brother of Queen Anna and a key ally for James I

Michael I – Tsar of Russia from 1613 to 1645 and founder of the Romanov dynasty, which ruled Russia until 1917

Attributed to Captain John Smith, one of the first English settlers at Jamestown, this detailed map of Virginia was published in 1612

The Jamestown fort was both a means to defend the settlement and to signal to the Indians the military might of the English

One of many pamphlets seeking to encourage new colonists to Virginia

An engraving of Pocahontas, 'The Lady Rebecca', during her visit to London in 1616

The bay of Hirado in 1621, where both the Dutch East India Company and the English East India Company traded. The English factory in Hirado was established in 1613 and was eventually closed in 1623

Armour sent as a gift to King James from Emperor Tokugawa Hidetada, now on display at the Tower of London

Letter from William Adams,
first Englishman in Japan,
to 'unknown friends and
countrymen', 1613

Emperor Tokugawa Ieyasu,
founder and first shogun of
the Tokugawa shogunate of
Japan, which effectively ruled
Japan from the Battle of
Sekigahara in 1600 until the
Meiji Restoration in 1868

The Mughal emperor Jahangir investing a courtier with a robe of honour watched by Sir Thomas Roe, English ambassador to the court of Jahangir at Agra

Sir Thomas Roe at the Court of Ajmir, 1614

SCHACH ABAS PERSARVM REX.

Abbas I, commonly known as Abbas the Great, was the fifth Safavīd shah of Iran from 1588 to 1629

A broadside on the wedding of Frederick V, Elector Palatine, and Princess Elizabeth of England

One of the masques held to celebrate Elizabeth and Frederick's wedding on 14 February 1613

Marriage procession of Princess Elizabeth and Elector Frederick, 1613

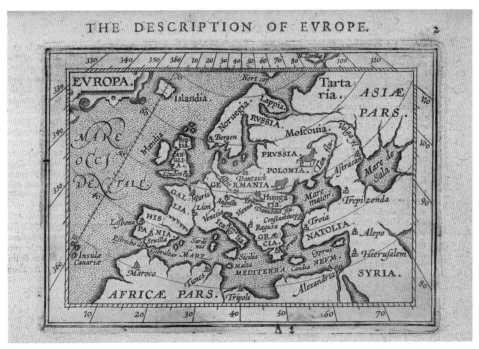

This map of Europe is from the 1603 edition of *Theatrum orbis terrarum* (*Theatre of the World*), first published in 1570 by Flemish map-maker Abraham Ortelius

Commissioned by his son Charles, the ceiling of Banqueting House in Whitehall celebrates James's wise and peaceful reign and the union of the crowns of England and Scotland

marked a period of intensified English interest in Chinese commodities brought in by the Portuguese. Decorating one's home with imported Chinese furniture or wallpaper (or domestically made imitations) was a way for Britain's newly monied merchant class to demonstrate their wealth, worldliness, success and sophistication, as the masque and the grand royal opening of Britain's Bourse had underlined.

Cocks came to believe that the chances of opening trade with China were good. Most of the silk to Japan was brought in by the Dutch East India Company (VOC) but, according to the chief English factor, they were hated by the Chinese for their attacks on Chinese shipping. Cocks also claimed the Portuguese were mistreated by the Chinese and were likely to be turned out of Macau, the Portuguese base off the southern coast of China from where they conducted their trading voyages to Nagasaki. Since 1557, Portugal had leased Macau from China in return for an annual rent.

Cocks concluded that the best way to gain access to the Chinese market was through a third party. He became convinced by a man called Li Dan, head of the Chinese community in Japan and known to the English as 'the China Captain'. On 25 November 1614, Cocks wrote from Hirado to the East India Company in London, describing: '3 or 4 Chinas, my friends, [who are labouring to] get us trade into their country and do not [doubt but it will] take effect'. The hope was that the English would secure trading access on an island near Nanjing, three or four days sailing from Hirado 'if the wind be good'. After this, Cocks continued, trade on the mainland would swiftly follow, 'for, as the Chinese themselves tell me, their Emperor is come to the knowledge how the Emperor of Japan hath received us and what large privileges he hath granted us'. He requested letters of introduction to the Chinese emperor from King James and asked the company that 'if it please God this take effect, then I hope your worships will let me have the credit in pursuing it.' Adding: 'my hope is great and, as the saying is, nothing seek, nothing find'.[27]

Hopeful that trade with China might finally be achieved, letters of introduction from James were sent via Bantam to Cocks in Japan. Whether at the instigation of the company or on the king's own initiative, efforts had been taken to prepare for every eventuality. One letter was described by Cocks 'in friendly sort', the other had 'some stricter terms'. Cocks advised the company that 'our China friends' – Li Dan and his brother 'Captain Whaw' – 'will not only translate them, but send then by such as shall see them delivered'. He added: 'Their opinion is, it is not good to send the threatening letter, for they are assured there will be nothing be done with the king [Emperor Shenzong of Ming] by force. But as we have a good name given of us of late, that we are peaceable people, so to go forward still in that sort.'[28] A little time later, Li Dan told Cocks that the letters had been well received 'by the noble men in China', and that soon a mandarin would be lodging a complaint with the shogunate over the continued Dutch presence in Japan.

When the emperor failed to respond to James's letters, Li Dan gave various excuses, while continuing to receive money and gifts from Cocks. Others were less trusting of Li Dan. Writing to the company in January 1618, George Ball, then president of the Bantam factory, sought to expose Cocks's costly naivety – 'to prove nothing but the plot of a nimble brain to serve his own turn'. Mr Cocks, he explained, 'having his imaginations levelled beyond the moon, hath the eyes of his understanding so blinded with the expectation of incredible wonders that is to be feared he will feel the loss before he will be made to see his error'.[29] Ball also believed the English should imitate the Dutch and force the Chinese to trade by capturing their merchant junks at sea. But whereas the Dutch experimented with multiple strategies, including launching an assault on Macao in order to gain a foothold on the Chinese mainland, the English pinned all their hopes on the fanciful promises that Li Dan could secure for them formal permission from the Ming court.

However, it was all lies, Cocks was being duped. Li Dan's claims to have influence at the imperial court were false; he was in no position to secure an opening for the English at Nanking, yet continued to string Cocks along in the hope of imminent Chinese trade.

***

The success of the Japanese venture came to rest on Richard Cocks's Eastern fantasy. As he had correctly acknowledged: 'I esteem our Japan trade altogether unprofitable if we procure not trade into China.'[30] But the window of opportunity for Britain to establish commercial contact with China and to expand trade in and with Japan was rapidly closing. With each passing month, the shogunate was developing a deeper hostility to the West because of the activities in the country of the Jesuits.

Having tolerated the Jesuits for more than half a century since the arrival of the Jesuit missionary Sir Francis Xavier, the 'Apostle of Japan' in 1549, the shogunate determined to do so no longer. In a letter of 10 December 1614 addressed to Cecil, who he was unaware had died two years before, Cocks described how the Japanese emperor 'had banished out of his dominions all Jesuits, papists, friars and nuns [and] pulled and burned down all their churches and monasteries'. Cocks added: 'They murmured and gave out many large reports that the arrival of our English nation in these parts is the chief reason of this alteration, although it is well known their own deserts are the cause thereof.'[31]

Cocks took every opportunity to distance the English from the Jesuits, explaining that 'the Roman Catholics' (in Spain and Portugal) were bent on conquest and describing the Jesuits as murderers of kings. In a meeting with the assistant to the shogun's chief secretary, Doi Toshikatsu, Cocks said that they need not doubt us, 'for that they the padres, were enemies to us, & to the state of England, & would destroy us all if they could'. He believed that the shogun was right to be wary of the Jesuits, 'lest they did not go about to serve him as they had done the Kings of England ... to kill & poison them or to blow them up with gunpowder & stirring up the subjects to rebel against the natural prince'.[32] Nevertheless, an official judgement on the subversiveness of Christianity drew no distinctions, stating that Christians generally were trying to take over Japan, subvert the native Japanese and the 'True Law' of Buddhism. Thereafter the shogun banned Christianity and began to persecute those people who had converted and refused to renounce the faith.[33]

With the death of Tokugawa Ieyasu, and his son Tokugawa Hidetada's full assumption of power, English difficulties escalated. When Cocks was called to the imperial court at Edo expecting company trading privileges to be renewed, he assumed it would be a formality. But Hidetada proceeded to restrict foreign trade into Hirado, forcing English merchants from Edo, Kyoto and Osaka. It was a serious blow. 'The Emperor might as well banish us right out of Japan as bind us to such an order,' Cocks noted in his diary, 'for that we could make no sales at that place.'[34] His frantic efforts to have the privileges restored proved futile. To make matters worse, an eruption of hostilities with the Dutch led to a period when the company's factory at Hirado was under siege, and four years passed with no English ships arriving.

It signalled the beginning of the end for English trade in Japan. By December 1621, it was being suggested within the company that the factory should close. Cocks initially resisted, believing that he was on the verge of a breakthrough in his dealings with the Chinese, but enough was enough. Cocks was accused of having squandered vast sums on his Chinese contacts 'who hath too long deluded you with your own simplicity'.[35] In December 1623, after just ten years of trading, a company ship was sent to collect Captain Cocks and his merchants. Dismayed by his fall from favour, Cocks died on the voyage home being wasted away of a consumption [tuberculosis].

The English had been naive at best, blinded by their desperation to find new markets for English broadcloth and to get silk and silver in return. Most could not see the reality that their cloth was not in demand in Japan, that the prospect of accessing the Chinese market was but a fantasy, and that Japanese trade would wither without access to China.

The East India Company now moved into a period of retrenchment, the closure of the factory in Hirado being followed by closures at Ayutthaya and Patani. The focus now fell on India as the great hope for trade.

19

A Passage to India

'Neither will this overgrown Elephant descend to Article or bind himself reciprocally to any Prince upon terms of Quality, but only by way of favour admire our stay so long as it either likes him or those that govern him.'

Sir Thomas Roe to the English Ambassador at Constantinople, 21 August 1617[1]

In February 1615, four English East Indiamen – the *Lion*, the *Expedition*, the *Peppercorn* and the *Dragon*, the flagship under the command of Captain William Keeling, left Tilbury in Essex for Surat – the bustling Mughal port in Gujarat on the western coast of India. The *Lion* was commanded by Christopher Newport who had proved himself a capable and loyal captain for his role carrying settlers and supplies from London to Virginia. In the service of the East India Company since 1612, Captain Newport was now charged with carrying the first ever official English ambassador to Mughal India, Sir Thomas Roe.

From a prominent City family of Kentish origin, Roe was a trusted courtier and diplomat. He had become close to the young Prince Henry and Princess Elizabeth after James's accession, and had been rewarded for his service with a knighthood in 1604, aged twenty-three. Roe had been part of the earl of Nottingham's delegation sent to Spain to ratify the Treaty of London in 1605, was a member of the King's Council of Virginia and had accompanied Elizabeth to Heidelberg after her marriage in 1613. He was described by the East India Company as a man of 'pregnant understanding, well spoken, learned, industrious, of a comely personage, and one of whom there are great hopes that he may work much good for the company'.[2] At the company's request, in 1615 Roe was created 'lord ambassador' by James for his 'Fidelity and Discretion'.[3]

As with Sir John Merrick in Russia, Roe had two masters: king and company. The 'Articles of Agreement' issued from the offices of the East India Company stipulated the ambitious commercial purpose of his mission: 'the better establishing and settling an absolute trade in any parts within the Dominions of the great Mogore'. Roe was to secure from the Mughal emperor Jahangir a permanent trade treaty with India. And, as the embassy was to be paid for by the company, all was to be achieved with much 'frugality'.[4] Meanwhile the ambassador's 'instructions', issued in the king's name from Whitehall, emphasised above all the need that Roe behave through his words and actions in a manner befitting the 'King of Great Britain'. The monarchs of Asia 'are most apt to seek to Maintain Correspondence with the greatest and Mightest Princes', the instructions explained, but 'their Countries being so far remote', they had to 'make their particular judgements much by fame and report'. Roe would therefore need to convince the Indian emperor that the King of Great Britain wielded such 'power and strength at sea, which gives us not only reputation and authority among the Greatest Princes of Christendom but Maketh us even a Terror to all Nations'. Moreover, he was to demonstrate that the king was a benevolent and most loved monarch, who was 'not only absolutely obeyed but universally beloved and admired of all our People'.

Besides this, the purpose of Sir Thomas's embassy remained vague, being given: 'full Power and Authority to treat ... and conclude concerning the Maintenance and Continuance of the Amity and Course of Merchandise between Us, and ... the said Great Mogul'.[5] As James sought to promote Stuart Britain in the world, the projection of his power and image abroad was the primary task of his first ambassador to India.

George Abbot, Privy Councillor and Archbishop of Canterbury, would later reflect on the significance of Roe's embassy: 'There is no place so remote, but that the consideration is mediately or immediately of consequence to our affaires here.' Not only was trade at stake, continued the archbishop, but it was also essential for the sovereigns of Europe to be aware that their wealth and reputation depended upon events distant from their courts.[6] Roe was to convince Emperor Jahangir of the importance of Britain as a European power worthy of both a formal and permanent trading agreement.

***

In the early seventeenth century, the Mughal empire was among the richest and most powerful empires in the world, covering northern and central India, modern-day Afghanistan and much of western Pakistan. The Mughals were a Muslim dynasty that traced its lineage back to Timur and Genghis Khan. They would reign in India from the sixteenth to the nineteenth century. The emperor ruled over an estimated 100 million subjects, with cities dwarfing those of Europe in terms of size, splendour, and wealth. Mirza Nur-ud-Din Beg Muhammad Salim, known by his imperial name Jahangir, acceded the throne in 1605 and was the fourth emperor of the Mughal dynasty. He was married to the indomitable and influential queen Mihr-un-Nissa or Nur Jahan.

The creation of direct sea links between Europe and India in the early sixteenth century saw representatives from Europe arrive at the Mughal court in Agra, on the banks of the Yumana River, seeking permission to trade. The Portuguese had come to India more than a century before, but the Dutch, who in 1616 had only been in the region for a decade, had already gained a significant foothold.

The East India Company had been in Mughal India since 1608, when a ship commanded by merchant and sea captain William Hawkins arrived at Surat in western India. Claiming fraudulently to be 'the king of England's ambassador', the following year Hawkins travelled to the imperial court at Agra where he petitioned Emperor Jahangir for a factory. However, his efforts were thwarted by the dominant presence of the Portuguese, who insisted that England was 'an island of no import', and that King James was merely a 'king of fishermen' and subject to Portugal.[7] As company merchants tried to ingratiate themselves with the Mughals, the Portuguese, who were already well established at the Mughal court, sought to convince the emperor that extending privileges to the London company – to mere merchants – would detract from his imperial dignity.[8]

It took the tenth voyage of the East India Company in 1612, led by Captain Thomas Best aboard the *Red Dragon*, to finally get the Mughal's attention. On his arrival at Surat on 5 September, Best sent the usual request to Agra seeking permission to trade and settle a factory, and then waited for the inevitable response. But then, on 29 November, a skirmish broke out between the English ships – the *Red Dragon* and the *Hosiander* – and four Portuguese galleons off the coast of Suvali (Swally), a village near Surat. Against the odds, Best managed to run the Portuguese ships aground and claim a spectacular victory. The Battle of Swally (as it became known) proved to be a turning point in relations between the English and Jahangir. The English had signalled that they might be more than mere 'fishermen' and could challenge Portuguese domination of Indian trade. Within days of Best's triumph, the company was issued a *farman* permitting a trading post at Surat. It fell short however, of being the specific permanent agreement that London sought.

At Jahangir's court the Portuguese stepped up their attempts to turn the emperor's mind against the English. East India Company merchant William Biddulph wrote to Sir Thomas Smythe advising the company of the need to secure its position, not only by increasing the armed strength of its fleets, but also by diplomatic intervention. He urged the company to send 'some proper man of account to reside in Agra with the King' who could challenge the influence of the Portuguese and the 'prating Jesuit Fathers' who were persuading the emperor that 'we are a base people and dwell in a little island, and of no force'.[9]

***

In late September 1615, after a seven-month voyage, the *Lion* dropped anchor off the coast of Surat. Roe did not go ashore immediately. He was determined to be received with sufficient dignity and splendour. The arrival of the king of Great Britain's first ambassador to India needed careful preparation. Having sent word of his arrival, all the English ships in the harbour were prepared with their ensigns aloft and flags flying from their mastheads, whilst a hundred men were sent ashore to form a guard of honour. Finally, on 26 September, amid a 48-gun salute from the fleet, the ambassador was rowed to shore.[10] It was the beginning of two years of image-making, as Roe sought to amplify the significance of James and Britain to the Mughal empire.

The initial reception was not quite what Roe had envisioned. On arrival, customs officials searched his belongings and that of his entourage, without his permission, to which Roe took great offence. 'I replied,' he wrote in his journal, 'That I was the Ambassador of a Mightie and free Prince: that I would never dishonour my Master so much, whose Person I bear, as to subject myself to so much slavery.'[11] At the 'name of an ambassador they laughed one upon another; it being become ridiculous, so many having assumed the title, and not performed the offices'. He continued: 'I mention these only to let the company understand how meanly an ambassador was esteemed at my landing.'[12] The assumption was that Roe was simply another merchant seeking to secure trading rights. Such previous merchant attempts, Roe believed, had undermined the honour of the ambassadorial office.

Roe's first experiences in India were little better. It quickly became clear that the diplomatic gifts the king and company had sent for Roe to present to the emperor – a set of virginals and a musician to play them, and an English coach and driver – lacked the largesse that was expected. Viewing the carriage as it was brought to shore, Surat's governor Zulfiqar Khan 'scorned it and said it was little and poor: that we bought ill velvet of the Chinese'.[13]

'The presents you have [sent] ... are extremely despised by those [who] have seen them,' an angered Roe wrote to Smythe at Philpot Lane. 'The lining of the coach and cover of the virginals scorned, being velvet of these parts and faded to a base tawny,' he went on. The company had failed to understand the lavish gifts that securing Mughal favour demanded. 'Here are nothing esteemed but of the best sorts: good cloth and fine, and rich pictures' and 'they laugh at us for such as we bring.' If favour 'depend on presents (as I am informed), I have small encouragement, and shall be ashamed to present in the king's name (being really his ambassador) things so mean, yea, worse than former messengers have had: the Mughal doubtless making judgement of what His Majestie is by what he sends.'[14]

In January 1616, after an arduous two-month journey from Surat to the Mughal court in Ajmer, Roe enjoyed his first audience with the forty-seven-year-old emperor. Jahangir welcomed Roe as the messenger of his royal 'brother' and graciously accepted both James's letter of introduction and the company's presents. After they left, however, Roe wrote again to London, explaining further humiliation: 'he [Jahangir] asked the Jesuit whether the King of England were a great King, that sent presents of so small value, and that he looked for some jewels'.[15] The emperor politely rode in the English carriage and flourished a scarf and sword the English had also given him.

When Roe next saw the coach, towards the end of the year, as the emperor prepared to go on a progress, both the English coachman and the coach had been redressed in sumptuous fabrics with Mughal grandeur. Brass nails had been replaced by silver nails and 'crimson China velvet', as Roe's chaplain described, by 'very rich stuff, the ground silver, wrought all over in spaces with variety of flowers of silk'.[16] Later, Jahangir would speak of his surprise that Roe as an ambassador was 'so slightly set' compared to the merchants sent before him who 'bought more curious toys that contented all.' What Roe had brought him 'was little, mean, and inferior to the other'.[17] Jahangir was subsequently presented with a collection of large oil paintings, which were more warmly received. Prominent among these were portraits of King James, Queen Anna and Princess Elizabeth, which, it was noted with relief, were displayed behind the Mughal emperor's throne at *nau ruz* (new year) ceremonies in March for two years in a row.[18]

Nonetheless Roe believed that his own audience with the emperor had gone well. He claimed to have been 'dismissed with more favour and outward grace (if by the Christians I were not flattered) then ever was showed to any Ambassador, either of the Turk or Persian, or other whatsoever'.[19] Indeed, in the long-awaited response to King James's letter, Jahangir wrote that Roe 'well deserved to be your trusted servant'.[20]

In mid-March 1616, after two months at court, Roe felt able to begin his campaign to establish a permanent trading alliance between Britain and Mughal India. He made clear that he was not seeking anything temporary or local, as had been previously secured by the company's merchants, but rather an agreement 'clear in all points, and a more formal and authentic confirmation'. A week later, Roe returned with a document translated into Persian outlining the privileges he sought, including free access to all ports belonging to the emperor; permission for English merchants to rent factories; suitable housing at fair prices; and that goods would move freely without payment of any duty beyond the normal customs. In return, the English would agree not to attack the ships of other nations 'except the enemies of the said English' or any other 'that shall seek to injure them'; their factors, while living ashore, 'should behave themselves peaceably and civilly' and, do their best to obtain 'rarities' for the Mughal, and provide him with 'any goods or furniture of war, which the said King shall reasonably desire at fair prices' and assist him against 'any Enemy to the Common Peace'.[21]

On 3 April, Roe received word that his demands were considered unreasonable and could not be signed.[22] Although the emperor had been courteous and considerate to Roe, the Indians held it to be derogatory for the emperor to sign a treaty with the representative of such an obscure and distant land.

Despite Britain's inferior wealth and status, Roe remained committed to pushing his claim that the composite kingdom he represented was at least as powerful – if not more so – than the Mughal empire. Roe wrote to James, insisting that he would restore the 'King's Honour' by improving the general opinion of and respect given to the English, or 'lay my life and fortune both in the ground' in trying.[23] He would 'at last by our force teach them to know your Majesty is Lord of all the Seas and can Compel that by your power, which you have sought with Courtesy, which this King cannot yet see for swelling'.[24]

At the same time, in letters to the king and to the Archbishop of Canterbury, Sir Thomas was happy to denigrate the Mughal court for various perceived moral failings, claiming to Abbot that 'their Pride endures no terms of equality', and that the Mughals are characterised by 'dull ignorance'. He bemoaned 'the pride and falsehood of these people, that attended only advantage and were governed by private interest and appetite' and refused to accept Christianity.[25] To James, Roe described how: 'The government [is] so uncertain, without written law, without Policy, the Customs mingled with barbarism, religions infinite, the buildings of mud (except the King's houses and some few others): that even this greatness and wealth that I admired in England (reserving due reverence to the Persons of Kings) is here, where I see it, almost contemptible.'[26] Nevertheless, as Roe noted in the same letter, 'the trade here will doubtless in time be very profitable for your Majesty's kingdoms, and may vend [sell] much cloth; but yet our condition and usage is so bad (notwithstanding fair words) that will require much patience to suffer, much industry to set upright'.[27] It would depend on Roe's ability to persuade the emperor that Britain was a country worth engaging with: a challenge greater than securing cloth sales.

***

While Roe laboured at court to improve England's trading position, trade itself proved sluggish. The chief of trade in India, Thomas Aldworth, had reported in 1614 that cloth was only selling 'in regard of the novelty to cover some of their elephants and to make some saddles for their horses; but for garments they use none in these parts'.[28] Muqarrab Khan, one of the emperor's courtiers, described English goods as being: 'Too much cloth and ill swords and almost nothing else, that every body was weary of it.' Muqarrab advised – as many others had – that the English 'bring all the rarities' from China and Japan, 'which were more acceptable here than gold'.[29]

Yet with limited demand for English broadcloth in India, as in Japan and across Southeast Asia, English merchants were struggling to purchase such 'rarities'. Roe made suggestions, unwelcome to the English factors, that they change how they traded in India – expressing views shared by many in England who criticised the East India Company. In a letter sent from Surat on 26 April 1616, he gave some 'general advises and observations'. Whilst acknowledging that trade depended on our 'good reception and privileges to be obtained' and was not yet 'permanent nor assured', failure to have commodities that sell was more important and 'will sooner and faster weaken us here'. As for English cloth, 'no man regards it' and unless some new goods can be discovered to sell, then trade there 'must fall to ground by the weakness of its own legs'.[30] Roe also argued against the export of silver from England that the merchants sought. The company 'apprehend[ed] it otherwise' and believed that goods from Asia purchased with bullion and then sold by English merchants in other European countries provided double customs revenue for the Crown, which could then be reinvested into the English economy, bringing 'Continual Profit both to the State and the Commonwealth'. The company, Roe said, should not sacrifice potential profits for the benefit of their European competitors, not least the Dutch and Portuguese.[31]

Roe, meanwhile, looked for any opportunity to stoke Mughal fears of Portuguese imperialism. In a letter to Prince Khurram, Jahangir's increasingly influential heir and the Crown prince of Surat, he described how 'contrary to all honour and justice, they [the Portuguese] call their King in Europe King of India'.[32] Roe was continually at pains to point out that the ambitions and activities of the English and Portuguese were entirely different. 'We,' he stressed, 'only desire open trade for all Nations, to the enriching of your highness kingdoms and the advancing of your customs, whereas they have ever sought to keep in subjection your subjects, suffering none to traffic but themselves and exacting duties for licence to pass upon your seas.'[33]

When Prince Khurram asked Roe whether the Dutch were friends of the English, he replied, emphasising the continued support the English gave the United Provinces against Spain, that they 'were a nation depending on the King of England, but not welcome in all places; their business I knew not'.[34] Roe was very aware of the strong commercial threat represented by the 'Hollanders' in India, telling the directors in London: 'they wrong you in all parts and grow to insufferable insolences'. Yet confrontation between the Dutch and English would only be to the advantage of the Portuguese. 'If we fall foul here, the common enemy will laugh and repeat the fruit of our contention,' he concluded.[35]

***

After four years at the Mughal court, Roe had had enough. He wrote to Sir Thomas Smythe that he was 'infinitely weary of this unprofitable employment, the success whereof is not that I aimed at for you'.[36] In his yearly report to the company in London in February 1618, Roe told them he had abandoned all hopes of securing a formal treaty with Jahangir: 'You can never expect to trade here upon capitulations that shall be permanent', he said, although he believed he could, before his departure, obtain all that was practically necessary for day-to-day trade.[37]

Taking formal leave of the emperor, Roe was presented with a letter for King James detailing the instructions he had given to all his 'subjects and vassals', that English merchants were to be given freedom and residence 'to their own content and safety.' They were to be allowed to trade freely throughout his dominions and their ships were to be free to enter his ports whenever they wished to do so.[38] These represented clear improvements in trading conditions but fell short of London's requirements.

Prince Khurram of Surat, who had once been so antagonistic towards the English, granted similar concessions on the eve of Roe's departure. Merchants would be allowed to trade freely, 'with honour and courtesy', and English goods would pass without hindrance. Englishmen in Surat were to be allowed to live under their own religion and their own laws, and to rent a 'good, strong and sufficient' house in the town.[39] A small but not insignificant success was that the English were given formal permission for a company trading post at Surat: a toehold in India at last.

The factors in Surat complained, however, that Roe had not procured 'the gift of a house nor ground' – in other words, garrisons – 'nor licence to build us a habitation' and no permanent settlement of trade.[40] Yet Roe rejected the idea that the company should seek onshore garrisons in India. 'Experience teaches me we are refused it at our advantage,' he told London. 'It is the beggaring of the Portugal [the Portuguese], notwithstanding his many rich residences and territories that he keeps soldiers ... He never profited by the Indies, since he defended them ... It hath been also the error of the Dutch who seek plantation here by the sword.' The East India Company, he stressed, should avoid unnecessary expense and follow a peaceful course: 'Let this be received as a rule that if you will Profit, seek it at Sea, and in quiet trade,' as he continued, 'it is an error to affect Garrisons and Land wars in India ... at sea you may take and leave' without 'your Designs' being 'published.'[41] Roe argued that the company should be driven by profit, not 'plantation'.

Roe had been tasked with two very ambitious commissions: to impress upon Emperor Jahangir the greatness of the king of Great Britain, a monarch whose gifts were generally laughed at in court; and to secure on behalf of the East India Company, whose goods were not in demand, a permanent trade treaty with Mughal India. In both Roe might be said to have failed. However, he had earned the gradual, grudging respect of the emperor, had challenged the dominance of Portuguese interests at court, and eventually, as he prepared to depart, secured improved trading rights from the emperor and Prince Khurram.

In February 1619, the company ship *Anne Royal* took Sir Thomas back to England. In its hold was a cargo full of indigo and Indian cotton textiles together with presents from the emperor to King James, including: 'a rich tent, rare carpets, certain umbrellas and other trinkets, and several antelopes'. One outcome of the long homeward voyage was the production of the first British map of the Mughal empire with all its cities and rivers. A map of the empire detailing its main cities and rivers had been requested by the East India Company in 1614, a year before Roe's departure, and it seems Roe used his visit to collect geographical information.[42] The map was then completed by William Baffin, Arctic explorer and surveyor, who was the master's mate on the *Anne Royal*. Known as 'Sir Thomas Roe's map', and published in London later that year, it provided the basis for all European maps of India for the next century.[43]

James did not appoint another ambassador to replace Roe. Perhaps he was loath to promote British interests further and risk contining to antagonise Philip III, King of Spain and Portugal, with whom James sought to maintain peace and secure a marriage alliance for Prince Charles. Perhaps the king believed Roe had achieved all that he had asked of him, that he might be seen as a 'great and mighty prince' with whom the emperor would 'seek to maintain correspondence'.

And if imitation might be seen as flattery, then so too Roe might be said to have succeeded. For if Roe's claims are to be believed, 'they [the Indians] imitate everything we bring, and embroider now as well as we', and even looked to employ British workers.[44] Jahangir asked Roe to provide 'a pattern of a Quiver and case for my Bow, a Coat to wear, a Cushion ... and a pair of Boots, which you shall cause to be embroidered in England ... for I know in your Country they can work better than any I have seen'.[45]

Britain's first official encounter with India had been for trade, not territory. The first ambassador and the English merchants were from a country still in its infancy in overseas trading. They had ventured to trade with one of the richest empires in the world from a position of weakness and inferiority. They came cap in hand, seeking a treaty which acknowledged them as worthy trading partners. Roe's embassy on behalf of king and company was a polite introduction to a Britain that, centuries later, would prove anything but – conquering and colonising with devastating brutality.

20

Pocahontas and a New Britain

'She renounced publicly her country Idolatry, openly confessed her
Christian faith ... was baptised, and is since married to an English
Gentleman of good understanding.'

Sir Thomas Dale, deputy governor, Virginia Colony, 18 June 1614[1]

Unlike the East India Company, which in these years was
an exclusively commercial venture 'for the Increase of our
Navigation, and Advancement of Trade', the Virginia Company had
an additional, religious mission.[2] Whilst seeking profit and a return
for company investors, its first charter, signed by James, explic-
itly stated that its purpose, 'to make habitation, plantation, and to
deduce a colony of sundry of our people', was intended to bring 'the
infidels and savages, living in those parts, to human civility, and to a
settled and quiet government'.[3] Yet while East India Company merchants in India adopted a largely 'peaceful course', as Roe described
it, from 1609 and the outbreak of the first 'Anglo-Powhatan war',
Virginia Company settlers increasingly justified the use of violence
to achieve their ends, burning settlements, and killing and capturing
indigenous peoples.

In the spring of 1613, Captain Samuel Argall had taken captive
the young daughter of powerful tribal chieftain Wahunsonacock
and held her hostage in return for prisoners and arms captured
by the Powhatan confederacy tribes, and as leverage to negotiate

a favourable peace. Matoaka ('Pocahontas') was made to live with English settlers, first at Jamestown and then along the James River at the new settlement of Henrico, where she resided with Reverend Alexander Whitaker, an Anglican theologian who taught her Bible studies in the hope of converting her to Christianity.[4] It was during this time that Pocahontas met widower John Rolfe, a survivor of the *Sea Venture* shipwreck.

Since arriving in the colony Rolfe had established a successful plantation further upriver at Varina Farms, where he cultivated tobacco seeds acquired from Trinidad. In March 1614, he exported his first four barrels of tobacco leaf to England. This strain was to prove extremely popular: sweeter and more fragrant than the tobacco that was native to the Chesapeake Bay region, it was more akin to the tobacco from the Spanish settlements that was so popular with European smokers. This quickly became Virginia's first cash crop.

In early 1614, Rolfe wrote to Jamestown Deputy Governor Sir Thomas Dale requesting permission to marry the young Powhatan 'princess'. Rolfe was at pains to reassure the governor that he was 'in no way led ... by unbridled desire or carnal affection' and marvelled that he should 'be in love with one whose education hath been rude, her manners barbarous, her generation accursed, and so discrepant in all nature from myself'. However, in fulfilment of the Virginia Council's declaration that the colony's 'main ends' were 'first to preach and baptise into Christian religion, and by propagation of the Gospel, to recover out of the arms of the Devil, a number of poor and miserable souls', Rolfe proposed to marry 'an unbelieving creature, namely Pocahontas'. It would be, the Englishman claimed, 'for the good of this plantation, for the honour of our country, for the glory of God, [and] for my own salvation'.[5] Following her conversion to Christianity, Pocahontas was given the Old Testament name Rebecca.

Dale granted permission for the marriage as did Wahunsonacock, Pocahontas' father. It is believed he saw the union of his daughter with Rolfe as a means of securing peace with the British after five years of conflict, and he sent one of his brothers to represent him at the wedding in Jamestown on 5 April 1614.

The marriage signalled the beginning of what would prove to be an eight-year peace. As settler Ralph Hamor described in his *A True Discourse of the Present State of Virginia*: 'Ever since [the marriage] we had friendly commerce and trade, not only with Powhatan himself, but also with his subjects round about us; so as now I see no reason why the colony should not thrive apace.'[6] When the couple had a son, Thomas, in January 1615, it was welcomed as strengthening the peace and increasing prospects of future cooperation between the settlers and the Powhatan.

For many, the conversion of the 'Indian princess' was in itself proof of the success of educational evangelism, as promoted in the booklet *Nova Britannia* (*'New Britain'*). From London, it was seen as evidence that James's vision for a 'New Britain' was working. In time, it was hoped, all the 'infidels and savages' might be brought into the Church of England, as James's charter to the Virginia Company demanded.[7]

***

From Newmarket on 26 February 1615, James wrote to the archbishops of Canterbury and York, acknowledging 'there is good progress made' in the Virginia colony as to 'the propagation of the gospel amongst infidels', and called on them to authorise collections for 'the erecting of some churches and schools for the education of the children of those Barbarians in Virginia'. First, the king instructed, a school was to be built, 'for training Indian children in the true knowledge of God and in some useful employment' and for the education of the sons of the white planters, who 'through want thereof have been hitherto constrained to their great costs to send their children from thence to be taught'.[8] Collections were to be made in every parish, and the sums collected were to be forwarded to the bishops and sent on every six months to the archbishops, who would pass them to the Virginia Company.

James was taking an increasingly active role in the colony. As Thomas Edwards, an official of the Bishop of London, wrote to the archdeacon of St Albans: 'You may see by these things sent unto you from my Lord of London what care his Majestie hath of the plantation in Virginia ... It is a thing very religious in itself and will be acceptable to God and honourable to the King and our Country.'[9]

In March 1616, Virginia Company treasurer Sir Thomas Smythe presented a receipt to the archbishop of Canterbury for £300 (around £65,000 today), 'in part of Monies collected within the diocese of London ... for the erecting of a college in Virginia for the education of the children of those Savages to the true knowledge of God and Christianity'.[10] Eight days later, a payment was approved for Rolfe and his wife of £100, 'out of the particular Cash of the Collections aforesaid'. These funds were for 'works to be performed for the planting & propagating of Christian religion in those heathen parts'.[11]

To celebrate the success of Pocahontas's conversion, to raise further funds for the college, and to attract more settlers for their North American plantation, the Virginia Company resolved to bring the 'civilised savage', and her husband and child to England.

***

In the spring of 1616, a delegation led by Sir Thomas Dale comprising the Rolfes, Pocahontas's uncle Uttamatomakkin (known as Tomocomo for short) and around a dozen other Powhatans, set sail on the company ship the *Treasurer* for England.

In London, the former governor of Jamestown John Smith, wrote to Queen Anna, briefing her ahead of the visit. Smith had been among the first settlers in Jamestown and spent the early months in the colony exploring Chesapeake Bay. He was taken prisoner and brought before Wahunsonacock, the chief of the Powhatan tribe. As Smith's letter relayed, Pocahontas, the chieftain's daughter had saved him from the wrath of her father and had played a critical role in fostering peace between the settlers and the 'savages'. Smith stressed the importance of Pocahontas's conversion. She was 'the first Christian ever of that nation', he wrote, 'the first Virginian who ever spoke English or had a child in marriage to an Englishman'. Reaffirming King James's vision of imperium, Smith added: 'Seeing this Kingdom [Britain] may rightly have a Kingdom [America] by her means.' He worried, however, that if Pocahontas were to be treated badly, her 'present love to us and Christianity might turn to … scorn and fury' and Britain might lose the chance to 'rightly have a Kingdom by her means'.[12]

The delegation arrived at Plymouth on 3 June and travelled by coach to London, where they stayed at the Bell Savage Inn (Savage was a reference to a former proprietor, William Savage), just off Ludgate Hill. Immediately 'Lady Rebecca', as she was known throughout the visit, was thrust into public life, attending receptions and masques hosted by the king and queen, as well as by the bishop of London at Lambeth Palace. According to Samuel Purchas, rector of St Martin's, who attended the bishop's reception, Pocahontas was received 'with festival state and pomp beyond what I have seen in his great hospitality to other ladies'. It was observed that she 'did not only accustom her self to civility, but still carried herself as the Daughter of a King, and was accordingly respected, not only by the Company … but of diverse particular persons of Honor, in their hopeful zeal by her to advance Christianity.'[13]

On Twelfth Night, 6 January 1617, Pocahontas and Tomocomo were brought before King James at the Banqueting House in the Palace of Whitehall for a performance of *The Vision of Delight*, an event hosted by Queen Anna.[14] Written by Ben Jonson and produced by Inigo Jones, the masque portrayed 'civilisation' emanating from London; the 'Empire's Seat' was the hub of political, religious and commercial power, subsuming the whole of the natural world. It was an allegorical depiction of the process of colonisation, which cast Pocahontas and her uncle both as spectators and participants – as the 'civilised convert' and the 'barbarous heathen'.[15] It was but one assertion of Britain's assumed racial superiority that defined Pocahontas's entire visit.

Wahunsonacock had only given permission that his daughter travel to London if she was accompanied by Tomocomo. For his part, Tomocomo made it clear he did not trust the English, causing Sir Thomas Dale and his company colleagues, great social embarrassment. He refused to engage with anyone who he suspected wished to convert him, leading the Anglican cleric Purchas, to describe him as a man who is 'a blasphemer of what he knew not' who preferred 'his God to ours.'[16]

After Jonson's masque, Pocahontas sat for a portrait engraving by the young Dutchman Simon van de Passe.[17] Likely commissioned by the Virginia Company, the engraving was deliberately intended as an image of successful assimilation and was produced in multiple copies to be circulated as a souvenir of her visit. The Latin and English inscriptions around the edge of the engraving identify her as: '*MATOAKA ALS REBECCA FILIA POTENTISS: PRINC: POWHATANI IMP: VIRGINIA*' – 'Matoaka, alias Rebecca, daughter of the most powerful prince of the Powhatan Empire of Virginia'. On 22 February, the ever-acerbic John Chamberlain sent a copy of the engraving to his friend and regular correspondent Sir Dudley Carleton with the comment: 'Here is a fine picture of no fair Lady and yet with her tricking up and high style and titles you might think her and her worshipful husband to be somebody, if you did not know that the Virginia Company out of their poverty [only] allow her four pound a week for her maintenance.'[18]

John Rolfe wrote a promotional tract for the Virginia Company's publicity campaign during their ten-month stay in London. It sought to present the colony as thriving and attractive both to investors and potential planters. *A True Relation of the State of Virginia* told 'how happily and plenteously the good blessings of God have fallen upon the people and colony'. Spacious, temperate and rich in resources, 'scarce any or no country known to man' is more 'abundantly furnished'. After years when many died of starvation or disease, the piece continued, it now 'tis more rare to hear of a man's death than in England amongst so many people as are there resident'. Rolfe stressed that the colonised lands were safe, prosperous and ripe for development. There 'is good and sufficient men as well of birth and quality to command soldiers to march, discover, and defend the country from invasions', as well as all manner of farmers, labourers and craftsman to ensure the colony was well provided for.[19]

***

In early 1617, as the delegation prepared for the return voyage to Virginia, Pocahontas was taken seriously ill near Gravesend. Her subsequent death, aged twenty-one, was most likely due to tuberculosis or pneumonia. She was buried on 21 March in the nearby cemetery of St George's Church.

Claiming Pocahontas in the name of 'Nova Britannia', Samuel Purchas declared that she had 'given great demonstration of her Christian sincerity as the fruits of Virginia conversion, leaving here a godly memory'.[20] Of his wife's death, Rolfe wrote to Virginia Company-man Sir Edwin Sandys:

> Although great is my loss, and much my sorrow to be deprived of so great a comfort, and hopes I had to effect my zealous intentions and desires as well in others … [I will] … trust that He, who hath preserved my child … will give me strength and courage to undertake any religious and charitable employment, yo'self and the Honourable Company shall command me, and which in duty I am bound to do.[21]

Rolfe left his son Thomas in the care of his English uncle and returned to Virginia. Twenty years later, Thomas migrated to Virginia where he spent the remainder of his life. He prospered by growing the variety of tobacco that his father had introduced, on lands that had originally belonged to his mother's people.[22]

On his return to Virginia, Tomocomo immediately sought to convince Opechancanough, who had become chief on Wahunsonacock's death in 1618, of the duplicity of the English, citing incidents he had seen and heard in London. Captain Samuel Argall reported that Tomocomo 'rails against England' and its people.[23] Concerned about how the Virginia Company would receive this news and the damage it would do to the project, Argall tried to discredit Tomocomo, writing that by his actions, he 'is disgraced'.[24] With time, Opechancanough would come to see that Tomocomo was right and the English could not be trusted.

***

On 29 November 1618, King James met with the new governor of Virginia, Sir George Yeardley, at the royal residence at Newmarket over dinner. Also present were Prince Charles and senior courtiers, including twenty-six-year-old George Villiers who, after coming to court only four years before, had rapidly risen in the king's affections, becoming marquess of Buckingham and a member of the Privy Council. Yeardley had been formally appointed governor just ten days before and knighted at Newmarket on the 24th in recognition of his role in restoring order in the colony in the period after the 'starving time' in the winter of 1609–1610 when many settlers died of starvation and disease.

During dinner, James and Yeardley spoke together for over an hour, reflecting on Pocahontas's visit and the prospects for further Christian conversions within the colony. James enquired as to 'what inclination the savages had to Christian religion, and how many of them had been converted or christened', and pressed upon Yeardley the need to induce them to Christianity by 'fair means and good example of life', and not to 'tyrannise them like the Spaniards'. The king expressed his concern with the 'quality of our ministers in Virginia', and 'wished that both now & hereafter they would ever conform themselves to the church of England, & would in no sort (albeit so far from home) become authors of Novelty or singularity'.[25] For James, conformity to the Church of England, both at home and in the plantations, was of singular importance for political stability, for his vision of imperium, and for the establishment of 'civility'. He insisted that in Virginia, '[our] churches should not be built like Theatres or Cockpits, but in a decent form, & in imitation of the churches in England'.[26]

James also addressed his other major concern: tobacco. The king's views on the 'filthy novelty' of smoking were well known. Early in his reign in England he had made clear his views in the *Counterblaste to Tobacco*, in which he also expressed his antipathy towards 'the Indians' who he claimed had introduced 'the corrupted baseness' of smoking into the realm during the reign of Queen Elizabeth. 'What honour or policy,' James had then asked, 'can move us to imitate the barbarous and beastly manners of the wild, godless, and slavish Indians, especially in so vile and stinking a custom?' Why, he mocked, do we not 'as well imitate them in walking naked as they do? In preferring glasses, feathers, and such toys, to gold and precious stones, as they do?'[27]

Nevertheless, he accepted that tobacco had been a commercial success. After the dinner, Yeardley reported that the king had agreed its cultivation could continue on 'certain conditions'. First, that the planting of corn to feed settlers is not neglected, and that 'we should daily endeavour o[ur] selves to raise more rich and stable commodities' and so might grow 'into contempt, & so into disuse' of tobacco, that 'fantastical herb'.[28] Second, James encouraged the 'planting of vines', as wine would both bring profitable trade, and the 'precious liquor' would 'draw much good company to come & live there'.[29] Lastly, James encouraged Yeardley 'to cherish up silkworms' and to 'plant and preserve Mulberry trees' in all parts of Virginia.

During the previous decade, significant efforts had been put into the ambitious plan to extend raw silk production to Virginia. In the autumn of 1608, specialist 'silkmen' had arrived in Jamestown as part of the 'Second Supply' which had brought a number of other European craftsman, including 'eight Dutch men and Poles' skilled in the production of potash glass and naval supplies, and seventy new settlers, to the plantation.[30] The silkmen carried with them a precious cargo of *Bombyx* silkworm eggs, most likely sourced from King James's estates around London. Having survived their Atlantic passage, these first English eggs hatched the following spring, but success was short-lived. When the 'master workman' on the project fell sick, the silkworms, left unattended, were eaten by rats which had come to the colony on board English ships.[31]

Nevertheless, the brief thriving of this cohort of silkworms and the discovery of an indigenous species of mulberry tree along the James River and on the Somers Isles (Bermuda), transformed sericulture into a key economic activity for the Virginia Company. On his return to England from Virginia in 1610, Sir Thomas Gates, who had been stranded on Bermuda with Yeardley, proclaimed to the company that there were enough mulberry trees 'to cherish and feed millions of silkworms, and return us in a very short time, as great a plenty of silks as is vented into the whole world from all the parts of Italy'. Reports from Bermuda likewise celebrated the mulberry trees as being 'altogether resemblant' of those seen 'in the best silk making places' in the world.[32]

News from the colony of the potential for silk production was enthusiastically received at a court engaged in its own extensive mulberry plantings on royal estates, and with a king who was passionate about his sericulture. In the summer months, when James went hunting or on progress through the southern counties, the itinerant court included 'his Majestie's silk-worms', for which Richard Lecavill, Groom of the Chamber, was paid for the 'pains and charges in carrying'.[33] It was both a reflection of the king's deep commitment to the project and a high-profile way to promote domestic silk production.

Queen Anna seems to have embraced her husband's pet project. In a portrait from 1609, she is depicted wearing a magnificent dress embroidered with silkworms, thereby demonstrating an interest in and patronage of sericulture.[34] By 1618, a bespoke building had been constructed for 'the Queens Silkworms' at Oatlands palace, by keeper Sir John Trevor. It boasted state-of-the-art heating and ventilation, complete with chimney and 'Iron work of Several Sorts' for 'cocoon reeling'. The two-storey silkworm house of four small rooms and a larger space upstairs with shelving for the growing of silkworms, bore Queen Anna's coat of arms: the royal coat of arms of England, Scotland and Ireland, impaled with her father's arms as King of Denmark.[35]

In a foreword to a publication on sericulture written by the Keeper of the King's Silkworms, Jean Bonoeil, James declared what he called his 'royal commandment' to the Virginia Council, that 'a speedy course be taken for the setting up of Silkworms … throughout the whole Colony'. He urged planters to apply their efforts to this 'rich and solid commodity' rather than to tobacco.[36] Those who scoffed at, or railed against, colonisation, Bonoeil's book declared, were 'next a kin, indeed, to the hateful Savages, enemies herein to God, their King, and Country'.[37]

With the king's support, the Virginia and Somers Isles [Bermuda] companies issued repeated instructions to the governors in Virginia and Bermuda to prioritise silk production and to procure the experts and materials required.[38] To try to stimulate competition and thereby jumpstart production, the Virginia Company offered a parallel bounty to the settlers, promising £50 'to him that shall first obtain and send over ten pounds of silk or ten gallons of *cocoons*'.[39] During the next few years, eight Frenchmen from Languedoc (described as '*Vignerons* … who are very skilful also in breeding of the *Silke*-worms, and making *Silk*') agreed to migrate to the colony, along with 'some Englishmen', and a silkman trained by Bonoeil.[40] For his part in helping to develop silk production in the colony, Bonoeil was admitted into the Virginia Company and granted two shares of land.[41]

By 1612 William Strachey was describing sericulture in Virginia as 'seriously considered of, and order taken that it shall be duly followed'.[42] With silk production apparently flourishing in the colony, it was only natural that when John Rolfe and Pocahontas were sent to London on the company's behalf, they took with them a sample of Virginia-grown silk.

Yet tobacco remained the colony's principal crop, and exports continued to grow significantly. With profit to be made, in 1619 the king introduced an unprecedented duty on Virginia tobacco, in what was a naked attempt to generate additional revenue for the Crown.[43] As cultivation of the 'sweet smelling' tobacco became more established in Bermuda and Virginia, the king's interest and interventions grew. It was not a little ironic that the commodity against which the king had spoken out so vociferously and for so long, was ultimately the crop that saved the plantation.

***

During the summer of 1619, the first African slaves arrived in the Virginia plantation. They had come from the port city of Luanda, which was then a Portuguese colony. Tens of thousands of men, women and children were enslaved there. About 350 men and women were loaded onto a Portuguese slave ship, the *San Juan Bautista*. As it made its way to the Spanish colony of Veracruz, two English privateer ships, the *White Lion* and the *Treasurer*, sailing under a Dutch flag, intercepted it and seized approximately fifty slaves. The ships, which were owned by Richard Rich, Earl of Warwick, sailed to Virginia where some of the men were traded to work on the colony's tobacco plantations. John Rolfe wrote to Sir Edwin Sandys in London that the *White Lion*, a 'Dutch man of war' arrived in the colony where its crew sold '20-odd Negroes' in exchange for provisions.[44] The Africans were most likely put to work in the tobacco fields that had recently been established in the area, providing the colony with much-needed labour.

And so was established the 'triangular slave trade' between Britain, Africa and the New World of the Caribbean and America, which had begun under Elizabeth I in the mid-sixteenth century – most notably by John Hawkins of Plymouth, the first English trader of enslaved people from West Africa to the Americas. English goods were traded in Africa, from where enslaved people were carried across the Atlantic. Goods produced in the New World were transported back to Britain. As Britain acquired more colonies in America and the Caribbean, so demand grew for enslaved Africans to cultivate and harvest the tobacco, rice, sugar, and other plantation crops.

Today, in Old Point Comfort in Hampton, Virginia, a monument stands where the *White Lion* docked. A proclamation was read by President Barack Obama in 2011, making the fort a national monument, and stating: 'The first enslaved Africans in England's colonies in America were brought to this peninsula on a ship flying the Dutch flag in 1619, beginning a long ignoble period of slavery in the colonies and, later, this Nation.'[45]

In fact, the first mention of the Virginia Company seeking African slaves in its American colonies came in 1616, in a commission from the company to Captain Daniel Tucker, the new governor of Bermuda. It demanded that he order a 'Mr Wilmott' to go to the 'Savage Islands and trade there for things fit for England as for the Plantation, such as Cattle, Cassava, Sugar Canes, Negroes to dive for pearls, plants'.[46] The following August, George Bargrave, a sea captain from Kent, returned with a variety of items, including sugar cane, figs, plantains and pineapples, but also an 'Indian and a Negro' that Nathaniel Butler, later governor of the colony, would declare as being 'the first these Islands ever had'.[47] The Africans who were taken to Bermuda – and to Virginia – contributed to the agricultural development of the colonies to provide food and stave off the thread of future 'starving times'.

A number of these first enslaved people were freed after a tenure of around seven years, which suggests that they most likely had the status of indentured servants. Racial slavery, therefore, was not imposed on these first African people upon their arrival in 1619, but instead evolved over the next decades in Virginia and the rest of English North America.

21

Shah Abbas's Silk

'It cannot be gainsaid but the silks bought at the first
hand is the best husbandry.'

George, Lord Carew, 1615[1]

With King James's efforts to develop a silk-weaving industry in Britain, the need for raw silk grew. The king had sought to address this through encouraging silk production at home and in Virginia, but that was never going to be enough. The demand for silk across Europe, and in Britain, was growing exponentially. Raw silk accounted for a rise from around 1 per cent in 1600 to around 29 per cent of the total value of London imports in 1622. As Privy Councillor Lord Carew complained in January 1617: 'There is such a madness in England as that we cannot endure our homemade cloth but must needs be clothed in silk.'[2] The heyday of English woollen cloth was over, as the wealthy spurned it in favour of silk furnishings, silk clothing, embroidered silk cloths and other accessories.

Britain needed a reliable supply of raw silk. Buying raw silk 'at the first hand' made most sense, as Carew conceded, thereby bypassing the costs and challenges of access through the overland trading routes and the vulnerability to foreign merchants.[3] And trade 'at the first hand' primarily meant trade with Persia. As the then ambassador to India Sir Thomas Roe observed: There is no better 'place for the benefit of our Nation to settle a trade for venting cloth and buying silk' than Persia.⁴ However, access to one of the main sources at Aleppo in Ottoman Syria, which served as the headquarters of the English Levant Company, could be subject to wars between the Ottoman Empire and the Safavīd state of Persia.

The ruler of Persia, Shah Abbas I, then known as 'Abbas the Great', is now regarded as the most important ruler of the over 200-year-old Safavīd dynasty that ended in the eighteenth century. For Shah Abbas and King James of Great Britain, there came to be something of a meeting of minds. Both men were preoccupied with silk, and both were vehemently opposed to the Ottoman Turk. For the shah, taking control of silk production through his reconquest of the Caspian provinces from the Ottomans and the establishment of a royal silk monopoly, was part of a policy of centralising the state under his personal authority.⁵ Abbas and James both sought an alliance of European princes to act against the Ottomans, and this was the ultimate goal of James's vision for a reunited Christendom. As the Venetian ambassador Nicolò Molin had earlier written of James: 'The king speaks of the Grand Turk with disdain. He hates him and wishes that the Christian powers would unite to drive him out.'⁶

Shah Abbas had inherited the throne of the Safavīd empire in 1589 at the age of sixteen after the forced abdication of his father. Determined to regain territories lost to the Turks and challenge the Ottomans, the shah led military campaigns against the Turks, and since the turn of the century, he had sent many envoys west, to establish an alliance with Christian Europe, in an attempt to redirect the silk trade and simultaneously land a blow to the Ottoman economy.

Among his envoys were two English travellers, brothers Anthony and Robert Sherley, who had arrived at the Safavīd court during the last years of Elizabeth I's reign.⁷ First Anthony, who deserted his mission, and then Robert in 1608 were sent to Europe to seek support for the shah's plans. Wearing 'Persian habit', Robert, together with his wife and the Persian ambassador Husain 'Ali Beg, travelled to Prague,

Rome and Madrid, before arriving at Hampton Court for an audience with King James in October 1611. Here Robert proposed the advantages of Persian trade and delivered a letter from the shah.[8]

It was a missive deliberately designed to flatter and enthuse. James was heralded as one whose 'kingdoms are many, both ancient and famous' and 'whose crown resembles the brightness of the sun'. Acknowledging James's reputation as a peacemaker who sought a reunion of Christendom to direct action against the Ottomans, Abbas added: 'You are so dear to the Christian commonwealth.'[9] The shah's proposal was to channel exports to Europe on English ships through the Persian Gulf, thereby depriving the Ottoman sultan of valuable customs revenue. For James it promised direct trade and plentiful supplies of Persian silk at cheaper rates. The proviso was that English merchants must be prepared to take the entire annual stock of silk and pay cash for half of it.

Both the Levant Company and the East India companies were opposed to the shah's proposal as presented by Sherley. Diverting trade through the Persian Gulf meant going against the interests of the Levant Company merchants at Aleppo, whilst the East India Company was already finding great difficulty in raising sufficient funds to carry on its existing operations. The prospect of exporting more bullion from the realm was sure to provoke further opposition.[10] Reflecting the views of both companies, John Chamberlain wrote to Sir Dudley Carleton: 'The way is long, the trade uncertain, and must quite cut off our traffic with the Turk.'[11] Despite James's enthusiasm for the shah's proposition, he had no means to dictate the course of action, and by the terms of their charters, all such commercial activity was ultimately determined by the companies.

***

As it became clear that English cloth was not selling in India, the East India Company came to revise their initial reservations. In 1614, doubtless aware of the company's struggles, Sherley travelled from Persia to meet with English merchants in Surat to repeat the shah's offer, thereby presenting the opportunity both for the company merchants to sell their cloth and secure new revenue by carrying Persian silk on company ships bound for Europe.[12] It was now an irresistible prospect; the company desperately needed a new outlet for their cloth and Persia seemed to be it.

Thomas Aldworth, chief factor in India, resolved to send two company merchants, Richard Steele and William Crowther, to Persia to investigate further the possibilities for trade and to obtain the necessary permissions from the shah.[13] They left Ajmer in India in March 1615 and travelled to Isfahan, Abbas's new Persian capital, where they arrived in September.

Having assessed the market, Steele concluded that there was opportunity for the sale of English broadcloth, particularly the lighter-coloured cloth, and other goods that the company could export both from England and from India, 'for the Persian country is so cold that for six months in the year they wear cloth; and also there is divers commodities of India will give great profit there'.[14] On Aldworth's instruction and with Sherley's help, Steele secured a farman ordering the governors of the Persian seaports to receive and assist any English vessels that might arrive.

When, in February 1616, news of Steele's mission reached Sir Thomas Roe at the Mughal court in Ajmer, Roe immediately wrote to the company factors in Surat of his concerns, not least that the strength of the Portuguese in the Persian Gulf would continually disrupt English trade there. Moreover, he doubted whether the shah would remain favourable to trading silk with the English if he were to make peace with the Ottomans. 'The silk is the Kings and if it avail him, he will do it; if not, a peace with the Turk will restore him to his old ways.'[15] The shah's monopoly on trade would also mean that merchants would have to buy direct from the shah's royal merchant in Isfahan. This would be costly in terms of money and human life, requiring merchants to make perilously long journeys back and forth between the Persian capital and Jask, or one of the other Persian ports. Unless the shah would make a concession and have local merchants ship the silk to port, Roe believed the East India Company should abandon their ambition for Safavīd silk.[16] As he made clear: 'We aim not at gnats and small flies, but at a commerce honourable and equal to two so mighty nations.'[17]

Thomas Kerridge and the other factors at Surat dismissed Roe's assessment, believing him 'in error of opinion concerning merchandising and merchant's affairs in these parts'.[18] On the arrival in the autumn of 1616 of a fresh fleet from London bringing a supply of broadcloth for which there was no hope of sale in India, they decided to send the cargo instead to Jask.

On 8 November 1616, the huge East Indiaman the *James* set sail from Suvali (Swally) in Surat and dropped anchor three weeks later off the coast at Jask. Among the merchants on board were Edward Connock, who had been appointed chief factor in Persia, and his deputy Thomas Barker. The ship's cargo included sixty-four bales of English broadcloth and about £6,333 sterling, all of which had recently arrived from London, together with a miscellaneous collection of other items such as knives, looking-glasses, vermilion (powdered cinnabar), drinking glasses and 'elephants' teeth'.[19]

Having been warmly received by the governor of Jask, Connock then met with Shah Abbas on 21 July 1617. He described himself as King James's 'messenger' and explained that he had a letter from the king to the shah – one of the commendatory letters left blank to be filled in as the occasion required. As Connock subsequently reported: 'In [the] presence of the whole Court, the King [Abbas] took His Majesty's letter, put it to his mouth, then on his head, examined the manner of the sealing of it, and then opened it, satisfied that it was a true letter, and demanded what His Majesty chiefly required.' According to his own account, Connock replied: 'Amity, trade, and commerce between the two Kings and their subjects.' The shah then called for wine, and in a large bowl drank his Majesty's health, saying 'that Connock was welcome, that the King of England should be his elder brother, that his friendship he did dearly esteem and tender, that he would grant us Jask or any other part we would require, and such freedom in every respect as in his honour he might grant.' No customs were to be paid on the silk exported from the company ships leaving Jask.[20]

Whereas in India, English merchants had struggled to secure the interest and attention of Emperor Jahangir, Shah Abbas received the merchants favourably and despite their modest cargo, he indicated that English cloth and many kinds of spices would find ready markets in Persia. 'To give life to our trades beginning,' as Connock put it, the shah offered to supply them at once 'with 3,000 bales' of the silk on' credit.[21] Connock had no doubt, that 'our new Persian trade ... in future and short time will produce as great benefit and satisfaction to our commonwealth of England as any other whatsoever commerce which she now in these parts enjoyeth'. The shah's desire, he said, was 'that the whole quantity of silk may be transported by sea for England, and not more through the Turk's dominions'. He added: 'It is worth all your [James's] other trades put together.'[22]

Such was the distance between Persia, India and England and the time taken for letters to be received, that it was not until January 1617 that Sir Thomas Smythe and the company directors had received a letter from Roe with details of Richard Steele's original reconnaissance mission of 1615, and the project 'for the opening of trade in Persia'.

They greeted the news with some caution. Many of the East India Company directors had also invested in the Levant Company and feared anything that might damage the trade in Persian silk via Aleppo. They were also very aware that trade in silk with Persia would require significant sums of money which would fuel the debate about the company's export of bullion for trade. In the end, the arguments of those in favour of the project won out; in spite of the risks and the cost, the potential prize was too great.

However, it was not only a commercial question but also a 'matter of state', requiring the approval of the king and the Privy

Council. This was swiftly secured. As Lord Carew wrote to Roe on 16 January 1617: 'The Lords like so well of it, and the merchants so willing to find it, as that it is concluded that a trial shall be made.'[23]

The East India Company prepared instructions for Roe. He was to make careful enquiry from native merchants about 'the quantity of silk that is yearly brought by merchants and exported out of Persia' together with the 'current price' and 'charges' to carry the silk to the port. If all was considered satisfactory, Roe could then send some 'fitting person or persons ... to treat with the King of Persia on our King's behalf for the establishment of such a trade with us as will answer with our means and vents of our commodities'. Certain stipulations were to be made as to customs duties and the provision of a 'safe and secure port', and at least one half of the price of the silk was to be taken in English goods, the remainder in 'ready money, spices and other Indian commodities'. Finally, the company insisted that the price of the silk, 'laden clear of all charges aboard our ships' must not exceed a rial [currency unit in Persia] and a half [6s] a pound, 'at which prices, and good conditions as aforesaid', the company assessed that they 'shall be able to take from the Persian yearly eight thousand bales of silk of 180 lb English each bale or thereabouts'.[24]

Accompanying the instructions was a letter for Roe from King James, written on 4 February 1617 from the Palace of Westminster. James considered a treaty with the shah essential for the commerce of silk and praised his ambassador's efforts to reach a trade agreement, 'for the opening of his Gulf [the Persian Gulf] and enlarging of the trade of our subjects into his dominions, especially for the traffic and commerce of silk'. James encouraged Roe to see that a treaty of commerce was concluded 'without further circumstance'.[25] On receipt of the company's instructions in October 1617, Roe drew up a commission for Connock to negotiate further with the shah, a role that was taken over by Thomas Barker after Connock's death in December.

The first fruits of trade in Persia came in early 1619 when an East Indiaman travelled from Jask to Surat with around seventy bales of raw silk, which arrived in time to be sent to London with Roe, sailing home on the *Royal Anne* at the end of his embassy.[26]

Whilst Roe had made clear his initial reservations as to the prospect of opening trade with Persia, now that he had a clear sense of James's approval of the project, he resolved to do all he could to support it. He acknowledged that if Britain succeeded in securing the trade, it would be a swipe against both the Ottoman Turkish and Spanish empires: securing the trade would 'alter the face of this part of the world' and would benefit the whole of Protestant Christendom.[27] Yet the price of failure would be the 'loss and disgrace to our nation' by making Spain a million crowns a year richer, and strengthening the reputation of the Portuguese in the East.[28]

Despite this extremely promising first shipment of silk, trade would prove difficult not least because of insufficient supplies, the hostile actions of local customs officials, 'Portuguese intrigue', and the challenge of transporting cargo across the country in extreme temperatures on the long, arduous road from Jask to Isfahan. It was exactly what Roe had feared. The shah stated that he was unwilling to ship silk to the gulf ports until he had secured Hormuz. The island kingdom – a thriving commercial centre situated at the mouth of the Persian Gulf, which was captured in the name of King Manuel I of Portugal in 1515 – was the point from which the Portuguese, and later the Iberian monarchy, dominated all sea-borne trade between Europe, Persia and the Indian Ocean.

***

In October 1619, Shah Abbas and his court hosted a lavish banquet in Isfahan. The shah had spent the previous years in the field fighting Ottoman forces in the north Caucasus, and the event was to celebrate his victories. After success against the Ottomans, the shah was now determined to move against the Portuguese and capture Hormuz. Yet despite its many military accomplishments, the Safavīd state did not possess a strong navy.

The English needed Persian silk, and the Shah needed English ships and crews.

Thomas Barker, the chief East India Company factor in Persia, hoped to use the occasion of the banquet to confirm the terms of trade and ensure the safety of his merchants, but whilst the shah promised to ensure his state officials respected the English merchants, he went much further. As Barker subsequently relayed in a letter to London, Shah Abbas had proposed to turn over the strategically and commercially valuable island of Hormuz to the English in exchange for naval support against the Portuguese. He noted that the shah expected the English to maintain 'secrecy until it were effected', and once the island was safely in their hands, 'the Safavīds' would deliver '[Castle Hormuz] unto the English'.[29] In return, the East India Company would receive special customs privileges, the right to establish an unfortified factory in Gombroon (near present-day Bandar Abbas) – a location better suited for English shipping than Jask – and a commitment that the shah would deliver a certain amount of raw silk to the English annually.[30] It was to be an alliance born of mutual need which saw the East India Company move beyond its trading brief, and provide ships to support the shah in direct military action against the Portuguese.

Meanwhile, the new king of Spain–Portugal, Philip IV, resolved to send reinforcements to add to the Portuguese presence in the Persian Gulf under the command of Ruy Freire de Andrade who was specifically instructed to ensure the Iberian attack was directed only upon 'foreigners', in other words the French, English and Dutch, and not 'upon the Persians or other vassals of the Shah' with whom it was necessary to maintain friendly exchanges.[31] If Ruy Freire judged his fleet was strong enough, he should repel the English from the Gulf regardless of the ongoing negotiations in Europe for a marriage between the Prince and the Spanish Infanta. The mission did not go to plan. On 25 December when the Portuguese fleet surrounded four East Indian ships under the command of Norfolk-born Captain Andrew Shilling, it was repelled with fierce cannon fire and forced to retreat.[32] It was a moment of considerable significance, not least in convincing the English merchants that an attack on Hormuz was now essential if they were to continue in their efforts to trade in Persia.

Nonetheless, Portuguese offensives against the ports on the southern coast of Persia intensified. Edward Connock looked to the company's agents in Surat for guidance who agreed that they could not protect their interests if the Portuguese remained in control of important ports in the Persian Gulf.

Back in London, and unaware of developments in Persia, on 19 March 1621 King James wrote to Shah Abbas, reaffirming his commitment to strengthening their relationship, but also complaining about apparent preferential treatment of Portuguese traders, whom he accused of wanting to expel the English from all commerce in the East. He thanked the shah for the 'many princely favours to ours residing within your Dominions and Territories' and proceeded to request certain further 'privileges and immunity' to encourage that trade. This included permission to buy silks nearer to the port of Jask, so that English merchants did not have to make the dangerous overland journey to Isfahan and expose themselves to the attempts of the Portuguese 'to drive our Subjects from all trade in those parts.' James also requested 'that our Merchants may have that freedom of Commerce and traffic with your Subjects as is usual among the Subjects of Princes in amity one with another', and that 'the native Commodities of our Kingdoms and such other Merchandizes as our People shall import into your Territories' may be exchanged for the 'Silk of your Dominions'.[33]

It was a greater level of involvement in trading company affairs than the king had demonstrated in either Japan or India, and reflected perhaps James's commitment to developing a domestic silk industry, and also his financial concerns. He had generally been reluctant to act against the Iberian monarchy, with whom he was still seeking a marriage alliance for Prince Charles. In response Shah Abbas assured James that the promises previously made would be faithfully kept and hinted to Barker, who delivered James's letter, of his intention to take Hormuz at the earliest opportunity and hand it to the English.

In January 1622, the East India Company confirmed their acceptance of the shah's proposal, resolving to assist him in taking Hormuz and other key ports or strongholds in the Persian Gulf. The terms established that plunder should be divided equally between both parties, and both an English and a Persian governor were to reside in the fortress; Muslim prisoners were to be taken by the Persians, and Christian men by the English.[34]

On 10 February, an English fleet transported and landed 3,000 Safavīd troops about two miles from the town of Hormuz, and then remained at sea to provide artillery support from their ships. By the beginning of May, the island had been captured by the Anglo–Safavīd force.

The news of the fall of Hormuz reached London in late 1622. The East India Company had acted beyond its authority and without the express permission of the Crown. Whilst James's letter to the shah had undoubtedly urged him to take steps to challenge the Portuguese in their attacks against English shipping, this was a conquest of territory claimed by a country with which James was officially at peace, and with whom he was seeking a marriage alliance. James knew the risk that the fall of Hormuz now represented to the Spanish match. From Madrid, Digby described how the news had created 'much storm' which he was seeking to calm.[35] He defended English actions, acknowledged the friendship of the two monarchs in Europe, and argued that the open hostility between the English and Iberian monarchy in the East justified any action the East Indian Company had taken.[36] The Spanish ambassador in London, Don Carlos Coloma, demanded justice. He had been ordered to ensure that James condemned the company's actions and receive assurance that the English would stop assisting the Persians and help to restore Hormuz to the Iberian monarchy.[37]

In taking Hormuz, the East India Company's military operation had seemed to resemble state action, which in turn raised complications for diplomatic relations in Europe.[38] Had the company's military action at Hormuz been in the name of the king? Clear precedent did not exist for dealing with the activities of British subjects or companies in far-flung places. Hormuz signalled the start of what would become domestic debates over decades, about the limits of company and state authority. As long as the East India Company was the only British presence in the region, it was the British state abroad.

When three of the company ships from Persia – the *Jonas*, the *London* and the *Lion* – arrived back in London in the summer of 1623, laden with the spoils from the conquest of Hormuz, the directors questioned the traders under whose authority had they collaborated with the Persians and provided them with military aid. One of the men claimed it had been the company's charter that gave them the right to 'defend and offend' and that they had consulted the company merchants in Surat.[39]

The Spanish ambassador requested that James seize the company's ships make restitution to Spain.[40] James complied, ordering the ships be sequestered (for the time being) and the men involved arrested.[41] Justice would be done, he assured the ambassador, and nothing would further damage relations between him and King Philip.[42] In fact James was merely buying time as he considered the prospect of yearly revenue from Hormuz.

In a letter written from the royal residence at Newmarket on 7 December 1624, James told Sir Thomas Smythe how he really viewed 'the business of Persia'. He described it as 'a matter of great advantage to the Trade of this our Kingdome'. And, he added: 'Our pleasure is that you take into your serious consideration and care both the furtherance and manner of settling of it, as may be best for the weal of our Kingdom.'[43]

Indeed, the successful action against the Portuguese greatly enhanced British access to Persian silk and other goods for the

European markets. It also gave merchants a foothold in Gombroon, where a dwelling was acquired in what would become the main British trading port in Persia for the next two decades. The English merchants were allowed to stay in Hormuz – though the fort was not handed over to them – and Shah Abbas permitted them to collect a percentage of the customs from incoming ships. Persia proved to be a good investment and customs revenues in London for all Persian imports – silk, carpets, velvets, damask, satins, taffetas, gold and silver cloth – rose. Thomas Barker, chief factor in Persia had been proved prescient when, in 1618, he had described trade there as the 'hopefullest without exception that ever England enjoyed'.[44] Meanwhile, as the English presence in the Persian Gulf tested Anglo–Iberian relations, tensions were growing with the Dutch in the Spice Islands of Indonesia.

22

The King of Pulo Run

'Mr Courthope, myself, and 32 men more hath maintained the possession of Pooloroon [Pulo Run], enduring much want and misery; for your worships' benefit and our country's credit...'

George Muschamp to the East India Company at Bantam,
12 March 1619[1]

In the early seventeenth century, Pulo Run, a tiny island of just two miles by half a mile in the Indonesian archipelago, was the sole supplier of the world's nutmeg. In 1616, after being violently subjugated by the Dutch, the Islamic inhabitants of Pulo Run, and their neighbours on Pulo Ai, swore allegiance to King James. He was to become 'by the grace of God, King of England, Scotland, Ireland, France, Pulo Ai and Pulo Run'. As a mark of their 'submission', the *orang kaya*, the island rulers, handed over their greatest treasure: a nutmeg sapling.[2]

Spices more than silk had been the great prize of Eastern commerce for decades, and had been the catalyst for the establishment of both the East India Company and its Dutch rival, the Verenigde Oostindische Compagnie (VOC). Of all the spices, the scarcest, and hence the most profitable, were nutmeg, mace and cloves. They were found in abundance in the Moluccas, Ambon and the Banda islands (collectively known as the Spice Islands). Nutmeg and mace came from Pulo Run, Pulo Ai, Lonthor and Neira in the Banda Sea.

It was only there that the nutmeg tree, *Myristica fragrans*, grew, and only there that nutmeg could be bought so cheaply. When sold in Europe, the value of nutmeg, the seed kernel inside the fruit of the nutmeg tree, increased by up to 32,000 per cent. It was highly coveted for its many culinary and medicinal properties – thought to cure everything from the plague to flatulence to the common cold – and so prized by the wealthy that it was exchanged as a gift and carried around with pocket-sized graters to add a dash of the spice whenever desired.

From the beginning of the seventeenth century, the seven small Banda islands became the primary theatre for the burgeoning conflict between the English and Dutch trading companies.[3] The Dutch had arrived there first in 1599 with a fleet under the command of Jacob Cornelisz van Neck. The voyage was deemed a stunning success, returning home with holds laden with spices, and sparking what would become known as the Spice Race, as European nations competed to acquire spices such as pepper, nutmeg and cinnamon.

Having arrived first and defeated the Portuguese at great cost, the Dutch considered themselves the sole inheritors of the monopoly on spices. The British were late to the spice race, but determined to access Eastern wealth, challenge Dutch dominance and secure access to the riches of the islands. Desperate to meet demand at home and to secure the profits that spice sales could bring, the East India Company rejected the theory of exclusive rights, maintaining instead that the seas were open to all, and that free trade was an inalienable right of every nation. Unlike the English company, the VOC had an arsenal of additional powers that allowed it to wage war, conduct diplomacy and plant colonies in Asia on behalf of the United Provinces.

Immediately the Dutch focused its efforts on the Spice Islands, determined to displace the Spanish and Portuguese by securing treaties with local rulers, and promising to protect them against Iberian aggression in return for control over the sales of their spices. Thereafter, the United Provinces claimed they had conquered the islands and secured the exclusive rights to trade there, which they were entitled to defend by any means. They established a fort (Fort Nassau) on the island of Banda Neira and imposed their control over the Bandanese people. By 1609, relations had deteriorated so much that the islanders ambushed and killed the Dutch admiral Pieter Verhoef, and forty of his men. The Dutch company responded with force and imposed a new treaty on the Bandanese demanding that all available spices would be delivered directly to them, 'without selling, trading, or exchanging in the slightest to any persons or nations other than the prescribed representatives'.[4]

Over the next few years repeated attempts by English merchants to trade in the islands were repelled by the Dutch. As news of such actions regularly filtered back to London, the East India Company directors looked to James to intervene, framing the events in the region not simply as commercial rivalry between the two trading companies, but rather hostile action by the Dutch against Britain. Sir Robert Naunton wrote to Sir Dudley Carleton in The Hague of the 'resentment which the Dutch had given to all that have any sense at all of the honour of his Majesty and of our whole nation'.[5] The Archbishop of Canterbury, George Abbot, whose brother Sir Maurice was a founder member of the East India Company, wrote similarly of the 'insufferable' acts of the Dutch against the king and the English nation.[6]

In an attempt to settle the differences between the two companies, it was resolved that English and Dutch commissioners meet to consider the points in dispute, not least the request of Governor Sir Thomas Smythe that his company trade in the Banda islands. The conference met in the spring of 1613 in London. Despite being head of one of the two states which were party to the negotiations, James – perhaps unsurprisingly, given his strong sense of divine right, and that his authority came from God – saw himself as something of an impartial mediator between the two sets of commissioners, leaving the Dutch feeling they could count on his sympathy and support against his own subjects. The conference sat for two months before being dissolved on the understanding that matters would be reconsidered at a later date.

Early in 1615, another expedition to the Banda islands was prepared at Bantam, and in February of that year, the chief merchants George Ball and George Cockayne sailed in the *Concord* and *Speedwell* to Banda Neira, where they found a Dutch squadron under the command of Gerard Reynst, governor-general of the Dutch East Indies. Reynst summoned them to Castle Nassau and accused them of being 'rogues and rascals.' He 'marveled whereof [they] should come to those places' which the Dutch claimed and forbade them to trade with the Bandanese. Having likely been briefed on the London conference before his departure from the Dutch Republic in June 1613, Reynst mocked the Englishmen for having a king who had taken the VOC's side. He claimed that James had not only 'silenced' Sir Thomas Smythe when Smythe requested permission for the company to trade in the Banda islands, but conceded that the VOC 'had all the right that might be [...] to these places of Banda'. Indeed, Reynst added, he could be forgiven for concluding that the VOC enjoyed 'more favour of his Majesty than the Company of England'.[7] James had apparently agreed with the Dutch that unless the VOC enjoyed a substantial income from the spice trade, they could not reasonably be expected to pay for the defence of the islands, which would otherwise be to the benefit of the Portuguese and the Spanish.

Refusing to be intimidated by Reynst, Ball and Cockayne continued their trading mission, leaving Neira for the adjacent island of Pulo Ai. Whilst the islanders welcomed the English merchants and made clear their loathing of the Dutch, they proved tough negotiators. As Cockayne subsequently reported to Smythe in London, the Bandanese were determined to secure a price that would be 'for [their] profit' and were resistant to the English establishing a trading post on the island.[8] Ball and Cockayne departed in late April 1615, leaving behind merchant Richard Hunt to continue to trade, together with Sophonias 'the Cossack', a Russian sent to England by the tsar a decade before and now EIC captain of the *Speedwell*. In early May, Dutch troops landed on the island but were driven back by the natives.

When the *Speedwell* left Pulo Ai in September with a large cargo of mace and nutmeg, Sophonias also had on board an *orang kaya* who was carrying a letter from the 'principal states' of Pulo Ai, Pulo Run and Neira, addressed to John Jourdain, 'the principal factor of the English at Bantam'. The letter explained that the Bandanese were vehemently opposed to the Dutch presence in their lands and appealed for help from the 'King of England' and claimed to have heard 'of the great love and peace, that [he] hath with all the world'. Since they believed that the king did not seek to invade other countries, but rather commanded his subjects to engage in peaceful trade, they wished to negotiate a treaty with him. They feared that the Dutch – described as those 'sons of Whores' and 'utter Enemies' – sought to conquer their land and destroy their Islamic religion. They pleaded with James to arrange deliveries of 'powder, shot, cloth and rice', and help them 'recover the Castle of Neira' (Castle Nassau). In return, they promised to sell their spices exclusively to the English, provided they would not seek to 'overthrow our religion' or 'commit offence with our Women'.⁹

Meanwhile, the Dutch had successfully landed at Pulo Ai and proceeded to conquer the island. A stone fortress, 'Castle Revenge' was to be constructed on the island to reinforce Dutch control. Many hundreds of Bandanese drowned at sea as they tried to escape. Richard Hunt did manage to slip away and on his return to Bantam, reported that eight days after the Dutch attack, the people of Pulo Ai had, he claimed, ceded their land 'for the use of the English nation' and drawn up 'articles' to protect 'their liberties'. As proof, Hunt had brought with him 'the earth of the country, sticks and stones', which he allegedly received from the Bandanese, 'in sign of possession of the country'.¹⁰

East India Company officer Nathaniel Courthope, together with Sophonis, Hunt and Thomas Spurway, was immediately dispatched to the Banda Islands with two East Indiamen, the *Defence* and *Swan*, and orders from John Jourdain, company president in Bantam. Jourdain warned Courthope to be cautious in his dealings with the

Bandanese, 'a peevish, perverse, diffident and perfidious people' but to find out whether the inhabitants of Pulo Ai and Pulo Run did indeed wish to be subjects of King James.[11] If they did, they should be induced to 'ratify under their hands and seals the former surrender, if lawfully made; if not, then to make a new surrender of all or part of such islands as are yet under their own commands and at their own dispose, leaving out those where the Flemings [the Dutch] are possessed and have command'.[12]

When Courthope and his ships arrived at Pulo Run on 25 December 1616, the islanders allegedly confirmed the 'surrender' of the island to the 'Crown of England' and pledged to put themselves under King James's protection as his subjects. They offered to send the king a 'branch of Nutmegs' as an annual gift and agreed to sell nutmeg and mace produced on the islands exclusively 'to the subjects of the King of England'. They assured Courthope that they made these promises not 'in madness or loosely as the breathing of the wind', but 'in their hearts'. They reiterated their demands, asking that James and his countrymen respect their property and persons, and prohibit any practices offensive to Islam, such as 'unreverent usage of women' and the 'maintaining of swine in our country'. Moreover, they asked that all inhabitants enjoy freedom of religion: any Englishman who wished to become a Muslim could do so, and any Bandanese would be free to convert to Christianity. The English flag, the 'ancient of Saint George', was flown across the island. The new treaty called on James to recover the neighbouring island of Pulo Ai, which had fallen into the 'hands and possession' of the Dutch, but which had previously 'absolutely surrendered to him'.[13]

John Davis, the captain of the *Swan*, meanwhile, disobeyed orders not to leave the island and sailed over to Lonthor, the largest of the Banda islands, in search of fresh water. The ship was promptly captured by the Dutch; five of its crew were killed and the rest apprehended. Now with English prisoners as hostages, Laurens Reael, the new Governor-General of the Dutch East Indies, opened negotiations with Courthope. He dismissed the treaty Courthope had made with the 'infidel moors' [the Bandanese] as 'against all right' and with no authorisation from King James. Surely, he argued, it could not be more important than 'the ancient alliance and confederation between the Crown of England and the United Provinces'?[14] Courthope and his men were given three days to make up their minds.

News of the ultimatum was immediately sent to Bantam. Letters were dispatched to Reael confirming that Pulo Run did now belong to the 'Crown of England' and that the English had not done anything unworthy of 'honest men or the honour of our nation'.[15] Reael was informed that when people decided of their own free will to 'become the vassals of a king or monarch', as the Bandanese had done by subjecting themselves to King James, they were received into the protection of the ruler or his representatives. In response to his reference to European politics, Reael was reminded that the English had given many testimonies of their 'sincere and true affection to your nation'.[16]

Courthope was going nowhere. He made it clear that he had no intention of withdrawing. It was his duty to maintain the rights of the East India Company and King James, 'our sovereign lord', and nor could he betray the Pulo Run people 'who have surrendered their islands and themselves unto his Majesty of England.'[17] With food scarce and no clean water supply, Courthope reinforced the island's defences and built a fort, Fort Swan, overlooking the main approaches to the east. Courthope prepared to dig in against the besieging Dutch forces.

***

Meanwhile, on 3 October 1618, Sir Dudley Carleton appeared at the Estates-General in The Hague to demand that the long-promised 'special embassy' should be sent to London without delay to discuss all the outstanding points of difference, as he saw them between the two nations – the East Indian spice trade; the refusal to admit English finished cloth into the Netherlands; James's questioning of the right of the Dutch to fish off the coasts of England and

Scotland; and clashes over whaling in Greenland – and to try and reach a settlement. Carleton had warned the Dutch government that James, though he had shown himself willing to 'bear much at their hands', had now reached the limit of his endurance. While Dutch representatives were sent to London, James appointed several Privy Councillors to oversee the negotiations, determined that the two countries would agree to a properly ratified treaty.[18]

Over the last five years, attempts had been made to broker a diplomatic arrangement between the East India Company and the Dutch company, to allow them both to enjoy the profits of trade in the East Indies. Despite consideration of a range of options – including even joining the companies together – negotiations had always failed to reach a resolution. One stumbling block, according to the East India Company, was their differing approaches to trade: whereas the English wanted a 'peaceable and quiet trade', war with Spain was 'the main scope and drift' of the Dutch company.[19] Crown and company were at one, on this point.

Despite the reticence of the English and Dutch companies to come to terms – with the twelve-year truce between Spain and the United Provinces, signed in 1609, due to expire, and faced with the prospect of renewed war between the Dutch and Spain – both governments sought a settlement to halt the further escalation of their conflict in Asia and push back against any renewed threats to Protestantism in Europe. The conflict between the two East India companies was considered increasingly counterproductive, especially after war broke out in central Europe in 1619.

After six months of negotiations at the Merchant Taylors' Hall, located between Threadneedle Street and Cornhill in the City of London, and after regular audiences with the king at Whitehall, Greenwich and at Newmarket, the Treaty of Defence was concluded in June 1619.[20] It was intended to eliminate the possibility of future disputes between the Dutch and English East India companies by binding them together as formal allies committed to sharing the profits of trade in 'the Molucca islands, Banda and Amboyna [Ambon island]', two-thirds to the VOC and one-third to the East India Company, to reflect their relative strength in the area. 'All irregularities, offences and misunderstandings' were to be forgotten. Conflict was to be replaced by 'assistance, friendship, and reciprocal correspondence'.[21] The agreement also required the two companies to cooperate by assembling a joint 'fleet of defence' comprising twenty ships split evenly between them, to strike at Iberian possessions and sea routes.[22] The East India Company was not to erect forts for its own defence, but was to contribute to those already established by the Dutch. The English company also agreed to contribute to the cost of maintaining the VOC's forts and garrisons spread across the Spice Islands. The treaty was to last twenty years and if disputes were to arise that could not be solved in the East Indies or by a discussion between the two companies, then they should be referred to the King of Great Britain and the States General, who should seek to resolve the conflict to the satisfaction of both companies.

Writing to Carleton in The Hague, John Chamberlain noted that only King James's direct intervention in the negotiations had allowed the two sides to reach a compromise: 'The king hath dissolved the difficulties of the East India business and by his own wisdom and authority brought them to accord, which being indeed said to be his own act, they are to acknowledge his gracious and pacifical disposition.'[23]

The East India Company signed only under pressure. While some members celebrated the suspension of conflict, many others believed they had been disadvantaged by the king's eagerness to secure an alliance with the United Provinces. While they got a share of the spice trade at long last, they also had to pay an unspecified sum to sustain the VOC's military establishment in Asia. They believed the treaty markedly favoured the Dutch in the East Indies and called on James to review the agreement. The king assured them that it would be beneficial and establish an end to the bitter competitive rivalry for at least the next two decades. He dismissed the concerns that the company had been put at a disadvantage, assuring them that 'the King esteems the East India Company a great ornament and strength unto his kingdoms'. By the terms of the treaty, if the Dutch went against them, the quarrel, 'should be no longer the company's but of the state'.[24]

Despite the treaty granting the English only one-third of the spice trade, even this much competition displeased the Dutch company. Jan Pieterszoon Coen, Reael's successor as governor-general, was defiantly opposed to the English in the Indies, maintaining they had 'no claim to a single grain of sand ... of the Moluccas, Amboyna or Banda'.[25] Coen was determined to do whatever lay in his power to enforce the Dutch monopoly and bring the islanders to heel. While he acknowledged the realities of European politics, stating: 'We are aware of how much the state of the United Provinces depends on the good friendship, correspondence and honour of the Crown of England,' he did not believe it justified the agreement at a time when the Dutch were on the verge of expelling the English from the spice trade.[26]

The ink on the treaty was hardly dry before hostilities broke out anew in the East. After years under siege, Courthope's resistance was finally broken. In October 1620, apparently lured off the island by the Dutch, Courthope and twenty-one men rowed to the neighbouring island of Lonthor. On the way back, they were surprised by two Dutch vessels. Courthope was shot in the chest and, refusing to surrender, rolled overboard to try to swim for shore, but he died trying. When the islanders of Pulo Run learned of the peace treaty two months after Courthope's death, they saw it as a great betrayal.

The following year, Coen ordered a military expedition to the Banda islands to suppress resistance and assert Dutch dominance. On 27 February 1621, Dutch forces under Coen's command launched a brutal assault against the Bandanese people. At least 2,500 people were killed and thousands fled to neighbouring islands. From 14,000 Bandanese, only 480 native people remained after the massacre. On 8 May, 44 *orang kaya* were put to death, their bodies mutilated, and their heads impaled on bamboo sticks. It was a ruthless display of colonial violence that solidified Dutch dominance in the Banda islands and the VOC's monopoly over the spice trade for the next two centuries.

Yet Pulo Run remained in British possession, with the islanders continuing to maintain they were subjects of King James. On several occasions, proposals for the formal occupation of the island were discussed by the East India Company, but it was generally thought to be too difficult to maintain such a distant 'possession'.

Decades later, on 31 July 1667, following the Treaty of Breda which ended the second Anglo–Dutch war, the two European nations, bartered territories and trading rights. Among the terms of the agreement the Dutch colony of Manhattan, then known as New Amsterdam – now New York, was formally exchanged for the British colony of Pulo Run.

23

Plymouth Plantation, New England

'Being thus arrived in a good harbour, and brought safe to land, they
fell upon their knees and blessed the God of Heaven who had brought
them over the vast and furious ocean.'

William Bradford, *Governor of Plymouth Plantation*, 1620[1]

Away from the challenges and brutality of commerce and the
relentless drive for new markets and profitable trade, Britain
continued the attempt to extend its global reach into new parts of the
world by encouraging people, from all manner of backgrounds, to
move to distant shores for a new life. As in Jamestown and Bermuda
(1607 and 1609), Ulster Plantation (1609) and Newfoundland
(1610), for some people it was the prospect of more land, greater
wealth and a better environment in which to bring up a family that
encouraged them to move; for others it was a desire to convert 'the
'uncivil' to the 'true faith'. For others again, it would be to flee from
religious persecution and establish a new society in the hope of finding religious freedom and security.

After many months of preparations, beset with delays and disasters
and a false start from Southampton, in September 1620, the *Mayflower*,
a battered 180-ton merchant vessel, left the port city of Plymouth in
Devon carrying 30 crew members, various livestock and 102 passengers: 74 men, and 38 women. There are thought to have been a further
31 children on the *Mayflower* including a number of orphans who had

been placed with guardians. For about a third of these people, this was a pilgrimage to the 'promised land'. These radical English Puritans, most in family groups, were embarking for a new life in fulfilment of 'God's design'. The remaining passengers comprised the pilgrim's servants as well as skilled craftsmen, labourers, indentured servants and soldiers from all over England to support the investors' interests and to provide practical assistance in the plantation. Already a cohesive community, the radical Puritans (religious separatists) were the dominant group, and termed themselves 'the pilgrims'. The rest of the fare-paying passengers, who were seeking a new life but not driven by religious convictions, were known as 'the strangers'.

Unlike the moderate Puritans who had participated in James's great religious conference in Hampton Court back in January 1604, and who sought to reform the Church of England from within, the *Mayflower* Puritans were 'separatists' who came to believe that their Christian faith was incompatible with the Church of England. They wanted forms of worship and church organisation that were closer to the teachings of the Bible, and, like many radical Catholics, they had become disappointed in James I and his kingship. For all his early promises of toleration and reform, he had offered only uniformity, a new translation of the Bible that stressed the role of the clergy, and an insistence that everybody follow the Book of Common Prayer to the letter. The separatists refused to attend their parish churches, challenged the authority of Church of England bishops, and began to secretly conduct their own religious services. When the government imposed fines upon them, some fled into exile to avoid the strictures of the established church. In spring 1609, one group, drawn largely from in and around the east of England, from Gainsborough in Lincolnshire, and an area around the village of Scrooby in Nottinghamshire, fled for the Dutch Republic where they were free to worship as they pleased.

For ten years the separatists lived in Leiden, famous for its large textile industry and its religious tolerance. But then, fearing the prospect of Catholic Spain regaining control over the United Provinces, and concerned that their children were becoming too influenced by Dutch culture and the Dutch church, some of the Leiden congregation resolved to move once more. Some had heard from contacts in the City of London that the Crown and the Virginia Company were looking for new planters to settle and build colonies in America.

The separatists knew it would be a risky venture, subject to 'many unconceivable perils and dangers' of the long voyage and the 'miseries of the land', where they would be 'liable to famine, and nakedness, and the want, in a manner, of all things', and facing the 'continual danger of the savage people, who are cruel, barbarous and most treacherous.'[2] But despite all the arguments against making the journey, their conviction that God wanted them to go held sway. As Pastor John Robinson and Elder William Brewster wrote to His Majesty's Privy Council for Virginia, from Leiden: 'We verily believe and trust the Lord is with us', and 'that He will graciously prosper our endeavours, according to the simplicity of our hearts therein'.[3]

In 1617, Robert Cushman and John Carver, two of the Leiden congregation, were sent across the Channel to London to meet with the Virginia Company directors in the hope of securing permission to establish a colony and 'to see what favour or acceptance such a thing might find with the King'. To demonstrate their acceptance of James's authority and the main doctrine of the Church of England, they drew up a 'Declaration of Faith and Church Polity'. Among the 'seven articles' they confirmed that they did 'assent wholly' to the 'Confession of Faith' published in the name of the Church of England and to King James as 'Supreme Governor in all his Dominions in all causes, and over all persons'.[4]

Cushman and Carver secured the support of Sir Edwyn Sandys (soon to become treasurer of the Virginia Company), who then petitioned Sir Robert Naunton (soon to be the king's 'principal secretary') to move his Majesty 'to give way to such a people (who could not so comfortably live under the government of another State) to enjoy their liberty of conscience under his gracious protection in America, where they would endeavour the advancement of his

Majesty's dominions and the enlargement of the Gospel by all due means'. A later account by Edward Winslow, a Leiden separatist originally from Droitwich in Worcestershire, describes that: 'This his Majesty said was a good and honest motion and asking what profits might arise in the part we intended, (for our eye was upon the most northern parts of Virginia) 'twas answered, Fishing. To which he replied with his ordinary asseveration, "So God have my soul, 'tis an honest trade; 'twas the Apostles' own calling."'[5]

On 9 June, the Virginia Company granted the Leiden Puritans a patent to establish a plantation under the company's charter in the 'Northern parts of Virginia'.[6] To fund the voyage and the establishment of the colony, the separatists secured the support of a consortium of seventy investors led by merchant Thomas Weston. Struggling with the adverse trading conditions in the Low Countries in the aftermath of William Cockayne's English cloth project, Weston saw an opportunity to make money by financing the *Mayflower* voyage in exchange for a share of the colony's anticipated profits from selling beaver pelts in England to make hats.

***

The journey began inauspiciously. On 23 August 1620, two ships, the *Mayflower* and the *Speedwell* had set out from Southampton but the *Speedwell*, heavily overloaded, proved to be unseaworthy and returned to port. After further false starts, those who still wanted to make the voyage all crowded onto the *Mayflower*. Captained by Christopher Jones, and with a crew of thirty men, they finally sailed from Plymouth on 6 September.

The hundred or so passengers spent the next eight weeks at sea in cramped conditions aboard the 106-feet (32 metres)-long ship. Many became ill with scurvy and seasickness, as they travelled through heavy storms which blew the ship off course. Finally, on 9 November they spied land, a peninsula named Cape Cod years earlier by English explorer Bartholomew Gosnold, but several hundred miles north of their intended destination of north Virginia. Although they tried to correct their course and sail south, the worsening weather meant they could go no further. Instead, Jones resolved that they would go back around Cape Cod to what their map identified as 'New England' – an area explored and named by John Smith of Jamestown in 1614 – and plant their colony there.

On 11 November, they dropped anchor at the site of today's Provincetown Harbor, Massachusetts. Amid complaints and threatened mutiny among 'the strangers' that the *Mayflower* had ventured to a territory beyond the domain of the Virginia Company, and so to an area with no legal force, 'it was thought good', wrote Pilgrim William Bradford, that 'there should be an association and agreement that we should combine together.'[7]

***

In the Name of God, Amen.

We whose names are underwritten, the loyal subjects of our dread Sovereign Lord King James, by the Grace of God of Great Britain, France, and Ireland King, Defender of the Faith, etc. Having undertaken, for the Glory of God and advancement of the Christian Faith and Honour of our King and Country, a Voyage to plant the First Colony in Northern Parts of Virginia, do by these present solemnly and mutually in the presence of God and one of another, Covenant and Combine ourselves together into a Civil Body Politic, for our better ordering and preservation and furtherance of the ends aforesaid; and by virtue hereof to enact, constitute and frame such just and equal Laws, Ordinances, Acts, Constitutions and Offices, from time to time, as shall be thought most meet and convenient for the general good of the Colony, unto which we promise all due submission and obedience.

In witness whereof we have hereunder subscribed our names at Cape Cod, the 11th of November, in the year of the reign of our Sovereign Lord King James, of England, France, and Ireland the eighteenth [year of his reign since accession], and of Scotland the fifty-fourth [year of his reign since accession]. Anno Domini 1620.[8]

This agreement, which came to be known as the Mayflower Compact, established a civil government to set up 'equal and just' laws for the common good. It was signed by the forty-one adult males in sufficient health to do so, on behalf of all members of the community. The compact made clear that signatories remained 'loyal subjects' of King James and that they were establishing the new colony in part for the 'Honour of our King and Country'. The separatists were not seeking to completely break from England, but rather their decision to settle in the 'New World' was 'for the Glory of God and advancement of the Christian Faith'.[9] With the agreement signed, Leiden separatist John Carver, who had helped secure funding for the voyage, was elected as the colony's first governor.

Sixteen 'well-armed men' then went ashore to what Yorkshireman William Bradford, one of the original Scrooby congregation, described as 'a hideous and desolate wilderness'.[10] In his history *Of Plymouth Plantation*, Bradford would chronicle their enterprise as an 'Exodus from England to the Promised Land', all part of God's divine plan. The pilgrims' belief that all was preordained fuelled their sense of entitlement towards this new world. As Bradford noted, it was a land 'fruitful and fit for habitation, though devoid of all civilised inhabitants and given over to savages, who range up and down, differing little from the wild beasts themselves'.[11]

Bradford's was one of a number of detailed accounts describing the early years of what would become the Plymouth Colony. Bradford also co-authored with Edward Winslow a narrative of the first thirteen months in the colony. The *Journal of the Pilgrims at Plymouth by certain English adventurers both merchants and others* celebrated the peaceful relations with 'the Indians', and 'when the fruits of the land became plenty'.[12] Winslow would write a sequel covering events up to 1623, which was titled: *Good News from New England*. These works framed the community as a model of morality, civility and true Christianity, and the creation of the colony as an example of divine providence.

Within a few weeks of their arrival, the party of men searched for a suitable site for their plantation amid abandoned villages, which they would soon discover belonged to members of the Wampanoag tribe, who had been wiped out after three epidemics swept across New England between 1614–20. On 11 December 1620, having ventured to the other side of Cape Cod Bay, the party found a site in a defensible position on an estuary, complete with harbour and flowing water; inland they found cornfields left by the indigenous peoples. Days later, the remaining *Mayflower* passengers disembarked and came ashore. Using maps that John Smith had published a few years earlier, the area was identified as 'New Plymouth'. The pilgrims elected to keep it as the name for their new colony, in honour of their final point of departure, Plymouth in Devon. They believed God had cleared the space for them to establish their Christian Commonwealth.

On Christmas Day, the pilgrims began to build a common house to provide temporary shelter, which by the end of January, with severe weather and sickness among many of them, remained unfinished.[13] Like the Jamestown colonists a decade before, the pilgrims' journal describes this first devastating winter as 'the starving time'. By late spring, half the *Mayflower* settlers were dead, mainly from starvation and disease. Among those who died were William Bradford's young wife Dorothy, and the colony's governor John Carver and his wife Katherine.

In March 1621, as the settlers were completing their fortifications, a tall Native American man, described as having long black hair swept back from a shaved forehead, and being almost naked, except for a leather loincloth, walked into the colony. 'He spoke to them in broken English,' recalled Bradford. The man introduced himself as Samoset, a member of the Wabanaki confederacy, from an area referred to as Pemaquid Point (later Maine). Since the turn of the century, English fishermen had made seasonal voyages to the region to take advantage of the significant shoals of cod. In broken English picked up from the fishermen, Samoset explained that 'Plymouth' was in fact Patuxet, a Wampanoag village, and that its people had been wiped out by disease.[14] Samoset told the settlers that Massasoit, the chieftain of the Wampanoag confederacy, lived in Pokanoket, forty miles to the southwest, at the head of Narragansett Bay.

Five days later, Samoset returned with another Native American, Tisquantum, who became known to the settlers as 'Squanto'. He had already had some direct experience of Englishmen, having been taken captive by one Captain Thomas Hunt, a member of John Smith's mission to New England in 1614, who had been left behind with instructions to continue fishing and trading in the area. Hunt, however, with one eye on profiting from the European slave trade, lured some twenty-seven Wampanoag men onto his ship on the promise of trade. He then captured and bound the men and carried them back across the Atlantic to be sold as slaves in Málaga, Spain. Tisquantum later escaped to London where he learned the language, before travelling back to America on a merchant ship.

Tisquantum would become an invaluable member of the Plymouth Colony, teaching the settlers where to hunt and fish, and how to plan and plant crops. He also acted as an interpreter between the English and Massasoit. According to Winslow, Tisquantum translated during negotiations for a treaty of peace and mutual defence between the settlers and the chief of the Wampanoag confederacy.[15] Hopeful that the settlers might be useful allies against the Narragansett, a neighbouring tribe, Chief Massasoit gifted them the land on which they were building their small settlement. In return, the pilgrims gave Massasoit two knives, a copper chain and, as Winslow described, 'the knowledge that king James saluted him as his Friend and Ally'.[16]

That autumn of 1621, aided by Tisquantum and the Wampanoag, the settlers enjoyed a bumper harvest of corn, squash, beans, barley and peas; there was also a plentiful supply of meat in the form of migrating birds such as ducks and geese. Now that they had 'gathered the fruit of our labours', it was time, William Bradford, now governor of the plantation, recorded, to 'rejoice together ... after a more special manner'. Massasoit and around ninety of his people arrived at the settlement with freshly killed deer and a 'good store of wild turkeys', and together with the settlers enjoyed a feast of 'thanksgiving'.[17] It was an occasion that came to be celebrated as America's first 'Thanksgiving'. Eleven months after their arrival at Cape Cod, as Bradford described it, they had found 'the Lord to be with them in all ways, and to bless their outgoings and incomings'.[18]

'The Indians', wrote Winslow, were 'very faithful in their Covenant of Peace with us; very loving and ready to pleasure us', not only 'the greatest' – Massasoit – 'but also all the Princes and peoples round about us' for fifty miles. The Englishman had heard that Corbitant, another *sachem* (chief) of the Wampanoag from as far away as Noepe (about 60 miles away, and now known as Martha's Vineyard), and seven others, like Massasoit, had submitted to King James, 'so that there is now great peace amongst the Indians themselves, which was not formerly, neither would have been but for us'.[19]

***

In May 1621, Captain Jones and his much-depleted crew arrived back in England on the *Mayflower*. On the 6th, they sailed up the Thames, bringing with them news of a new colony named 'Plymouth' but with an empty hold. The harsh winter and illness meant the settlers had not yet began to source the beaver pelts and other supplies upon which the financial success of the colony depended. It was the worst possible outcome for Thomas Weston and the other London merchants who had invested in the enterprise.

Determined to make a return on their money, the consortium hastily organised a second voyage. By June, a small ship, the *Fortune*, was ready to set sail, loaded with thirty-five new settlers, including more members of the Leiden congregation. Among them was Robert Cushman from Kent, who had been the agent in London for the separatists as they prepared for the *Mayflower* voyage. Now he was going to the colony as an overseer, to ensure that the colonists provided the goods the original contract with Weston and the other investors had specified.

Following the *Fortune*'s arrival in Plymouth Bay in late November 1621, Governor Bradford, Cushman and the settlers spent two weeks gathering what they could: beaver skins, sassafras (a genus of tree used for medicinal and culinary purposes) and clapboard. They hoped the haul would go some way to restoring confidence in the financial viability of the settlement and maintain the backing of the consortium. On 13 December, the *Fortune* left again for England with a fully loaded hold, and also a journal detailing the pilgrims' first thirteen months, which was given to Cushman for safekeeping. Known as *Mourt's Relation*, the detailed account went on sale in London in 1622, initially at a shop in Cornhill. This was primarily a publicity piece, aimed at attracting future investment in New England by engaging a reading public who were becoming increasingly interested in the world beyond their shores.

While the manuscript that became *Mourt's Relation* made it back to England, the *Fortune's* cargo did not. During the return voyage, disaster struck. Blown off course in a storm, the ship was intercepted by a French warship off the Vendée coast and taken into port. After thirteen days, the vessel was released but only after the French governor at Ile d'Yeu had seized the ship's cargo, guns and most of its rigging. The *Fortune* limped back to London on 17 February 1622, leaving Cushman to face Weston and the other *Mayflower* investors.

After two successive failures, Thomas Weston had run out of patience with the Plymouth colonists, and his London consortium began to disintegrate. Whilst believing the settlers were no longer worthy of investment, Weston was still convinced that money could be made across the Atlantic and resolved to establish his own colony under a separate patent with a determined focus on exploiting the fur trade. He fitted out another ship, the *Charity*, which together with a smaller fishing vessel, the *Swan*, left Portsmouth loaded with artillery and eighty planters who, by Weston's own admission, were not England's finest – 'many of our people were rude fellows'.[20]

As Weston's men set sail, Robert Cushman wrote to the pilgrims prophetically describing his fears that Master Weston's colonists would not 'deal so well with the savages as they should'. The situation on the ground was complex, and the settlers had found themselves out of their depth, not aware that they were often being used as pawns in power struggles between the Wampanoag confederacy and other tribes. Cushman urged the pilgrims to 'signify to Squanto [Tisquantum] that they are a distinct body from us, and we have nothing to do with them, neither must be blamed for their falls, much less can warrant their fidelity'.[21]

In June 1622, the *Charity* and the *Swan* arrived in Plymouth Bay. The pilgrims initially took in Weston's settlers and provided them with food and accommodation.

***

By late summer. the new planters, all but the sick and infirm, had left Plymouth for Massachusetts Bay, where they chose a site called Wessagusset (now North Weymouth) alongside what became known as Levett's River (now the Fore River in Maine).[22] Unlike New Plymouth, Wessagusset was still inhabited, and the indigenous peoples of the Massachusetts lived close by.

The newcomers quickly proved ill-prepared for the harsh conditions of life in the colony, arriving too late in the year to plant corn, and they soon ran out of victuals. Weston's men began conducting raids on the Massachusetts tribe, stealing their food and provisions. According to one of the new settlers, one Phineas Pratt of London, a member of their group 'turned salvage [sic]', foraging like animals in order to survive, for 'at last most of them left their dwellings and scattered up and down in the woods and by the watersides, where they could find ground nuts and clams, here six and there ten'. Another man, weakened with hunger, became stuck in the mud while searching for shellfish and died there. The rest 'were ready to starve both with cold and hunger also because they could not endure to get victuals by reason of their nakedness' as they had already traded all their clothing to the Indians.[23]

Governor Bradford saw these developments as a salutary lesson: whilst the Puritans' journey to America had been like the biblical crossing of the Red Sea, the fate of the Weston colony was compared to Saint Paul's account in Corinthians – of the sinful Israelites who ignored the law of Moses and turned to idolatry and fornication, suffering death as a result. As conditions and relations with the native peoples at Wessagusset deteriorated, Bradford interpreted all as evidence of God's unswerving justice. It would indeed be His guiding hand that would lead the pilgrims to take the steps that they did. Yet it is also clear from Bradford's account that the raids were antagonising the Indians in such a way that they did not make a distinction between the Wessagusset settlers and the Plymouth pilgrims. It was all just as Robert Cushman had feared.

The situation had not been helped by the sudden death in November 1622 of 'Squanto', the colonists' intermediary, translator, and someone they saw as a friend and ally. According to Bradford, Tisquantum 'fell sick of an Indian fever, bleeding much at the nose (which the Indians take for a symptom of death)', and died within a few days.[24] Months later, when Wampanoag chief Massasoit also fell ill, Winslow, now deputy governor, saw it as an opportunity to win back the trust of the local tribes. According to his own account, he travelled forty miles on foot to Massasoit's village, Sowams, where he fed Massasoit, washed his mouth and scraped his tongue, which was 'exceedingly furred', and then helped to make him a broth. When the chieftain recovered, he rewarded Winslow by reaffirming his commitment to an alliance with the English at Plymouth colony – and warning him of a plot afoot among the Massachusett to launch a mass attack involving a number of other tribes against the fledgling Wessagusset colony.

News of the attack by Powhatans on English settlements in the Virginia colony in March, had already put the Plymouth settlers on their guard and now with Massasoit's warning, they resolved to take no chances and launch a pre-emptive attack against the Massachusett. Miles Standish, who had travelled with the original contingent on the *Mayflower* as the pilgrims' militia leader, and Governor Bradford, apparently came up with the plan. Standish and eight men would sail to Wessagusset on the pretence of a trading mission and kill the chief of the Massachusett. They would then cut off his head and bring it back to the pilgrims to display at Plymouth as a warning to any enemies of the colony. In a letter to his assistant, Isaac Allerton, Bradford explained that there was a sense of moral obligation 'to rescue the lives of our countrymen, whom we thought (both by nature, and conscience) we were bound to deliver', even though it had been the 'evil and deboyst [debased] carriage' of the men at Wessagusset that had 'so exasperated the Indians against them'.[25] They also feared that the Massachusetts now threatened their Plymouth colony as well.

Standish and the raiding party reached Wessagusset on 26 March 1623, and shortly after, when the Massachusetts chief Wittawamut and his leading warrior Pecksuot arrived, he persuaded them to come to a house to discuss a possible peace. Standish proceeded to stab both Pecksuot and Wittawamut to death, and then hanged Wittawamut's brother from a tree. In total seven men of the Massachusetts tribe were killed.

Standish returned to Plymouth colony to a hero's welcome, bearing the head of one of the warriors wrapped in cloth, which was then placed on a pole on top of the newly completed roof of the colony's fort.[26] The pilgrims had delivered their message in an act of divine providence.

In a letter dated six months after the event to the project's investors in London, Bradford and Allerton wrote: 'We kil[le]d seven of the chief of them, and the head of one of them stands still on our fort for a terror unto others.' It was, they claimed, 'by the good providence of God' that the Indians' 'wickedness came upon their own pate [heads].[27] In his *Good News from New England*, Winslow claimed that God had secured 'our preservation from so many dangerous plots and treacheries, as have been intended against us.'[28]

However, away from the colony some of the original Leiden congregation struggled to fully reconcile Standish's actions at Wessagussett with their religious beliefs. In a letter of December 1623 to Governor Bradford, Pastor John Robinson, a separatist leader still living in exile in Leiden, referred to 'the killing of those poor Indians', and said he wished Standish had converted them to Christianity rather than murder them without evidence of their wrongdoing. Although the Indians may have 'deserved it', the pastor continued, he believed they had been provoked by 'those heathenish Christians' (Weston's men). It was obvious to Robinson that the pilgrims had intended to establish their superiority over the Indians through the murder of Wittawamut and his men, and he admonished them for such worldly motivations, reflecting: 'It is ... a thing more glorious, in men's eyes, than pleasing in God's or convenient for Christians, to be a terror to poor barbarous people.' Furthermore, Robinson cautioned, 'where blood is once begun to be shed, it is seldom staunched of a long time after ... And indeed I am afraid lest, by these occasions, others should be drawn to affect a kind of ruffling course in the world.'[29] In other words, once the spilling of blood had started, it would be difficult to stop.

London lawyer Thomas Morton, who had arrived in New England as a settler in 1624, was more outspoken. In his *New English Canaan*, published in Amsterdam in 1637, he criticised the pilgrims' treatment of native peoples as the 'new creed of Canaan' [the 'Promised Land'], in which 'the savages were seen as a 'dangerous people, subtle, secret and mischievous' and that violent action against them was therefore justified.[30] The Indians' name for the English, he added, was now *Wotawquenangem* – 'cut-throats'.[31]

24

The Powhatan Uprising

'For many do inform me, your coming is not for trade, but to invade my people and possess my Country.'

Powhatan (Wahunsonacock) to John Smith, 1609[1]

At Jamestown, Virginia, about 400 miles south of Plymouth colony, the arrival of George Yeardley as governor (in 1619), the successful visit to London of new Christian convert, the 'Lady Rebecca' (Pocahontas), and the fundraising efforts to build a school to educate the 'Barbarians in Virginia', had brought a new sense of optimism to the colony. There was hope that the native peoples might indeed be converted to the Christian faith and the colony made profitable. Funds continued to flow from Britain and relations between the settlers and the Indians appeared cordial. According to the observations of Sir Francis Wyatt, who became governor in 1621, much of this was due to the efforts of Yeardley and colonist George Thorpe, with 'the houses generally set open to the Savages, who were always friendly entertained at the tables of the English, and commonly lodged in their bed-chambers'.[2] The 'peace of Pocahontas' ending the first Anglo-Powhatan war had held for eight years. All in all, prospects seemed bright.

But on the morning of 22 March 1622, more than 500 men of the Powhatan confederacy launched a surprise attack against English settlements along the James River. A number of Indians had come into the settlers' homes to trade, socialise and share a meal, as had become the custom. Survivor accounts describe how the warriors suddenly drew knives and weapons concealed in their clothing and attacked every man, woman and child they could.[3] By noon, 347 settlers from the settlements around Jamestown, a third of the colony's population, lay dead. Many of the corpses were defaced and dismembered, cut 'into many pieces' with 'some parts' carried away.[4] Twenty women were taken prisoner, and an unknown number of Powhatan warriors killed.

On 18 April, a month before the news of the attack reached London, members of the Virginia Company filed into St Mary-le-Bow Church in the City of London for a special service of thanksgiving. Reverend Patrick Copland, the company's chaplain, preached a sermon celebrating all that the Virginia plantations had achieved.[5] It had now begun to overcome its dependence on tobacco as a cash crop and would soon produce an abundance of: 'Corn, Wine, Oil, Lemons, Oranges, Pomegranates, and all manner of fruits pleasant to the eye and wholesome for the belly', as well as silk, flax, hemp, cotton wool, iron and copper. Within a few years, Copland predicted, company investors could hope for a return of 'double, treble, yea, I may say of tenfold for one'. Virginia could provide nearly everything that he had 'heard and seen abroad in my travelling to India and Japan' and 'that the most opulent parts of Christendom do afford.'[6]

But of greater importance for Copland was evidence in the colony of the most 'wonderful works of the Lord', the 'happy league of Peace and Amity fondly concluded and faithfully kept, between the English and the Natives'. Hostility and conflict were hazards of the past. Virginia's native populations who 'seem to groan under the burden of the bondage of Satan ... want nothing but means to be delivered'. Opechancanough, who succeeded his brother Powhatan as chieftain, Copland continued, had 'willingly acknowledged that theirs was not the right way, desiring to be instructed in ours'.[7] It would prove to be an arrogant and fateful misjudgement.

The years immediately after the Virginia Company brought Pocahontas and her English husband John Rolfe to London, had seen not only peaceful relations, but rapid expansion in the colony. Efforts to convert the native populations had given way to a relentless pursuit of profit. As early as 1616, Rolfe, who had planted the first tobacco crop in Virginia, wrote that it was 'much to be mourned and lamented, how lightly the works of God are nowadays generally regarded, and less sought after: but the works of the World ... hungered for and thirsted after with unsatiable greediness'.[8] By 1620, the 'planting and providing of Corn [was] so utterly neglected that the dearth grew excessive', and the colonists 'reduced themselves into an extremity of being ready to starve'.[9] Large-scale tobacco production and King James's campaign to develop silk production had an even more detrimental impact upon the native populations, with more plantations being set up along the fertile banks of the James River and a 'daily fear' that the English would push them off their lands altogether, much as the Spanish had done to the native peoples of the West Indies.[10]

George Thorpe, MP for Portsmouth, landowner, a significant investor in the Virginia Company, and a man heavily involved in the king's silkworm project, arrived in Virginia in 1620. He had been appointed to serve as deputy of 11,000 acres of land, located on the north bank of the James River, which had been set aside for a university and an 'Indian school'.[11] Unlike many of the British settlers, Thorpe seemed genuinely committed to fostering better relations with the native population. As he described with dismay in a letter to company treasurer Sir Edwin Sandys in May 1621: 'There is scarce any man amongst us, that doeth so much as afford them a good thought in his heart, and most men w[i]th their mouths give them nothing but maledictions and bitter execrations ... if there be wrong on any side it is on ours.'[12]

Thorpe regarded the Powhatan as being 'of a peaceable and virtuous disposition' and believed that they could be 'brought round' by kindness and compassion. He punished those under his command for mistreating local peoples and, as a gesture of his commitment to peace, had some English mastiff dogs killed because they 'frightened the Indians'.[13] He promised the Powhatan that all the English comforts and material goods could be theirs if they would just accept the Christian God, and asserted to Sandys that, once the Powhatan had been won over by the 'book of the world', they would more readily embrace the spiritual book of 'the Word'.[14] Thorpe gave Opechancanough a number of gifts and built an English-style house for him, with a locking front door, which according to settler accounts, intrigued local tribesmen who opened and closed it a hundred times a day.[15] In an attempt to foster better relations, Thorpe urged the Virginia Company, 'to make some public declaration of their intent and desire of the conversion of this people and ... a testification of their love and hearty affection towards them ... thereby to mollify the minds of our people'.[16]

Thorpe's advice seems to have been taken on board back in London, for when the new governor Francis Wyatt arrived in Virginia in November 1621, his instructions were to 'have espe-cial care that no injury or oppression be wrought by the English against any of the natives of that country whereby the present peace may be disturbed, and ancient quarrels (now buried) might be revived'.[17] The colonists were told to procure Powhatan children 'by just means' for education and conversion, the most capable of whom were to be schooled for the 'Indian college'. In addition, the 'better disposed' of the Powhatan adults were to be given suitable rewards 'to converse with our people and labour amongst them ... that thereby they may grow to a liking and love of civility and finally be brought to the knowledge and love of God and true religion'.[18] The company directors hoped to remove 'all matter of scandal and reproach' that had been caused by the 'great neglect and remissness in the Governors of Virginia, from time to time (to the infinite prej-udice of that Plantation)'.[19] The company wanted Wyatt to promote the cohabitation of 'Indian and English families' – 'as being a great means to reduce that Nation to Civility and to the embracing of our Christian religion'.[20]

By the time Wyatt arrived in the colony Thorpe's peaceful conversion of the Powhatan seemed to be bearing fruit. When Thorpe met with Opechancanough to present greetings from the new governor, the Powhatan chief received him warmly and promised to conclude agreements with Wyatt on defence and exploration. He 'gave the English leave to seat themselves anywhere on his Rivers where the Natives ... [were] not actually seated'.[21] To Thorpe's astonishment, Opechancanough who had previously appeared intransigent, now seemed open to conversion: he 'willingly acknowledged that theirs [the Powhatan's religion] was not the right way, desiring to be instructed in ours and confessed that God loved us better than them'.[22] The chief said he would now permit his people to live among the colonists, and for English families to live in his settlements.[23]

And so, in his sermon to the company grandees at Cheapside, London, in April 1622, Reverend Copland proudly announced: 'there is no Danger ... either through wars, or famine, or want of convenient lodging'. For, he continued, 'blessed be God, there hath been a long time, and still is, a happy league of Peace and, Amity soundly concluded, and faithfully kept, between the English and the Natives, that the fear of killing each other is now vanished away'.[24]

It was not to be.

***

When Opechancanough became Powhatan chief, following his brother Wahunsonacock's death in 1618, 'the King of these Savages', as Edward Waterhouse, secretary to the Virginia Company in London later described him, had begun to plot a path of revenge.[25] Opechancanough was determined to finally stem the tide of encroachment on his people's tribal lands and to end the period of peaceful cooperation that had followed the marriage of Pocahontas and John Rolfe. Building new friendships with settlers, giving them gifts of fish and fowl, visiting them in their homes, all appears to have been part of a ruse designed to give the colonists a false sense of safety. As part of this, Opechancanough declared an interest in Christianity, even suggesting that the Christian 'God was a good God', much better than his own.[26]

By 1622, Opechancanough's mask of compliance had so relaxed security on the ground that settlers had begun teaching native peoples in the use of firearms, previously a capital offence. On the eve of the attack, there was no hint of concern, with Wyatt reporting to the Virginia Company directors that all was well.[27] Then the Powhatan launched their assault. Among those killed was George Thorpe. According to John Smith, his corpse had been abused 'with such spite and scorn ... as is unfitting to be heard with civil ears'.[28]

Wyatt wrote to London with news of the 'massacre'. The Powhatan had, 'under the Colour of unsuspected amity', attempted 'to have swept us away throughout the whole land had it not pleased God of his abundant mercy to prevent them in many places'. With no suggestion that the settlement should be abandoned, the governor requested resupply for the colonists, weapons to defend against further attacks and food.[29] The letter arrived in London in late June, and the company prepared their response.

In a report – *A Declaration of the State of the Colonie and Affaires in Virginia, With a Relation of the barbarous Massacre* – which was swiftly published and widely disseminated, company secretary Edward Waterhouse narrated the incident. His description of the various ways that vengeance might be wrought on the native populations was detailed and uncompromising. They were 'perfidious and inhumane people' who had acted 'contrary to all laws of God and men, of Nature & Nations'. Now, the colonists might justifiably seek retribution. 'Our hands, which before ... were tied with gentleness and fair usage, are now set at liberty by the treacherous violence of the Savages.' The settlers could by 'Right of War, and law of Nations' now invade the country and 'destroy them who sought to destroy us', to seize towns and land, and to kill without mercy.[30] The Powhatan could be attacked 'by force, by surprise, by famine in burning their Corn, by destroying and burning their Boats, Canoes, and Houses, by breaking their fishing Wares, by assailing them in their huntings', and 'by pursuing and chasing them with our horses, and blood-Hounds to draw after them, and Mastiffs to tear them'. Only children were to be spared. The Powhatan attack, it was claimed, would in the end prove to be a great advantage to the colony – liberating the British from efforts at amity, enabling them to 'kill Indians' with impunity, to seize their lands and compel them to 'servitude and drudgery'.[31]

Waterhouse's tract also called on King James to be more interventionist – to be more like the Spanish king in the West Indies and see 'the Plantation of this his lawful and rightful kingdom of VIRGINIA' as a fourth realm which he should govern in the same way as made him the 'absolute king of three of the most populous kingdoms'.[32] In other words, James needed to act as the King of Virginia.

***

On 13 November 1622, the poet John Donne – now the king's chaplain and Dean of St Paul's – preached the Virginia Company's annual sermon at St Michael's, Cornhill, in the City of London.[33] His words contrasted sharply with those of Copland just seven months before. While Copland had believed Virginia's native peoples were eager for instruction in the Christian faith, Donne now denounced them as pagans who enthusiastically and unrepentantly took delight in deceit, treachery and violence.[34] A 'flood of blood', had broken over Virginia, he said.[35] Donne exhorted that the company not to be put off by such adversities. He called upon investors to abandon their drive for profit and instead embrace a new vision 'to gain souls to the glory of God.'[36]

However, Donne's call for a renewed mission was drowned out by a chorus of incensed voices, outraged by the 'massacre' in Virginia and calling for retribution. The earlier view that the native populations were 'redeemable' was replaced by a belief that they were irretrievably debased. Plans for the Indian college were shelved, and voices such as Donne's for the wholesale conversion of Native Americans were ignored. England's leading champion of 'imperial Christianity', Samuel Purchas, joined the verbal onslaught. They 'be not worthy of the name of a Nation', Purchas proclaimed, 'being wild and Savage: yet as Slaves, bordering rebels, excommunicates and outlaws are liable to the punishments of Law, and not to the privileges'. The massacre, he believed, 'hath now confiscated whatsoever remainders of right the unnatural Naturals had and made both them and their Country wholly English'. While Purchas did not abandon all hope of conversion, he recognised the small chance of success of 'so bad a people, having little of Humanity but shape, ignorant of Civility, of Arts, of Religion; more brutish than the beasts they hunt'.[37]

It was all in sharp contrast to how the project started, as described thirteen years earlier by Robert Johnson – a man who, as alderman, chaplain to the Bishop of Lincoln, member of the Virginia company, and son-in-law of company powerhouse Sir Thomas Smythe, perfectly represented the commerce, business, Godly purpose, and territorial expansion of James's Britain. Articulating the king's vision, Johnson's *Nova Britannia* had boasted that, unlike the Spanish, Britain would gain a foothold in the New World not with swords and muskets, but through 'fair and loving means fitting to our English natures'. Now, coexistence and conversion were to be replaced by conquest and subjection. It was to be 'a perpetual war without peace or truce'.[38]

The company gathered weapons and supplies to send to Virginia, and James donated arms and ammunition from the Tower of London, which were found to be 'altogether unfit, and of no use for modern service'.[39] Governor Wyatt saw his task starkly: The 'expulsion of the Savages' by any means. 'For it is infinitely better,' he added, 'to have no heathen among us, who at best were but as thorns in our sides, then to be at peace and league with them.'[40]

Armed settlers set out to destroy every vestige of Powhatan presence in the areas between the James and York Rivers and beyond. By January 1623, the Virginia Council wrote victoriously that 'by Computation and Confession of the Indians themselves, we have slain more of them this year, then hath been slain before since the beginning of the Colony'.[41] When Opechancanough eluded all attempts to capture him, the settlers invited him to a sham peace parley, where they planned to poison him. But he managed to escape once more.

News of the failed poisoning caused disquiet among company members in London; while the Indians must be defeated, they agreed, it should be by 'honorable' means. Yet the colonists insisted on a free hand: 'Whereas we are advised by you to observe rules of Justice with these barbarous and perfidious enemies,' the council in Virginia responded, 'we hold nothing unjust, that may tend to their ruin, (except breach of faith). Stratagems were ever allowed against all enemies, but with these neither fair war nor good quarter is ever to be held, nor is there other hope of their subversion, whoever may inform you to the contrary.'[42]

***

By the winter of 1622–3, those planters hastily recruited to repopulate the colony in the aftermath of the Powhatan attack, found scenes of abject desperation, as famine and disease ravaged the settlements. Letters from the colony rang with plaintive pleas for deliverance. Sir Edwin Sandys's brother wrote that since the massacre, a 'general sickness' had taken almost five hundred lives, 'and not many of the rest have not knocked at the doors of death'. Virginia colonist Samuel Sharp declared: 'The Lord's hand hath been more heavy by sickness & death then by the sword of our Enemies.' Settler William Rowsley described how the colony had, 'felt the affliction of War, sense of sickness and death of a great number of men, likewise among the cattle for dog have eaten in this winter more flesh than the men'.[43] A year later, a report from Virginia noted that only 1,275 people occupied the colony, a fraction of the approximately 6,000 Britons who had migrated to the colony over the past seventeen years.[44]

On James's instruction, the Privy Council ordered an investigation into the conditions in the colony and the Virginia company's management thereof, and 'all wrongs and injuries done to any of the Adventurers and Planters'. Privy Councillors were ordered to travel to Virginia and confiscate company papers by force; the commissioners were also 'to examine whether all that have gone to the plantations have taken the Oath of Supremacy' as the 1609 charter had demanded.[45]

A review of the company's records in London and in the colony, quickly discovered that the Virginia Company was bankrupt and had been hopelessly mismanaged for years. Radical change and royal intervention were required.

To James, as to many observers, the company had proven itself incapable of proper government without his direct leadership. Yet Sandys, treasurer of the company, was accurate when he wrote that if the king disapproved of the company's governance, James would need to change its joint-stock system and the Crown take on more direct management.

Now with the colony's very survival threatened, the king finally intervened and 'reserved of the whole cause to his own hearing'.[46] As diplomat Francis Nethersole reported to Dudley Carleton in The Hague: 'There is a Commission of Privy Counsellors and others appointed to advise upon a fit Patent to be given to the Company of Virginia ... [at] last being overthrown. The Reformation intended as I hear is that there shall be a Company for trade, but not for Government of the Country' – of which his Majesty "will take care".'[47]

On 24 May 1624, James revoked the company's charter and took over Virginia as a royal colony. After fifteen years of relative freedom for the Virginia Company in managing overseas affairs, with successive charters granting the corporation increasing power, the king now *asserted* sovereignty over his subjects, wherever they were in the world. Colonisation, 'this worthy action reserved by the

Divine providence', was to 'be perfected and consummate by his Royal hands'.[48] Now, for the first time, the Crown would take direct responsibility for overseas colonies and their subjects.

One casualty of the Powhatan raid, which was doubtless a great sadness to James, was silk production. On 27 March 1622, the king had been heartened by reports from Virginia that the planters' efforts were yielding results, with their hopes 'now greater than ever [of] a flourishing country in a short time with that rich Commodity of Silk'. Yet unbeknown to James, all had been destroyed in the days before. The attacks devastated the plantations. As John Pory in Virginia put it: 'Having made these preparations, and the silkworms ready to be covered [that is, making their cocoons], all was lost, but my poor life and children, by the Massacre.'[49]

The only industry to survive the attack of 22 March was tobacco. James's hostility towards tobacco cultivation had been implacable, but now, as all else disintegrated in the colony, his position changed. With money to be made, James now created a royal monopoly for the crop. Whilst he maintained tobacco use 'tend[s] to the corruption both of the health and manners of Our people', he now supported it as a source of crown revenue. In a 'Proclamation on Tobacco of 1624', James banned the import and use of all tobacco (that is, Spanish tobacco) 'which is not of the proper growth of Our Colonies of Virginia and the Somers Islands [Bermuda]'. As the proclamation continued, to support, encourage, 'cherish and protect' the prosperity of these colonies, the Crown was 'contented to tolerate the use of Tobacco, of the growth of those Plantations for a time, until by more solid Commodities they be able to subsist otherwise'.[50] Principle for James might always be sacrificed for pragmatism, especially when it affected crown revenues.

'These Plantations, though furthered much by your Majesty's grace,' Sandys pointed out, were not upheld by the king's purse but by private adventurers who would naturally fail to take interest in 'the regulating and governing of their own business [if] their own votes had been excluded'.[51] It was a shrewd observation, as in other aspects of his foreign policy, James sought to extend Britain's reach and his own authority and reputation. In 1625, the *Discourse of the Old Company*, a tract written by members of the dissolved Virginia Company, whilst seeking to justify the colony's failure, acknowledged that Virginia's best hope for survival now rested in the king's direct control through which the colony 'might be annexed to the impartial Crown of this Realm'.[52]

Despite James's persistent belief in a monarch's divine right and absolute authority, the Virginia Company had not, in its early stages, been a domain where the king had sought to impose his authority with any real force. The early 1620s were a watershed, with the Crown recognising for the first time that it had certain responsibilities towards its colonies overseas.[53]

Part Three

25

Christendom on Fire

'This business in Bohemia is like[ly] to put all Christendom
in combustion.'

Sir Dudley Carleton, *British ambassador in The Hague*, 1619[1]

As violence erupted in parts of the world where Britain was trying to assert its identity and sense of purpose, so too in Europe,
during the final decade of James's reign, peace was increasingly
under threat and with it, James's vision for a reunited Christendom.

In 1619 a war of religion broke out in central Europe that would
last for thirty years seeding deep divisions in countries and communities and leading to the estimated deaths of between five and eight
million soldiers and civilians. It was exactly what James, through his
mediation, his calls for a general council of the church, and his mar-
ital diplomacy had always sought to avoid. Not only did it expose
the failings of James as self-styled European peacemaker but, with
humiliating irony, it was the actions of his son-in-law Frederick,
Elector Palatine, in 'usurping' the throne of Bohemia, that triggered
the war. The conflict between the Catholic League, led by Spain,
and the Union of Protestant German states, supported by the Dutch
and the British, would ultimately see Frederick evicted from the
Palatinate, his ancestral lands.

Amid calls for James to intervene militarily both to protect
Protestantism and to come to the aid of his daughter Elizabeth

and her husband, the king sought to apply the policy he had pursued throughout his reign: mediate and secure peace whilst, given the country's lack of funds for war, limit direct military action. It had been James' approach when called upon to intervene militarily in the Jülich-Cleves succession crisis, nine years earlier. But with Frederick's lands (and the inheritance of James's grandchildren) at stake, it would be tested as never before, with James adopting counterposing strategies in a desperate attempt to create balance and stability and to restore peace to the Palatinate. As British volunteer forces fought against the Austrian and Spanish Habsburgs in the Palatinate, James pushed ahead with negotiations for a marriage treaty involving Prince Charles and the Spanish infanta, Maria. It was a policy that would pit the king against Parliament, many of his Privy Councillors, his children and subjects in all of his kingdoms. The stakes could not have been higher.

As crisis erupted in Europe, a panegyric was published in London celebrating King James's achievements as a conciliator and seeking to generate support for the king's peace-making efforts. *The Peacemaker, or Great Brittaines Blessing*, written largely by Lancelot Andrews with some additions from the king himself, was 'fram'd for the continuance of mighty happiness', seeking to show 'the idleness of a quarrelling reputation wherein consists neither manhood nor wisdom', and therein to avoid 'blood-shedding'. The work was dedicated 'to all our true loving and peace-embracing subjects' and observed that England and Scotland had been reconciled in 'their loving Union', and that Ireland, 'that rebellious Outlaw', had been brought to heel. Spain, 'that great and long-lasting opposite, betwixt whom and England, the Ocean ran with blood not many years before', had shaken hands 'in friendly amity'. Between Spain and her 'with-standing Provinces' in the Netherlands, 'leagues of friendship' had been established. Other disputes had also been happily resolved: Denmark and Sweden, Sweden and Poland, Cleves and Brandenburg.[2] In the light of this considerable experience, James's first reaction to war in central Europe was to attempt negotiation.

In the same year, Paul van Somer's life-size portrait of James I, commissioned by the king himself, depicts him standing next to his crown, orb and sceptre. Around his neck the king has a plate metal gorget, a movable piece of armour that covered the throat; the rest of the suit is stacked at his feet. The mounting threat of continental events had meant that *Rex Pacificus* had been forced to don a gorget. With his armour adjacent to him, the message was clear: if necessity demanded it, James would go to war.

***

In the spring of 1618, three Catholic officials were thrown from a top-floor window of Prague Castle in Bohemia (now the Czech Republic) by an angry mob of Protestant rebels, in an act that came to be described as the 'defenestration of Prague'. It marked the beginning of a revolt of the Protestant nobility of Bohemia against their new, staunchly Catholic king, the Habsburg Archduke Ferdinand of Austria, cousin to King Philip III of Spain.

James immediately sought to mediate a peaceful settlement. On 27 September 1618, Francis Cottington, the English envoy in Spain, had an audience with Philip III. As Cottington explained to the Spanish king, such was James's 'respect to the general peace and quiet of Christendom and to the perfect friendship and brotherly amity' between Philip and himself, that 'he was resolved to use his utmost endeavours and to interpose his best credit and authority for compounding the difference' between the two parties. While the king of Spain insisted that the Bohemians' actions were 'without ground' and clearly amounted to an act of rebellion, he acknowledged 'that the King of Great Britain did every way give good demonstrations of his affection to the peace and quiet of Christendom' and would support him to 'interpose himself for the accommodating of the business of Bohemia'.[3]

In spring of 1619, an embassy of 150 people led by the Scotsman James Hay, now Viscount Doncaster, was sent to Germany to open negotiations with both parties for a peaceful settlement. Neither the

Bohemian rebels nor Ferdinand II, King of Bohemia, were prepared to accept the king's mediation and Doncaster returned home having made no progress. Ferdinand thought 'his Ma[jesty] of Great Britain was not well informed how the Bohemians his subjects had behaved themselves toward him'.⁴ Just weeks later, James was to be left in no doubt, and in the most dramatic and ironic manner. On 26 August, Ferdinand II was deposed and the Bohemian Crown offered to Frederick, Elector Palatine, James's twenty-two-year-old son-in-law.

Europe held its breath. Frederick's acceptance of the Bohemian Crown would mean the deposition of a legitimate monarch, King Ferdinand, who had also just been elected Holy Roman Emperor following the death of the last emperor, Matthias, in late March. It would inevitably lead to an invasion of Frederick's own territory, the Palatinate, and ignite – in the words of James's envoy in Brussels, William Trumbull – 'a cruel, and an almost eternal war' in Christendom, pitting the Austrian and Spanish Habsburgs against the Protestant states of Europe.⁵

As Frederick considered the Bohemian estates' offer, his envoy arrived in London with letters from Elizabeth as Electress Palatinate seeking advice and support both from her father and her brother Charles, and from George Villiers, Marquess of Buckingham, now her father's closest companion – who besides being rumoured to share the king's bed, was now the most influential figure in government. Elizabeth urged Buckingham to use his 'best means in persuading his Majestie to show himself, now in his helping of the Prince here, a true loving father to us both'.⁶

It would have been doubtless a great source of pain that, at a time when she needed the help of her family most, Elizabeth could not write a letter to her mother. Queen Anna had passed away just months earlier, on 2 March 1619, after several years of failing health, which the royal physician had diagnosed variously as being caused by gynaecological problems, an ulcerated leg, and gout. She died at Hampton Court of consumption and dropsy, aged forty-four. James was at Theobalds when she died, then unwell himself.

Indeed, in the last years of their marriage, not least as James became distracted by Buckingham, husband and wife had grown apart. However, James had always respected Anna as his queen and cherished the Danish alliance that she had brought. Indeed, on the day of her death, the king wasted no time in writing to Anna's brother, Christian IV. Whilst praising his wife's 'keen judgment' and 'sharp senses' and lamenting the long illness she had suffered, he reassured Christian that 'the intimacy of our future affairs might continue as long as it seems too good to the one who dispenses lifetimes to kingdoms'.[7] James acknowledged the significant role that Anna had played in strengthening the dynasty and stressed that her death should not signal the end of the Stuart–Oldenburg alliance.

One of Anna's last acts had been pleading for her husband's mercy for Sir Walter Ralegh. Two years before, Ralegh had convinced James to release him from the Tower on the promise that he would enrich the crown by finally finding the gold of the fabled city of El Dorado. Despite express orders to respect the peace with Spain, Ralegh's son Wat, who had accompanied him on the voyage, led an attack against the Spanish at San Thomé on the Orinoco River in South America. On his return to London Ralegh was tried and sentenced to death. Grateful to Ralegh for his friendship with her son Prince Henry and for the medical remedies he had sent as Henry lay dying, Anna begged that his life 'may not be called into question'.[8] Her pleadings had no effect, Pressed by the Spanish ambassador Diego Sarmiento de Acuña, Count of Gondomar, James was determined to grant no reprieve. Ralegh was executed on the morning of 29 October 1618, at Westminster.

Anna's spectacularly lavish (and expensive) funeral was used by James, like so many other ceremonial occasions during his reign, with a European audience in mind. Now, with war on the continent, James took the opportunity presented by his wife's funeral to remind Catholic Europe of Anna of Denmark's Protestant kinship with many German princes, and the diplomatic and dynastic strength of the Stuart monarchy whether as ally or foe.[9] James had his motto '*Beati pacifici*' (Blessed are the peacemakers) repeated across his wife's catafalque, taking the opportunity to once again broadcast his desire for peace in Europe.[10]

Anna's passing doubtless added to James own sense of vulnerability and mortality particularly as, shortly after her death, his health suddenly deteriorated. He was suffering from a 'shrewd fit of the [kidney] stone', diarrhoea and arthritis. Many thought he was dying. When his health improved, Chamberlain reflected: 'Men apprehend what a loss we should have if God should take him from us and do earnestly inquire and in general heartily wish and pray for his safety.'[11]

***

At the end of September 1619, Frederick V of the Palatinate accepted the Bohemian Crown, upending James's dynastic diplomacy and efforts for peace in the most spectacular fashion. The king of Great Britain was now drawn into the heart of the conflict. Frederick had accepted the crown after making it known that he'd been seeking his father-in-law's advice, and James now feared that his own integrity had been impugned. As James confided in Doncaster, 'Since not the least blemish or stain', must be suspected, the 'first care must be to vindicate and to clear' his actions and ensure there was no suggestion he had supported Frederick's actions. James hoped he would not be thought capable of 'so unworthy a deed, as publicly to profess mediation of peace between a king and his subjects' while secretly conspiring to depose a legitimate ruler.[12] A belief in divine right monarchy that precluded such acts was exactly what his many writings against the 'assumed' powers of the 'papal Antichrist' had argued against.

The stance James chose to take as king meant effectively abandoning his daughter. He refused to recognise Frederick as King of Bohemia, forbade the clergy from offering prayers for Frederick and Elizabeth and their new kingdom, and banned any celebratory bonfires or bell-ringing in London.[13] He assured Phillip of Spain that he felt nothing but abhorrence for his son-in-law's actions, describing Frederick to Ambassador Gondomar as a 'Godless man and a usurper.' James added: 'The Princes of the Union want my help, but I give you my word, they shall not have it.'[14]

Yet James had by now a reputation, not just as a peacemaker but so too as a dissembler. Gondomar believed James was keeping his options open: if Frederick succeeded in Germany and defeated the Habsburgs, he would abandon the Spanish match for Prince Charles; if not he would continue to mediate and seek restitution of the Palatinate as part of the agreement for a Spanish marriage alliance.[15] Batta van Male, the Flemish envoy in London, took it 'as an infallible maxim that this king governs himself in these affairs with much artifice', believing, as did many, that what James said about the matter of the restitution of the Palatinate could not be believed, that 'words are no deeds'.[16]

Certainly, James's assurance to Gondomar is difficult to reconcile with the steps that he did ultimately take, and whilst the king refused to publicly acknowledge Frederick's accession to the Bohemian Crown, he could not ignore the threat now posed to Frederick's territories in the Palatinate and the serious consequences for James's grandchildren: five-year-old Fredrick Henry, Charles Louis, then two, Elisabeth, just one, and Prince Rupert, born in Prague just a month after his parents' coronation as king and queen of Bohemia.

Indeed, for many in Britain, Frederick and Elizabeth were the heroic standard-bearers of the Protestant cause, inheritors of the late Prince Henry's mantle. In his 1619 tract *Messiah Already Come*, John Harrison, a former member of the prince's household, described Frederick 'as the chief bulwark of the Christian religion', the prince to defeat the Antichrist and unite the church.[17] And on 12 September, George Abbot, Archbishop of Canterbury, wrote to Robert Naunton, secretary of state, sending his apologies for absence ahead of the next Privy Council meeting, and making plain his views on the European situation, which he wished to be relayed to his fellow Privy Councillors. He urged intervention and support for Frederick, a prince whom God had chosen 'to be a mark of honour thro' all

Christendom, to propagate his gospel, and to protect the oppressed'. Therefore, he urged, 'with all the spirits you have put life into this business and let a return be made into *Germany* with speed, and with comfort, and let it really be prosecuted, that it may appear to the World that we are awake when God in this sort calleth us.'[18]

And so emerged a situation whereby James sought to appease the Spanish, and attempted to mediate a settlement, whilst also taking steps to support Frederick militarily.

In April 1620, James sent Sir Robert Anstruther to his brother-in-law's Danish court to try and raise money for Frederick. Christian somewhat reluctantly agreed to loan James £100,000 (with a yearly interest charge of £6,000).[19] These were funds, James insisted, to promote peace not war.[20] As he wrote to Christian in early June, no money should be used 'to support a war in Bohemia but only to protect our son-in-law's inherited lands in the Palatinate, and our grandson's [Frederick Henry] there ... for we do not want to commit ourselves to do anything by which we may be rendered useless for the purpose of conciliating peace in some ways between the parties'.[21]

In March, James allowed George Abbot to permit the clergy to collect a voluntary contribution for Frederick, albeit with the instruction that the conflict should not be represented 'as one of religion, which would stir up Europe'.[22] At the same time the king gave permission to Scottish mercenary leader Sir Andrew Gray to levy 2,000 foot soldiers, an equal split of Scotsmen and English in what would be a deliberately 'British' force. Gray was, as James initially specified, to do so quietly and not to 'beat the drum'.[23] The restriction did not last long: soon drums were beating in London on the very day that the Spanish ambassador returned to London, as Gondomar swiftly reported to Phillip III. In Scotland, orders were issued to those who had enrolled to fight, to assemble in Edinburgh, and by July 1620 Gray and his British force had arrived in Lusatia.[24] One anonymous observer described Gray's 'Britons' as being 'so well governed and so good discipline amongst them, they are praised by all men above other nations that are there'.[25]

In *An English-Mans Love to Bohemia*, printed in London in 1620 and dedicated to Gray, John Taylor, Thames waterman and self-proclaimed 'Water Poet', describes an emerging 'British' national unity which was based on support for Frederick and Elizabeth. The Scottish and the English – 'true borne Britain's worthy countrymen' – came together in their determination to 'emblaze their worth' in the war; the two parts of the joined polity spur each other to greater things: 'I know your valiant minds are sharp and keen/To serve your Sovereigns daughter, Bohem[ia]s Queene', and in that they were united.[26]

Gray's force was recognised as the first 'British' regiment to march and fight united under the new Union flag.

***

On 30 August 1620, 25,000 Spanish troops led by General Ambrogio Spinola entered Frederick's lands in the Lower Palatinate and advanced rapidly towards Heidelberg. It was exactly what James had feared. The territories of his son-in law had been invaded, and he would now have to respond. Writing from Prague on 15 September, Elizabeth urged Buckingham to appeal to her father to abandon his efforts to negotiate, to commit to decisive military action and to 'show himself a loving father to us, and not suffer his children's inheritance to be taken away'. The enemy, she added, 'will more regard his blows than his words'.[27]

The anger felt in London was palpable. As the Venetian ambassador Girolamo Londo reported: the 'whole court is boiling over with rage at the news' of the Spanish invasion.[28] There were now very real fears that European Protestantism was in danger of being crushed by a revitalised Catholic advance. That James continued to negotiate for a Spanish match seemed beyond comprehension and something his ambassadors found impossible to justify. Writing from Brussels in October, William Trumbull described how he was 'looked upon like an owl [and] interrogated upon such terms' that he 'dare not appear in the street'.[29]

Anti-Spanish demonstrations were staged in London and preachers and pamphleteers raged against the Spanish. Thomas Scott's
satirical account, *Vox Populi, or Newes from Spayne*, first printed
anonymously in mid-November 1620, gave a scathing account
of royal inaction and Spanish manipulation, claiming the Spanish
sought a universal monarchy and universal church, 'to get the whole
possession of the world'.[30] While King James 'extremely hunts after
peace', and 'so affects the true name of a Peacemaker, as that for it he
will do or suffer any thing', the Spanish deceived him.[31]

When James became aware of the pamphlet, he reacted furi-
ously, believing it could seriously damage his diplomatic relations
with Spain. Simonds D'Ewes, diarist and antiquarian, noted: 'The
king himself, hoping to get the Prince Elector, his son-in-law, to be
restored to the Palatinate by an amicable treaty, was much incensed
at the sight of it, as being published at an unseasonable time.'[32]

On 24 December 1620, James issued 'A Proclamation against
Excess of Lavish and Licentious Speech of Matters of State', in
which he promised to punish not only those who 'did intermeddle
by pen or speech' with matters of state 'either at home or abroad',
but also those who gave 'attention', 'applause' or 'entertainment'
to 'any such discourse' without informing the Privy Council as to
where such speeches were being made.[33] When the identity of *Vox
Populi*'s author was revealed a matter of weeks later, Thomas Scott
fled to the Dutch Republic, where he continued to publish a range of
political tracts against the Spanish match and James's appeasement
of Spain. Under pressure from James, the Dutch States General
issued a proclamation in January lambasting unlicensed publications
in 'Latin, French, English, Scots, and various other languages', and
prohibiting their overseas export, 'especially one against the King of
Great Britain and his principal ministers'.[34]

The events in Bohemia and the Palatinate – and the fate of
Elizabeth, Frederick and their young family in particular – captured
the attention of contemporary Britons like never before, as did the
actions involving British volunteer forces, who continued to defend

the remaining three Palatine towns which had remained loyal to Frederick: Frankenthal, Mannheim and Frederick's hereditary capital, Heidelberg. John Taylor's report of his visit to the new king and queen of Bohemia, *News From Bohemia*, was published in response to what he described as continual requests from Londoners for information about the couple. As Taylor described, '[I] cannot pass the streets but I am continually stayed by one or the other, to know what news, so that sometimes I am four hours before I can go the length of two pairs of butts.'[35]

In August 1621, a single sheet of news entitled *Corrant out of Italy, Germany etc.* was published in London. It had been previously produced in Amsterdam, a centre for the publication of news, and was the first *coranto* to be published in England. Thomas Archer, the bookseller who printed it, was promptly imprisoned.[36] Despite Archer's treatment, the *Corrant out of Italy ... etc.* appeared at regular intervals that year, as did other corantos translated from the Dutch. Each consisted of a series of short entries, each headed by the place and date of the news. They provided updates of events in Bohemia and in the war zones, which fed a growing appetite among Britons for foreign news: printed pamphlets advertising 'news from the Palatinate' on their title pages proliferated in London's stationers' shops.

Such pamphlets printed in the capital and the news gleaned from them, circulated via networks of correspondents across the English counties, and north as far as Scotland. One news diary of an unknown Edinburgh merchant burgess is packed with details of events from the Palatinate, with considerable focus on the debates of the English Parliament and views of significant figures such as the Marquess of Buckingham. The merchant took it for granted, with no resentment, that a 'British' foreign policy was now made in London by the King of Great Britain.[37] The events in the Palatinate and responses to them, served to unite most Scottish and English as Britons who saw the necessity of a united force abroad.

Whilst the outbreak of a major war in central Europe, and the centrality of James's own son-in-law in it, signalled the nadir of

James's policy for a reunited Christendom, it was, at the same time, the means by which a united British Protestant identity began to be found and expressed.

***

On 8 November 1620, Frederick's forces were routed at the Battle of White Mountain, on the outskirts of Prague. Prague fell, and Frederick, Elizabeth and their children, fled the country, and Emperor Ferdinand regained the Bohemian Crown. The couple's brief reign as King and Queen of Bohemia was over. Now all efforts could be focussed on the return of the Palatinate. As Sir John Digby wrote to Sir Walter Aston, ambassador in Madrid, a peaceful resolution now seemed possible: with 'the Business of Bohemia' now settled 'to the liking of the Emperor', King James would now 'employ his full Power and authority with the Emperor, for the freeing and settling of the Patrimonial Inheritance of his Son in law & Grand Children upon reasonable & equitable terms'.[38] But if such mediation failed, James now promised to send money and men to Frederick's aid. Having avoided calling parliament for seven years, James now resolved, reluctantly, that the Lords and Commons would need to be summoned.

James's view of the absolute power of a monarchy meant he resisted recognising Parliament's rights but now, with a parliamentary grant of funds the only means whereby he could make a meaningful military intervention to restore the Palatinate, and amid pressure from Privy Councillors, including Buckingham and the Archbishop of Canterbury, to move against the Spanish, he had little choice. A council of war was established to cost a campaign. Their detailed report estimated that an army of 30,000 men would come at an immediate cost of £250,000 (more than £60 million today) to be followed by an annual sum of £900,000 (c.£191 million today). The scale of funds required perhaps vindicated James's long-standing approach to kingship; it was money he knew he would never secure from a cash-strapped Parliament.

When Parliament opened on 30 January 1621, James had to be carried into the Lords because of the weakness in his legs caused by his gout and arthritis. It was an apt image for a king struggling to maintain his strategic footing. In his opening speech he spoke with anger and regret as to 'the miserable and torn estate of Christendom', which, he added, 'none that hath an honest heart can look on without a weeping eye'. As James explained, with the Palatinate – his grandchildren's future inheritance – looking set to fall, he needed funds in case negotiations failed and war became unavoidable: 'wherein I declare, that if by fair means I cannot get it, my crown, and honour and all shall be spent with my son's blood also.'[39]

The Commons immediately voted him two subsidies to the value of £160,000, sufficient to support the garrisons already in the Palatinate but not to send additional British troops, and declared 'unto his most excellent Majesty and the whole world', that it considered itself to be 'members of the same body' as the 'afflicted' Protestants on the continent. It would therefore support, with universal consent, the king's interventions 'with his sword' to effect that 'which by a peaceable course shall not be effected'.[40] Parliament's declaration of defiance was quickly reported, translated into Dutch and German, and circulated abroad.

But much to Parliament's frustration, James did not give up his search for peace by negotiation. In May, Sir John Digby was sent to Vienna to urge a ceasefire and seek a reconciliation between the Emperor Ferdinand and Frederick, but the truce he secured was soon broken by both sides.[41] James made one final appeal to his son-in-law for peace. He urged Frederick to accept the terms Digby had sought to negotiate in Vienna, including the stipulation that he must 'upon his knee, crave pardon of the Imperial Majesty', while at the same time suggesting to Emperor Ferdinand that Frederick had already capitulated.[42] However, Frederick remained defiant. He refused to abandon his Protestant allies in Bohemia. From The Hague, where they were now in exile, Frederick and Elizabeth, mounted a sustained propaganda campaign to promote military action. Their cause, they maintained, was a 'common' one for all Protestants.

It was a call reflected in a sermon delivered in July 1621, by Thomas Gataker, rector of Rotherhithe in Surrey and subsequently printed in Fleet Street. In *A Spark Towards the Kindling of Sorrow for Sion*, Gataker presented in apocalyptic terms the indifference of Britain to the fate of Protestants in Europe. 'We are grown insensible of our own evils,' he wrote, and many take little notice of the 'insupportable afflictions' of 'our Brethren, and fellow members in Christ Jesus' except as 'a matter of news and novelty'. Referring, in a manner of words, to James's policy of mediation and moderation, Gataker described a kind of 'negative Christianity' whereby men 'are neither Papist, nor Puritans, Heretics or Schismatics, they can easily tell what they are not; not so easily what they are'.[43]

However, with the failure of negotiations between Frederick and Ferdinand, James now appeared to have little choice but to begin military preparations and recall Parliament.

***

With MPs and peers gathered again in November 1621, James made it clear that their sole business was money for the Palatinate. The subsidy granted in January had already been spent on maintaining the garrisons there and James now demanded immediate funds to support Frederick's army through the winter, and then a further £900,000 in the spring to maintain an army for a year.[44]

Yet rather than the immediate grant of funds that James expected, the debate's focus shifted to the threat posed by Spain, with members calling on James to first abandon negotiations for Prince Charles's marriage to the infanta. The price of the Spanish match, they argued, would be abandoning the Protestant cause in Europe, the fate of the Palatinate and the king's own daughter.[45] To many, England's troubles stemmed from failing to uphold the Lord's cause. 'God is angry with us for not keeping the Crown of Bohemia,' declared leading parliamentarian and MP for Bath, Sir Robert Phelips.[46] Digby recounted the details of his mission for peace, emphasising that diplomacy had failed, after which Sir Edward Coke declared, 'the King for a Peace could descend no Lower but must resolve either to abandon his children or engage yourself in a war'. James must now 'on this just occasion, speedily and effectually to take the sword in your hand'.[47]

The Commons' petition to the king was bold and uncompromising. He must make war on Spain, break off the ongoing negotiations for the Spanish match, and see that 'our most noble prince may be timely and happily married to one of our own religion'.[48]

James was furious. Writing to the Speaker of the House, he railed against 'some fiery and popular spirits' who meddled with 'matters far above their capacities, tending to our high dishonour and breach of the prerogative royal'.[49] The House was directed 'that none therein shall presume hence forth to meddle with anything concerning our government or deep matters of state, namely not to deal with our dear son's match with the daughter of Spain, nor to touch the honour of that king'.[50] James affirmed his commitment to the Spanish marriage, and insisted that the origins 'of this miserable war, which hath set all Christendom on Fire' had been 'only caused by our son-in-law's hasty and rash resolution, following evil counsel' to accept the Bohemian Crown.[51]

But for all the Commons' calls for action, the funds that James had requested remained to be granted. Some baulked at the potentially devastating cost; others demanded that James address their concerns first, and agree to break off the Spanish marriage negotiations, before money would be granted. Sir Edward Giles MP exposed what he saw as the absurdity of James's approach: 'We must fight the Spaniards in the Palatinate and be friends with them everywhere else.'[52]

The House was more inclined to talk, than provide money. It was an opportunity to hold their divinely appointed monarch to ransom as a means to try and dictate policy.

Ultimately the concern of the Commons for Protestantism and Frederick's cause, was not matched by a willingness to pay the high costs of intervention at a time when the economy was struggling in a trade slump and there had been poor harvests. Whilst the Commons talked of assisting Elizabeth and Frederick with their 'lives and fortunes', they ultimately wanted a cheap war, voting just one subsidy for the support of troops already in the Palatinate.[53] Yet when Parliament continued to assert its 'ancient and undoubted right' to free speech, James hastily ended the session, before even that grant of subsidies for the war effort could be approved.

For Gondomar, the Spanish ambassador, this was 'the best news in a century', for it removed any realistic prospect of British forces launching meaningful military action on the continent.[54]

With all prospects of sending a significant army to the Palatinate abandoned, James's only hope was that the restitution of the Palatinate might be achieved as a prerequisite to a Spanish match. The successful conclusion of the marriage negotiations with Madrid now took on an even great urgency.

26

A Game at Chess

Black Knight: What we have done Hath been dissemblance ever,
White Knight: There you lie then, And the game's ours; we give thee
check-mate by Discovery ...

Thomas Middleton, *A Game at Chess* (1624)[1]

On 18 February 1623, two heavily disguised men with fake beards, claiming to be brothers Jack and Tom Smith, set sail from Dover for the continent. Incognito were twenty-three-year-old Prince Charles and George Villiers, Marquess of Buckingham, eight years his senior. The pair accompanied by a small entourage were heading for Madrid, and the Spanish court, where they hoped to conclude the negotiations for a marriage alliance and secure a commitment for the peaceful resolution of the Palatinate crisis. With Philip IV having acceded to the throne aged sixteen, following the death of his father Philip III in 1621, it was hoped the stalled negotiations might be re-energised with a new king. The future of peace in Europe was, it seems, held in the hands of these three young men.

According to King James, it was 'the business of Christendom' that had lured Prince Charles to Madrid, as much as 'the cod piece point' as the king crudely described the proposition that his son marry the Spanish infanta, sixteen-year-old Maria Anna.[2] For 'at bottom', as Charles had acknowledged to Gondomar, 'this concerns my sister'.[3] Given the impasse in Parliament over funds for war, and Elizabeth's impassioned pleas for help as the Palatinate was over-run, Charles sought to bring the negotiations for a Spanish match to a conclusion. While it was not unprecedented to fetch a bride from her country of origin once the marriage was concluded – as James had done with Anna of Denmark – the king recognised that it was 'without example in many ages' for a king's only son to travel to meet another king's daughter before the marriage articles were agreed upon, let alone in disguise and completely unannounced. As diplomat Sir Henry Wotton later observed, the thought of 'so great a prince and favourite so suddenly metamorphosed into travellers, with no greater train, was enough to make any man living unbelieve his five senses'.[4]

James had initially been reluctant to support his son's high-risk venture to Madrid, but after the failure of the 1621 Parliament he knew that finalising the marriage negotiations was his best chance of restoring the Palatinate. It was the last throw of the dice. As James wrote, 'If my baby's credit in Spain, mend not these things' – meaning the Palatine question – 'I will bid farewell to peace in Christendom, during our times at least.'[5] It was an audacious attempt to checkmate Philip IV, the new young king.

Now, eighteen years after an Anglo–Spanish match had first been mooted, so much seemed to depend upon the outcome of these negotiations. They were, as Buckingham noted, carrying out 'the business of most consequence in Christendom'.[6] But time was running out. The situation on the ground in the Rhineland was rapidly deteriorating. Renewed attempts to secure a ceasefire had failed, and on 19 September 1622, after eleven weeks of resistance, the capital Heidelberg fell. Three days later, Emperor Ferdinand secretly transferred the electorship of the Palatinate to Maximilian, Duke of Bavaria. Elizabeth and Frederick had lost both the Crown of Bohemia and the ancestral lands in the Palatinate.

Charles, Buckingham and their entourage crossed the Channel to Boulogne, before travelling through France. They arrived in Paris on 21 February 1623 and secretly visited the Louvre palace, where they saw Louis XIII and his wife Queen Anna dine in public and watched the king's sister Henrietta Maria dancing. When the French government later learned of Prince Charles's clandestine visit, they deemed his behaviour 'an affront and a great insult'.[7]

After hastily departing France, the royal party crossed the Pyrenees, arriving unannounced at the English ambassador's residence in Madrid on 7 March. A shocked Sir John Digby wrote to Dudley Carleton in The Hague: 'Nothing could have happened more strange and unexpected unto me.' If informed in advance of the project, he said, he would have done everything he could to stop the prince from embarking on such a dangerous journey.[8] Not only were there the perils of travel – accidents, bandits in the mountains, exposure to the elements – but Sir John was (rightly) worried that the presence of the Stuart heir at the Madrid court might strengthen the Spanish king's hand in the marriage negotiations. As one contemporary noted: 'Whiles our Prince is in Spain, the Spaniard get what they wished from us.'[9]

***

The previous February 1622, James had sent Sir John Digby to the Spanish court to test the new king's commitment to the match, to a marriage treaty and towards negotiating terms for the restoration of the Palatinate to Frederick and his heirs. By August, Digby had been persuaded that Philip IV was committed to both the marriage and to the Palatinate's return. He observed that the two issues had become inseparable in Anglo–Spanish relations: the Spanish 'would not make the match without resolving to restore the Palatinate, nor restore the Palatinate without resolving to make the match'.[10] Now, all that was needed was for the pope to issue a dispensation to allow a Protestant prince to marry a Catholic infanta. Arrangements would be made for the Infanta Maria to move to England the following spring.

However, while reassuring James that the negotiations were on track, Philip IV had in late 1622 asked his chief minister Count

Olivares to find a way out of the Anglo–Spanish match. His father had apparently advised him on his death bed, that the infanta, his sister, should not go through with the marriage. As Philip IV wrote to Olivares: 'I think it is now time to find a way out of it; wheretofore I require you to find some other way to content the King of England, to whom I think myself bound for his many expressions of friendship.'[11] Yet talk of the marriage continued.

By January 1623, word had spread in England that the marriage alliance was now a foregone conclusion, and that Gondomar would be sent to the Emperor Ferdinand to arrange the return of Frederick's lands. James rewarded Digby by making him Earl of Bristol.[12] Such was James's optimism, that he commissioned Inigo Jones to build a new Banqueting House at Whitehall (the previous one had burned down in 1619) as a suitable venue to stage the festivities and entertainments for the marriage.

***

In early March 1623, Charles and Buckingham arrived at the Spanish court in Madrid, and, disguises discarded, their true identities revealed. Their entry was, in the words of court chronicler, Gil González de Ávila, 'a singular mark of confidence in Spain that has astonished the entire world'.[13]

Prince Charles's unheralded arrival in Spain shocked observers across Europe and aroused considerable interest. Pamphlets and corantos published and translated in various languages relayed details of the visit.[14] It seemed that finally the king of Spain and the king of Great Britain were going to put aside their country's differences and sign the marriage agreement.

The Dutch looked on with trepidation, fearing Charles's presence in Madrid signalled that negotiations for the Spanish match were now complete and, with it, England's imminent defection from the Protestant cause. Sir Dudley Carleton writing from The Hague expressed the concerns of many. 'When I consider that Spain and these United Provinces are at this present the two most diametrically opposite and hostile countries of the whole world,' he told Chamberlain, 'and that they two only children of the king our sovereign are, one with the other, the otherwise the other, it passeth my capacity how they can be long well looked on in both places.'[15] With Anglo–Dutch relations already strained by trade conflicts, Carleton, like many European observers, believed a marriage would inevitably lead to a full Anglo–Dutch naval conflict: a 'bloody war at sea'.[16]

After hastily arranged preparations, Charles made his official entry into Madrid and then moved into the royal palace. In the weeks and months that followed, banquets, entertainments and religious festivities were laid on by Philip IV to showcase the riches and splendour of the Habsburg Empire and the Catholic Church.[17] For the Spanish, the match was, at it had always been, desirable as a means to secure the conversion of Prince Charles – and Britain – to the Catholic religion. The prince's arrival in Madrid was seen as a sign that he was willing to convert in order to marry the devoutly Catholic Infanta Maria Anna.[18]

The celebrations were therefore tempered when Charles made it clear that conversion was unthinkable, and that he would rather renounce the match than change his religion. Olivares reluctantly conceded that a papal dispensation would be needed for the marriage to go ahead and agreed to send a letter to Rome to press the pope to grant permission at his earliest convenience.[19] To make matters even more uncomfortable for Charles at the Spanish court, in spring the first reports had reached Madrid of the capture of the Portuguese fort of Hormuz by Anglo–Persian forces.[20] The timing could not have been worse. The Spanish considered the attack as a direct violation not only of the 1604 peace treaty, but also as a reason to question English commitment towards a dynastic union with the Habsburgs. Digby wrote that the news created 'much storm' in Madrid, which was then exacerbated when 'richly laden' ships loaded with booty won at Hormuz arrived back in England.[21]

When the prince was formally introduced to the young infanta on Easter Day, 6 April, he seemed enamoured. Shortly after seeing her, he had said that 'all he ever yet saw, is nothing to her, and [swore] that if he want her, there shall be blows'.[22]

Meanwhile, parallel Habsburg negotiations concerning the Palatinate proposed that the region's restitution would be achieved through another marriage treaty, that of Frederick's eldest son Frederick Henry and Emperor Ferdinand's second daughter, Cecilia Renata. James readily endorsed the idea, writing to Charles and Buckingham: 'if either that way, or any other, this business be brought to a good end'.[23] Frederick instructed his agent in England, Johannes Joachim von Rusdorf, to try to dissuade James from agreeing to such a treaty. He was convinced that Emperor Ferdinand would never agree to Frederick's restoration whatever the terms. Meanwhile Elizabeth and Frederick sent messages to Charles in Spain urging him not to come to an agreement with the Spanish king knowing that Philip's promises to restore the palatinate would be meaningless.

On 4 May 1623, the papal dispensation finally arrived in Madrid – but filled with impossible conditions. The pope insisted that in England the Spanish infanta must have a strictly Spanish and Catholic household, and a bishop and twenty-four priests who were to be exempt from English law. It also stipulated that the Catholic chapel (of the infanta or when she was queen) be open to *any* worshippers. There were additional clauses that required James to ensure freedom of worship and conscience for all English Catholics (which would require the alteration of the Oath of Allegiance). Finally, James would have one year to secure Parliament's agreement to all the terms.[24] Appalled by the pope's demands, Charles and Buckingham wrote immediately to James for guidance as to what to do next.

Believing that his son and his favourite were now effectively prisoners at the Spanish court, James resolved to agree to anything that the Spanish demanded in order to bring them home. He sent a letter telling Charles and Buckingham of his shock when Sir Francis Cottington had told him of their situation, which 'hath stricken me dead. I feel it shall very much shorten my days, and I am perplexed that I know not how to satisfy the people's expectations here, neither know I what to say to the council.' As he continued: 'But as for my advice and directions that ye crave, in case they will not alter their decree, it is in a word, to come speedily away, and if ye can get leave, give over all treaty.'[25]

The prince followed his father's advice and, much to the surprise of the Spanish court, on 9 July confirmed that he would accept all the conditions of the papal dispensation. Bonfires were lit and celebrations erupted throughout Madrid.

Ten days later, James formally ratified the treaty in the Chapel Royal at Whitehall before the Spanish ambassadors – Juan de Mendoza, Marquis de la Hinojosa, and Don Carlos Coloma – and priests from the Spanish embassy.[26] His determination for the marriage to be the key instrument by which the Palatinate might be restored without committing full scale to war, and his son and Buckingham's impromptu visit to the Spanish court, had left James facing the prospect of having to allow Catholicism to be practised in England and his own Oath of Allegiance rendered meaningless.

The news that James had sworn to uphold the terms of the marriage was greeted with horror in The Hague – where Elizabeth and Frederick remained in exile – and among the German princes. James's nephew, Christian of Brunswick-Lüneburg, railed at his uncle, for his commitment to diplomacy over military action. He wrote that in comparison to historical figures, such as Alexander the Great, Julius Caesar and Henri IV of France – all 'esteemed and celebrated as the most outstanding heroes of the world' – King James was 'the old pants-shitter, the old English bed-shitter.' 'Because of his stupidity', he was 'the greatest ass in the world'.[27]

Charles signed the marriage treaty on 4 August, after the death of Pope Gregory XV in July, knowing that nothing could happen until a new dispensation was issued by the new pope, Urban VIII. He was now determined to return to England, with or without the infanta. He had come to believe that the Spanish had no genuine commitment to restoring his sister and Frederick's lands and titles.[28]

Charles concluded it was time to go home: in Buckingham's words, they 'saw there was no more to be gained here' with regard to the Palatinate.[29] Nevertheless, keen not to jeopardise what had been achieved, on 7 September 1623 Prince Charles and Philip IV vowed to abide by the marriage contract. Charles signed a document, entrusted to Digby, authorising his marriage to take place in his absence once the pope's dispensation arrived. It was valid until Christmas.

Finally, after six long months at the Spanish court, Charles and Buckingham left Madrid and made their way to the northern coast for their departure. En route, at Segovia, they met Sir Francis Nethersole, who had been sent by Elizabeth to urge her brother not to go through with the marriage until he had obtained adequate promises for her husband's full restoration to his lands and titles.[30] With guile worthy of his father, Charles immediately sent one of his servants back to Madrid with instructions that when the papal dispensation arrived, the servant should give Digby a letter instructing him not to proceed with the marriage until Digby had received assurance that after the formal betrothal, the infanta would not enter a nunnery. It was a bizarre condition, to top a bizarre few months; but it was not completely without foundation. Previously the Infanta Maria had let it be known that she would rather become a nun than marry a heretic. Charles's letter was calculated, by raising a valid question, to delay matters indefinitely without undermining the oath that he had made.[31]

From The Hague, Elizabeth expressed her disappointment with her father's policies to Sir Edward Conway, secretary of state. 'I hope his Majesty will one day see the falsehood of our enemies,' she wrote, 'but I pray God send my dear brother safe in England again and then I shall be more quiet in my mind.'[32] She prayed that Charles and Buckingham's return would bring a change in James's position. She would soon learn that Prince Charles was now determined to wage war against Spain to secure the return of the Palatinate to his sister and brother-in-law.

**

Charles and Buckingham arrived back in England on Sunday 5 October 1623. Finding that, contrary to rumour and expectation, the prince had returned home a Protestant and without a Catholic bride in tow, the kingdom was engulfed in widespread rejoicing, and church bells rung across the country. Despite the wet weather, more than 300 bonfires were counted in the City between Whitehall and Temple Bar alone. Diarist Simonds D'Ewes noted: 'I dare be bold to say this, London never before saw so many bonfires at one time,' adding, 'the only thing to be lamented was the great excess and drunkenness of this day, the two usual fault[s] of Englishmen upon any good hap ...'[33] An anonymous printed report, *The Joyfull Returne of the most illustrious Prince Charles*, described the day as: 'This English masterpiece of ours' and predicted, 'it will be a legacy for young men when they grow old to read (by the fire side) the chronicle of this day to their children.'[34]

Celebrations spread from London across the country to Coventry and Cambridge, Great Yarmouth and Oxford. According to one commentator, when the news reached Edinburgh, eight days after Charles's homecoming, there was 'great thanksgiving' accompanied by bonfires, sermons and the shooting of ordnance.[35] Similar scenes took place in Aberdeen, where the citizens sought to 'express the joy and gladness of the hearts of the people' with trumpets and drums, and ringing the city's bells.[36] In the Irish plantations there were no bells; settlers celebrated the prince's return with martial displays of drill formations. In his dedication to *Irelands Jubilee*, Stephen Jerome wrote that celebrations were held: 'from Ulster to Connacht, as all in

Great Britain, even from Dan to Beersheba, from Berwick to Dover, from Edinburgh to utmost Orcades [Orkneys]'.[37]

What Charles's return meant for the Spanish alliance and the match was far from clear. As Alvise Vallaresso, the Venetian ambassador, succinctly surmised: 'As he went without reason, so he reasonably returns without results.'[38] Writing to Digby on 8 October, James made clear that the marriage could only proceed if agreement had been reached on the restitution of the Palatinate. He could not, he maintained, 'give joy to our only son', but 'give our only daughter her portion [dowry] in tears'.[39]

Charles too was determined that Spain should give a firm undertaking to restore the Palatinate before he would finally commit to the marriage. He wrote to Digby telling him 'to try what the King of Spain will do concerning the business of the Palatinate before I be contracted'. His purpose, he added, was 'in no ways to break the marriage but in this dull interim of looking for my mistress, to put an end to the miseries of my sister and her children'.[40] But as Digby wrote to James, the Spanish believed that the restitution of the Palatinate was too complicated to be hurriedly appended to a marriage treaty, and 'held it fit to treat of them distinctly'.[41]

Finally, on 24 November 1623, Pope Urban VIII confirmed the dispensation granted by his predecessor and gave his blessing for the union between Prince Charles and the Spanish infanta.[42] When Philip IV announced that the betrothal ceremony would take place two weeks later, on 9 December, Charles sent Digby instructions to revoke his proxy and make the marriage contingent upon an agreement about the Palatinate.[43] The marriage was to be postponed indefinitely.

Charles and Buckingham were now determined to commit Britain to entering the war in Europe as the means to restore the Palatinate. It was, as poet and politician Sir Benjamin Rudyerd described it, 'the turn of Christendom'.[44] Charles called on his father to summon Parliament for the specific purpose of funding a war against Spain, to recover the Palatinate. As Elizabeth told the Venetian ambassador in The Hague, while 'she did not trust her father', she was now 'compelled to trust his son and Buckingham'.[45]

***

For nine days in August 1624, crowds flocked to the Globe Theatre in London for sold-out performances of Thomas Middleton's new play, *A Game at Chess*. The drama, depicted as a chess game between Britain and Spain, was an openly satirical depiction of the game of Machiavellian diplomacy that had played out during the prince's time at the Spanish court.

The White King represented King James. The White Knight was Prince Charles – and the 'White Duke', or rook, was the Duke of Buckingham. Philip IV was the Black King. The Black Knight was the outgoing former Spanish ambassador, the Count of Gondomar.[46] Aided and abetted by the Jesuits, Spain was depicted as plotting to achieve world domination, starting with the conquest of Britain via the conversion of Charles, Prince of Wales. The denouement saw the complete defeat of Spain (allegorised as 'the Black House') by England ('the White House').

Outraged, the new Spanish ambassador Carlos Coloma wrote to Olivares in Madrid on 20 August: 'The king of the Blacks has easily been taken for our lord the King, because of his youth, dress, and other details.'[47] Indeed, the actors had gone to such lengths to make the main characters recognisable that they had got hold of a commode-like 'chair of ease' for the Black Knight (Gondomar), on account of the ambassador's anal fistula, which had become common knowledge.[48] Coloma's account to Olivares described how playgoers, 'came out of the theatre so inflamed against Spain that, as a few Catholics have told me who went secretly to see the play, my person would not be safe in the streets.' He went on to recount his 'sufferings here as a true Hell', seeing the 'sacred name of my king so outraged in so many ways by such low, vile people, nor his holy and glorious acts so unworthily interpreted'.[49]

Following complaints from Coloma that it was 'so scandalous, so impious, so barbarous and so offensive to my royal master', the play was banned on James's instructions.⁵⁰ *A Game at Chess* had reflected the depth of popular hostility to the Spanish and to the Spanish match, which wasn't just shared by Londoners, or even Englishmen, but by Scottish and some Irish people too. Scottish Presbyterian David Calderwood recounted in his memoirs how militant Protestants both north and south of the border were of the same mind: the whole isle 'of Britain, specially the professors of true religion, were astonished, and feared alteration both in the state of the kirk and commonwealth'.⁵¹ In Ireland, concern that the Spanish match would see Catholic toleration caused great anxiety for Protestants in the Ulster plantations, whose position was both precarious and still in the minority. In October 1622, the Lord Deputy in Ireland wrote to the Privy Council in London that some 'corrupt and ill affected men' (meaning Catholics) had been encouraged by 'swarming' priests who led them to believe that toleration would soon be introduced.⁵² Indeed, throughout the following year, regular reports came from Ireland of how 'out of confidence of the match', the Catholic majority had become unbridled.⁵³

Opposition to the Spanish marriage united James's kingdoms, as did a sense of how the 'united' kingdom – Britain – should respond to 'the Spanish threat', which had been identified by Thomas Scott in his pamphlet *Vox Populi*, as being Spain's ambition for a universal Catholic monarchy. Scott, an Englishman educated in Scotland, saw Spain, through Gondomar, as seeking to prevent 'perfect union' in church and commonwealth between Scotland and England.⁵⁴ For Scott, as for a number of other writers, a united Britain must wage war against Spain and Catholicism: 'England and Scotland should be united in this'.⁵⁵ Like Middleton in *A Game at Chess*, Scott emphasised the duplicity of a Spain that would eventually claim Britain as its own. The only way to prevent such Spanish domination was war. And with Prince Charles's safe return, war was now widely expected.

When Parliament was called on 30 December 1623, Simonds D'Ewes wrote in his journal how it was 'verily hoped to see [the Palatinate] recovered and the Gospel again settled in Germany by the armies and assistances of the King of Great Britain'.[56]

27

Endgame

'One victory obtained by the joint valour of the English and Scots, will more indelibly Christen your Majesty's Empire of Great Britaine than an Act of Parliament or Artifice of State.'

Tom Tell Troath or A Free Discourse Touching the Manners of the Tyme, (1622)[1]

On Monday 19 February 1624, Parliament opened amid great expectation that was reported on both in Britain and across the continent. In Germany and the United Provinces, in Spain, France and in Denmark, all attention was on Whitehall. 'All our discourses,' wrote Carleton from the Hague, focused on events in Westminster,[2] 'Everything remains in suspense', wrote the English agent in Mainz in French, with attention on 'le Parlement de la grande Bretagne.'[3] If the negotiations with Spain on the match were to be broken off, as Charles and Buckingham believed they should be, the only route to restoring the Palatinate was war. For James it would mark an upending of his vision for European peace through mediation and the marriages of his children.

For some time now ambassadors had also been reporting a marked decline in the king's health and disposition. He had been experiencing kidney problems, low spirits and recurrent attacks of gout and arthritis. As James now visibly aged, Charles emerged resolute and emboldened after his experiences in Madrid. This was to be a struggle for Britain's future between father and son, the king and his heir. As Thomas Erskine, the Earl of Kellie, remarked shortly before Parliament gathered: 'It may come that the young folks shall have their world. I know not if that will be.'[4]

It seems that Charles had come of age, as John Chamberlain observed on seeing the prince at Westminster that February: he 'indeed is grown a fine gentlemen and beyond the expectation I had of him last which was not these seven years, and indeed I think he never looked nor became himself better in all his life'.[5] Charles had left the sickliness of his boyhood, and now exuded confidence and poise. He had developed a steely guile and political resolve, and an ability to impose his will. Through his experiences chairing the council when his father was indisposed, he had increasingly begun to look like a king-in-waiting. In November 1623, when ill health once again took the king away to Newmarket, one observer remarked that the prince 'is now entering into command of affairs by reasons of the king's absence and sickness, and all men address themselves unto him'.[6]

***

James's opening speech to Parliament three months later was unchar-acteristically defensive and reflective, revealing much of his state of mind, and body. He began by drawing attention to the 'fruits' of his government: peace 'when all neighbour countries are at war'. His desire for the maintenance of peace had led him to conduct exten-sive negotiations, including for a marriage between his son and the infanta. Yet, after the prince's time in Madrid and the disingenuous reassurances of the Spanish over the Palatinate, he had 'awaked as a man out of a dream', seeing that 'the business is nothing advanced neither of the match nor of the palat[inate] for all the long treaties & great p[ro]mises'.[7]

Now, in an extraordinary move which broke with precedent, James called on members of Parliament to give their advice on for-eign policy, which was 'the greatest matter that could ever concern a king.' 'Give me,' he requested, 'your free and faithful counsels in the matter I propose, of which you have often heard, the Match of my Son. I desire your best assistance to advise me what is best and fittest for me to do for the good of the Commonwealth, and the advancement of Religion, and the good of my Son and my Grand-children.' He asked his subjects: 'Consider with yourselves the state of Christendom, my children and this my own kingdom. Consider of these, and upon all, give me your advice.'[8]

It was very different from 1621 when Parliament had been acri-moniously dissolved by James after he considered MPs to have encroached on the royal prerogative when they criticised the Spanish match. Now he invited their advice and insisted his desire for 'a happy conclusion of this our meeting'.[9]

As the debate in Parliament commenced, impassioned speeches spoke of the threat posed by Spain and the action that must now be taken. Sir Benjamin Rudyerd led calls for the immediate repudiation of the marriage treaty which had already cost so much: 'We have lost the Palatinate altogether and almost all our party of the religion abroad, besides a great bulk of papistry grown and knotted within our bowels at home.' The projected match had 'exceedingly threat-ened' the United Provinces; 'the whole power of the Emperor and King of Spain coming down up on it'. The Dutch might have objec-tionable characteristics he said – a reference perhaps to their much-talked of conduct in the East Indies – but they have provided refuge to Elizabeth – 'the inestimable jewel of this Crown' – and had 'performed our outwork, which, if it be taken, we shall be more in danger'.[10]

The Commons were determined that negotiations with the Spanish should immediately be broken off and the Palatinate recov-ered. Rudyerd, like many others who spoke in the debate, rejected intervention limited to just the Palatinate but instead argued that the Spanish should be the focus of the offensive both on land, in the Low Countries, and at sea where the bullion from the New World which financed the Spanish and imperial armies might be seized. This would also provide much needed support for the English economy at a time when the conflict in Europe had caused an economic depression. As politician and jurist Sir Edward Coke reminded the Commons: the country had grown weak with 'want of trade and traffic which is the lifeblood of the state'.[11]

On 8 March, at Theobalds in Hertfordshire, George Abbot, Archbishop of Canterbury, and a small delegation from Parliament presented James with the unanimous advice of both Houses: 'The treaties both for the marriage and the Palatinate may not any longer be continued, with the honour of your Majesty, the safety of your People, the welfare of your Children and Posterity, as also the assurance of your ancient Allies and Confederates.'[12] The king had asked for Parliament's advice, and it had been given definitively.

James's response was characteristically couched in equivocation. As a 'peaceable king' all his life, he was reluctant 'without Necessity, to embroil myself with War', even though he remained committed to the restitution of the Palatinate. If there was no other way to recover the Palatinate, he would consider war, but only if he had sufficient funds to support it. Otherwise, he would only be able 'to show my teeth and do no more'.[13]

The king requested a huge grant of funds for 'this great business'; five subsidies and ten-fifteenths [a fifteenth was a tax on goods] for war and one subsidy and one-fifteenth for his own necessities and debts. It would add up to an audacious amount: more than had been granted to Elizabeth I during her decade and a half long war with Spain. For James it was a test of the assumption that he had maintained through his reign, as had been evidenced in the Parliament of 1621: that though Parliament might talk of war and urge it in the most passionate terms, they were less committed to funding it.

As the House reassembled, Richard Weston, Chancellor of the Exchequer, began with a long statement of the king's expenses on foreign affairs and the size of the grant that would be needed if the king was to have sufficient funds for war.[14]

After much debate, Parliament agreed to grant three subsides and three-fifteenths amounting to over £400,000. But there were conditions: the Spanish marriage negotiations had to be abandoned, and a council of war, established in 1621 and accountable to Parliament, would approve how the money was spent. Parliament promised that this grant was only the 'first fruits of our hearty oblation' and that 'if you shall be engaged in a real war, we your loyal and loving subjects will never fail to assist your Majesty in a Parliamentary way'.[15]

Finally, in a speech to a parliamentary delegation at Whitehall on 23 March, James conceded, and agreed to break off negotiations with Spain. He outlined what was to be his new bellicose foreign policy. For two decades he had sought conciliation, 'for sparing the effusion of Christian blood, and as the most easy and probable way to recover the Palatinate for my Children.'[16] Now, confident of the righteousness of the cause, he promised that the funds raised would be devoted solely to securing the Palatinate by military means. For the conduct of the war, he required 'a faithful secret Council of War' and assured them that the spending of the subsidies granted would be supervised by those appointed by Parliament. However, he insisted, the ultimate responsibility for military operations and for foreign policy remained his – 'whether I shall send 200, or 2,000 men? whether by Sea or Land, East or West, by Diversion or otherwise by Invasion upon the Bavarian or Emperor you must leave that to your King'.[17]

Having agreed to break with Spain and commit to war, James had given, as the Speaker Sir Thomas Crewe declared in his speech before Parliament adjourned on the 29 May, 'the true believers at home and our neighbours & confederates abroad' have cause to 'rejoice and sing a new song of joy'.[18]

***

For James it was a very different song. For the first time in his reign, he had committed to war. When the archbishop of Canterbury requested permission for popular demonstrations of joy, he was refused. The king 'thought it not fit in regard the war was not yet begun and so what the success might be not known, and to rejoice before victory was presumptuous before it and contemptible without it'.[19] James had ended his speech expressing his desire that 'he end his days in accord with his people through Parliament'.[20]

It was a comment that perhaps revealed an awareness of his declining health, and the growing influence of his son. Towards the end of the year, 1624, the Venetian ambassador Vallaresso reported that the king seemed 'practically lost; he comes to various decisions and inclines to his usual negotiations; he does not care to fall in with the wishes of his son-in-law and the favourite. He now protests, not weeps, but finally gave in.'[21] Beset by worsening arthritis that limited his mobility, James appeared increasingly frail and depressed. 'It seems to me', noted the French ambassador Tanneguy Le Veneur, the Comte de Tillières, 'that the intelligence of this King has diminished. Not that he cannot act firmly and well at times and particularly when the peace of the kingdom is involved. But such efforts are not continuous as they once were.' He pointed to what he saw as a growing timidity: 'His mind uses its powers only for a short time … old age carries him into apprehension.'[22]

Perhaps through 'apprehension' or more through his long-held aversion to war, James had, despite parliamentary subsidies and his own expressed intent, still not declared war. He continued to believed that an Anglo–Spanish union was possible and so too the peaceful restitution of the Palatinate, and despite the opposition of his son, he was still in almost daily contact with envoys from Madrid.

Yet Charles and Buckingham had already started laying plans for a full-scale assault on Spain by land and sea, in cooperation with all the anti-Habsburg states of Europe. They had made overtures to the Venetians, the French and the Dutch. In addition, unofficial embassies were criss-crossing the Channel between London and Paris conducting negotiations for a marriage between Charles and the French princess Henrietta Maria, daughter of Henri IV, to cement a new Anglo-French alliance against Spain. It was the final humiliation for James, not least given that the French made no commitment as part of the treaty to secure the restoration of the Palatinate. Now Britain was on the brink of all-out war with Spain. The die had been cast.

***

In December 1624, James met with the French ambassadors at Theobalds, before travelling to Cambridge for the swearing of the marriage articles. Having been received publicly in the presence of members of the council and of the court, James, Charles, Buckingham and Secretary Conway withdrew in private for the oath-taking and signing. The king played his part from bed, on account of his gout and arthritis. Such was the pain in his hand, that when the marriage treaty was signed, a stamp of James's signature was used, despite his Majesty being present. For the state banquet that followed, Charles took his father's place.

Over Christmas James remained in his chambers at Whitehall but emerged on 9 January 1625, to watch the Ben Jonson masque, *Fortunate Isles and the Union*, in the presence of the French, Spanish and Dutch ambassadors. Its theme was a unified British kingdom which, guided by a wise king, takes pride in being a land of peace, separate from Europe. It alluded to Charles's impending accession and the prince's plans to marry Henrietta Maria.[23]

In the new year, James withdrew to Newmarket, and in early March, he moved to Theobalds. Within a week his physicians reported the king was having 'some Indisposition of body'. He was wracked with pain and experiencing bouts of intense fever. By the middle of the month, as the fever broke, he appeared to recover, but then on 22 March he suffered an 'apoplectic fit' – a stroke. By the 26th he had lost the ability to speak, his jawbone loosened, and his tongue enlarged. Finally, he succumbed, his body experiencing a violent dysentery, excreting 'burned, bilious and putrid things.'[24] James, 'King of Great Britain, France and Ireland' died just before noon on Sunday 27 March 1625, aged fifty-eight.

***

Shortly after his death an official report in Latin documented the king's final illness and the results of the post-mortem examination of his body. Among its conclusions were that the pressures of kingship – 'continuously concerned for the peace and tranquillity of the whole Christian world' – had taken a toll. It was also noted that James suffered from 'low spirits', melancholy, and 'afflictions of the mind'.[25]

King Charles I was immediately proclaimed at the gates of Theobalds by the knight marshal, Edward Zouch. The earl of Kellie advised the Privy Council that proclamations should speak of the 'King of Great Britain', as James had preferred, rather than putting one nation of the union first, as in 'England and Scotland' or 'Scotland and England'.[26]

On the night of 4 April, a torch-lit procession of carriages, with twenty-four-year-old King Charles I at its head, escorted James's coffin the thirty miles from Theobalds to Denmark House on the Strand, where his body would lie in state for six weeks. The privy apartments there had been prepared, draped with black cloth. James's coffin was covered with black velvet and a life-size wooden effigy of the king dressed in royal robes was placed on top.[27] His servants remained in attendance – 'as if his majesty had been living' – in a bedchamber illuminated by candles mounted in six silver candlesticks, bought by Prince Charles in Spain in 1623.[28]

28

Great Britain's Solomon

His pen restrain'd the strong, reliev'd the weak
And graciously he could write, doe and speak
And had more force and vigour in his words
Then neigh'bring Princes could have in their swords

John Taylor, 'A Living Sadnes[s]' (1625)[1]

On 7 May 1625, James made his final journey to Westminster Abbey. A procession of thousands of mourners, dressed in black and ranked according to their status, escorted the body and effigy of the late king, 'richly dressed and crowned', borne on a funeral chariot drawn by six horses, caparisoned in black velvet through the city's streets. The chief heralds carried embroidered banners emblazoned with heraldic insignia and with the king's motto '*Beati Pacifici*', together with the Union Flag. The presence of all the leading members of the English and Scottish nobility was a final act of union of which James would have been proud.[2] Following behind as 'Chief Mourner', in a significant break with tradition, was the new king dressed in a long black robe with a black hood.[3] Charles's presence at his father's funeral was a powerful display of filial love and dynastic continuity.

At the abbey, the bier and effigy were placed in a spectacular catafalque built by Inigo Jones. Above an elevated platform on, which the bier rested was a domed roof supported by eight columns all draped in black velvet, embroidered with the 'arms of his Kingdoms and Dominions'. On the base stood twelve statues of female figures personifying the king's virtues and accomplishments, including Fame, Justice, Glory, Peace, Learning, and Religion. Accompanying inscriptions heralded James's achievements, including the Anglo-Scottish union, the Ulster plantation and colonies in America, and the expansion of trade.[4]

The two-hour long funeral sermon, entitled 'Great Britain's Solomon' and delivered by John Williams, the Bishop of Lincoln and Lord Keeper of the Great Seal, reflected many of the same themes. Williams took as his text the Old Testament account of the death of Solomon in 1 Kings 11.41–3, and proceeded to draw a long and flattering comparison between James and Solomon, which focussed on King James's wisdom and desire for peace.[5] 'None can be honoured by all of Europe, but he that held the Balance of all Europe, and, for the space of twenty years at the least, preserved the peace of all Europe,'[6] said Williams. This peace, he continued, had been remarkably beneficial to James's own realms:

The Schools of the Prophets newly adorned, all kinds of learning highly improved, manufactures at home daily invented, Trading abroad exceedingly multiplied, the Borders of Scotland peaceably governed, the North of Ireland religiously planted, the Navy Royal magnificently furnished, Virginia, Newfoundland, and New England peopled, the East India well traded, Persia, China, and the Mogor visited, lastly, all the ports of Europe, Africa, Asia, and America to our red Crosses freed, and opened. And they are all the Actions, and true-borne Children of King James his Peace.[7]

Williams closed by looking to the future – 'the magnificence' of James's funeral testifying to the filial devotion of a 'pious son of a most pious father'. James's immortal kingly body lived on, not in statues or effigies, said Williams, but in Charles, 'a breathing statue of all his Virtues'. Though his father was dead, it was as though he was not, 'for he hath left One behind him most like himself'.[8] Charles listened, seated at the head of the catafalque.

Finally, with the obsequies over, King James VI and I was laid to rest in the Henry VII Chapel, underneath the central monument, next to the Tudor king who had founded a renowned dynasty. It was the place James had specifically created for himself when he moved Queen Elizabeth I's body to the north aisle of the chapel almost twenty years before.

***

James's 'desire and intention', as John Donne declared in a sermon delivered a year after the king's death, had been to be 'Peacemaker of all the Christian world' and to silence 'all Field-drums'.[9] It was a vision King James ultimately failed to achieve. His diplomatic efforts, including those to make alliances through the marriages of his children, had not healed divisions. The outbreak of war in Europe in 1618 – a conflict ignited by the actions of his son-in-law which would last for thirty years – shattered any hope of a unified Christendom. And James's attempts to unite Britain in peace imploded with the civil wars of the three kingdoms and the execution of Charles I outside Banqueting House in 1649.

Yet a 'short peace' in Europe had endured for fifteen years after James's accession, enabling the English gunships of the Armada to become trading and sailing ships transporting planters, supplies, samples of wares, factors, ambassadors, diplomats and people of commerce. Increasingly merchants, adventurers and those seeking new lives and opportunities sailed all over the globe. From the return of the first voyage of the East India Company in 1603, the year of James's accession, overseas trade expansion developed in places as far flung as Russia, the Moluccas, India, Persia, Japan and Virginia. By the time of James's death, Britain had challenged Spanish dominion over the Americas and established new long-distance trade routes to the Eastern Mediterranean and the East Indies. Union Jacks had been flown in ports in all the known continents.

More members of the population at large in 'New Britain' became exposed to foreign products, cultures and customs than at any time in the kingdoms' histories. So too language changed, not least through the publication and dissemination of the King James Bible (which gave us phrases such as 'salt of the earth', 'skin of their teeth', 'apple of his eye'). It would become the book of the British Empire: where the empire spread, the Bible went. It was used to both challenge and defend the slave trade. It would shape the religious experience, language, thoughts, beliefs, and expressions of generations of readers all over the globe. Along with the works of William Shakespeare – the majority of which were written during James's reign in England – the King James Bible is cited as one of the greatest influences on the development of modern English.

The unprecedented growth in interest in foreign affairs, which saw the emergence of the first news-sheets and newspapers, brought news of conflicts on the continent, 'developments in the colonies', and also tapped into a range of related concerns about the perceived threat of Catholicism, the 'Turk', and the role of Britain on the international stage. Such interest in and discussion of foreign affairs encouraged greater comment and scrutiny of the monarch's action, and began to raise questions about the relationship between the king and Parliament, between Britain and Europe, and between Britain and indigenous peoples in territories Britain occupied as its own.

The Crown's limited finances meant that James was unable to assume the traditional role of a monarch leading armies into foreign fields, had he wanted it. Rather, continuing where Elizabeth I had left off, James enthusiastically granted and renewed charters to consortiums who were prepared to bear the cost of the long, risky voyages overseas to develop new trading routes and establish new markets. These charters delegated royal authority and with it powers to engage in trade and diplomacy, establish laws and governments and construct forts. Under James the Crown outsourced Britain's expansion overseas. In the words of Robert Wilkinson, the king's chaplain, in his sermon entitled 'The Merchant Royall' delivered at

Whitehall in 1607, 'by this trade we have gotten acquaintance with foreign nations and the kingdom of Christ enlarged, by this we have leagues of amity contracted with people of divers languages ...'[10]

Expansion and enterprise, the forging of an overseas 'British' identity, the fraught and increasingly violent emergence of Britain in the world, owed as much to those Jacobean 'entrepreneurs' as to the king himself. They represented a new London elite based not at court but in the hub of commercial London, merchants and financiers in the Royal Exchange and the New Exchange, in the newly built residences along the Strand and in the back rooms of Sir Thomas Smythe's house in Philpot Lane. It was men like Smythe, Hudson, Rolfe, and Roe who assumed the main responsibility for advancing English trade, exploration and expansion beyond Europe. And it was clerics, preachers and pamphleteers like Robert Johnson, William Crashaw, Robert Gray and Richard Crankthorpe that articulated a vision of Britain's imperial destiny. The Jacobean years, from 1603 to 1625, saw the coming together of vested interests – political, commercial and religious – to begin the work of building 'a new Britain in another world'.

In this James was often a supporting character. He sought opportunities to make money from customs revenues or from compounding imports, such as pepper and nutmeg, so the Crown could sell them at inflated prices. He also relished the opportunities such enterprises afforded, to enhance his honour and reputation, and to export his identity as king of Great Britain. And so he corresponded with the shah of Persia, the emperor of Mughal India, as well as countless other rulers and princes in the East, introducing himself and Britain, and requesting rights for his merchants. Aside from commerce, James saw colonisation, be it in Ireland or across the Atlantic, as the Christian moral imperative, a means of creating new British societies of 'civilised' subjects. 'How great a part of wide and wild America, is now new encompassed with this His Crowne?' Samuel Purchas rejoiced.[11]

While James failed to achieve his ambition of full union with Scotland, he set a path that drew England and Scotland together, and so too parts of conquered Ireland. Moreover, a British national identity did begin to evolve, but not through James's naive attempts to enshrine it in common laws and institutions; rather union evolved through a new common cause with the world beyond its shores: through the support of and identification with Protestants in Europe and a determination that the Protestant state of Great Britain, that James had created, play an active military role abroad. Given James's determination to maintain peace and not go to war in Europe, this nascent British identity ironically stands as much in opposition to as it does in celebration of James as king of Great Britain.

ACKNOWLEDGEMENTS

Writing a book is an endeavour at once solitary and entirely dependent on the support, patience and reassurance of friends, family, and colleagues. It is a journey that begins and ends with the commitment of a publisher, and the team at Bloomsbury have remained unwavering in their support throughout. My editor Jasmine Horsey immediately understood and encouraged my ambition to attempt a global history of the first King of Great Britain and gave me the confidence to believe that I could deliver it. Kate Johnson is the most fantastic copyeditor and so much more. She made a huge contribution with her insightful questions and thoughtful suggestions. Catherine Clarke, at the incomparable Felicity Bryan Associates, can hardly be summed up as my agent. She is the ultimate champion, friend, and confidant. Never have I come off a call with Catherine or finished a coffee – or cocktail – without feeling affirmed, inspired and refreshed.

I began writing this book as an academic within the history department at Royal Holloway, University of London, spending long days of a research sabbatical in the Cambridge University Library, in the British Library, and the National Archives. From then on, many conversations and email exchanges with archivists, librarians and countless scholars have helped me navigate unfamiliar terrain and new global perspectives. There are too many brilliant minds to mention, but the works cited in the bibliography are evidence of the breadth of scholarship upon which I have relied.

I finally delivered the book after endless weekends and holidays spent researching and writing and many months working through the night, before setting off for the day job as Executive Dean of the School of Communication and Creativity at City St. Georges, University of London. Whilst a full and varied work life has been hugely rewarding and energizing, I have not been much fun. Friends and family have had to not only endure my endlessly repeated refrain, 'I have to work on the book' but the false hopes raised by my repeated failure to predict how long things would take to get done. Plans have been routinely made and then unmade.

My parents, Celia and Paul Whitelock have been constant in their love, support and concern as has my sister Emily and nephew Sam. My sister Amy and nephew and niece Lilly and Baillie have seen much less of me than I would have liked as has the 'family in the north.' My parents-in-law David and Linda Downes have never failed to support and accept me and their love and patience, and that of Sally and Olive Hastings and Lucy and the Gratton girls, has made all the difference.

Friends are everything. All have played a part in ways impossible to summarize and thanks and huge appreciation goes to Vicky Alcock, Daniel Beer, Mel Bunce, Layla and Max, Bluebelle and Phoenix Evans-Delderfield, Chez Hall, Isobel and Peter Maddison, Emma Spearing, Chris Reynolds, Rosie Peppin Vaughan, Pedro Ramos Pinto and Martha, Robin, Katie, Oak and Margot D'Arcy, Pip and Jonathan Edwards, Matt and Vicky Edwards, Susi Fabbri, James McConnachie, Marc Newman, Sandra and David Swarbrick, Kate and James, Charlotte and Oliver Preston, Andrew (RRDJ), Hayley and Grayson Swarbrick, and Penny. The 'Women of Altitude', led by Rosie Tween, have shown how challenges can be overcome against all odds. Together we climbed a mountain, and the bonds we forged then and since, have been precious and life affirming. Alice Hunt has been as kind and caring as she is smart and inspiring: a fantastic writer, scholar, and reader whose wisdom and friendship I rely on hugely.

ACKNOWLEDGEMENTS

During the writing of this book, I have lost some great friends, among them two 'Women of Altitude'. The deaths of the Cambridge legend that was Rosie Tween, and of the sparkling Amanda Morris-Drake show how life is precious and all too short, but so too how some people use their time to touch so many. Life has never been the same since the death of my brilliant, beautiful, much loved, and greatest friend Rebecca Edwards Newman. She inspired me endlessly – and continues to do so – her boys Oscar, Alexander and Max are a credit to her. It is to Becky that this book is dedicated.

And finally, of course, Kate. Hopeful without expectation that the book would 'soon' be finished, encouraging without being pressuring, supportive whilst making it clear that there is a life waiting to be lived, and never ever failing to make me smile. Kate is the person anyone would want on their team; I got very lucky that she chose to be on mine. I now hope that I can live up to my pledge that, once the book was finished, I would be the funnest person she knows. That is the next big challenge.

NOTES

EPIGRAPHS

1   Lewes Roberts, *The treasure of traffike, or, A discourse of forraigne trade wherein is shewed the benefit and commoditie arising to a commonwealth or kingdome, by the skilfull merchant, and by a well ordered commerce and regular traffike* (London, 1641)
2   John Williams, *Great Britains Salomon* (London, 1625)

INTRODUCTION

1   *Letters from Sir Robert Cecil to Sir George Carew*, ed. Sir John Maclean (London, 1864) pp. 147–8
2   *Letters from Sir Robert Cecil to Sir George Carew*, ed. Sir John Maclean (London, 1864) pp.147–8
3   The phrase is from Rupali Mishra, *A Business of State: Commerce, Politics, and the Birth of the East India Company* (Cambridge, MA, 2018) p.545
4   'James I speech in Parliament: 8 March 1624', in *Journal of the House of Lords: Volume 3, 1620–1628* (London, 1767–1830), British History Online pp.249–51
5   See for example Thomas Palmer, *An Essay of the Meanes how to make our Travailes, into foraine Countries, the more profitable and honourable* (London, 1606); Fynes Moryson, *An itinerary vvritten by Fynes Moryson Gent. First in the Latine tongue, and then translated by him into English: containing his ten yeeres trauell through the tvvelue dominions of Germany, Bohmerland, Sweitzerland, Netherland, Denmarke, Poland, Jtaly, Turky, France, England, Scotland, and Ireland. Diuided into III parts* (London, 1617)
6   BN MSS. Français 15,989, fol. 61, cited in Malcolm R. Smuts, *Political Culture, the State, and the Problem of Religious War in Britain and Ireland, 1578–1625* (Oxford, 2023) p.546

1 SORROWS JOY

1   *Sorrowes Joy. Or, A lamentation for our late deceased soveraigne Eliʒabeth, with a triumph for the prosperous succession of our gratious King, James, &c.* (London, 1603)

2   William Camden, *The Historie of the Most Renowned and Victorious Princesse Eliʒabeth, Late Queene of England* (London, 1630) p.222

3   Godfrey Goodman, *The Court of King James the First*, ed. J.S. Brewer, 2 vols (London, 1839) vol. 1, pp.96–7

4   Rowland Whyte to Robert Sidney, 29 August 1599, in *Report on the Manuscripts of Lord de l'Isle & Dudley Preserved at Penshurst Place*, ed. William A. Shaw and Geraint Dyfnallt Owen, 6 vols (London, 1934) vol. 2, p.386

5   Sir Henry Ellis (ed.), *Original Letters illustrative of English History*, 2nd series (London, 1827) vol. 3, p.193

6   23 Eliz. C.2 (1581) in *The Statutes of the Realm: Printed by Command of His Majesty King George the Third, In Pursuance of an Address of the House of Commons of Great Britain. From Original Records And Authentic Manuscripts* (London, 1819) vol. 4, pp.659–661

7   See for example 'Report of the council of state to Philip III on the English succession, 1 Feb 1603', *Calendar of State Papers, Spain (Simancas)*, [hereafter *CSP Span*] *Volume 4, 1587–1603*, ed. Martin A.S. Hume (London, 1899) p.720

8   *The State of England Anno Dom. 1600* by Thomas Wilson, ed. F.J. Fisher (London, 1936) pp.2, 5

9   23 Eliz I., C.2 (1581) in *Statutes of the Realm* vol.4 pp.659–61

10 William Fowler, *A true reportarie of the most triumphant, and royal accomplishment of the baptisme of the most excellent, right high, and mightie prince, Frederik Henry; by the grace of God, Prince of Scotland Solemniʒed the 30. day of August. 1594* (Edinburgh, 1594)

11 Andrew Melville, *Principis Scoti-Britannorum Natalia and Gathelus* (Edinburgh, 1594) printed in *George Buchanan: The Political Poetry*, ed. and trans. Paul J. McGinnis and Arthur H. Williamson (Edinburgh, 1995), pp.276–9

12 Quoted in Christian Schneider, 'A Kingdom for a Catholic? Pope Clement VIII, King James VI/I, and the English Succession in International Diplomacy (1592–1605)', *The International History Review* 37/1 (2015) pp.119–41, p.121

13 See Cynthia Fry, 'Diplomacy and Deception: King James VI of Scotland's Foreign Relations with Europe (c.1584–1603)', University of St Andrews (2014)

14   See for example *CSP Span* IV pp.632, 675; 683; 724, 782

15   See Albert, J. Loomie, 'Philip III and the Stuart Succession in England, 1600–1603', *Revue Belge de Philologie et d'Histoire* 43 (1965) pp.492–514

16   James VI, *The true lavv of free monarchy, or The reciprocall and mutuall duty betvvixt a free king and his naturall subjects.: By a well affected subject of the kingdome of Scotland* (Edinburgh, 1598) printed in Johann P. Somerville (ed.) *King James VI and I: Political Writings* (Cambridge, 1994) pp.62–84; TNA SP 52/61 no.65 cited in Alexander Courtney, *James VI, Britannic Prince. King of Scots and Elizabeth's Heir, 1566–1603* (London, 2024) p.197

17   *Calendar Of State Papers Relating To Scotland And Mary, Queen Of Scots, Volume 13, Part 1 (1597–1599)*, ed. J.D. Mackie (London, 1969) pp.136–37

18   *Correspondence of King James VI of Scotland with Sir Robert Cecil and Others in England, During the Reign of Queen Elizabeth: With An Appendix Containing Papers Illustrative of Transactions Between King James and Robert Earl of Essex...* ed. John Bruce (London, 1861) pp.xxxvi

19   Ibid. p.4

20   Ibid. p.10

21   Cited in D.H. Willson, *King James VI and I* (London, 1967) p.154

22   Printed in *The Secret Correspondence of Sir Robert Cecil with James VI King of Scotland: Now First Published*, ed. Edmund Goldsmid (Edinburgh, 1887) pp.5, 8–9

23   TNA SP 52/67 no.32; *Letters of Queen Elizabeth and King James of Scotland*, ed. J. Bruce (London, 1849) pp.135–38

24   See Richard Dutton, 'Hamlet and Succession', in Susan Doran and Paulina Kewes (eds.), *Doubtful and Dangerous: The Question of Succession in late Elizabethan England* (Manchester, 2014) pp.173–91

25   G.B. Harrison (ed.) *A Last Elizabethan Journal* (London, 1933) p.323; TNA, SP 14/1 fols.68.73; John Stow, *A Summarie of the Chronicles of England* (London, 1604) p.439; Bruce (ed.) *Correspondence of King James VI of Scotland with Sir Robert Cecil and Others* p.73

26   *Calendar of State Papers Relating To English Affairs in the Archives of Venice, Volume 9, 1592–1603*, ed. Horatio F. Brown (London, 1897) [hereafter *CSP Ven*] no.1166

27   *Acts of the Privy Council (APC), 1601–1604*, ed. J.R. Dasent (London, 1907), pp.491–2

28   John Manningham, *The Diary of John Manningham of the Middle Temple, 1602–03*, ed. Robert Parker Solein (Hanover, NH, 1976) p.208; John Clapham, *Elizabeth of England: Certain Observations concerning the Life*

and Reign of Queen Elizabeth, ed. Evelyn Plummer Read and Conyers Read (Philadelphia, 1951) p.99; *The Journal of Sir Roger Wilbraham for the Years 1593–1616*, ed. H.S. Scott (London, 1902) p.54

29   *CSP Ven*, vol.9 No. 563

30   Clapham, *Certain Observations* p.99

31   *APC 1601–4* p.492; HMC, *The manuscripts of His Grace the Duke of Rutland: preserved at Belvoir castle Rutland* (London, 1888) p.388

32   Cited in Michael G. Cornelius, *John Donne and the Metaphysical Poets* (London, 2008) p.39

33   *Correspondence of King James VI of Scotland with Sir Robert Cecil and Others* p.47

34   *The Memoirs of Robert Carey*, ed. Walter Scott (London, 1808) p.117

35   Ibid. p.118

36   William Weston, *The Autobiography of an Elizabethan*, tr. Philip Carman (London, 1955) p.222

37   *The Memoirs of Robert Carey* pp.119–20

38   Clapham, *Certain Observations* p.99

39   *The Diary of John Manningham* p. 169; *Journal of Sir Roger Wilbraham* p.54; Goodman, *The Court of King James the First* vol.1, pp.55–58

40   'By the King. A Proclamation, declaring the undoubted Right of our Sovereign Lord King James, to the Crown of the Realms of England, France and Ireland. [London, 24 March 1603]' in James F. Larkin and Paul L. Hughes (eds), *Stuart Royal Proclamations: Vol.1, Royal Proclamations of King James I 1603–1625* (Oxford, 2013)

41   Ibid.

42   *The Diary of John Manningham* pp.208–9

43   *CSP Ven*, vol. 9 No. 1169

44   *The Diary of John Manningham* pp.208–9

45   Clapham, *Certain Observations* p.99

46   The claim to throne of France, which had been maintained since the reign of Edward III, was merely nominal.

47   *The Memoirs of Robert Carey* pp.124–8

48   John Nichols, *The Progresses, Processions and Magnificent Festivities of King James the First*, 4 vols (London 1828) vol. 1 p.33

49   *Letters of King James VI and I*, ed. G.P.V. Akrigg (London, 1984) p.209

50   *CSP Ven* vol.10 No. 40

51   Amy L Juhala, 'The Household and Court of King James VI', PhD, University of Edinburgh (2000) p.170

52   TNA SP 15/6/179

53 J.H. Burton et al., eds, *Register of the Privy Council of Scotland* (16 vols), Edinburgh, 1877–90) vol.6 p.560; *Stuart Royal Proclamations*, vol. 1 pp.18–20

54 J. Duncan Mackie (ed.), '"A Loyall Subiectes Advertisement" as to the Unpopularity of James I's Government in England, 1603–4', *The Scottish Historical Review*, 23 (1925) pp.1–4 at p.2

55 Quoted in Willson, *King James VI and I* p.171

56 Mackie (ed.), '"A Loyall Subiectes Advertisement"' p.2

57 John Stow and Edmond Howes, *The annales, or a general chronicle of England* (London, 1615) p.823

58 Lambeth Palace Library, MS Talbot papers, vol. K, fol. 83, as printed in Edmund Lodge, *Illustrations of British History, Biography, and Manners in the Reigns of Henry VIII, Edward VI. Mary, Elizabeth and James I, Exhibited in a Series of Original Papers* (London, 1791) vol.3, pp.163–5. See also Nadine Akkerman, 'The Goddess of the Household: the Masquing Politics of Lucy Harington-Russell, 1601–1604' in Nadine Akkerman and Birgit Houben (eds.), *The Politics of Female Households: Ladies-in-waiting across Early Modern Europe* (Leiden, 2013), pp.287–309 at pp.290–92

59 'By the King. A Proclamation inhibiting the use and execution of any Charter or Graunt made by the late Queen Elizabeth, of any kind of Monopolies, &c. [Theobalds 7 May 1603]', in *Stuart Royal Proclamations* vol.1

60 G.B. Harrison, *A Jacobean Journal: Being a Record of Those Things Most Talked of During the Years, 1603–1606* (London, 1941) pp.16–17

2 THE WONDERFUL YEAR

1 Thomas Dekker, *The Wonderfull Yeare: 1603* (London, 1603)

2 Samuel Daniel, *A Panegyrike Congratulatorie Delivered to the Kings most Excellent Majestie* (London, 1603)

3 John Nichols, *The progresses, processions, and magnificent festivities, of King James the First, his royal consort, family, and court*, 4 vols (London 1828) vol. 1 pp.128–30

4 Ibid. vol. 1 p.129

5 Ben Jonson, *The Masque of Blackness* (1605), ed. David Lindley in *The Cambridge Edition of the works of Ben Jonson Online*, https://universitypublishingonline.org/cambridge/benjonson.

6 Dekker, *The Wonderfull Yeare: 1603* unnumbered

7 Robert Cotton, *Discourse of his Majesty's Descent from the Saxon Kings* (London, 1603)

8 George Owen Harry, *The genealogy of the High and Mighty Monarch, James, by the Grace of God, King of Great Brittayne* (London, 1604)

9   See Linda Levy Peck (ed.), *The Mental World of the Jacobean Court* (Cambridge, 1991) p.5 and plate 1.

10   'By the King. A Proclamation for the uniting of England and Scotland. [Greenwich 19 May 1603]' (1603) in James F. Larkin, and Paul L. Hughes (eds.), *Stuart Royal Proclamations: Vol.1, Royal Proclamations of King James I 1603–1625* (Oxford, 2013)

11   *The Register of the Privy Council of Scotland A.D.1599–1604*, vol. 6 p.553

12   See Maurice Lee Jr, 'James VI's "Government of Scotland after 1603"', *The Scottish Historical Review*, 55 (1976) pp.41–53 at p.41

13   For the postal service see William Taylor, 'The King's Mails, 1603–1625', *The Scottish Historical Review*, 42 (1963), pp.143–47

14   Mark Kishlansky, *A Monarchy Transformed: Britain 1603–1714* (London, 1996) p.78

15   Bruce (ed.), *Correspondence of King James VI of Scotland with Sir Robert Cecil and Others* p.56

16   Gervase Holles, *Memorials of the Holles Family, 1493–1656* (London, 1937), p.94

17   See Keith M. Brown, 'The Scottish Aristocracy, Anglicization and the Court, 1603–38', *The Historical Journal*, 36 (1993) 543–76

18   *CSP Ven* vol. 10 No.55

19   *Translation and Facsimiles of the Original Latin Letters of King James I of England (VI of Scotland), to his Royal Brother-in-Law, King Christian IV of Denmark*, ed. Ronald M. Meldrum, (Washington, DC, 1977) p.9

20   'By the King. A Proclamation signifying the Kings Majesty's pleasure, touching the resort of people to his Coronation. [Windsor Castle 6 July 1603]', in. Larkin and Hughes (eds), *Stuart Royal Proclamations*

21   W.B. Rye, 'The Coronation of King James I, 1603', *The Antiquary*, 22 (1890) pp.18–23 at p.19

22   See Sybil M. Jack, '"A Pattern for a King's Inauguration": The Coronation of James I in England', *Parergon*, 21 (2004) pp.67–91; Alice Hunt, 'The Bright Star of the North: James I and his English Coronation', *Medieval English Theatre*, 38 (2016), pp.22–37

23   Rye, 'The Coronation of King James I', p.19

24   Thomas Bilson, *A sermon preached at Westminster before the King and Queen's Maiesties at their Coronation on St James his day being the 28 [sic] July* (London, 1603) sig.A [5]

25   James VI, *The True Law of Free Monarchies: or, The Reciprock and Mutual Duetie betwixt a Free King, and His Naturall Subjects* (Edinburgh, 1598) printed in Sommerville (ed.), *Political Writings* pp.62–85

26   James VI, *The Trew Law* in Sommerville (ed.), *Political Writings* p.65

27 BL, G.3, EM.316 quoted in Susan Doran, *From Tudor to Stuart: The Regime Change from Elizabeth I to James I* (Oxford, 2024) p.392

28 *CSP Ven* vol. 10 No. 105

3 THE EYES OF ALL MEN

1 Francis Bacon, 'The Beginning of the History of Great Britain', in B. Vickers (ed.) *The History of the Reign of King Henry VII and Selected Works* (Cambridge 1998) pp.215–220

2 See Fry, 'Diplomacy and Deception'

3 *Calendar of the Cecil Papers in Hatfield House: Volume 15, 1603*, ed. M.S. Giuseppi (London, 1930), British History Online

4 Smuts, *Political Culture*, p.546

5 *Correspondance de la cour d'Espagne sur les affaires des Pays-Bas au XVIIe siècle*, ed. Henri Lonchay and Joseph Cuvelier, 2 vols (Brussels, 1923), vol. 1 pp.141–2 quoted by Fry, 'Diplomacy and Deception', p.131

6 *Correspondance de la cour d'Espagne*, p.144 quoted in Smuts, *Political Culture*, p.546

7 Maximilien de Béthune duc de Sully, *The Memoirs of the Duke of Sully, Prime Minister to Henry the Great*, trans. Charlotte Lennox, 4 vols (London, 1861), vol. 2 p.358 quoted in R. Cross, 'To Counterbalance the World: England, Spain and Peace in the Early 17th century' PhD, University of Princeton (2012) p.107

8 James I, 'Speech to Parliament of 31 March 1604', in Sommerville (ed.), *Political Writings* p.169

9 See Cross, 'Counterbalance the World' p.104

10 Walter Ralegh, 'A Discourse Touching a War with Spain, and of the Protecting of the Netherlands', (1603) printed in *The Works of Sir Walter Ralegh, Kt*, 8 vols (Oxford, 1829), vol. 8, p.314

11 Pierre Paul Laffleeur de Kermaingant, *L'ambassade de France En Angleterre Sous Henri IV. Mission de Christophe de Harlay, Comte de Beaumont (1602–1605)* (Paris, 1895) vol.2 p.109 cited in Cross, 'Counterbalance the World' p.105

12 *Correspondence de la Cour d'Espagne* vol.1 p. 148 cited in Cross, 'Counterbalance the World' p.108

13 *Memoirs of the Duke of Sully*, vol. 2 p.363 quoted in Cross, 'Counterbalance the World' pp.135–6

14 *Archives ou correspondence inédite de la maison Orange-Nassau*, ed. G. Groen van Prinsterer, series 2,(Utrecht, 1858), vol.2 pp.229–30 quoted in Smuts, *Political Culture* p.551

15   Kermaingant (ed.), *Mission de Harlay*, vol.2 p.283 quoted in Smuts, *Political Culture* p.552

16   *Correspondence de la Cour d'Espagne* vol.1 pp.170–71 cited in Cross, 'Counterbalance the World' p.112

17   AGS Estado, leg. 840, doc 181, ff.2v-3 cited in Cross, 'Counterbalance the World' p.150

18   *A calendar of the manuscripts of the Most Hon. The marquis of Salisbury, KG, &c, preserved at Hatfield House, Hertfordshire* (24 vols, London, 1883–1976) [*HMC Salisbury*] vol. 15 p.260

19   Maurice Lee Jr. (ed.), *Dudley Carleton to John Chamberlain, 1603–1624: Jacobean Letters* (New Brunswick, NJ, 1972), p.42

20   Ibid. p.55

21   AGS Estado, leg. 842, docs 147–8, f. 2 cited and quoted in Cross, 'Counterbalance the World', p.153

22   Lee (ed.), *Jacobean Letters* p.55

23   Beaumont to Henri IV, 23 January 1604, in Mary Sullivan, *Court Masques of James I: Their Influence on Shakespeare and the Public Theaters* (New York, 1913) p.193

4 THE REUNION OF CHRISTENDOM

1   James I Speech to the English Parliament in *Political Writings* ed. Sommerville pp.132–146 at p.140

2   ABSJ, PC, p.1337 (ABSJ, Stonyhurst Collectanea P/ii, p.492a) cited in Michael C. Questier, Dynastic *Politics and the British Reformations, 1558–1630* (Oxford, 2019) p.271

3   *CSP Ven* vol. 10 No.73

4   ABSJ, PC, p.1338 (ABSJ, Stonyhurst Collectanea P/ii, p.492a) in Questier, *Dynastic Politics* p.271

5   Henry Gee and William John Hardy (eds), *Documents Illustrative of English Church History* (New York, 1896) pp.508–11

6   TNA SP 14/1, fols 110r–110v

7   Bodleian Library Ashmolean MS 1729, no. 37, fols. 68r–v; Diana Newton, *The Making of the Jacobean Regime: James VI and I and the Government of England, 1603–1605* (Woodbridge, 2005), p.28

8   *CSP Ven* vol.10 No.22; Stanley Rypins, 'The Printing of "Basilikòn Dôron", 1603', *The Papers of the Bibliographical Society of America*, 64.4 (1970) pp.393–417

9   See James Doelman, '"A King of Thine Own Heart": The English Reception of King James VI and I's *Basilikon Doron*', *The Seventeenth Century* 9 (1994), pp.1–9

10   'Basilikon Doron' in *Political Writings*, ed. Sommerville pp.1–61 at p.5

11   Patrick Adamson, *Genethliacum serenissimi Scotiae, Angliae, et Hiberniae principis, IACOBI VI, Mariae Regnae filii* (1566), printed and trans. in Steven J. Reid and David McOmish (eds.), *Corona Borealis: Scottish Neo-Latin Poets on King James VI and His Reign, 1566–1603* (Glasgow, 2020)

12   George Buchanan, 'Genethliacon' in *George Buchanan: The Political Poetry*, ed. and trans. Paul J.McGinnis and Arthur H.Williamson (Edinburgh, 1995), pp.154–5

13   See Reid and McOmish (eds.), *Corona Borealis: Scottish Neo Latin Poets on King James VI and his Reign 1566–1603* (Glasgow 2020)

14   James Melville, *The Autobiography and Diary of Mr. James Melvill* (Edinburgh, 1842) p.48

15   Roger A. Mason, 'George Buchanan, James VI and the Presbyterians' in Roger A. Mason (ed.), *Scots and Britons: Scottish Political Thought* (Cambridge, 1994) pp.113–37

16   'Basilikon Doron' p.25

17   Ibid. p.18–19

18   Ibid. p.27

19   James VI, 'Trew Law', in *Political Writings*, ed. Sommerville, p.61

20   Annie I. Cameron and Robert S. Rait (eds.), *The Warrender Papers*, (Edinburgh, 1932), II, vol. 2, pp.131–2; 133–41 cited in Franklin L. Baumer, 'England, the Turk, and the Common Corps of Christendom', *American Historical Review*, 50.1 (1944) pp.26–48 at p.43

21   See Franklin Le Van Baumer. 'The Conception of Christendom in Renaissance England.' *Journal of the History of Ideas*, 6.2 (1945), pp.131–56

22   'Henry VIII to Wotton, *State Papers of Henry VIII*, X 25–26' cited in Baumer, 'England, the Turk, and the Common Corps of Christendom', p.43

23   *CSP Ven* vol. 10 No.36

24   BL Kings MS 123 fol.326v quoted and trans. Smuts, *Political Culture* pp.557–8

25   Ibid. fol.327

26   Ibid. fol.324

27   Ibid. fol.327

28   BL Kings MS 124, fol. 39v

29   Jacques-Auguste de Thou, *Historiarum sui temporis, pars prima* (Paris, 1604)

30 Jacques-Auguste de Thou, *Histoire universelle*, 11 vols (The Hague, 1740), vol. 1 p.xlvii cited in W.B. Patterson, *James VI and I and the Reunion of Christendom* (Cambridge, 1997) p.2

31 *CSP Ven* vol.10, no. 739

32 'By the King. A Proclamation commanding all Jesuits, Seminaries, and other Priests, to depart the Realm by a day appointed. [Westminster 22 February 1604]' in J. Larkin and Hughes (eds), *Stuart Royal Proclamations*

33 *Stuart Royal Proclamations*, I. 60–63

34 See Nichols, *Progresses* vol.1 p.315

35 'By the King. A Proclamation commanding all Jesuits, Seminaries, and other Priests, to depart the Realm by a day appointed' [Westminster 22 February 1604] in Larkin and Hughes (eds), *Stuart Royal Proclamations*

36 William Barlow, The *Summe and Substance of the Conference Which, It Pleased his Excellent Majestie to Have...at Hampton Court: January 14.1603* (London, 1603) (London, 1804) p.35

37 British Library MS Lansdowne 988, fols 274v, 297r

38 Printed in Alfred W. Pollard, ed., *Records of the English Bible: The Documents Relating to the Translation and Publication of the Bible in English, 1525–1611* (New York, 1911), pp.53–5

39 *The Bible: Authorized King James Version* (London 1612), ed. Robert Carroll and Stephen Prickett (Oxford, 1998) p.lxxi

40 Ibid. p.lxxii

5 THE KING OF GREAT BRITAIN

1 Ben Jonson, *The Masque of Blackness* (1605), in *The Cambridge Edition of the Works of Ben Jonson Online* (Cambridge, 2014)

2 Harrison, *A Jacobean Journal* pp.110–13

3 See Mark Hutchings and Berta Cano-Echevarría, 'The Spanish Ambassador's account of James I's entry into London, 1604 [with Text], *The Seventeenth Century*, 33 (2017) pp.255–77

4 Gilbert Dugdale, *The Time Triumphant Declaring in Briefe, the Arival of our Soveraigne Liedge Lord, King James into England, his Coronation at Westminster: Together with his Late Royal Progresse, from the Towre of London Through the Cittie, to his Hignes Manor of White Hall...*(London, 1604), sig A3, B4

5 Nichols, *Progresses* vol.1 p.324

6 *CSP Ven* vol.10 No.201

7 Dugdale, *The Time Triumphant*

8 John Fenton, *King James his welcome to London* (London, 1603) B3v

9   See Maureen M. Meikle, 'A Meddlesome Princess: Anna of Denmark and Scottish Court Politics, 1589–1603' in Julian Goodare and Michael Lynch (eds.), *The Reign of James VI* (Edinburgh, 2008) pp.126–41

10 Thomas Dekker, *The Whole Magnificent Entertainment given to King James* (London, 1604); (Triumphant Passage of the King through London, 160r) in Nichols, *Progresses* vol. 1 pp.337–76 at pp.357, 358

11 Texts of the procession was subsequently produced by Thomas Dekker, *The Whole Magnificent Entertainment given to King James* (London, 1604); Ben Jonson, *B. Jon: His Part of King James his Royall and Magnificent Entertainment* (London, 1604); Stephen Harrison, *The Arches of Triumph Erected in Honor of the High and Mighty Prince. James the First of That Name, King, of England and the Sixt of Scotland* (London, 1604)

12 Kevin Sharpe, *Image Wars: Promoting King and Commonwealths in England, 1603–1660* (New Haven, CT, and London, 2010)

13 Ben Jonson, *B. Jon: His Part of King James his Royall and Magnificent Entertainment* in Nichols, *Progresses* vol. 1 pp.377–99 at p.378

14 Ibid. p.383

15 Ibid. p.383

16 Graham Parry, *The Golden Age Restor'd: The Culture of the Stuart Court, 1603–42* (Cambridge, 1981) p.6

17 Jonson, *B. Jon: His Part of King James his Royall and Magnificent Entertainment* in Nichols, *Progresses* in Nichols, *Progresses* vol. 1 p.386

18 Johnson in Nichols, *Progresses* vol. 1 p.387

19 R. Dutton (ed.), *Jacobean Civic Pageants* (Keele, 1995) p.54

20 See Gervase Hood, 'A Netherlandic Triumphal Arch for James I' in Susan Roach (ed.), *Across the Narrow Seas: Studies in the History and Bibliography of Britan and the Low Countries*. Presented to Amma E.C. Simoni (London, 1991) pp.67–82

21 Dekker in Nichols, *Progresses* vol. 1 pp.337–376 at pp.357, 358

22 Ibid. p.362

23 Ibid. p.371

24 Jonson in Nichols, *Progresses* vol. 1 p.391

25 King's Speech to Parliament, 19 March 1604 in Somerville (ed.) *Political Writings* pp.132–46 at p.133

26 Ibid. pp.132–46

27 Ibid. pp.134, 135–36, 137

28 Ibid. pp. 132–46

29 'A letter to the Earl of Northumberland after he had been with the King' in Francis Bacon, *The remaines of the Right Honorable Francis, Lord Verulam, Viscount of St. Albanes, sometimes Lord Chancellour of England*

being essayes and severall letters to severall great personages (London 1648) p.65

30 Francis Bacon, *A discourse of the happy union of the kingdoms of England & Scotland dedicated in private to King James I / by Francis Lord Bacon* (London, 1700) p.5

31 William Cobbett, *Parliamentary History of England from the Norman, in 1066 to the Year 1803*, 36 vols (London, 1819) vol. 34 p.934

32 'House of Commons Journal Volume 1: 24 April 1604', in *Journal of the House of Commons: Volume 1, 1547–1629* (London, 1802), British History Online p.178

33 *Commons Journal* vol. 1 pp.186–7

34 *Commons Journal* vol. 1 p.186

35 *Commons Journal* vol. 1 p.183

36 TNA SP 14/7/85, fol.284

37 *HMC Report on the manuscripts of the Duke of Buccleuch and Queensberry, K.G., K.T., preserved at Montagu House, Whitehall*, 3 vols. (1899–1926) vol. 3 p.86

38 *A discourse of the happy union of the kingdoms of England & Scotland dedicated in private to King James I* by Francis Lord Bacon (London, 1700); *Commons Journal* vol. 1 pp.177–8, 184

39 *Commons Journal* vol. 1 p.184

40 Nichols, *Progresses* vol. 1, fn. 25

41 'A Treatise about the Union of England and Scotland', in Bruce R. Galloway and Brian P. Levack (eds.), *The Jacobean Union: Six Tracts of 1604* (Edinburgh, 1985) 47

42 John Gordon, *England and Scotland's Happinesse in Being Reducted to Unitie of Religion, Under Our Invincible Monarke King James* (London, 1604) pp.5–6

43 Quoted in Jason White, *Militant Protestantism and British Identity, 1603–1642* (Abingdon, 2015) p.19

44 'James I Speech to Parliament, 19 March 1604' in Sommerville (ed.), *Political Writings* pp.132–46 at p.140

45 See for example William Cornwallis, *The Miraculous and Happy Union between England and Scotland by how admirable meanes it is effected* (London, 1604) and John Thornborough, *A Discourse Plainly Proving the Evident Utilitie and Urgent Necessitie of the Desired Happie Union of the Two Famous Kingdomes of England and Scotland...* (London, 1604)

46 Walles Notestein, *The House of Commons 1604–1610* (New Haven, CT, 1971), pp.80, 83–5

47 'A most joyful and just recognition of the immediate, lawful and undoubted Succession, Descent and Right of the Crown' is the full title of the Succession to the Crown Act 1603 (1 Jas. 1. c. 1) *Statutes of the Realm*: vol. 4, 1603–25, ed. John Raithby (London, 1819) pp.1017–18

48 'By the King. A Proclamation for the uniting of England and Scotland. [Greenwich 19 May 1603]' in Larkin and Hughes (eds.), *Stuart Royal Proclamations*

49 Ibid.

50 'By the King. A Proclamation concerning the Kings Majesty's Stile, of King of Great Britain, &c. [Westminster 20 October 1604]' in Larkin and Hughes (eds.), *Stuart Royal Proclamations*

51 Ibid.

52 *Register of the Privy Council of Scotland* vol. 6 p.597

53 *The Acts of the Parliament of Scotland 1593–1625*, 12 vols (London, 1814–44) vol. 4 p.276

6 REX PACIFICUS (KING OF PEACE)

1 Thomas Middleton, *The peace-maker: or Great Brittaines blessing,* ... (London, 1618) B2

2 *CSP Ven* 10 No.97

3 'Speech to Parliament of 19 March 1604' in Sommerville (ed.) *Political Writings* pp.133–4

4 See P. Croft, 'Trading with the Enemy, 1585–1604', *The Historical Journal*, 32 (1989), pp.281–302

5 Richard Martin, *A Speech Delivered, to the King's Most Excellent Majestie in the Name of the Sheriffes of London and Middlesex* (London, 1603) unnumbered (printed in Nichols, *Progresses* vol. 1, 1.131*.)

6 *The Register of Letters etc. of the Governour and Company of Merchants of London trading into the East indies*, ed. George Birdwood and William Foster (London, 1893) p.28

7 Hatfield House, Cecil Papers 190/12.

8 T.N.A., SP 14/4, fol. 146r, 7 Nov. 1603 cited in Alexandra Gajda, 'War, Peace and Commerce and the Treaty of London (1604)', *Historical Research*, 96.274 p.466

9 AGS Estado, leg. 842, doc 135, fol.1, trans. and citation made in Cross, 'Counterbalance the World' p.182

10 AGS Estado leg 842 doc.140 fol.6, trans. and citation made in Cross, 'Counterbalance the World' p.176 who adds the Constable had given Villamediana permission to claim a diplomatic illness

11 AGS Estado, leg. 842, doc 140, fol.8v cited in Cross, 'Counterbalance the World' p.180

12 AGS Estado, leg. 842, doc 73, fol. 3 cited in Cross, 'Counterbalance the World' p.185

13 AGS Estado, leg. 842, docs 88, 90–92, fol.2 cited in Cross, 'Counterbalance the World' p.186

14 AGS Estado, leg. 842, doc 94 fol.1 cited in Cross, 'Counterbalance the World' pp.186–7

15 Henry Howard, earl of Northampton, 'Reason against Permission of the Indias', BL Cotton MS., Vespasian C XIII, fol. 401r. See Gajda, 'War, Peace and Commerce' pp.459–72

16 'A Treaty of Perpetual Peace and Alliance between Philip III, King of Spain, and the Archduke and Archdutches Albert and Isabella on the one side, and James I of England on the other side, 1604', in *A general collection of treaties, manifesto's, contracts of marriage, renunciations, and other publick papers* (London, 1713) [hereafter *Treaties*] pp.131–46

17 Ibid.

18 'The Proclamation Upon the peace with Spain and the Archdukes. [Whitehall 19 August 1604] (1604)' in Larkin and Hughes (eds.), *Stuart Royal Proclamations*

19 S.R. Gardiner, *History of England from the Accession of James I to the Outbreak of the Civil War, 1603–1642*, 10 vols (London, 1887–91) vol. 1 p.214

20 *CSP Ven* vol. 10 No. 278

21 (Bl Add MS 38, 139 fol.70); Bl Sloane 1851 fol.120

22 For example *Calendar of State Papers Domestic* [hereafter *CSP Dom*]: *James I, 1603–1610*, ed. Mary Anna Everett Green (London, 1857), British History Online p.127

23 *Relación de la Jornada del Excelentissimo Condestable de Castilla, a las pazes entre España y Inglaterra, que se concluyeron y juraron en Londres por el mes de Agosto, Año 1604* (Valencia, 1604) fol.14 cited in Cross, 'Counterbalance the World' p.335

24 TNA SP 94/11 fol.196

25 TNA SP 94/11 fol.196, 172

26 TNA SP 94/12 fol.128

7 THE POWDER PLOT AND PAPER WAR

1 *Journal of the House of Commons: Volume 1, 1547–1629* (London, 1802) British History Online p.302

2 *Letters of King James VI & I* pp.276–7

3   TNA SP 14/216/176

4   TNA SP 14/216/ part 1 no.38

5   TNA SP 14/216 fol.1

6   TNA SP 14/216 fols. 44–5

7   Ibid.

8   Sir John Harington, *Nugæ Antiquæ: Being a Miscellaneous Collection of Original Papers in Prose and Verse: Written in the Reigns of Henry VIII. Queen Mary, Elizabeth, King James, &c.* (London, 1792), vol. 2 pp.239–40

9   'By the King. A Proclamation denouncing Thomas Percy and other his adherents to be Traitors. [Westminster 7 November 1605]' in Larkin and Hughes (eds.), *Stuart Royal Proclamations*

10 *His Maiesties Speach in This Last Seßion of Parliament, as Neere His Very Words as Could Be Gathered at the Instant* (London, 1605), printed in Sommerville (ed.), *Political Writings* pp.147–158

11 *A Discourse of the Maner of the Discovery of the Late Intended Treason, was published with His Majesties Speech in This Last Session of Parliament* (London, 1605). The volume is customarily referred to as *The King's Book*

12 A *True and Perfect Relation of the proceedings at the several Arraignments of THE LATE MOST barbarous Traitors* (London 1606), A3. On the King's Printing House see Graham Rees and Maria Wakely, *Publishing, Politics, and Culture: The King's Printers in the Reign of James VI and I* (Oxford, 2009)

13 Anon, *A True and Perfect Relation of the Whole Proceedings Against the Late Most Barbarous Traitors, Garnet a Jesuite, and His Confederats Contayning Sundry Speeches Delivered by the Lord Commissioners at Their Arraignment...* (London, 1606) sig A2v

14 'The Trial of Henry Garnet, Superior of the Jesuits in England, at the Guildhall of London, for a High Treason, being a Conspirator in the Gunpowder Plot', 28 March 1606, in T.B. Howell (ed.), *State Trials*, (London, 1816), vol. 2 p.234

15 William Camden, *Actio in Henricum Garnetum Societatis Iesuiticae in Anglia superiorem ...*(London, 1607)

16 Thomas Dekker, *The Double PP. 1605* (London, 1605)

17 J[ohn] H[eath] *The Divell of the Vault. Or, the Vnmasking of Murther in a Briefe Declaration of the Catholike-complotted Treason, lately discouered* (London, 1606). sigs D2v, D3

18 See for example Robert Abbot, *Antichristi Demonstratio* (London, 1603) and *Antilogia* (London, 1613); George Downame, *Treatise Concerning Anti-christ* (London, 1603)

19 'Act for the better discovering and repressing of popish recusants' 3 & 4 Jac.1.c.4: *Statues of the Realm*, iv 1071.

20 BL Kings MS 123 fol.327

21 James I, Tripilici nodo, triplex in Sommerville (ed.) *Political Writings* p.90

22 George Blackwell, *His Answeres vpon Sundry His Examinations; Together with His Approbation and Taking of the Oath of Allegeance; And His Letter Written to His Assistants and Brethren, Moouing Them Not Onely to Take the Said Oath but to Aduise All Romish Catholikes So to Doe* (London, 1607), p.9

23 Ibid. pp.23–4, 39

24 James I, 'Tripilici nodo, triplex' in Sommerville (ed.) *Political Writings* p.97

25 Ibid. p.99

26 George Blackwell, *A Large Examination Taken at Lambeth According to His Maiesties Direction, Point by Point, of M. George Blakwell, Made Archpriest of England by Pope Clement 8, vpon Occasion of a Certaine Answere of His, without the Priuitie of the State, to a Letter Lately Sent unto Him from Cardinall Bellarmine Blaming Him for Taking the Oath of Allegeance* (London, 1607), p.158

27 James I, 'Tripilici nodo, triplex' p.86

28 Ibid. p.111

29 Ibid. p.131

30 Robert Bellarmine, *Matthaei Torti, presbyteri & theology papiensis, responsio ad librvm inscriptum, Triplico nodo, triplex cuneus, sive apologia pro iuramento fidelitatis* (St Omer, 1608) See for pamphlets and tracts produced Peter Milward, *Religious Controversies of the Jacobean Age: A Survey of Printed Sources* (London, 1978) pp.89–131

31 A reference to Psalm 22:12 which sees demons represented by bulls surrounding Christ on the Cross

32 James I, *The Workes of the Most High and Mightie Prince, James* (London, 1616) sig. d2

33 TNA SP 99/3 fol.153v

34 TNA SP 99/3 fol.154v

35 *Ambassades de Monsieur de la Boderie en Angleterre sous le règne d'Henri IV. & la minorité de Louis XIII., depuis les années 1606 jusqu'en 1611*, ed. Paul Denis Burtin, 5 vols (Paris, 1750) vol. 2 p.68, quoted and trans. in Smuts, *Political Culture* p.566

36 TNA SP 99/3 fols. 187v–188

37 *Ambassades de la Boderie* ed. Burdin, vol. 2 p.160, quoted and trans. in Smuts, *Political Culture* p.566

38 *CSP Ven* vol. 10 No. 728; *CSP Ven* vol. 11 No. 3

39 George Marcelline, *The Triumphs of King James* ...(London, 1610) m2v–m3r

40 A point made by Linda Levy Peck (ed.), *The Mental World of the Jacobean Court* (Cambridge, 1991) p.8

41 James I, *An Apologie....together with a Promonition* (1609) printed in Sommerville (ed.), *Political Writings* pp.62–85

42 *Ambassades de la Boderie* ed. Burdin, vol. 4 pp.378–9, quoted and trans. in Smuts, *Political Culture* p.563

43 James I, 'Tripilici nodo, triplex' p.112

8 THE MONARCHS MEETING

1 John Ford, *Honor Trivmphant. Or The Peeres Challenge, by Armes defensible, at Tilt, Turney, and Barriers . . . Also The Monarches meeting: The King of Denmarkes welcome into England* (London, 1606) F2r

2 Point made by pamphleteer William Drummond in a letter dated 18 July 1606 and printed in John Nichols, *Progresses* vol. 2, p.53

3 John Ford, *Honor Trivmphant* F1v

4 Ibid. F2r

5 Edward P Cheyney, 'England and Denmark in the Later Days of Queen Elizabeth', *The Journal of Modern History* 1.1 (1929), pp.9–39 at p.24

6 *Letters of King James I ...to King Christian IV of Denmark* p.15

7 See Steve Murdoch, *Britain, Denmark-Norway and the House of Stuart, 1603–1660: A Diplomatic and Military Analysis* (East Linton, 2000) p.37

8 Henry Robarts, *The King of Denmarkes Welcome: Containing his ariuall, abode, and entertainement, both in the Citie and other places* (London, 1606), A3r; John Davies, *Bien Venv. Greate Britaines Welcome to Hir Greate Friendes, and Deere Brethren The Danes* (London, 1606), C1v

9 From James Shapiro, *1606. William Shakespeare and the Year of Lear* (London, 2015) p.291; See Paul Douglas Lockart, *The Activist Monarchy of Christian IV of Denmark, 1513–1660: The Rise and Decline of a Renaissance Monarchy* (Oxford, 2007)

10 Ford, *Honor Trivmphant* F1r.

11 *The King of Denmarkes Welcome* A2v

12 Hatfield House, Cecil Papers, vol. 119, 16 August 1606

13 Sir John Harington, *Nugæ Antiquæ: Being a Miscellaneous Collection of Original Papers in Prose and Verse: Written in the Reigns of Henry VIII. Queen Mary, Elizabeth, King James, &c.* (London, 1792), vol. 2 p.130

14 Ibid. vol. 2 p.128

15   Ibid. vol. 2 p.126

16   Ibid. vol. 2 p.131

17   Nichols, *Progresses* vol. 2 p.84

18   *The King of Denmarkes Welcome*, A2v

19   Sir John Harington, *Nugæ Antiquæ* vol. 2 p. 129

20   *The King of Denmarkes Welcome* p.22

21   Henry Roberts, *Most royall and Honourable entertaine-ment, of the famous and renowmed King, Christiern the fourth, King of Denmarke, &c...for his gracious welcome By H. R.* (London, 1606) [*The King of Denmarkes Welcome*]

22   *The King of Denmarkes Welcome* p.2

23   Nichols, *Progresses* vol. 2 p.68. See Hatfield House, Cecil Papers vol. 193

24   Nichols, *Progresses* vol. 2 p.68

25   *King of Denmark Welcome* sig D2r

26   Henry Roberts, *Englands farevvell to Christian the fourth, famous king of Denmarke* (London, 1606) unnumbered

27   Ibid.

28   *Letters of King James VI and I* pp.326–7

29   *Sermons by the Right Honourable and Reverend Father in God, Lancelot Andrewes, Late Lord Bishop of Winchester. Published, by His Majesties speciall command. . The fovrth edition. With an alphabeticall table of the principall contents. Whereunto is added, a sermon preached before two Kings, on the fift of August. 1606* (London, 1641)

30   *Letters of King James I ... to King Christian IV of Denmark*, pp.59 and 53

31   John Davies, *Bien Venv. Great Britaines Welcome to Hir Greate Friendes, and Deere Brethren The Danes* (London, 1606) B4v

32   Davies, *Bien Venv* B3r, B2v

33   *Letters of King James I ... to King Christian IV of Denmark* p.98

34   Ibid. pp.97–8

35   *CSP Ven* vol. 10 No. 617

36   Ibid. No. 566

37   Nichols, *Progresses* vol. 2 p.92

38   Phineas Pett, *The Autobiography of Phineas Pett*, ed. W.G. Perrin (London, 1918) pp.20–22

39   See Martin Bellamy, *Christian IV and his Navy: A Political and Administrative History of the Danish Navy 1596–1648* (Leiden, 2006). See Sarah Fraser, *The Prince Who Would Be King: The Life and Death of Henry Stuart* (London, 2018) p.91

9 UNION JACK

1   'House of Commons Journal Volume 1: 02 May 1607', in *Journal of the House of Commons: Volume 1, 1547–1629* (London, 1802), British History Online pp. 366–7

2   'By the King. A Proclamation declaring what Flags South and North Britain shall bear at Sea. [Westminster 12 April 1606]' in Larkin and Hughes (eds.), *Stuart Royal Proclamations*

3   Ibid.

4   'House of Commons Journal Volume 1: 16–18 November 1606', in *Journal of the House of 1547–1629* (London, 1802), British History Online pp.314–15

5   John Rushworth (ed.), *Historical Collections of Private Passages of State, Weighty Matters In Law, Remarkable Proceedings In Five Parliaments: Beginning the Sixteenth Year of King James. Anno 1618, And Ending the Fifth Year of King Charls [sic], Anno 1629* (London, 1701) vol. 1 p.161

6   Thomas Campion, *The discription of a maske, presented before the Kinges Maiestie at White-Hall, on Twelfth Night last in honour of the Lord Hayes, and his bride* (London, 1607). See David Lindley, 'Campion's 'Lord Hay's Masque' and Anglo-Scottish Union', *Huntington Library Quarterly*, 43.1 (Winter, 1979), pp.1–11

7   BL Harleian MS 1314 fol.44

8   Cobbett, *Parliamentary History* vol. 1, p.1097

9   *The Parliamentary Diary of Robert Bowyer, 1606–1607*, ed. David Harris Willson (Minneapolis, 1931) p.356

10 BL Harleian MS 5191 fols 17–18; Michelle O'Callaghan, 'Performing Politics: The Circulation of the "Parliament Fart"', *Huntington Library Quarterly*, 69 (2006), pp.121–38

11 'House of Commons Journal Volume 1: 14 February 1607', in *Journal of the House of Commons: Volume 1, 1547–1629* (London, 1802), British History Online pp.334–5

12 *The Letters and Life of Francis Bacon*, ed. J. Speeding, 7 vols (London, 1868) vol. 3. p.315

13 *The Register of the Privy Council of Scotland, 1545–1625*, vol. 7 pp.535–6

14 'A Speach to Both The Houses of Parliament, Delivered in the Great Chamber at White-Hall. The Last Day of March 1607', in Sommerville (ed.), *Political Writings* pp.159–78 at p.163

15 Ibid. p.178

16 Ibid. p.164

17 *CSP Ven* vol.10 No. 733

18 *Commons Journal* vol. 1 pp.339–40

19 *Commons Journal* vol. 1 pp.366–8

20 See Calvin v. Smith, 77 Eng. Rep. 377, 378 (K.B. 1608) cited in Polly Price, 'Natural Law and Birthright Citizenship in Calvin's Case (1608)', *Yale Journal of Law and the Humanities*, 9. / 1 (1997), pp.73–145, p.82

21 Gardiner, *History of England* vol.1 pp.301–57

22 John Speed, *The History of Great Britaine...* (London, 1611) pp.155–61

23 John Speed, *Theatre of the Empire of Great Britaine* (London, 1612)

24 See Steve Murdoch, Steve Murdoch, 'James VI and the formation of a Scottish British Military Identity' in Andrew MacKillop and Steve Murdoch (eds.), *Fighting for Identity. Scottish Military Experiences c.1550–1900* (Edinburgh, 2002), pp.x

25 John Davies, *The Muses-Teares for the Losse of Henry, Prince of Wales* (London, 1613) A2r

10 PRINCE HENRY AND THE GRAND TOUR

1 Francis Bacon, *On Travel* (London, 1625) printed in *The Essays of Francis Bacon*, Clark Sutherland Northup (New York, 1998) pp.56–8 at p.56

2 Thomas Palmer, *An essay of meanes how to make our Travailes, into forraine Countries, the more profitable and honorable* (London, 1606) sig. A2v

3 Clare Williams, *Thomas Platter's Travels in England 1599* (London, 1937) p.170

4 Bacon, *On Travel* pp.56–8

5 Thomas Palmer, *An Essay of the meanes to make our travails into forraine Countries, the most profitable and honourable* p.44

6 Joseph Hall, *Quo vadis? A iust censure of travell as it is commonly vndertaken by the gentlemen of our nation* (London, 1617)

7 *The Life and Letters of Sir Henry Wotton*, ed. Logan Pearsall Smith, 2 vols (Oxford, 1907), vol. 1, p.70; note 3

8 Ibid. vol. 1, p.434

9 See Thomas Wilks, 'The Court Culture of Prince Henry and his Circle 1603–1613', unpublished DPhil dissertation (University of Oxford, 1987)

10 Thomas Birch, *The Life of Henry, Prince of Wales, Eldest Son of King James I* (London, 1760) p.97

11 James Cleland *Hēro-paideia, or The institution of a young noble man* (London, 1607). p.35

12 Archivo di Stato di Firenze, MDP 5157 fol. 37 quoted in Thomas Wilks 'Introduction', in Catherine MacLeod (ed.), *The Lost Prince: The Life and Death of Henry Stuart* (London, 2012) p.13

13 Anna Banti (ed.), *Europa Milleseicentosei Diario di Viaggio di Bernardo Bizoni* (Milan, 1944) p.118 quoted in Thomas Wilks 'Introduction' in MacLeod (ed.), *The Lost Prince* p.13

14 'Basilikon Doron' pp.45–59

15 See Birch, *Life of Henry, Prince of Wales* pp.69–70

16 Ibid. p.90

17 Ibid. p.89

18 BL Harleian MS 7007 quoted ibid. p.168

19 *CSP Ven* vol.11 No. 407

20 BL Harleian MS 7007, fol. 224; *CSP Ven.* vol. 11 No.406

21 BL Lansdowne MS 91, fol. 35

22 BL Harleian MS 7007, fol. 319

23 BL Lansdowne MS 91, fol. 35

24 BL Harleian MS 7007, fol. 319

25 *Calendar of the State Papers, Relating to Ireland, of the Reign of James I* [hereafter *CSP Ireland*], 5 vols (London, 1872–80), vol. 2 p.656; *Life and Letters of Sir Henry Wotton* vol. 1 p.445

26 *Life and Letters of Sir Henry Wotton* vol. 1. pp.456–7

27 BL Harleian MS 7007, f.299; see Birch, *Life of Henry, Prince of Wales*

28 *CSP Ven* vol. 11 No.513

29 Birch, *Life of Henry, Prince of Wales*, p.175

11 JAMESTOWN, VIRGINIA

1 Michael Drayton, 'To the Virginian Voyage', 1606, in *Poems of Michael Drayton*, ed. John Buxton, 2 vols. (Cambridge, 1953), vol. 1. p.123

2 See Alexander Brown, *The Genesis of the United States*, 2 vols (London, 1890) vol.1 p.27

3 'The First Charter, 10 April 1606' printed in *The Three Charters of the Virginia Company of London: With Seven Related Documents: 1606–1621*, ed. Bemiss, Samuel B. (Williamsburg, VA, 1957) pp.1–13

4 Ibid.

5 Ibid.

6 Ibid.

7 See David Beers Quinn, *Set Fair For Roanoke: Voyages and Colonies, 1584–1606* (Chapel Hill, NC, 1985)

8 Richard Hakluyt in his *Discourse Concerning Western Planting*, and in his *Principal Navigations, Voyages, Traffiques and Discoveries of the English Nation* (London, 1599–1600) p.4

9 BL Harleian 7007, f.139 printed in Brown, *The Genesis of the United States* vol. 1 p.109

10 'George Percy, Observations gathered out of a discourse of the plantation of the southern colony in Virginia by the English 1606', in Edward Wright Haile (ed.), *Jamestown Narratives: Eyewitness Accounts of the Virginia Colony, the First Decade: 1607–1617* (Champlaign, VA, 1998), p.91

11 'Instructions from the Virginia Company of London to the First Settlers, 1606', Thomas Jefferson Papers Series 8, Manuscript Division, Library of Congress. Available online at the Library of Congress

12 'The Council in Virginia to the Council in England' in Brown, The *Genesis of the United States* vol.1 pp.106–8 at p.108

13 William Brewster, 'Letter from Virginia (1607)', in Haile (ed.), *Jamestown Narratives*, p.127

14 John Smith, *The generall historie of Virginia, New-England and the Summer Iles* (London, 1624) p.53

15 Ibid. p.55

16 Ibid. p.68

17 Ibid.

18 Robert Johnson, *Nova Britannia Offring most excellent fruites by planting in Virginia*...(London, 1609)

19 Robert Johnson, *The nevv life of Virginea declaring the former successe and present estate of that plantation, being the second part of Noua Britannia* (London, 1612)

20 Johnson, *Nova Britannia* unnumbered

21 Zunga to Philip III, 15 March 1609, in Philip L. Barbour (ed.), *The Jamestown Voyages under the First Charter, 1607–1609*, 2 vols (Cambridge, 1969) vol. 2 pp.254–7

22 Pedro de Zuñiga to Philip III, 8 October 1607, in Barbour (ed.), *The Jamestown Voyages* vol. 2 p.118

23 'Justification for planting Virginia', before 1609, in *Records of the Virginia Company*, ed. Susan Myra Kingsbury, 5 vols (Washington, DC, 1906) vol. 3 pp.1–2

24 *Nova Britannia*, unnumbered

25 *CSP Ven* vol. 11 No.449

26 William Crashaw, *A sermon preached in London Before the Right Honorable the Lord Lawarre* (London, 1610)

27 *CSP Ven* vol. 11 No. 449

28 *CSP Ven* vol. 12 No.534

29 'The First Charter, 10 April 1606', printed in Samuel M. Bemiss (ed.), *The Three Charters of the Virginia Company of London: With Seven Related Documents: 1606–1621* ed. Bemiss, Samuel B. (Williamsburg, VA, 1957) pp.1–12

30   *CSP Ven*, vol.11 Nos. 237, 249. Marc Antonio Correr to the doge and senate, Feb 1609, quoted in 'Events in England, 1608', in Barbour (ed.), *The Jamestown Voyages* vol. 2 p.212

31   'The Second Charter, 23 May 1609' printed in Bemiss (ed.), *The Three Charters of the Virginia Company of London* pp.27–54

32   William Crashaw, *A Sermon Preached in London before the right honorable Lord Lavvarre, Lord Gouernour and Captaine Generall of Virginea* (London, 1610); William Symonds, *Virginia: a sermon preached at White-Chappel* (London, 1609); Robert Gray, *A Good Speed to Virginia* (London, 1609)

33   Gray, *A Good Speed to Virginia*, sig. C2r

34   Ibid.

35   Richard Crakanthorpe, *A sermon at the solemnizing of the Happie Inauguration of Our Most Gracious and Religious Soveraigne King James* (London, 1609)

36   Barbour (ed.), *The Jamestown Voyages* vol. 2 pp.116–17

37   Silvester Jourdain, *A Discovery of the Bermudas, Otherwise Called the Isle of Devils* (London, 1610). William Strachey's account was published posthumously by Samuel Purchas in *A true Reportory of the Wreck, and Redemption of Sir Thomas Gates Knight upon and from the Islands of the 'Bermudas: His Coming to Virginia and the Estate of the Colony Then and After, under the Government of the Lord La Warr, July 15 1610, written by William Strachey* (London, 1625)

38   *Council for Virginia, A true declaration of the estate of the colony in Virginia with a confutation of such scandalous reports as have tended to the disgrace of so worthy an enterprise* (London, 1610), pp.1–2

39   Alonso de Velasco to Philip III, 12 July 1613, in Brown, *Genesis of the United States*, vol. 2 pp.638–9

40   Smith, *The generall historie of Virginia* p.204. See also George Percy, *A True Relation of the Proceedings and Occurances of Moment which have happened in Virginia from the Time Sir Thomas Gates shipwrecked upon the Bermudes anno 1609 until my departure out of the Country which was in anno Domini 1612* (London, 1624)

41   William Strachey, 'A True Reportory of the Wreck and Redemption of Sir Thomas Gates, Knight, upon and from the Islands of the Bermudas', in *A Voyage to Virginia in 1609: Two Narratives: Strachey's 'True Reportory' and Jourdain's 'Discovery of the Bermudas'*, ed. Louis B. Wright (Charlottesville, VA, 2013) pp.1–102 at p.92

12 THE PLANTATION OF ULSTER

1   *CSP Ireland* vol. 3 p.520

2   Quoted in Nicholas P. Canny, *Making Ireland British, 1580–1650* (Oxford, 2001), p.192

3   Tim Harris, *Rebellion: Britain's First Stuart Kings* (Oxford, 2014) p.147

4   *CSP Ireland* vol. 3 p.81

5   'Basilikon Doron', p.24

6   Ibid.

7   Sir John Davies, *A discovery of the true causes* (London, 1612) p.282

8   See discussion in David Armitage, *The Ideological Origins of the British Empire* (Cambridge, 2000) p.57

9   Articles of Agreement, 28 January 1609 printed in D.A. Chart (ed.) *Londonderry and the London Companies 1609–1629, Being a Survey and other Documents Submitted to King Charles I by Sir Thomas Phillips* (Belfast, 1928)

10   *CSP Ireland* vol. 3 p.474

11   Lochlainn Ó Dálaigh, *Cáit ar ghabhadar Gaoidhil? [Where have the Gaels Gone?]*, printed and translated in W. Gillies, 'A poem on the downfall of the Gaoidhil', *Éigse*, XIII (1969–70), pp.203–10

12   See Jane Ohlmeyer, *Making Ireland English: The Irish Aristocracy in the Seventeenth Century* (London, 2012)

13   Haus- Hof- und Staatsarchiv (Vienna) [HHStA] Belgien PC46, fols 166v–67 cited and described in Smuts, *Political Culture* p.526

14   TNA SP77/10, fols. 332, 337v, 358v

15   HHStA Belgien PC47, fol. 27v cited in Smuts, *Political Culture*, p.526

16   *CSP Ireland* 1615–25 vol. 5 p.167

17   Sir John Davies, *Historical relations: or, a discovery of the true causes why Ireland was never entirely subdued, nor brought under obedience of the crown of England, until the beginning of the reign of King James the First* (London, 1733) p.117

18   Luke Gernon, *Discourse of Ireland, anno 1620* (Cork 1620), p.356

19   See Library Company of Philadelphia, MS 25 1175.F, James VI and I to Sir Arthur Chichester, 5 June 1614 as cited in Joseph Wagner, 'The First "British" Colony in the Americas: Inter-kingdom Cooperation and Stuart-British Ideology in the Colonisation of Newfoundland, 1616–1640', *Britain and the World* 15.1 (2022) pp.1–23 at p.4

20   John Speed, *The theatre of the empire of Great Britaine presenting an exact geography of the kingdomes of England, Scotland, Ireland, and the iles adioyning...*(London, 1612) p.139; Fynes Moryson, *An Itinerary: Containing His Ten Yeeres Travell...*, 4 vols ([1617]; Glasgow, 1907–8) vol. 4 p.85

21   Joseph Wagner makes this argument in 'The First "British" Colony'

13 BRITAIN'S BOURSE

1 Dekker, *The Wonderfull Yeare: 1603*

2 John Stow, *Abridgement of the Chronicles of England* (London, 1611), dedication

3 *CSP Ven* vol 11, No.497

4 *Register of Letters* p.130

5 *The Entertainment at Britain's Burse* (London, 1609), TNA SP14/44.62 printed in *Re-Presenting Ben Jonson: Text, History, Performance*, ed. Martin Butler (Basingstoke, 1999) pp.132–148 at p.134

6 Ibid. p.140

7 Humphrey Gilbert, *A Discourse of a Discoverie for a New Passage to Cataia* (London, 1576), H1–2

8 Geffe, Nicholas, *Discourse ... of the meanes and Sufficiencue of England, for to Have Abundance of Fine Silke, by Feeding of Silk Wormes within the Same...For the general use and universal benefit of all those his Country- men which embrace it* (London, 1607); *CSP Dom James I, 1611–1618*, ed. Mary Anna Everett Green (London, 1858), British History Online pp.126, 194

9 Olivier de Serres, *The Perfect Use of Silk-Wormes, and Their Benefit... Done out of the French original of D'Olivier de Serres Lord of Pradel into English by Nicholas Geffe Esquire* (London, 1607)

10 Geffe, *Discourse*, pp.10–11

11 Ibid. p.13

12 Hatfield House, Cecil Papers 193/28 (1606) cited in Ben Marsh, *Unravelled Dreams: Silk and the Atlantic World, 1500–1840* (Cambridge, 2020) p.105

13 *CSP Dom* 1603–10, p.540

14 *CSP Dom* 1603–10, pp.344, 398, 540; 1611–18, pp.246, 555; BL Harleian MS 4807, nos. 25, 29, 30

15 William Stallenge, *Instructions for the Increasing of Mulberie Trees, and the Breeding of Silke-Wormes for the Making of Silke in This Kingdom* (London, 1609)

16 'Charter Granted by James I and dates 31st May 1609, Confirming and Extending the Charter of Elizabeth' printed in *Charters Related to the East India Company from 1600–1761*, John Shaw (London, 1887) pp.16–31 at p.26

17 BL IOR B/3, fol.139v

18 BL IOR B/3, fol.140v, 141

19 BL IOR B/3, fol.142

20 BL IOR B/3, fol.144v–145

21 *Chamberlain Letters*, vol. 1 p.294

22 See Richmond Barbour, *The Loss of Trades Increase: An Early Modern Maritime Catastrophe* (Philadelphia, 2021)

23 Robert Kyall, *The trades increase* (London, 1615)

24 Ibid. pp.53–5

25 Dudley Digges, *The Defense of Trade. In a Letter to Sir Thomas Smith Knight, Governor of the East India Company &c From One of That Society* (London, 1615) pp.2–3

26 Ibid. p.32

14 THE WAY OF THE NORTH

1 Thomas Blundevile, *M. Blundeuile his exercises* (London, 1613)

2 Cited in J. Winter Jones (ed.), *Divers Voyages touching the Discovery of America and the Lands Adjacent* (London, 1850) p.25

3 Samuel Purchas, *Pvrchas His Pilgrimes* (London, 1625)

4 Ibid. p.728

5 *Henry Hudson the navigator: the original documents in which his career is recorded, collected, partly translated, and annotated by G.M. Asher* (London, 1860) p.192

6 Edward Wright, *Certain errors in navigation* (London, 1612) sig*4

7 J. Davis, 'Motives inducing a project for the discovery of the North Pole Terrestrial; The Straights of Anian into the South Sea and the coasts thereof'. It is unclear whether or not Digges was the author of this separate sheet. Nevertheless, it was clearly addressed to the prince

8 This document is in Appendix C, *The Voyages of Captain Luke Foxe and Captain Thomas James [...] with Narratives of the Earlier North-West Voyages* 2 vols, Miller Christy (London, 1894) vol. 2 pp.639–41

9 Abacuk Prickett, 'A Larger Discourse of the Same Voyage, and the Success Thereof, Written by Abacuk Prickett', printed in Asher (ed.), *Henry Hudson the Navigator: The Original Documents in Which His Career Is Recorded.* (Cambridge, 2010) pp.98–134 at pp.104–5

10 Christy (ed.), *The Voyages*, vol.2 p.634

11 Ibid. p.635

12 Ibid.

13 'A Charter Granted to the Company of the Merchants Discoverers of the North-West Passage' in Christy (ed.), *The Voyages*, vol. 2 pp.642–64

14 *Henry Hudson the navigator*) p.255

15 Printed in Christy (ed.), *The Voyages* vol. 2 p. 644; *CSP Ven*, vol. 12, No. 265

16 D. Digges, *Of the Circumference of the Earth; Or a Treatise of the North West Passage* (London, 1612)

15 A THIRST FOR GLORY

1 Daniel Price, *The Defence of Trvth Against a Booke Falsely Called the Trivmph of Trvth Sent over from Arras A. D. 1609. by Hvmfrey Leech Late Minister. Which Booke in All Particulars Is Answered, and the Adioning Motiues of His Revolt Confuted* (Oxford, 1610), sig. Av

2 D. Digges, *Of the Circumference of the Earth; Or a Treatise of the North West Passage*

3 Birch, *Life of Henry, Prince of Wales*, p.43

4 P Du Mornay, *The Mysterie of Iniquitie: that is to say, the historie of the papacie*, trans S. Leannard (London, 1612) sig. A2

5 A point made by Thomas Wilks, 'The Pike Charged: Henry as Militant Prince' in Wilks (ed.), *Prince Henry Revived: Image and Exemplarity in Early Modern England* (London, 2007) pp.180–211 at p.195

6 *Memorials of affairs of state in the reigns of Q. Elizabeth and K. James I. Collected (chiefly) from the original papers of the Right Honourable Sir Ralph Winwood, Kt. Sometime one of the Principal Secretarie*, ed. Edmund Sawyer [hereafter Winwood, *Memorials*], 3 vols (London, 1725) vol. 3 p.114

7 Winwood, *Memorials* vol. 3 p.114

8 Ibid. p.63

9 Ibid. pp.114–16

10 'Propositions of Warre and Peace delivered to his Highness Prince Henry by some of his Military servants: Arguments for Warre', printed in Sir Robert Cotton, *An Answer made by Command of Prince Henry, to Certain Propositions of Warre and Peace* (London, 1655)

11 See discussion and argument made in Noah Millstone, 'Sir Robert Cotton, Manuscript Pamphleteering, and the Making of Jacobean Kingship during the Short Peace, ca. 1609–1613'. *Journal of British Studies* 62.1 (2023) pp.134–160

12 BL, Cotton MS, Cleopatra F VI, fols. 9r–v quoted and discussed in Millstone, 'Short Peace' p.142

13 BL. Cotton MS Cleopatra F VI, fols. 37v–38r; see Millstone, 'Short Peace' p.145

14 Winwood, *Memorials* vol. 3 p.81. See Smuts, *Political Culture* p.569

15 Winwood, *Memorials* vol. 3 p.97

16 TNA SP 31/2/41 quoted and trans. in Smuts, *Political Culture* pp.569–70

17 *Ambassades de Monsieur de la Boderie* vol. 4 pp.330–31

18 RGP 135, 44–5 no. 249, 22 March 1610 cited in Murdoch, 'James VI and the Formation of a Scottish British Military Identity' in Andrew MacKillop and Steve Murdoch (eds), *Fighting for Identity. Scottish Military Experiences c.1550–1900* (Edinburgh, 2002) p.13

19 Larkin and Hughes (eds.), *Stuart Royal Proclamations*

20 *CSP Ven* vol.11 No. 945; C. Pagnini, 'Henry Stuart 'The Rising Sun of England': The Creation of a Prince of Wales (June 1610)', *Drammaturgia*, 16 (2020) pp.261–9

21 Jean l'Oiseau de Tourval, . *The French Herald Svmmoning All Trve Christian Princes to a generall Croisade, for a holy warr against the great Enemy of Christendome, and all his slaues. Vpon the Occasion of the most execrable murther of Henry the grat. To the Prince. London: Edward Allde for Mathew Lownes, 1611. Loiseau de toruval, the French herald* sig. A2v quoted in Rebecca A. Calgano, 'Publishing the Stuarts: Occasional Literature and Politics from 1603 to 1625', Columbia University PhD (2011) p.104

22 BL Harl MS 7007 fols. 387, 398 quoted in Birch, *Life of Henry, Prince of Wales*, pp.198–203

23 HHStA [Haus- Hof- und Staatsarchiv (Vienna)] Belgien PC46, fols. 78v, 131r, 167r, 171v, cited in Smuts, *Political Culture* p.570

24 HHStA Belgien PC47, fol. 257 cited in Smuts, *Political Culture* p.570

25 Nadine Akkerman (ed.), *The Correspondence of Elizabeth Stuart: Queen of Bohemia, vol. 1, 1603–1631* (Oxford, 2015) p.108 (no.66)

26 *A collection of scarce and valuable tracts*, ed. Baron John Somers (London, 1809–10) vol. 2 p.210

27 *HMC Report on the Manuscripts of His Grace the Duke of Portland, present at Welbeck Abbey*, vol. 9 (Norwich, 1923) p.45

28 *A collection of scarce and valuable tracts*, vol 2. p.206

29 Nichols, *Progresses* vol. 2 pp.471–2

30 *Chamberlain Letters* vol. I p.388

31 Nichols, *Progresses* vol. 2 p.485

32 *Letters of King James I ... to King Christian IV of Denmark* p.142

33 *CSP Ven* vol. 12 No. 692

34 Ibid.

35 Francis Bacon, *The Works of Francis Bacon*, ed. James Spedding, Robert Leslie Ellis and Douglas Denon Heath (London, 1870) vol. 6 p.328

36 Sir Arthur Gorges, *The Olympian Catastrophe* (London, 1612) printed in *The Olympian catastrophe, by Sir Arthur Gorges* (London, 1925)

37 See Elizabeth Goldring, '"So iust a sorrowe so well expressed": Henry, Prince of Wales and the Art of Commemoration', in T.Wilks (ed.), *Prince Henry Revived: Image and Exemplarity in Early Modern England* (London, 2007) pp.280–300

38 W.G. Perrin (ed.), *The Autobiography of Phineas Pett* (London, 1918) p.100

39 *CSP Ven* vol. 12 No.696

40 *HMC Report on the manuscripts of the Marquess of Downshire* (London, 1938) vol. 3 p.417

41 *CSP Ven* vol. 12 No.690

42 *CSP Ven* vol. 12 No.692

43 *Calendar of State Papers Colonial, America and West Indies: Volume 1, 1574–1660*, ed. W. Noel Sainsbury (London, 1860), British History Online No.29

44 Letter printed in Ralph Hamor, *A True discourse of the present state of Virginia* (London, 1615) fol.51

45 *CSP Ven* vol. 12 No.698

46 *CSP Ven* vol. 12 No.693

47 *Chamberlain Letters* vol. 1 p.398

48 *CSP Ven* vol. 12 No.698

49 *CSP Ven* vol. 12 No.698

16 UNION OF THAMES AND RHINE

1 John Donne, 'An Epithalamion, Or mariage Song on the Lady Elizabeth, and Count Palatine being married on St. Valentines day' in *Poems of John Donne*, vol. 1, ed. E.K. Chambers (London, 1896) pp.83–7

2 *CSP Ven* vol. 12 No.734

3 TNA SP14/71 fols.134r-v cited in Akkerman, *Eliƶabeth Stuart* p.71

4 *CSP Ven* vol. 12 No.734

5 *Chamberlain Letters*, vol.1 p.418

6 *Poems of John Donne*, pp.83–7

7 *Chamberlain Letters* vol. 1 pp.420–22 at p.421

8 *CSP Domestic, James I, 1611–18*, ed. Mary Anne Everett-Green (London, 1858), vol. 72, No. 7

9 John Taylor, *Heavens Blessings and Earths Joy* (London, 1613)

10 Nichols, *Progresses* vol. 2 p.541

11 *Chamberlain Letters* vol. 1 p.415

12 Anthony Nixon, *Great Brittanes Generall Joyes* (London, 1613) sig. B3v

13 Nichols, *Progresses* vol. 2 p.542

14 Anon., *The Marriage*, sig. Br–B2r cited in Akkerman, *Elizabeth Stuart* p.82
15 Ibid.
16 *Chamberlain Letters*, vol. 1 pp.423–6 at p.424
17 See Akkerman, *Elizabeth Stuart* p.83
18 'The Charge of the Lady Elisabeths marriage[…]', BL Add MS58833, fols.18v–19v cited in Akkerman, *Elizabeth Stuart* p.85
19 *Journal of Roger Wilbraham* p.110
20 *Chamberlain Letters* vol. 1 p.425
21 *CSP Ven* vol. 12 No.775
22 Nichols, *Progresses* vol. 2 pp.601–5
23 *Thomas Campion, 'Lords' Masque' in English Masques*, ed. Herbert Arthur Evans (New York, 1898) pp.72–87 at p.84
24 George Chapman, *The Memorable Maske of the two Honorable Houses or Inns of Court; the Middle Temple, and Lyncolns Inne* … (London, 1613)
25 Ibid. sig. A[1]. See Tucker Orbison, ed., *The Middle Temple Documents Relating to George Chapman's The Memorable Masque* (Oxford, 1983)
26 *CSP Ven.* vol.12 No.775
27 See Lauren Working, 'Locating Colonization at the Jacobean Inns of Court', *The Historical Journal*, 61 (2018), pp.29–51
28 Chapman, *The Memorable Maske* sig. A2v
29 Ibid. sig. Bv
30 Ibid. sig. A[1]
31 Ibid. sig. A2
32 *The autobiography of Phineas Pett*, ed. W.G Perrin (London, 1918) pp.35, 86
33 Akkerman, *Elizabeth Stuart* vol. 1. p.114
34 Winwood, *Memorials* vol. 3 p.467

17 A RUSSIAN PROPOSITION

1 TNA SP 91/1 fols. 220–21 printed and trans. in Chester S.L. Dunning, 'A Letter to James I Concerning the English Plan for Military Intervention in Russia', *The Slavonic and East European Review*, 67.1 (1989) pp.107–8
2 William Shakespeare, *The Winters Tale*, ed. Stephen Orgel (Oxford, 2008)
3 *HMC Salisbury* vol.16 p.459
4 See Alexia Grosjean, *An Unofficial Alliance: Scotland and Sweden 1569–1654* (Leiden, 2003)
5 TNA SP 88/3/ fols.42–47v
6 TNA SP 88/3/fol.36–36v

7   See Geraldine M. Phipps, *Sir John Merrick, English Merchant-Diplomat in Seventeenth Century Russia* (Newtonville, MA, 1983) p.69

8   TNA SP 91/1-228r-231v, 'Proposition of the Muscovites to render them subjects to the King of England [1613]', printed in Inna Lubimenko, 'A Project for the Acquisition of Russia by James I', *The English Historical Review*, 29.114 (April 1914) pp.246–56

9   Lubimenko, 'A Project for the Acquisition of Russia' p.249

10   Ibid. p.252

11   Ibid. p.252

12   *Chamberlain Letters* vol. I p.448

13   Ibid. p.445

14   BL Lansdowne MS 142 fol.395.

15   TNA 22/60-20 James I to Russian Representatives 3 May 1613; Treaty Roll C76/217-m23 Commission to Merrick and Russell, p.72 ft 53. 1613: Treaty Roll C76/217-m23 Second Commission to Merrick and Russell, 1613 cited in Phipps, *Sir John Merrick*, p.72 ft 53

16   Treaty Roll C76/217-m23 cited in Phipps, *Sir John Merrick*, p.72 ft.54

17   TNA SP 91/1 240r-241v

18   Printed in *HMC Buccleuch and Queensbury* vol.1 pp.136–7

19   Ibid.

20   See full printed account of embassy see Maija Jansson and Nikolai Rogozhin (eds.), trans. Paul Bushkovitch, *England and the North: The Russian Embassy of 1613–1614* (Philadelphia, 1944) pp.145–81

21   *Chamberlain Letters* vol. 1 p.482

22   TNA SP 102 49-6 Mikhail to James I, 11 June 1613, cited in Phipps, *Sir John Merrick* p.76

23   TNA SP 91/1 242r-243v

24   TNA SP 75/5 fols. 63 and 73 cited in Steve Murdoch, 'Stolbovo in Perspective, Jacobean Diplomacy in the Baltic Region, 1589–1618' in *Sweden, Russia, and the 1617 Peace of Stolbovo*, ed. Arne Jonsson and Arseneii Vertushko-Kalevich (Turnhout, Belgium, 2023)

25   TNA SP 91/1-58r-59v

26   Cobbett, *Parliamentary History* vol. 1 p.1153

27   *APC* vol. 33, 1613–1614 p.451

28   TNA PC 2/27 fol.174

29   *Chamberlain Letters* vol. 1, p.542

30   Treaty Roll C76/217 mm.18 and 19 ', Commission to Merrick, 18 June 1614, cited in Phipps, *Sir John Merrick*. 83 ft 22

31   Ibid.

32   TNA SP 91/1 50r-53v

33   See Phipps, *Sir John Merrick* p.79

34   Longleat House, Papers of the Marquis of Bath, Whitelocke Collection, vol. 1 fol.182

35   *Purchas His Pilgrimes* pp.792–7

36   Italics are my emphasis. TNA SP 91/2 fol 23 cited in Murdoch, 'Stolbovo in Perspective' pp.47–66 at p.60

37   This point made ibid. p.60

38   See Phipps, *Sir John Merrick* p.118

18   EASTERN FANTASY

1   BL IOR: B/7/p.42 printed in Anthony Farrington (ed.), *The English Factory in Japan, 1613–1623* vol. 1 (London, 1991) p.1

2   *Register of Letters* p.412

3   Farrington (ed.), *The English Factory in Japan*, vol. 1. No.4 p.62

4   *The Voyage of Captain Saris to Japan, 1613*, ed. Sir Ernst Mason Satow (London, 1900), pp.212–30

5   BL IOR E/3/1 no.78 printed in Farrington (ed.), *The English Factory in Japan*, vol. 1, No.6 pp.65–73 at p.72

6   IOR E/3/1 no. 96; Farrington (ed.), *The English Factory in Japan*, vol. 1, No. 8 pp.76–9

7   *The Voyage of Captain John Saris to Japan, 1613*, p.79

8   Adam Clulow, 'Commemorating Failure: The Four Hundredth Anniversary of England's Trading Outpost in Japan', *Monumenta Nipponica*, 68. 2 (2013) pp.207–31 at p.217

9   *The Voyage of Captain John Saris to Japan, 1613*, p.107

10   BL IOR B/2.fol. 150 printed in Farrington (ed.), *The English Factory in Japan*, vol. 1 No.4 p.62

11   See Timon Screech, *The Shogun's Silver Telescope: God, Art, and Money in the English Quest for Japan, 1600–1625* (Oxford, 2020)

12   Letter of the emperor to James printed in Robert Kerr, *A General History and Collection of Voyages and Travels*, 18 vols (London, 1813) vol. 9 p.31

13   BL IOR: E/3/1 no.22 printed in Farrington (ed.), *The English Factory in Japan*, vol. 1 No.19 pp.103–9 at p.103

14   *Letters Received by the East India Company from its Servants in the East* [hereafter *EIC Letters*], ed. F. C. Danvers and W. M. Foster, 2 vols (London, 1896) vol. 2 (1613–15) pp.4–9

15   C.J. Purnell (ed.), *The Log-book of William Adams 1614–1619, with the Journal of Edward Saris and other Documents Relations to Japan, Cochin-China* (London, 1916), p.293

16 *Calendar of State Papers Colonial, East Indies, China and Japan, Volume 2, 1513–1616,* ed. W. Noel Sainsbury (London, 1864), British History Online No.769

17 BL IPR B/5/pp.225–6 printed in Farrington (ed.), *The English Factory in Japan,* vol. 1 No.68 pp.205–6

18 BL IOR G/40/25 pp.132–136 printed in Farrington, (ed.), *The English Factory in Japan,* vol. 1 No.70 pp.209–14

19 *Proceedings in Parliament, 1614,* ed. Maija Jansson (Philadelphia, PA, 1988) p.298 n.22

20 BL IOR G/40/25 pp.132–6 printed in Farrington (ed.), *The English Factory in Japan* vol. 1 No.70 p.213

21 BL IOR G/12/15 p.56 printed in Farrington (ed.), *The English Factory in Japan* vol. 1 No.232 pp.574–5

22 Farrington (ed.), *The English Factory in Japan* vol. 1 No.229 p.562

23 BL IOR G/12/15 pp.64–5 printed in Farrington (ed.), *The English Factory in Japan* vol. 1 No 235 pp.585–7 at p.585

24 *Diary of Richard Cocks, Cape-Merchant in the English Factory in Japan, 1615–1622: With Correspondence,* ed. Edward Maunde Thompson, 2 vols (Cambridge, 2010) vol. 2 p.288

25 Frère Hayton, *Here begynneth a lytell cronycle translated [and] imprinted at the cost [and] charges of Rycharde Pynson* (London, 1520), sig. A3r.

26 Richard Hakluyt, *The principal navigations voyages traffiques & discoveries of the English nation: made by sea or over-land to the remote and farthest distant quarters of the earth at any time within the compasse of these 1600 yeeres,* 12 vols (Glasgow, 1903–5), vol. 3, p.256; Richard Hakluyt, *The Principal Navigations, Voyages, Traffiques, And Discoveries of the English Nation,* ed. Richard Hakluyt and Edmund Goldsmid, 16 vols (Edinburgh, 1885–90)

27 BL IOR E/3/2 no. 189 & 201 printed in Farrington (ed.), *The English Factory in Japan* vol. 1 No.75 pp.224–7 at pp.226–7

28 *Diary of Richard Cock* vol. 2 pp.298–9

29 BL IOR E/3/5 no.595 printed in Farrington (ed.), *The English Factory in Japan* vol. 1 No.266 pp.655–74 at p.65

30 *Diary of Richard Cocks* vol. 2 p.311

31 TNA CO 77/1 no. 42 printed in Farrington (ed.), *The English Factory in Japan* vol. 1 No.85 pp.256–61 at p.256

32 *Diary of Richard Cocks* vol. 1 p.173

33 Timon Screech, 'The English and the Control of Christianity in the Early Edo Period' *Japan Review* 24 (2012) pp.3–40

34 *Diary of Richard Cocks* vol. 1 p.186

35   Ibid. p.xl

19 A PASSAGE TO INDIA

1   *EIC Letters*, vol. 6 pp.298–9
2   *Calendar of State Papers Colonial, East Indies, China and Japan, Volume 2, 1513–1616*, ed. W Noel Sainsbury (London, 1864), British History Online p.317
3   *The Embassy of Sir Thomas Roe to the Court of the Great Mogul, 1615–1619: As Narrated in his journal and correspondence*, ed. Sir William Foster 2 vols (London, 1899) vol. 2 pp.551–3
4   *The Embassy of Sir Thomas Roe* vol. 2 pp.547–9
5   Ibid. pp.551–3
6   TNA, SP 14/90/34
7   *Register of Letters*, pp.105–6
8   *EIC Letters*, vol. 1, p.158
9   *EIC Letters* vol. 1, p.300
10   *The Embassy of Sir Thomas Roe* vol. 1 p.46
11   Ibid. pp.47–8
12   Ibid. p.45
13   Ibid. p.67
14   Ibid. p.97
15   Ibid. p.119
16   Ibid. vol. 2 p.323
17   Ibid. p.390
18   Ibid. vol. 1 p.143
19   Ibid. p.109
20   Ibid. vol. 2 p.558
21   Ibid. vol. 1 pp.154–5
22   Ibid. p.156
23   Ibid. p.46
24   Ibid. vol. 2 p.497
25   Ibid. vol.1 pp.310, 496, 508
26   Ibid. p.120
27   Ibid.
28   *EIC Letters* vol. 2. p.97
29   Ibid.
30   *The Embassy of Sir Thomas Roe* vol. 1 p.165
31   Ibid. p.166
32   Ibid. p.209
33   Ibid.

34   Ibid. vol. 2 p.459
35   Ibid. p.481
36   Ibid. p.501
37   Ibid. p.469
38   Ibid. p.558
39   Ibid. pp.506–14 at p.509
40   Ibid. p.516
41   Ibid. p.344
42   Ibid. pp.531–41
43   Baffin's chart is BL, Add. MS. 12206, fol. 6;
44   *The Embassy of Sir Thomas Roe* vol. 2 p.478
45   Ibid. p.391

20 POCAHONTAS AND A NEW BRITAIN

1   Cited in Ralph Hamor, *A True discourse of the present estate of Virginia and the successe of the affaires there till the 18 of Iune 1614.* (London, 1615) p.55

2   BL IOR/A/1/2

3   'The First Charter, April 10, 1606' in *The Three Charters of the Virginia Company of London with Seven Related Documents: 1606–1621*, ed. Bemiss, Samuel B. (Williamsburg, VA, 1957) pp.1–12

4   Hamor, *A True discourse* p.31

5   Ibid. p.63

6   Ibid. p.11

7   'The First Charter, April 10, 1606' in *The Three Charters of the Virginia Company of London with Seven Related Documents: 1606–1621*, ed. Bemiss, Samuel B. (Williamsburg, VA, 1957) p.3

8   *Records of the Virginia Company* vol. 1–2

9   H[erts] R[ecord] O[ffice] reference ASA 5/4, no. 219 printed in Peter Walne, 'The Collections for Henrico College, 1616–1618', *The Virginia Magazine of History and Biography*, 80. 3 (1972) pp.259–66 at p.263

10 *Records of the Virginia Company* vol.1 p.163

11 'Sir Edwin Sandys and John Wrothe to Sir Thomas Smith, warrant, 10 March 1616/17', printed in *The Virginia Magazine of History and Biography*, 99.1 (1991), pp.81–94 at p.94

12 John Smith, *The generall historie of Virginia, New-England, and the Summer Isles with the names of the adventurers, planters, and governours from their first beginning. anº: 1584. to this present 1624* (London, 1624) p.122

13 Samuel Purchas, *Purchas his pilgrimes. part 4 In fiue bookes* (London, 1625) p.1774

14   *Chamberlain Letters* vol.2 pp.49–50

15   See Karen Robertson, 'Pocahontas at the Masque,' *Signs* 21.3 (Spring 1996) pp.551–83

16   *Purchas his pilgrimes* p.1774

17   See Charlotte Ickes, 'The Sartorial and the Skin: Portraits of Pocahontas and Allegories of English Empire', *American Art* 29.1 (2015) pp.82–105

18   *Chamberlain Letters* vol. 2 p.57

19   John Rolfe, *A true relation of the State of Virginia lefte by Sir Thomas Dale, knight, in May last 1616* (New Haven, CT, 1951) p.34

20   *Purchas his pilgrimes* p.1774

21   John Rolfe, Letter to Sir Edwin Sandys, 8 June 1617, in *Records of the Virginia Company* vol. 3 p.72

22   Ibid. p.73

23   Ibid.

24   'A report of S[i]r Yeardlyes going Governor to Virginia', 5 December 1618, Magdalene College, Cambridge, Ferrar Papers (FP) 93

25   Ibid.

26   King James I, *A Counterblaste to Tobacco* (London, 1604), B1–B2

27   'A report of S[i]r Yeardlyes going Governor to Virginia,' FP 93

28   Ibid.

29   Smith, *The generall historie of Virginia*, p.66

30   *The Complete Works of Captain John Smith (1580–1631)*, ed. Philip L. Barbour, 3 vols (Williamsburg, VA, 2011) vol. 1 p.151

31   Richard Hakluyt, *The Principal Navigations, Voyages, Traffiques, And Discoveries of the English Nation*, ed. Richard Hakluyt and Edmund Goldsmid, 16 vols (Edinburgh, 1885–90) vol. 15 p.187; Nathaniel Butler, *The Historye of the Bermudaes or Summer Islands*, ed. J. Henry Lefroy (London, 1882), p.218

32   Acts of the Privy Council of England [hereafter APC] vol. 34, 1615–16, ed. E.G. Atkinson (London, 1925), p.129

33   See T.B. Pugh, 'A Portrait of Queen Anna of Denmark at Parham Park, Sussex', *The Seventeenth Century*, 8.2 (1993) pp.167–80

34   See Ben Marsh, *Unravelled Dreams: Silk and the Atlantic World 1500–1840* (Cambridge, 2020) p.108

35   John Bonoeil, *A Treatise of the Art of Making Silke, or, Directions for Making Lodgings, and the Breeding, and Ordering of Silkewormes, for the Planting of Mulberry Trees, and All Other Things Belonging to the Silke Art . . .* (London, 1622); *Records of the Virginia Company* vol. 2 p.101

36   John Bonoeil, *His Maiesties gracious letter to the Earle of South-Hampton* (London, 1622), M3v.

37   Charles E. Hatch, 'Mulberry Trees and Silkworms: Sericulture in Early
     Virginia', *The Virginia Magazine of History and Biography* 65 (1957) p.7

38   J. Henry Lefroy, *Memorials of the Discovery and Early Settlement of the
     Bermudas or Somers Islands, 1515–1685*, 2 vols (London, 1877), vol. 1
     p.500

39   *Records of the Virginia Company* vol. 3 p.240

40   *Records of the Virginia Company* vol. 3 p.63

41   W. Strachey, *The Historie of Travaile into Virginia Britannia* (1612), ed.
     R.H. Major (London, 1849), p.117

42   'A Proclamation concerning the viewing and distinguishing of Tobacco
     in England and Ireland, the Dominion of Wales, and Town of Barwicke.
     [Theobalds 10 November 1619]' in Larkin and Hughes (eds.), *Stuart
     Royal Proclamations*

43   See John Thornton, 'The African Experience of the "20. and Odd
     Negroes" Arriving in Virginia in 1619', *The William and Mary Quarterly*,
     55.3 (1998) pp.421–34; Alden T. Vaughan in 'Blacks in Virginia: A
     Note on the First Decade', *The William and Mary Quarterly* 29:3
     (1973) pp.469–78

44   *Records of the Virginia Company* vol. 3 pp.241–8 at p.243

45   'Establishment of the Fort Monrow National Monument by the President
     of the United States of America: A Proclamation', 1 November 2011

46   A. C. Hollis Hallett, *Bermuda under Sommer Islands Company 1612–1684*,
     3 vols (Bermuda 2005) vol. 1 p.5

47   *Butler's History of the Bermuda: a Contemporary Account of Bermuda's
     Earliest Government*, transcribed and ed. C.F.E. Hollis Hallett
     (Bermuda, 2007) p.11

21 SHAH ABBAS'S SILK

1   *Letters from George Lord Carew to Sir Thomas Roe, Ambassador to the Court
     of the Great Mogul. 1615–1617*, ed. John Mclean (London, 1860) p.77

2   Ibid. p.77

3   Ibid.

4   *The Embassy of Sir Thomas Roe* vol. 1 p.96

5   See Linda. K Steinmann, 'Shah 'Abbas and the Royal Silk Trade
     1599–1629', *Bulletin (British Society for Middle Eastern Studies)* 14.1
     (1987) pp.68–74

6   *CSP Ven* vol. 10 No. 739

7   See Anthony Sherley, *Sir Anthony Sheirley His Relation of his Travels into
     Persia* (London, 1613)

8 See R.W. Ferrier, 'The European Diplomacy of Shāh 'Abbās I and the First Persian Embassy to England', *Iran*, 11(1973) pp.75–92

9 Translated and printed in Philip Evelyn Shirley, *The Sherley brothers, an historical memoir of the lives of Sir Thomas Sherley, Sir Anthony Sherley, and Sir Robert Sherley, knights* (London, 1848) p.61

10 BL Lansdowne MS 160 No.36 fol.144

11 *Chamberlain Letters*, vol. 1 p.313

12 *EIC Letters*, vol. 2 pp.171, 267

13 Ibid. pp.266–8

14 Ibid. p. 237

15 Ibid. vol. 4 p.330

16 Ibid. pp.328–32

17 Ibid. p.52

18 Ibid. p.190

19 Ibid. p.56

20 *EIC Letters*, vol. 6 pp.32–3

21 Ibid. p.37

22 Ibid. vol. 5 pp.66, 191

23 *Letters of George Lord Carew to Sir Thomas Roe, ambassador to the court of the Great Mogul, 1615–1617*, ed. John Maclean (London, 1860) p.77

24 *The Embassy of Sir Thomas Roe* vol. 2 pp.554–6

25 Ibid. pp.556–7

26 William Foster, *England Quest of Eastern Trade* (London, 1933) p.304

27 BL Add.MS.6115, fol.208r

28 BL Add. MS.6115, fol. 80r–v

29 BL IOR/E/3/7, fol.44v–45

30 BL IOR/E/3/7, fol.108v

31 'The King's Letter for Ruy Freire de Andrade, containing the Instructions for his expedition, 15 January 1622', in *Commentaries of Ruy Freire de Andrada*, ed. C. R. Boxer (London, 1930), Appendix I, pp.211–18 at p. 215 cited in Valentina Caldari, 'The End of the Anglo-Spanish Match in Global Context, 1617–1624,' PhD, University of Kent (2015) p.142

32 BL IOR/E/3/7, f. 342

33 BL IOR G/29/1, transcribed in Sultan bin Muhammad al-Qasimi, 'Power Struggles and Trade in the Gulf, 1620–1680' unpublished PhD thesis, Durham University (1999), p.305

34 BL IOR/G/29/1, ff. 79v–80

35 TNA SP 94/25 fol.339r

36 *CSP Ven* vol. 17 No.732

37 AGS, E., Leg. 2516, docs. 32 and 33, Council of State, Madrid, 26 April 1623, quoted and discussed in Caldari, 'The End of the Anglo-Spanish Match in Global Context, 1617–1624'

38 Point made by Mishra, *A Business of State. Commerce, Politics and the Birth of the East India Company* (London, 2018) p.179

39 BL IOR B/8

40 TNA SP 94/27/189r

41 TNA SP 14/151/38

42 TNA SP 94/27/211

43 *Calendar of State Papers Colonial, East Indies and Persia, Volume 8, 1630–1634*, ed. W. Noel Sainsbury (London, 1892), British History Online No.642

44 *Calendar of State Papers Colonial, East Indies, China and Japan, Volume 2, 1513–1616*, British History Online No.340

22 THE KING OF PULO RUN

1 *Calendar of State Papers Colonial, East Indies, China and Japan, Volume 3, 1617–1621*, ed. W. Noel Sainsbury (London, 1870), British History Online No.623

2 Purchas, Hakluytus *Posthumus*, V, 1pp, 81–83;

3 See Martine Julia van Ittersum, 'Debating Natural Law in the Banda Islands: A Case Study in Anglo–Dutch Imperial Competition in the East Indies, 1609–1621', *History of European Ideas*, 42.4 (2016) pp.459–501

4 J.E. Heeres and F.W. Stapel (eds.) *Corpus Diplomaticum Neerlando-Indicum*, 6 vols (The Hague, 1907–55) vol. 1 p.67 cited in Adam Clulow, *Ambonia, 1623* (New York, 2019) p.35

5 *Calendar of State Papers Colonial, East Indies, China and Japan, Volume 3, 1617–1621*, Ibid. British History Online No.425

6 Ibid. British History Online No.468

7 *EIC Letters*, vol. 3 p.141

8 Ibid. p.142

9 *The Register of Letters* pp.492–3

10 *The Journal of John Jourdain, 1608–1617*, ed, William Foster (Cambridge, 1905) pp.328–29

11 *The Journal of John Jourdain*, pp.328–9; *Calendar of State Papers Colonial, East Indies, China and Japan, Volume 2, 1513–1616, ed.* W Noel Sainsbury (London, 1864), British History Online no. 1171

12 *EIC Letters*, vol.4, pp.215–220, at p.217

13 Purchas, *Hakluytus Posthumus*, V, (London, 1995) pp.181–3

14 TNA, CO 77/1 f. 109v, 110r cited in Ittersum, 'Debating Natural Law in the Banda Islands' p.481

15 *EIC Letters*, vol. 6, p.310

16 Ibid.

17 Ibid. pp.345–52 at pp.349–50

18 *Calendar of State Papers Colonial, East Indies, China and Japan, Volume 3, 1617–1621*, ed. W Noel Sainsbury(London, 1870), British History Online No. 527

19 TNA CO 77/1/48, fol.92r

20 The treaty can be found in Charles Jenkinson, *A Collection of Treaties of Peace, Commerce, and Alliance Between Great-Britain and Other Powers: From Year 1619 to 1734* (London, 1781), pp.1–16

21 Ibid. p.3

22 Ibid. p.5

23 *Chamberlain Letters* vol. 2 p.239

24 *Calendar of State Papers Colonial, East Indies, China and Japan, Volume 3, 1617–21*, British History Online No.700

25 Coen to Heeren 17, 11 May 1620 quoted in Adam Clulow, *Amboina, 1623: Fear and Conspiracy on the Edge of Empire* (New York, 2019) p.108

26 Ibid.

23 PLYMOUTH PLANTATION, NEW ENGLAND

1 William Bradford, *Of Plymouth Plantation, 1620–1647: The Complete Text*, ed. Samuel Eliot Morison (New York, 1952) p.155

2 Ibid. p.26

3 Printed in Walter H. Burgess, *John Robinson, Past of the Pilgrim Fathers, a study of his life and times* (London, 1920) pp.214–15

4 Ibid. pp.212–13

5 Edward Winslow, *Hypocrisie Unmasked* (London, 1646) p.90

6 Bradford, *Of Plymouth Plantation* p.38

7 Ibid. p.76

8 Ibid.

9 Ibid.

10 Ibid. p.62

11 Ibid. p.25

12 *Relation or Journal of the beginning and proceedings of the English Plantation settled at Plymouth in New England, by certain English adventurers both merchants and others.... Mourt's Relation.* (London, 1622) p.66

13 Ibid. p.50

14 Bradford, *Of Plymouth Plantation* p.79

15 *Mourt's Relation* pp.36–7

16 Ibid. p.55

17 Bradford, *Of Plymouth Plantation* p.90

18 Ibid. p.90

19 *Mourt's Relation* p.61

20 Bradford, *Of Plymouth Plantation* p.106

21 Ibid. p.108

22 Named after Capt. Christopher Levett – 'His Majesty's Woodward'

23 Bradford, *Of Plymouth Plantation* p.291

24 Ibid. p.114

25 'A Letter of William Bradford and Isaac Allerton, 1623', *American Historical Review* 8.2 (1903) pp.294–301 at p.298

26 Bradford, *Of Plymouth Plantation* p.83

27 'Letter of William Bradford and Isaac Allerton', p.298

28 Edward Winslow, *Good newes from New-England* (London, 1624) n.3.

29 Bradford, *Of Plymouth Plantation* p.375

30 Thomas Morton, *New English Canaan* (1632), printed in Charles Francis Adams, in *The English Canaan of Thomas Morton* (Boston, 1883) p.256

31 Ibid. p.254

24 THE POWHATAN UPRISING

1 *Travels and Works of Captain John Smith President of Virginia, and Admiral of New England 1580–1631*, vol. 1, ed. Edward Arber, 2 vols (London, 1910) vol.1 p.134

2 Edward Waterhouse, *A declaration of the state of the colony and affairs in Virginia . . .* (London, 1622) p.12

3 Waterhouse, *A declaration* pp.13–14

4 Ibid. p.14

5 Patrick Copland, *Virginia's God Be Thanked; or, A Sermon of Thanksgiving for the Happie Successe of the Affayres in Virginia This Last Yeare; Preached by Patrick Copland at Bow-Church in Cheapside, before the Honorable Virginia Company, on Thursday, the 18. of Aprill 1622; and Now Published by the Commandement of the Said Honorable Company* (London, 1622)

6 Ibid. p.12

7 Ibid. pp.28–9

8 John Rolfe, *True Relation of the State of Virginia lefte vt Sir Thomas Dlae, knight, in May last 1616* (New Haven, 1951) p.40

9 *Records of the Virginia Company* vol. 1 pp.266, 351

10 Waterhouse, *A declaration* p.22

11 See 'The First University in America, 1619–1622', *The Virginia Magazine of History and Biography*, 30.2 (1922), pp.133–56 at p.148

12 *Records of the Virginia Company* vol. 3 p.446

13 Ibid.

14 Ibid.

15 *Travels and Works of Smith* vol. 2 p.574; Samuel Purchas, *Hakluytus Posthumus Or Purchas His Pilgrimes* vol. 19 (London, 1906) p.153

16 *Records of the Virginia Company* vol. 3 p.446

17 'Instructions to the Governor and Council of State in Virginia, July 24, 1621', in *The Three Charters of the Virginia Company of London with Seven Related Documents: 1606–1621*, ed. Bemiss, Samuel B. (Williamsburg, VA, 1957) p.110

18 Ibid. p.111

19 *Records of the Virginia Company* vol. 1 pp.269–449

20 *Records of the Virginia Company* vol. 3 p.487

21 Purchas, *Pilgrimes* vol. 19 p.153

22 *Records of the Virginia Company* vol. 3 p.584

23 Ibid. vol. 3 p.128

24 *Virginia's God Be Thanked* pp.9–10

25 Waterhouse, *A declaration* p.13

26 Ibid. p.16

27 Ibid. p.12

28 Edward Arber ed., *Travels and Works of Captain John Smith* vol. 2 p.575

29 *Records of the Virginia Company* vol. 3 p.612

30 Waterhouse, *A declaration* p.23

31 Ibid. pp.24–5

32 Ibid. p.33

33 See Noel Malcolm, 'Hobbes, Sandys and the Virginia Company', *The Historical Journal* 24.2 (1981) pp.297–321

34 John Donne, 'Sermon CLVI. Preached to the Virginian Company, 1622', in *The Works of John Donne, D.D., Dean of St. Paul's, 1621–1631, With a Memoir of His Life*, ed. Henry Alford, 6 vols (London, 1839), vol. 6 pp.225–42 at p.236

35 Ibid. p.231

36 Ibid. p.235

37 Purchas, *Pilgrimes*, vol. 19 p.231

38 Robert Johnson, *Nova Britannia offering most excellent fruites by planting in Virginia: exciting all such as be well affected to further the same.* (London, 1609) pp.13–14

39 Privy Council, William A. Fitzroy, James Munro and W.L. Grant (eds.), *Acts of the Privy Council of England, Colonial Series, Vol. 1 1613–1680* (London, 1908) p.54

40 Francis Wyatt, 'Letter of Sir Francis Wyatt, Governor of Virginia, 1621– 1626', *The William and Mary College Quarterly Historical Magazine* 6. 2 (1926) pp.114–21 at p.118

41 'Report of Governor and Council, Jan. 20, 1623', in Edward D. Neill, *History of the Virginia Company of London* (Albany, NY, 1869) p.365

42 *Records of the Virginia Company* vol. 3 p.451

43 Ibid. vol.4 p.235

44 'A Declaration of the State of the Colony and Affairs in Virginia. List of the Names of the Living in Virginia', 16 February 1624, in *Calendar of State Papers Colonial, America and West Indies: Volume 1, 1574–1660*, British History Online No.2

45 *Records of the Virginia Company*, vol. 4 p.118

46 *Chamberlain Letters*, vol. 2 p.555

47 TNA 14/169, f. 19r quoted in Lauren Working, *The Making of an Imperial Polity: Civility and America in the Jacobean Metropolis* (Cambridge, 2020) p.89

48 'Documents of Sir Francis Wyatt, Governor', *The William and Mary Quarterly*, 8 (1928), pp.157–67, at p.166

49 *Complete Works of John Smith*, vol.2 p.312

50 James I, *A Proclamation Concerning Tobacco* (London, 1624), in Larkin and Hughes (eds.), *Stuart Royal Proclamations*

51 In Wesley Frank Craven, *Dissolution of the Virginia Company. The Failure of a Colonial Experiment* (Gloucester, MA, 1964), p.284

52 *Records of the Virginia Company* vol.4 p.547

53 Point made by Working, *The Making of an Imperial Polity* p.94

25 CHRISTENDOM ON FIRE

1 *Jacobean Letters* pp.270–71

2 Thomas Middleton, *The peace-maker: or, Great Brittaines blessing* (London, 1618) unnumbered

3 S.R. Gardiner (ed.), *Letters and other documents illustrating the relations between England and Germany at the commencement of the Thirty Years' War* (London, 1968) vol. 1 p.10

4 Ibid. vol. 1 pp.144–8; p.118–27

5 Quoted by Brennan C. Pursell, *The Winter King, Frederick V of the Palatinate and the Coming of the Thirty Years War* (Farnham, 2003) p.80

6   Akkerman, *Elizabeth Stuart* vol.1 letter 150 p.205

7   *Letters of King James I ... to King Christian IV of Denmark* p.198

8   Letter from Anna to Buckingham printed in Agnes Strickland, *Lives of the Queens of England, From the Norman Conquest,* 12 vols (London, 1885) vol. 7 p.175

9   See Jemma Field, '"Orderinge Things Accordinge to his Majesties Comaundment": The Funeral of the Stuart Queen Consort Anna of Denmark', *Women's History Review,* 30.5 (2021) pp.835–55

10 Ibid. p.849

11 *Chamberlain Letters* vol. 2 pp.225–6

12 *Gardiner* (ed.), *Letters and other documents* pp.41, 42

13 Ibid. p.44

14 Gardiner, *History of England* vol.2 p.350

15 *Coleccion de documentos ineditos para la historia de España,* 113 vols (Madrid, 1842–95) vol. 2 p.133 cited in Smuts, *Political Culture* p.609

16 C.H. Carter, *The Secret Diplomacy of the Habsburgs, 1598–1625* (London, 1964) p.187

17 John Harrison, *The Messiah Already Come* (London, 1619)

18 *Cabala, mysteries of state: in letters of the great ministers of K. James and K. Charles. Wherein much of the publique manage of affaires is related. / Faithfully collected by a noble hand* (London, 1654) p.169

19 *Calendar of State Papers Domestic: James I, 1619–23,* ed. Mary Anna Everett Green (London, 1858), British History Online p.437

20 See Steve Murdoch, *Britain, Denmark-Norway, and the House of Stuart, 1603–1660* (East Linton, 2000) p.49

21 *Letters of King James I ... to King Christian IV of Denmark* p.206

22 TNA SP 14/113/33–34

23 *Calendar of State Papers Domestic: James I, 1619–23,* ed. Green, British History Online p.125

24 *Register of the Privy Council of Scotland, 1619–1622* (Edinburgh, 1877) vol.12 p.255 quoted in Steve Murdoch, *Britain, Denmark–Norway and the House of Stuart,* p.49

25 Anon., *A most true relation of the late proceedings in Bohemia, Germany, and Hungaria Dated the 1. the 10. and 13. of Iuly, this present yeere 1620. As also of the happie arriuall of Sir Andrew Gray into Lusatia. Together with the articles of peace betweene the Catholikes, and the princes of the reformed religion, in the citie of Vlme, the third of Iuly last. ... Faithfully translated out of the high Dutch* (London, 1620), p.10

26 John Taylor, *An English-Mans Love to Bohemia* (London, 1620) sigs. A2r-2 v. See Murdoch, 'James VI and the Formation of Scottish-British

Military Identity', in *Fighting for Identity: Scottish Military Experience C. 1550–1900*, ed. by Murdoch and Andrew Mackillop (Leiden: Brill, 2002), pp.3–31, at p.19

27 Akkermann, *Eliȝabeth Stuart* vol. 1 letter 186 p.254

28 *CSP Ven* vol.16 No.559

29 Quoted in Robert Zaller, *The Parliament of 1621: A Study in Constitutional Conflict* (Berkeley, CA, 1971) p.17

30 Thomas Scott, *Vox Populi, or Newes from Spayne Translated according to the Spanish Coppie; which may Serve to Forwarn both England and the Vnited Provinces how farre to Trust to Spanish Pretences.* (London, 1620) A4r

31 Ibid. B1

32 Sir Simonds D. 'Ewes, *The Autobiography and Correspondence of Sir Simonds D'Ewes, Bart., During the Reigns of James I and Charles I*, ed. J.O. Halliwell (London, 1845) p.159

33 James I and VI, *A Proclamation against Excesse of Lauish and Licentious Speech of Matters of State, 24 December 1620*, Stuart Royal Proclamations

34 Quoted in Jayne E.E. Boys, *London's News Press and the Thirty Years War* (Cambridge, 2014) p.68

35 John Taylor, *Taylor his trauels: from the citty of London in England, to the citty of Prague in Bohemia* (London, 1620), unnumbered.; *Newes from Bohemia. A true relation of the now present warres in Bohemia* (London, 1619)

36 Folke Dahl, *A bibliography of English corantos and Periodicals Newsbooks 1620–1642* (Stockholm, 1953) p.49

37 'Diary of an Unknown Edinburgh Merchant Burgess', the National Library of Scotland Wodrow collection Quarto IX, fol.129 cited in Jason White, *Militant Protestantism and British Identity 1603–1642* (London, 2012) p.47

38 BL Add MSS 36444, fol.248 cited in Robert Zaller, '"Interest of State"; James I and the Palatinate', *Albion: A Quarterly Journal Concerned with British Studies*, 6.2 (1974) pp.144–75 at p.150

39 Cobbett, *Parliamentary History of England* vol. 1 pp.1175–80 at p.1178

40 Gardiner, *History of England* vol.4 p.129

41 TNA SP 80/4, fols. 22–3 cited in Zaller, '"Interest"' p.160

42 BL, Egerton MSS 2594, fol. 163 cited ibid. p.173

43 Thomas Gataker, *A sparke tovvard the kindling of sorrow for Sion* (London, 1621) p.10

44 Commons Debates, 1621, ed. Wallace Notestein, Frances Helen Rolf and Hartley Simpson, 7 vols (New Haven, CT, 1935) vol.3 pp.419–24; vol. 4 pp.426–8

45 House of Commons, Thomas Tyrwhitt and Edward Nicholas, *The Proceedings and Debates of the House of Commons in 1620 and 1621* (Oxford, 1766) vol. 2 p.45

46 Ibid. p.212

47 Ibid. pp.290, 264

48 The petition is printed in Rushworth (ed.), *Historical Collections*, vol. 1 pp.40–43

49 Ibid. vol. 1 p.43

50 Ibid.

51 'His Majesty's Declaration. Touching his Proceedings in the late Assembly and Convention of Parliament (1622)' in Sommerville (ed.), *Political Writings* p.257

52 Conrad Russell, *Parliaments and English Politics 1621–29* (Oxford, 1979) p.125

53 *Commons Debates, 1621* p.464

54 Quoted by Thomas Cogswell, 'England and the Spanish Match', in R. Cust and A. Hughes (eds.), *Conflict in Early Stuart England: Studies in Religion and Politics 1603–42* (London, 1989), pp.107–13 at p. 115

26 A GAME AT CHESS

1 Thomas Middleton, *A Game at Chess* (1624) ed. T.H. Howard-Hill (Manchester, 1997)

2 *Letters of King James VI and I* p.420

3 *CSP Ven* vol.16 p.576

4 Sir Henry Wotton, *Reliquiae Wottonianae: or a Collection of Lives, Letters, Poems, with characters of Sundry personages: and other incomparable pieces of Languages and Art* (London, 1651) p.214

5 *Letters of King James VI and I* p.394

6 TNA SP 94/27/22 quoted in Roger Lockyer, *Buckingham, the Life and Political Career of George Villiers, First Duke of Buckingham, 1592–1628* (London, 1981), p.158

7 *CSP Ven* vol.17 No. 801

8 TNA, SP 94/26, fol. 81

9 Cited in Thomas Cogswell, *The Blessed Revolution: English Politics and the Coming of War, 1621–1624* (New York, 1989) p.37

10 TNA 94/25/166–168v quoted in Lockyer, *Buckingham* p.125

11 Samuel Rawson Gardiner, *Prince Charles and the Spanish Marriage: 1617–1623*, 2 vols (London, 1869) vol. 2 p.276

12 Brennan C. Pursell, 'The End of the Spanish Match', *The Historical Journal* 45.4 (2003) pp.699–726 p.703

13 Quoted by Henry Ettinghause, *Prince Charles and the King of Spain's Sister – What the Papers Said: An Inaugural Lecture Delivered on 28 February 1985* (Southampton, 1987) p.8

14 For a list of newsletters and pamphlets on Charles's visit, see Alexander Samson, '1623 and the Politics of Translation' in Samson (ed.), *The Spanish Match: Prince Charles' Journey to Madrid 1623* (Abingdon, 2006), p.91, fn 2

15 Lee (ed.), *Jacobean Letters* p.298

16 Ibid.

17 See David Sánchez Cano, 'Entertainments in Madrid for the Prince of Wales: Political Functions of Festivals', in Samson (ed.), *The Spanish Match*, pp.51–74

18 *CSP Ven*, vol.17 No. 870

19 Francisco de Jesús, *Narrative of the Spanish Marriage Treaty*, ed. Samuel R. Gardiner (London, 1869), p.208

20 Archivo General de Simancas [hereafter AGS], E., Leg. 2516, doc. 32, cited in Caldari, 'The End of the Anglo-Spanish Match in Global Context, 1617–1624' p.225

21 TNA SP 94/25 fol.339r

22 Philip Yorke, Earl of Hardwicke, *Miscellaneous State Papers: From 1501 to 1726*, 2 vols (London, 1778) vol. 1 p.410

23 Ibid. p.404

24 *Calendar of State Papers Domestic: James I, 1619–23*, ed. Green, British History Online No.143; *CSP Ven* vol.17 No.849

25 BL Harl MS 6987 art.48 printed in *Letters of the Kings of England, now first collected from the originals in royal archives, and from other authentic sources, private as well as public*, ed. J.O. Halliwell-Phillipps (London, 1846) pp.207–8

26 Rushworth (ed.), *Historical Collections* vol. 1 pp.86–9

27 Cited in Brennan C. Pursell, *The Winter King: Frederick V of the Palatinate and the Coming of the Thirty Years' War* (Aldershot, 2003) p.198

28 Hardwicke, *Papers*, vol. 1 pp.449–50

29 Ibid. vol. 1 p.451

30 Rushworth (ed.), *Historical Collections* vol. 1 p.102

31 See Lockyer, *Buckingham* p.164

32 Akkerman, *Elizabeth Stuart* vol. 1 No. 305 pp.433–4 at p.434

33　The *Diary of Sir Simonds D'Ewes 1622–24*, ed. Elisabeth Bourchier (Paris, 1974) pp.163–4

34　*The Joifull Returne of the most illustrious Prince, Charles… from the court of spain* (London, 1623) pp.37–8

35　'Diary of an Unknown Edinburgh Merchant Burgess', National Library of Scotland Wodrow collection Quarto IX, fol.129

36　*Extracts from the Council Register of…Aberdeene, 1570–1625*, 2 vols (Aberdeen, 1848), vol. 2 pp.389–90 cited in Thomas Cogswell, *Blessed Revolution: English Politics and the Coming of War, 1621–1624* (Cambridge, 1989) p.10

37　Stephen Jerome, *Irelands Jubilee or Joyes Io-paen for Prince Charles his welcome home* (Dublin, 1624)

38　*CSP Ven* vol.18 1623–5 No.149

39　*Scrina Sacra; Secrets of Empire, in Letters of Illustrious Persons: A Supplement of the Cabala &c.* (London, 1654) p.136

40　TNA SP 31/8 vol. 198

41　Hardwicke, *Papers* vol. 1 pp.484–5

42　Francisco de Jesús, *Narrative of the Spanish Marriage Treaty*, ed. and trans. Samuel R. Gardiner (London, 1869) p.261

43　Gardiner, *History of England from the Accession of James I to the Outbreak of the Civil War, 1603–1642* 7 vols. (London, 1884–1890), vol. 5 p.153

44　Quoted in Lockyer, *Buckingham* p.168

45　*CSP Ven* vol.18 No 235

46　See Thomas Cogwell, 'Thomas Middleton and the Court, 1624: A Game at Chess in Context', *Huntington Library Quarterly* 47 (1984): pp.273–88

47　Cited and translated in Edward M. Wilson and Olga Turner, 'The Spanish Protest against "A Game at Chesse"', *The Modern Language Review* 44.4 (1949) pp.476–82 at p.477

48　John Reynolds, *Vox coeli, or, Newes from Heaven* (London, 1624), p.45. See also *Chamberlain Letters* vol. 2 pp.577–8

49　Cited in Wilson and Turner 'The Spanish Protest' pp.480–81

50　Ibid.

51　David Calderwood, *History of the Kirk of the Scotland* (Edinburgh, 1845) vol. 7 p.570

52　*Calendar of State Papers, Ireland 1615–1625*, ed. C.W. Russell and John P. Prendergast (London, 1872) p.393 No.954

53　*CSP Ireland 1615–1625* p.455 No.1129

54　Scott, *Vox Populi*

55　Thomas Scott, *Digitus Dei* (Holland, 1623) p.5

56　*The Autobiography and Correspondence of Sir Simonds D'Ewes*, vol. 1 p.242

27 ENDGAME

1 Bodleian Library, Tanner MS 73 fols.199r–230v, *Tom Tell-Troth, or A free discourse touching the murmurs of the Times, Directed to His Majesty, by way of Humble Advertisement* (1622)

2 TNA SP 84/116/204

3 TNA SP 81/30/73 cited by Cogswell, *The Blessed Revolution* p.143

4 *HMC Report on the manuscripts of the Earl of Mar and Kellie. Supplementary report on the manuscripts of the Earl of Mar & Kellie, preserved at Alloa house, Clackmannanshire*, ed. Rev. Henry Paton (London, 1930) p.183

5 *Chamberlain Letters* vol. 2 p.546

6 Dudley Carleton to Sir Dudley Carleton, 10 November 1623 TNA SP 14/154/19

7 BL Harleian MS 159 fol. 59 cited in Robert E. Ruigh, *The Parliament of 1624: Politics and Foreign Policy* (Cambridge, MA, 1971) p.156

8 Ibid.

9 Cobbett, *The Parliamentary History of England* vol. 1, p.1376

10 Northamptonshire Record Office, Finch-Hatton MSS 50 fols. 10–11 cited in Cogswell, *The Blessed Revolution* p.175

11 Cited in Stephen D.White, *Sir Edward Coke and 'The Grievances of the Commonwealth', 1621–1628* (Chapel Hill, NC, 1979) p.94

12 Rushworth (ed.), *Historical Collections* vol. 1, p.128

13 Ibid. p.130

14 'House of Commons Journal Volume 1: 11 March 1624', in *Journal of the House of Commons: Volume 1, 1547–1629* (London, 1802), British History Online p.682

15 J.R. Tanner, ed., *Constitutional Documents of the Reign of James I* (Cambridge, 1961) p.299

16 Folger MS.X d, 150 fol.1v cited in Patterson, *Reunion of Christendom* p.348. Alternative version of speech in Rushworth (ed.), *Historical Collections*, vol. 1 p.139

17 Folger MS.X d, 150 fol.1v cited in Patterson, *Reunion of Christendom* p.348. Version in Rushworth (ed.), *Historical Collections*, vol. 1 p.140 has '2000 pounds and 10000 pounds' instead of a reference to the number of men.

18 Folger MS. V. a. 205, pp.138, 144 cited in Patterson, *Reunion of Christendom* p.350

19 TNA SP 14/161/36, cited in Ruigh, *The Parliament of 1624* p.232

20 *CSP Ven* vol.18 No.309

21 *CSP Ven* vol.18 No.225

22 Quoted in Willson, *King James VI and I* p.412

23 Ben Jonson, *The fortunate isles and their vnion Celebrated in a masque design'd for the court, on the Twelfth night. 1624* (London, 1625)

24 Bodleian MS Barlow 54 fol.3r quoted in Alastair Bellany and Thomas Cogswell, *The Murder of King James I* (New Haven, CT, 2015) p.40

25 Ibid. p.41

26 HMC, Henry Paton, Walter John Francis Erskine Mar and Kellie, and Thomas Erskine Kellie, *Report On the Manuscripts of the Earl of Mar and Kellie: Preserved at Alloa House, Clackmannanshire.* (London, 1930) p.226

27 *HMC Eleventh report: appendix. Part 1, The manuscripts of Henry Duncan Skrine, Esq.: Salvetti correspondence* (London, 1877), pp.4, 15

28 Nichols, *Progresses* vol. 4 p.1039

28 GREAT BRITAIN'S SOLOMON

1   John Taylor, *A Living Sadnes, In Duty Conscreated to the Immortal Memory of Our Late Deceasased Albe-Loued Soueraugne Lord, the Peereles Paragon of Princes, James, King of Great Brittaine* (1625) p.2

2   *HMC 11th Report, Skrine: Salvetti Correspondence* pp.15–17

3   BL Lansdowne MS 885 fol.127v; 'Procession to the King's Funeral, 1625', in Nichols, *Progresses* vol. 4 pp.1039–48

4   This paragraph draws directly from Alastair Bellany and Thomas Cogswell, *The Murder of King James I* (New Haven, CT, 2015) p.51 Images are in John Peacock, 'Inigo Jones Catafalque for James I', *Architectural History* 25 (1982) pp.6–7

5   John Williams, *Great Britains Salomon: A Sermon Preached at the Magnificent Funerall, of the most high and mighty King, James, the late King of Great Britaine, France, and Ireland, defender of the Faith* (London, 1625)

6   Ibid. p.60

7   Ibid. p.57

8   Ibid. pp.75–6

9   Evelyn M. Simpson and George R. Potter (eds.), *The Sermons of John Donne*, 10 vols. (Berkeley, CA, 1953) vol. 7 p.166

10 R. Wilkinson, *The Merchant Royall. A Sermon Preached at Whitehall* (London, 1607) p.17

11 Samuel Purchas, *The kings towre* (London, 1623) sig. D4v

SELECT BIBLIOGRAPHY

Primary Sources

Unpublished manuscript references appear in endnotes

Acts of the Privy Council, ed. J. R. Dasent (London, 1890).

The Acts of the Parliament of Scotland 1593–1625, ed. Thomas Thomson and C. Innes, 12 vols (Edinburgh, 1814–44).

'A Journal of the Conference Betwixt His Majesty's Commissioners, and the Commissioners of the King of Spain, and Arch-Dukes of Austria, Dukes of Burgundy, &C. At the Treating and Concluding of a Peace with the Aforesaid Princes at Somerset-House in London, Anno 1604', In *The History of the Reign of Philip the Third, King of Spain*, ed. Robert Watson and William Thomson (New York, 1818).

Alexander, William, Earl of Stirling, *An Elegie on the Death of Prince Henrie* (Edinburgh, 1612).

Akkerman, Nadine (ed.), *The Correspondence of Eliȥabeth Stuart: Queen of Bohemia, Vol.1 1603–1631* (Oxford, 2015).

Akrigg, G.P.V. (ed.), *Letters of King James VI and I* (Berkeley, 1984).

Andrewes, Lancelot, *Sermons by the Right Honourable and Reverend Father in God, Lancelot Andrewes, Late Lord Bishop of Winchester. Published, by His Majesties speciall command. . .The fovrth edition. With an alphabeticall table of the principall contents. Whereunto is added, a sermon preached before two Kings, on the fift of August. 1606* (London, 1641).

Anon., *Articles of Peace, Entercourse, and Commerce, Concluded... In a Treatie at London... the 18. Day of August after the Old Stile in the Yeere of our Lord God 1604* (London, 1605).

Anon., *The King of Denmarkes welcome: Containing his ariuall, abode, and entertainement, both in the Citie and other places* (London, 1606).

Anon., *A most true relation of the late proceedings in Bohemia, Germany, and Hungaria Dated the 1. the 10. and 13. of Iuly, this present yeere 1620. As also of the happie arriuall of Sir Andrew Gray into Lusatia. Together with the articles of peace betweene the Catholikes, and the princes of the reformed religion, in the citie of Vlme, the third of Iuly last. …. Faithfully translated out of the high Dutch* (London, 1620).

Anon., *Sir Thomas Smithes voyage and entertainment in Rushia* (London, 1605).

Anon., *A True and Perfect Relation of the Whole Proceedings Against the Late Most Barbarous Traitors, Garnet a Jesuite, and His Confederats Contayning Sundry Speeches Delivered by the Lord Commissioners at Their Arraignments…* (London, 1606).

Anon., *A True and Perfect Relation of the proceedings at the several Arraignments of The Late Most barbarous Traitors* (London, 1606).

Anon., *The King of Demarkes's Welcome Containing his Arivall, Abode, and Entertainment, both in the Citie and Other Places* (London, 1606).

Arber, Edward and A.G. Bradley (eds.) *Travels and Works of Captain John Smith President of Virginia, and Admiral of New England 1580–1631*, vol. 1 (London, 1910).

Asher, G.M. (ed.) *Henry Hudson the Navigator: The Original Documents in Which His Career Is Recorded collected, partly translated, and annotated* (London, 1860).

Bacon, Francis, A *discourse of the happy union of the kingdoms of England & Scotland dedicated in private to King James I / by Francis Lord Bacon* (London, 1603).

Bacon. Francis, *On Travel* (London, 1625).

Barbour, Philip I (ed.), *The Jamestown Voyages under the First Charter, 1607–1609, Vol. 1* (Cambridge, 1969).

Barlow, William, The *Summe and Substance of the Conference Which, It Pleased his Excellent Majestie to Have…at Hampton Court: January 14.1603* (London, 1604).

Beaumont, Francis, *The Masque of the Inner Temple and Grayes Inne* (London, 1613).

Bellarmine, Robert, *Responsio Matthaei Torti Presbyteri et Theologi Papiensis, ad Librum inscriptum, Triplici Nodo Triplex Cuneus* (Cologne, 1608).

Blackwell, George, *A Large Examination Taken at Lambeth, according to his Maiesties direction, point by point, of M. George Blackwell, made Archpriest of England, by Pope Clement 8. Vpon occasion of a certaine answere of his, without the priuitie of the State, to a Letter lately sent vnto him for Cardinall Bellarmine, blaming him for taking the oath of Allegiance. Together with the Cardinals Letter, and M. Blackwels said answere vnto it. 234 Also M. Blackwels Letter to the Romish Catholickes in England, aswell Ecclesiasticall, as Lay.* (London, 1607).

Blackwell, George, *Mr. George Blackwel, (Made by Pope Clement 8. Archpriest of England), his Aunsweres vpon sundry his Examinations: Together, with his Approbation and taking of the Oath of Allegeance: And his Letter written to his Assistants, and brethren, moouing them not onely to take the said Oath, but to aduise all Romish Catholikes so.* (London, 1607).

Bemiss, Samuel B. (ed.), *The Three Charters of the Virginia Company of London with Seven Related Documents: 1606–1621* (Williamsburg, VA, 1957).

Bilson, Thomas, *A Sermon Preached at Westminster before the King and Queen's Maiesties at their Coronation on St James his day being the 28 [sic] July* (London, 1603).

Birch, Thomas, *The Life of Henry Prince of Wales, Eldest Son of King James I. Compiled chiefly from his own Papers, and other Manuscripts, never before published* (London, 1760).

Birdwood, Sir George, and Sir William Foster (eds.), *The Register of Letters etc. of the Governour and Company of Merchants of London trading into the East indies* (London, 1893).

Blundevile, Thomas, *M. Blundeile his exercises* (London, 1613).

Bonoeil, John, *His Majesties gracious letter to the Earle of South-Hampton* (London, 1622).

Bonoeil, John, *A Treatise of the Art of Making Silke, or, Directions for Making Lodgings, and the Breeding, and Ordering of Silkewormes, for the Planting of Mulberry Trees, and All Other Things Belonging to the Silke Art . . .* (London, 1622).

Bourcier, Elisabeth (ed.), *The Diary of Sir Simonds D'Ewes 1622–1624* (Paris, 1975).

Bradford, William, *Of Plymouth Plantation, 1620–1647: The Complete Text*, ed. Samuel Eliot Morison (New York, 1952).

Bradford, William [with Edward Winslow], *A relation or journall of the beginning and proceedings of the English plantation settled at Plimoth* (London, 1622).

Bradford, William, 'A Letter of William Bradford and Isaac Allerton, 1623', *American Historical Review*, 13.2 (1903) pp.294–301.

Brooke, Christopher, 'A Poem on the Late Massacre in Virginia (1622)', reproduced in *The Virginia Magazine of History and Biography*, 72 (1964), pp.259–92.

Brown, Alexander, *The Genesis of the United States: A Narrative of the Movement in England, 1605–1615: Vol. 1* (Boston, 1890).

Bruce. John (ed.), *Correspondence of King James VI of Scotland with Sir Robert Cecil and Others in England, During the Reign of Queen Elizabeth: With an*

Appendix Containe Papers Illustrative of Transactions Between King James and Robert Earl of Essex...Camden Society, 78 (London, 1861).

Burtin, Paul Denis (ed.) *Ambassades de Monsieur de la Boderie, en Angleterre Sous La Regne d'Henri IV et La Minorite de Louis XIII,* 5 vols (Paris, 1750).

Butler, Nathaniel, *The Historye of the Bermudaes or Summer Islands,* ed. J. Henry Lefroy (London, 1882).

Calderwood, David, *History of the Kirk of the Scotland,* vol. 7 (Edinburgh, 1845).

Calendar of State Papers, Colonial, East Indies, China and Japan. Vols. 2, 3, 4, 1513–1616, 1617–21 and 1622–24 ed. W. Noel Sainsbury (London, 1857–1878), British History Online.

Calendar of State Papers, Colonial, America and West Indies: Volume 1, 1574–1660, ed. W. Noel Sainsbury (London, 1860), British History Online.

Calendar of State Papers, Domestic Series: James I, 1603–1610, 1611–18, 1619–1623, 1623–1625, ed. Mary Anne Everett (London, 1857–8).

Calendar of State Papers, Spain (Simancas), Volume 4, 1587–1603, ed. Martin A.S. Hume (London, 1899), British History Online.

Calendar of State Papers and manuscripts, relating to English affairs, existing in the archives and collections of Venice, Vols. 9, 10, 11, 12, 1592–1603, 1603–1607, 1607–1610, and 1610–1613, ed. Horatio Brown (London, 1897–1905) British History Online.

Calendar of State Papers and manuscripts, relating to English affairs, existing in the archives and collections of Venice, Vols. 13, 14, 15, 16, 17, 18 1613–1615, 1615–1617, 1617–1619, 1619–1621, 1621–1623, 1623–1625, ed. Allen B. Hinds (London, 1907–12) British History Online.

Calendar of State papers relating to Ireland in the reign of James I, ed. C.W. Russell and John Prendergast, 5 vols (London, 1872–80).

Calendar of the Manuscripts of the Most Honourable the Marquess of Salisbury Preserved at Hatfield House, Hertfordshire, 24 vols (London, 1883–1976).

Camden, William, *Actio in Henricum Garnetum Societatis Iesuiticae in Anglia superiorem* ...(London, 1607).

Camden, William, *The Historie of the Most Renowned and Victorious Princesse Elizabeth, Late Queene of England* (London, 1630).

Cameron, Annie I., and Robert S. Rait (eds.), *The Warrender Papers* (Edinburgh, 1932).

Cano-Echevarria, Berta, and Mark Hutchings, 'The Spanish Ambassador and Samuel Daniel's Vision of the Twelve Goddesses: A New Document', *English Literary Renaissance* 24 (2012) pp. 223–57.

Carey, Robert, *The Memoirs of Robert Carey,* ed. Walter Scott (London, 1808).

Carleton, Dudley, *Letters from and to Sir Dudley Carleton, Knight During Hus Embassy in Holland, from January 1615/1616 to December 1620* (London, 1775).

Campion, Thomas, *The discription of a maske, presented before the Kinges Maiestie at White-Hall, on Twelfth Night last in honour of the Lord Hayes, and his bride* (London, 1607).

Chamberlain, John, *The Letters of John Chamberlain*, ed. N.E. McClure, 2 vols (Philadelphia, 1939).

Chapman, George, *An epicede or funerall song* (London, 1613).

Chapman, George, *The memorable masque of the two honorable houses or Innes of Court; the Middle Temple, and Lyncolns Inne* (London, 1614).

Clapham, John, *Elizabeth of England: certain observations concerning the life and reign of Queen Elizabeth*, ed. Evelyn Plummer Read and Conyers Read (Philadelphia, 1951).

Cleland, James, *Hēro-paideia, or The institution of a young noble man* (London, 1607).

Cobbett, William, *Parliamentary History of England from the Norman, in 1066 to the Year 1803*, 36 vols. (London, 1806–20).

Copland, Patrick, *Virginia's God be thanked, or a sermon of thanksgiving for the happie success of the affayres of Virginia this late yeare, Preached by Patrick Copland at Bow Church in Cheapside, before the Honorable Virginia Company on Thursday the 18 of April, 1622* (London, 1622).

Cotton, Sir Robert, *An Answer made by Command of Prince Henry, to Certain Propositions of Warre and Peace*(London, 1655).

Cotton, Sir Robert, *Discourse of his Majesty's Descent from the Saxon Kings* (London, 1603).

Council for Virginia, *A declaration of the state of the colonie and affaires in Virginia* (London, 1620).

Crakanthorpe, Richard, *A sermon at the solemnizing of the happie inauguration* (London, 1609).

Crashaw, William, *A sermon preached in London before the right honorable the Lord Lawarre* (London, 1610).

Cushman, Robert, *A sermon preached at Plimmoth in New-England* (London, 1622).

Daniel, Samuel, *A Panegyrike congratulatory to the Kings Majestie* (London, 1603).

Danvers, F.C., and W.M. Foster (eds.), *Letters Received by the East India Company from its Servants in the East*, 6 vols (London, 1896–1902).

Davies, John, *Bien Venv. Great Britaines Welcome to Hir Great Friendes, and Deere Brethren The Danes* (London, 1606).

Davies, John, *The Muses-Teares for the Losse of Henry, Prince of Wales*, (London, 1613).

Davys, John, *A discourse of the true causes why Ireland was never entirely subdued* (London, 1612).

Dekker, Thomas, *The Whole Magnificent Entertainment given to King James, Queen Anne His Wife and Henry Frederick the Prince*... (London, 1604).

Dekker, Thomas, *The Wonderfull Yeare: 1603* (London, 1603).

Dekker, Thomas, *The Double PP. 1605* (London, 1605).

Digges, Dudley, *Of the Circumference of the Earth; Or a Treatise of the North West Passage* (London, 1612).

Digges, Sir Dudley, *The defense of trade in a letter to Sir Thomas Smith Knight, governor of the East India Company etc From One of That Societie* (London, 1615).

Donne, John, *The Works of John Donne, D.D., Dean of St. Paul's, 1621–1631, With a Memoir of His Life*, ed. Henry Alford, 6 vols (London, 1839).

Drayton, Michael, *Poems of Michael Drayton*, ed. John Buxton, 2 vols (Cambridge, 1953).

Drayton, Michael, *Poly-Olbion* (London, 1612).

Dugdale, Gilbert, *The Time Triumphant Declaring in Briefe, the Arival of our Soveraigne Liedge Kord, King James into England, his Coronation at Westminster: Together with his Late Royal Progress from the Towre of London Through the Citie to his Hignes Maner of White Hall* ... (London, 1604).

Eburne, Richard, *A plaine path-way to plantations* (London, 1624).

Ellis, Henry, *Original Letters illustrative of English History*, second series in 4 vols (London, 1827).

Farrington, Anthony (ed.), *The English Factory in Japan 1613–1623*, 2 vols (London, 1991).

Fenton, John, *King James his welcome to London* (London, 1603).

Ford, John, *Honor Trivmphant. Or The Peeres Challenge, by Armes defensible, at Tilt, Turney, and Barriers ... Also The Monarches meeting: The King of Denmarkes welcome into England* (London, 1606).

Foster, William (ed.), *The Embassy of Sir Thomas Roe to the Court of the Great Mogul, 1615–1619, as Narrated in his Journal and Correspondence*, 2 vols (London, 1899).

Foster, William (ed.), *The Journal of John Jourdain, 1608–1617, describing his Experiences in Arabia, India and the Malay Archipelago* (Cambridge, 1905).

Foster, William (ed.), *The English Factories in India, 1618–1621; a Calendar of Documents in the India Office, British Museum and Public Record Office* (Oxford, 1906).

Fowler, William, *A true reportarie of the most triumphant, and royal accomplishment of the baptisme of the most excellent, right high, and mightie prince, Frederik Henry; by the grace of God, Prince of Scotland Solemnized the 30. day of August. 1594* (Edinburgh, 1594).

Galloway, Bruce R., and Brian P. Levack (eds.), *The Jacobean Union: Six Tracts of 1604* (Edinburgh, 1985).

Gardiner, Samuel R., *Prince Charles and the Spanish Marriage 1617–1623. A Chapter in English History*, 2 vols (London, 1869).

Gardiner, Samuel R. (ed.), 'The earl of Bristol's Defence of His Negotiations in Spain', in *The Camden Miscellany*, vol. 6 (London, 1871).

Gardiner, Samuel R., (ed.) *Letters and other Documents Illustrating the Relations between England and Germany at the Commencement of the Thirty Years War* (London, 1865).

Gataker, Thomas, *A sparke tovvard the kindling of sorrow for Sion* (London, 1621).

Geffe, Nicholas, *Discourse ... of the meanes and Sufficiencue of England, for to Have Abundance of Fine Silke, by Feeding of Silk Wormes within the Same... For the general use and universal benefit of all those his Country- men which embrace it* (London, 1607).

Gilbert, Humphrey, *A Discourse of a Discoverie for a New Passage to Cataia* (London, 1576).

Good newes from Virginia. Sent from Iames his Towne this present Moneth of March, 1623 by a Gentleman in that Country (London, 1624).

Goodman, Godfrey, *The Court of King James the First*, ed. J.S. Brewer, 2 vols (London, 1839).

Gordon, John *England and Scotland's Happinesse in Being Reducted to Unitie of Religion, Under Our Invincible Monarke King James* (London, 1604).

Gorges, Sir Arthur, *The Olympian catastrophe* (London, 1612).

Goldsmid, Edmund (ed.), *The Secret Correspondence of Sir Robert Cecil with James VI King of Scotland: Now First Published* (Edinburgh, 1887).

Gray, Robert, *A good speed to Virginia* (London, 1609).

Hall, Joseph, *Quo vadis? A iust censure of travell as it is commonly vndertaken by the gentlemen of our nation* (London, 1617).

Halliwell, James Orchard, *The Autobiography and Correspondence of Sir Simonds d'Ewes*, vol. 1 (London, 1845).

Hakluyt, Richard, *The principal navigations, voyages, traffiques and discoveries of the English Nation* ...3 vols (London, 1598–1600).

Hardwicke, Philip Yorke, Earl of, *Miscellaneous State Papers: From 1501 to 1726*, 2 vols (London, 1778).

Harington, Sir John, *Nugæ Antiquæ: Being a Miscellaneous Collection of Original Papers in Prose and Verse: Written in the Reigns of Henry VIII. Queen Mary, Elizabeth, King James, &c.* 2 vols (London, 1792).

Harrison, John, *The Messiah Already Come* (London, 1619).

Harrison, G.B., *A Jacobean Journal: Being a Record of Those Things Most Talked of During the Years, 1603–1606* (London, 1941).

Harrison, Stephen, *The Arches of Triumph Erected in Honor of the High and Mighty Prince. James the First of That Name, King, of England and the Sixt of Scotland* (London, 1604).

Harry, George Owen, *The genealogy of the High and Mighty Monarch, James, by the Grace of God, King of Great Brittayne* (London, 1604).

Hamor, Ralph, *A true discourse of the present state of Virginia* (London, 1615).

Heath, Jonn, *The Divell of the Vault. Or, the Vnmasking of Murther in a Briefe Declaration of the Catholike-complotted Treason, lately discouered* (London, 1606).

Historical MSS Commission, *The manuscripts of His Grace the Duke of Rutland: preserved at Belvoir Castle*, 4 vols (London, 1888–1905).

Historical MSS Commission, *Report on the Manuscripts of the Duke of Buccleuch and Queensberry, K.G., K.T., preserved at Montagu House, Whitehall*, 3 vols (London, 1899–1926).

Historical MSS Commission, *Report on the Manuscripts of Lord de l'Isle & Dudley Preserved at Penshurst Place*, ed. William A. Shaw and Geraint Dyfnallt Owen, 6 vols (London, 1934).

Historical MSS Commission, *Calendar of the Manuscripts of the Most Honourable the Marquess of Salisbury, K.G., Preserved at Hatfield House*, 24 parts (London, 1883–1976).

Historical MSS Commission, *Mar and Kellie Manuscripts* (London, 1904).

The Holy Bible, Conteyning the Old Testament and the New: Newly Translated out of the Originall Tongues and with the Former Translations Diligently Compared and Reuised, by his Maiesties Speciall Comandement. (London, 1611).

Holles, Gervase, *Memorials of the Holles Family, 1493–1656* (London, 1937).

Hollis Hallett, A.C., *Bermuda Under Sommer Islands Company 1612–1684*, 3 vols (Bermuda, 2005).

Hubbock, William, *An oration gratulatory to the high and mighty Iames of England, Scotland, France and Ireland, King, defendor of the faith, &c.* (London, 1604).

Ives, Vernon A. (ed.), *The Rich Papers: Letters from Bermuda, 1615–1646* (Toronto, 1984).

James VI, *The true lavv of free monarchy, or The reciprocall and mutuall duty betvvixt a free king and his naturall subjects: By a well affected subject of the kingdome of Scotland* (Edinburgh, 1598).

James VI and I, *Basilikon Doron, Or His Majesties Instructions to His Dearest Sonne, Henry the Prince* (London, 1603).

James I, *An Apologie for the Oath of Allegiance First Set Foorth Without a Name, and Now Acknowledged By The Authour, the Right High and Mightie Prince, James…Together with a Premonition of His Maesjtie's, to Most Mightie Monarches, Kings, Free Princes and States of Christendome* (London, 1609).

James I, *A counterblaste to tobacco* (London, 1604).

James I, *The King's Majesties Speech, as it was Delivered by Him in the Upper House of the Parliament* (London, 1604).

James I, *His Maiesties Declaration, Touching his Proceedings in the Late Assemblie and Conuention of Parliament* (London, 1622).

James I, *Meditation upon the Lords prayer* (London, 1619).

James I, *The workes of the most high and mightie prince, James by the grace of God, King of Great Britaine, France and Ireland, defender of the faith.* (London, 1616).

[James I], *Triplici Nodo, Trimplex Cuneu.Sive Apologia Pro Iuramento Fidelitatis: Adversus Duo Brevia P.Pauli Quinti, & Epistolam Cardinalis Bellarmini, ad G.Blackwellum Antipresbytereum Nuper Scriptam, Authoritate Regia* (London, 1607).

Meldrum, Ronald M. (ed.), *Translation and Facsimiles of the Original Latin Letters of King James I of England (VI of Scotland), to his Royal Brother-in-Law, King Christian IV of Denmark* (Washington, DC, 1977).

Haile, Edward Wright (ed.), *Jamestown Narratives: Eyewitness Accounts of the Virginia Colony: The First Decade: 1607–1617* (Champlain, VA, 1998).

Jansson, Maija, *Proceedings in Parliament 1614 (House of Commons)*. (Philadelphia, 1988).

Jansson, Maija, and Nikolai M. Rogozhin (eds.), *England and the North: The Russian Embassy of 1613–1614*, trans. Paul Bushkovitch (Philadelphia, 1944).

Jenkinson, Charles (ed.), *Collection of Treaties of Peace, Commerce, and Alliance Between Great- Britain and Other Powers: From Year 1619 to 1734* (London, 1781).

Jerome, Stephen, *Irelands Jubilee or Joyes Io-paen for Prince Charles his welcome home* (Dublin, 1624).

Johnson, Robert C., 'The Indian Massacre of 1622: Some Correspondence of the Reverend Joseph Mead', *The Virginia Magazine of History and Biography*, 71 (1963), pp.408–10.

Johnson, Robert, *Nova Britannia offering most excellent fruites by planting in Virginia: exciting all such as be well affected to further the same.* (London, 1609).

Jonson, Ben, *B. Jon: His Part of King James his Royall and Magnificent Entertainment* (London, 1604).

Jonson, Ben, *The Cambridge Edition of the Works of Ben Jonson Online.*

Jonson, Ben, *The fortunate isles and their vnion Celebrated in a masque design'd for the court, on the Twelfth night. 1624* (London, 1625).

Jonson, Ben, *The Masque of Blackness* (1605), ed. David Lindley in *The Cambridge Edition of the works of Ben Jonson Online.*

Jonson, Ben, *The staple of news* (London, 1631).

Jourdain, Silvester, *A Discovery of the Bermudas, Otherwise Called the Isle of Devils* (London, 1610).

Journal of the House of Burgesses of Virginia, ed. Henry Read McIlwaine and John Pendleton (Richmond, 1915).

Journal of the House of Commons, Volume 1: 1547–1629 (London, 1802) British History Online.

Journal of the House of Lords, Volume 2: 1578–1614 and Volume 3: 1620–1628 (London, 1767–1830) British History Online.

Kayll, Robert. *The Trades Increase* (London, 1615).

King, John, *A sermon preached at White-Hall* (London, 1608).

Kingsbury, Susan Myra, *Records of the Virginia Company of London*, 4 vols (Washington, DC, 1906–35).

Laffleur de Kermaingant, Pierre Paul, *L'Ambassade de France en Angleteere Sous Henri IV. Mission de Christophe de Harlay, Come de Beaumont*, 2 vols (Paris, 1895).

Larkin, James E., and Paul L. Hughes (eds.), *Stuart Royal Proclamations: Vol.1, Royal Proclamations of King James I 1603–1625* (Oxford, 2013).

Lee, Jr., Maurice, ed. *Dudley Carleton to John Chamberlain 1603–1624: Jacobean Letters.* (New Brunswick, NJ, 1972).

Lefroy, Sir John Henry, Memorials *of the Discovery and Early Settlement of the Bermudas or Somers Islands, 1515–1685*, 2 vols (London, 1877).

Lochay, Henri, and Joseph Cuvelier (eds.), *Correspondance de la Cour d'Espagne sur les Affaires des Pays-Bas au XVII Siècle*, 2 vols (Brussels, 1923).

Lodge, Edmund (ed.), Illustrations *of British History, Biography, and Manners in the Reigns of Henry VIII, Edward VI. Mary, Elizabeth and James I, Exhibited in a Series of Original Papers* (London, 1791).

Mackie, J. Duncan (ed.), '"A Loyall Subiectes Advertisement" as to the Unpopularity of James I.'s Government in England, 1603–4', *The Scottish Historical Review*, 23 (1925) pp.1–17.

Maclean, John (ed.), *Letters from Sir Robert Cecil to Sir George Carew*, ed. Sir John Maclean (London, 1864).

Maclean, John (ed.), *Letters from George Lord Carew to Sir Thomas Roe, Ambassador to the Court of the Great Moghul 1615–1617* (London, 1860).

Manningham, John, *The Diary of John Manningham of the Middle Temple, 1602–03*, ed. Robert Parker Solein (Hanover, NH, 1976).

Marcelline, George, *The Triumphs of King Iames the First of Great Brittaine, France, and Ireland* (London, 1610).

Martin, Richard, *A Speech Delivered, to the King's Most Excellent Majestie in the Name of the Sheriffes of London and Middlesex* (London, 1603).

Masson, David (ed.), *The Register of the Privy Council of Scotland, 1604–1607. Vol. 7; 1619–1622 vol 12.* (Edinburgh, 1885–95).

Melville, Andrew, *Principis Scoti-Britannorum Natalia and Gathelus* (Edinburgh, 1594).

Melville, James, *The Autobiography and Diary of Mr. James Melvill* (Edinburgh, 1842).

Middleton, Thomas, *The peace-maker: or, Great Brittaines blessing* (London, 1618).

Middleton, Thomas, *A Game at Chess* (1624), ed. T.H. Howard-Hill (Manchester, 1993).

Mornay, P. Du *The Mysterie of Iniquitie: that is to say, the historie of the papacie*, trans. S. Leannard (London, 1612).

Morton, Thomas, *New English Canaan* (1632).

Moryson, Fynes, *An itinerary vvritten by Fynes Moryson Gent. First in the Latine tongue, and then translated by him into English: containing his ten yeeres trauell through the tvvelue dominions of Germany, Bohmerland, Sweitzerland, Netherland, Denmarke, Poland, Jtaly, Turky, France, England, Scotland, and Ireland. Diuided into III parts* (London, 1617).

Mun, Thomas, *England's treasure by forraign trade, or the Balamce of our Foreign Trade is the Rule of our Treasure* (London, 1664).

Nichols, John (ed.), *The Progresses, Processions, and Magnificent Festivities, of King James the First*, 4 vols (London, 1828).

Nixon, Anthony, *Great Brittaines Generall Ioyes. Londons Glorious Triumphes...* (London, 1613).

Notestein, Wallace, *The House of Commons 1604–1610* (New Haven, CT, 1971).

Notestein, Wallace (ed.), *Commons Debates, 1621*, 7 vols (New Haven, CT, 1935).

Palmer, Thomas, *An Essay of the Meanes how to make our Travailes, into foraine Countries, the more profitable and honourable* (London, 1606).

Pett Phineas, *The Autobiography of Phineas Pett*, ed. W.G. Perrin (London, 1918).

Price, Daniel, *The Defence of Trvth Against a Booke Falsely Called the Trivmph of Trvth Sent over from Arras A. D. 1609. by Hvmfrey Leech Late Minister. Which Booke in All Particulars Is Answered, and the Adioning Motiues of His Revolt Confuted* (Oxford, 1610).

Purchas, Samuel, *The kings towre* (London, 1623).

Purchas, Samuel, *Purchas his pilgrimes. part 4 In fiue bookes* (London, 1625).

Purnell, C.J. (ed.), *The Log-book of William Adams 1614–1619, with the Journal of Edward Saris and other Documents Relations to Japan, Cochin-China* (London, 1916).

Raleigh, Walter, 'A Discourse Touching a War with Spain, and of the Protecting of the Netherlands', in *The Works of Sir Walter Ralegh, Kt, 299–316* (Oxford, 1829).

Reid, Steven J., and David McOmish (eds.), *Corona Borealis Scottish Neo-Latin Poets on King James VI and His Reign, 1566–1603* (Glasgow, 2020).

Reynolds, John, *Vox coeli, or, Newes from Heaven* (London, 1624).

Roberts, Lewis, *Treasure of Traffike or a Discourse of Forraigne Trade* (London, 1641).

Robarts, Henry, *Englands Farewell to Christian the Fourth, Famous King of Denmarke:..* (London, 1606).

Robarts, Henry, *The Most royall and Honourable entertainment, of the famous and renowmed King, Christiern the fourth, King of Denmarke...*(London, 1606).

Rolfe, John, *A True Relation of the State of Virginia lefte by Sir Thomas Dale, knight, in May last 1616* (New Haven, CT, 1951).

Rushworth, John, *Historical Collections of Private Passages of State, Weighty Measures in Law, Remarkable Proceedings in Five Parliaments*, 8 vols (London, 1721–2).

Rye, W.B., 'The Coronation of King James I, 1603', *The Antiquary*, 22 (1890) pp.18–23

Satow, Sir Ernest Mason (ed.), *The Voyage of Captain Saris to Japan, 1613* (London, 1900).

Sawyer, Edmund (ed.), *Memorials of Affairs of State in the Reigns of Q. Eliȝabeth and K. James I, Collected (chiefly) from the Original Papers of the Right Honourable Sir Ralph Winwood*, 2 vols. (London, 1725).

Scott, Thomas, *Digitus Dei* (Holland, 1623).

Scott, Thomas, *Vox Populi, or Newes from Spayne Translated according to the Spanish Coppie; which may Serve to Forwarn both England and the Vnited Provinces how farre to Trust to Spanish Pretences.* (London, 1620).

Scrina Sacra; Secrets of Empire, in Letters of Illustrious Persons: A Supplement of the Cabala &c. (London, 1654).

Serres, Olivier, *The Perfect Use of Silk-Wormes, and Their Benefit...Done out of the French original of D'Olivier de Serres Lord of Pradel into English by Nicholas Geffe Esquire* (London, 1607).

Shakespeare, William, *The Winter's Tale*, ed. Stephen Orgel (Oxford, 2008).

Sherley, Anthony, *Sir Anthony Sheirley His Relation of his Travels into Persia* (London, 1613).

Smith, John, *The generall historie of Virginia, New-England, and the Summer Isles with the names of the adventurers, planters, and governours from their first beginning. an⁰: 1584. to this present 1624* (London, 1624).

Smith, Logan Pearsall, *The Life and Letters of Sir Henry Wotton*, 2 vols (Oxford, 1907).

Sommerville, Johann P. (ed.), *King James VI and I: Political Writings* (Cambridge, 1994).

Sorrowes Joy. Or, A lamentation for our late deceased soveraigne Elizabeth, with a triumph for the prosperous succession of our gratious King, James, &c. (London, 1603).

Speed, John, *The History of Great Britaine...* (London, 1611).

Speed, John, *Theatre of the Empire of Great Britaine* (London, 1612).

Speeding, J. (ed.), *Life and Letters of Francis Bacon*, 7 vols (London, 1869).

Stallenge, William, *Instructions for the Increasing of Mulberie Trees, and the Breeding of Silke-Wormes for the Making of Silke in This Kingdom* (London, 1609).

Statutes of the Realm, Volume 4: 1547–1624, ed. John Raithby (London, 1819).

Stow, John, *The Annales, or a General Chronicle of England, Begun First by Maiester John Stow, and After him Continued and Augmented with Matters Forreyne, and Domestique, Auncient and Moderne, Unto the Ende of This Present Yeare 1614 by Edmond Howes* (London, 1615).

Strachey, William, *For the colony in Virginea Britannia. Lawes divine, morall and martiall* (London, 1612).

Strachey, William, *A true repertory of the wracke, and redemption of Sir Thomas Gates, Knight, upon, and from the Islands oof the Bermudes: his coming to Virginia, and the estate of that Colonie then, and after, under the government of Lord La Warre*, in Samuel Purchas, *Purchas his Pilgrimes* (London, 1625).

Sully, Maximilien de Béthune, duc de, *Memoirs of the Duke of Sully, Prime Minister to Henry the Great*, trans. Charlotte Lennox, 4 vols (London, 1861).

Symonds, Williams, *Virginia: a sermon preached at White-Chappel* (London, 1609).

Tanner, J.R. (ed.), *Constitutional Documents of the Reign of James I* (Cambridge, 1961).

Taylor, John, *A Living Sadnes, In Duty Conscreated to the Immortal Memory of Our Late Decesased Albe-Loued Soueraugne Lord, the Peereles Paragon of Princes, James, King of Great Brittaine* (London, 1625).

Taylor, John, *Newes from Bohemia. A true relation of the now present warres in Bohemia* (London, 1619).

Taylor, John, *Taylor his trauels: from the citty of London in England, to the citty of Prague in Bohemia* (London, 1620).

Thompson, Sir Edward Maunde (ed.), *Diary of Richard Cocks, Cape-Merchant in the English Factory in Japan, 1615–1622: With Correspondence*, 2 vols (London, 1883).

Thornborough John, *A Discourse Plainly Proving the Evident Utilitie and Urgent Necessitie of the Desired Happie Union of the Two Famous Kingdomes of England and Scotland by Way of Answer to Certaine Objections Against the Same* (London, 1604).

Thou de, Jacques-Auguste, *Historiarum sui temporis, pars prima* (Paris, 1604).

Tourval, Jean l'Oiseau de, *The French Herald Svmmoning All Trve Christian Princes to a generall Croisade, for a holy warr against the great Enemy of Christendome, and all his slaues. Vpon the Occasion of the most execrable murther of Henry the grat. To the Prince.* (London, 1611).

Waterhouse, Edward, A *declaration of the state of the colony and affairs in Virginia* ... (London, 1622).

Weston, William, *The Autobiography of an Elizabethan*, trans. Philip Carman (London, 1955).

Whitaker, Alexander, *Good newes from Virginia* (London, 1613).

Wilkinson, R., *The Merchant Royall. A Sermon Preached at Whitehall* (London, 1607).

Wilbraham, Roger, *The Journal of Sir Roger Wilbraham for the Years 1593–1616*, ed. H.S. Scott (London, 1902).

Williams, John, *Great Britains Salomon: A Sermon Preached at the Magnificent Funerall, of the most high and mighty King, James, the late King of Great Britaine, France, and Ireland, defender of the Faith* (London, 1625).

Willson, David Harris (ed.), *The Parliamentary Diary of Robert Bowyer, 1606–1607* (Minneapolis, 1977).

Winslow, Edward, *Good newes from New-England* (London, 1624).

Winslow, Edward, *Hypocrisie Unmasked* (London, 1646).

Winwood, Ralph, *Memoirs of Affairs of State in the Reigns of Q.Elizabeth and K.James I, Collected (Chiefly) from the Original Papers of ... Sir Ralph Winwood*, ed. E. Sawyer, 3 vols (London, 1725).

Wright, Edward, *Certain errors in navigation or navigators* (London, 1612).

Wright, Louis B. *A Voyage to Virginia in 1609: Two Narratives: Strachey's 'True Reportory' and Jourdain's 'Discovery of the Bermudas'* (Charlottesville, VA, 2013).

Wotton, Sir Henry, *Letters and Dispatches from Sir Henry Wotton to James the First and His Ministers in the Years MDCXVII–XX* (London, 1850).

Wotton, Sir Henry, *Reliquiae Wottonianae: or a Collection of Lives, Letters, Poems, with characters of Sundry personages: and other incomparable pieces of Languages and Art* (London, 1651).

Secondary Sources

Adams, Simon, 'Spain or the Netherlands? The Dilemmas of Early Stuart Foreign Policy', in *Before the English Civil War: Essays on Early Stuart Politics and Government*, ed. Howard Tomlinson, (New York, 1983) pp.79–101.

Adams, Simon, 'Foreign Policy and the Parliaments of 1621 and 1624', in *Faction and Parliament: Essays on Early Stuart History*, ed. Kevin Sharpe (Oxford, 1978), pp.139–71.

Akkerman, Nadine, *Elizabeth Stuart, Queen of Hearts* (Oxford, 2021).

Akkerman, Nadine, 'The Goddess of the Household: the Masquing Politics of Lucy Harington-Russell, 1601–1604', in Nadine Akkerman and Birgit Houben (eds.), *The Politics of Female Households: Ladies-in-waiting across Early Modern Europe* (Leiden, 2013), pp.287–309.

Andrews, Kenneth R., 'Caribbean Rivalry and the Anglo-Spanish Peace of 1604', *History* 59 (1974) pp.1–17.

Archer, Ian., 'The City of London and the Ulster Plantation', in *The Plantation of Ulster*, ed. Ó Ciardha and Ó Siochrú, (Manchester, 2012) pp.78–97.

Arel, Maria Salomon, *English Trade and Adventure in Russia in the Early Modern Era* (London, 2019).

Armitage, David., *The Ideological Origins of the British Empire* (Cambridge, 2000).

Barbour, Richmond, 'Power and Distant Display: Early English "Ambassadors" in Moghul India', *Huntingdon Library Quarterly* 61.3 (1988) pp.343–68.

Baron, Samuel H, 'Thrust and Parry: Anglo-Russian Relations in the Muscovite North', *Oxford Slavonic Papers* 21 (1988) pp.19–40.

Barroll, J. Leeds, *Anna of Denmark, Queen of England: A Cultural Biography* (Philadelphia, 2001).

Barroll, J. Leeds, 'The Arts at the English Court of Anna of Denmark', in *Readings in Renaissance Women's Drama: Criticism, History, and Performance, 1594–1998*, ed. Susan P. Cerasano and Marion Wynne-Davies, (London, 1998) pp.47–59.

Barroll, J. Leeds, 'The Court of the First Stuart Queen', in *The Mental World of the Jacobean Court*, ed. Linda Levy Peck (Cambridge, 1991) pp.191–208.

Bassett, D.K., 'English Trade in the Far East, 1623–1684', *Journal of the Royal Asiatic Society*, (1960), pp.32–47.

Baumer, Franklin Le Van, 'The Church of England and the Common Corps of Christendom', *The Journal of Modern History* 16.1 (1944) pp.1–21.

Baumer Franklin Le Van, 'The Conception of Christendom in Renaissance England', *Journal of the History of Ideas*, 6.2 (1945), pp.131–56.

Baumer, Franklin Le Van, 'England, the Turk, and the Common Corps of Christendom', *The American Historical Review* 50.1 (1944) pp.26–48.

Bellamy, Martin, *Christian IV and his Navy: A Political and Administrative History of the Danish Navy 1596–1648* (Boston, 2006).

Bellany, Alastair, and Thomas Cogswell, *The Murder of King James* (New Haven, CT, 2015).

Bernhard, Virginia, 'Bermuda and Virginia in the Seventeenth Century: A Comparative View', *Journal of Social History*, 19 (1985), pp.57–70.

Bevington, David, and Peter Holbrook (eds.), *The Politics of the Stuart Court Masque* (Cambridge, 1998).

Bindoff, S.T., 'The Stuarts and their Style', *English Historical Review*, 60.237 (1945) pp.208–11.

Brenner, Robert, *Merchants and Revolution: Commercial Change, Political Conflict, and London's Overseas Traders, 1550–1653* (Cambridge, 1993).

Brown, Keith M., 'The Scottish Aristocracy, Anglicization and the Court, 1603–38', *The Historical Journal*, 36 (1993) pp.543–76.

Burgess, Walter H., *John Robinson, Past of the Pilgrim Fathers, a study of his life and times* (London, 1920).

Boys, Jayne E.E. *London's News Press and the Thirty Years War* (Cambridge, 2014).

Carroll, Robert, and Stephen Prickett (eds.) *The Bible: Authorized King James Version* (Oxford, 1998).

Carter, Charles Howard, 'Gondomar: Ambassador to James I', *The Historical Journal* 7.2 (1964) pp.189–208.

Carter, Charles Howard, *The Secret Diplomacy of the Habsburgs, 1598–1625* (New York, 1964).

Canny, Nicholas P., 'The Ideology of English Colonization: From Ireland to America,' *William and Mary Quarterly* 30.3 (October 1973) pp.575–98.

Canny, Nicholas P., *Kingdom and Colony: Ireland in the Atlantic World 1560–1800* (Baltimore, 1988).

Canny, Nicholas P. (ed.), *The Origins of Empire: British Overseas Enterprise to the Close of the Seventeenth Century*, (Oxford, 1998).

Chaudhuri, K.N., *The English East India Company: The Study of an Early Joint-Stock Company 1600–1640* (London, 1965).

Cheyney, Edward P., 'England and Denmark in the Later Days of Queen Elizabeth', *The Journal of Modern History*, 1.1 (1929), pp.9–39.

Clark, G.N., *The Colonial Conferences between England and the Netherlands in 1613 and 1615* (Leyden, 1951).

Clegg, Cyndia S., *Press Censorship in Jacobean England* (Cambridge, 2001).

Clulow, Adam, 'Commemorating Failure: The Four Hundredth Anniversary of England's Trading Outpost in Japan', *Monumenta Nipponica*, 68.2 (2013) pp.207–31.

Clulow, Adam, 'From Global Entrepôt to Early Modern Domain: Hirado, 1609–1641', *Monumenta Nipponica* 65.1 (2010) pp.1–35.

Clulow, Adam, and Tristan Mostert (eds.). *The Dutch and English East India Companies: Diplomacy, Trade and Violence in Early Modern Asia* (Amsterdam, 2018).

Coast, David, *News and Rumour in Jacobean England: Information, Court Politics and Diplomacy, 1618–1625* (Manchester, 2014).

Cogswell, Thomas, *The Blessed Revolution: English Politics and the Coming of War, 1621–1624* (Cambridge, 1989).

Cogswell, Thomas, 'England and the Spanish Match', in *Conflict in Early Stuart England: Studies in Religion and Politics 1603–1642*, ed. Richard Cust and Ann Hughes (London, 1989) pp.107–33.

Cogswell, Thomas, *James I: The Phoenix King* (London, 2017).

Cogswell, Thomas, 'A Low Road to Extinction? Supply and Redress of Grievances in the Parliaments of the 1620s', *The Historical Journal*, 33.2 (1990) pp.283–303.

Cogswell, Thomas, 'Phaeton's Chariot: The Parliament-Men and the Continental Crisis in 1621', in *The Political World of Thomas Wentworth, Earl of Strafford, 1621–1641*, ed. J.F. Merritt (Cambridge, 1996) pp.24–46.

Cogswell, Thomas, Richard Cust and Peter Lake (eds.), *Politics, Religion and Popularity in Early Stuart Britain* (Cambridge, 2002).

Cogswell, Thomas, 'Thomas Middleton and the Court, 1624: A Game at Chess in Context', *Huntington Library Quarterly*, 47.4 (1984) pp.273–88.

Cooper, Michael, 'The Second Englishman in Japan: The Trials and Travails of Richard Cocks, 1613–1624', *Transactions of the Asiatic Society of Japan* 17 (1982) pp.121–59.

Cornelius, Michael G., *John Donne and the Metaphysical Poets* (London, 2008).

Cramsie, John, 'Commercial Projects and the Fiscal Policy of James VI and I', *The Historical Journal*, 43 (2000) pp.345–64.

Cramsie, John, *Kingship and Crown Finance under James VI and I, 1603–1625* (Woodbridge, CT, 2002).

Craven, Wesley Frank, *Dissolution of the Virginia Company: The Failure of a Colonial Experiment* (Gloucester, MA, 1964).

Croft, Pauline, *King James* (New York, 2003).

Croft, Pauline, 'Rex Pacificus, Robert Cecil, and the 1604 Peace with Spain', in *The Accession of James I: Historical and Cultural Consequences*, ed. Glenn Burgess, Rowland Wymer and Jason Lawrence (New York, 2006) pp. 140–54.

Croft, Pauline, 'Serving the Archduke: Robert Cecil's Management of the Parliamentary Session of 1606', *Historical Research*, 64 (1991) pp.289–304.

Croft, Pauline, 'Trading with the Enemy, 1585–1604', *Historical Journal*, 32 (1989), pp.281–302.

Crouch, Patricia, 'Patronage and Competing Visions of Virginia in George Chapman's 'The Memorable Masque' (1613)', *English Literary Renaissance* 40.3 (2010) pp.393–426.

Cross, Robert, 'Pretense and Perception in the Spanish Match, or History in a Fake Beard', *Journal of Interdisciplinary History* 37.4 (2007) pp.563–83.

Curran, Kevin, 'James I and Fictional Authority at the Palatine Wedding Celebrations', *Renaissance Studies* 20.1 (2006) pp.51–67.

Cust, Richard, 'News and Politics in Early Seventeenth-Century England', *Past and Present* 112 (1986) pp.60–90.

Das, Nandini, *Courting India: Seventeenth-Century England, Mughal India, and the Origins of Empire* (London, 2003).

Das, Nandini, 'Encounter as Process: England and Japan in the Sixteenth Century', *Renaissance Quarterly*, 69 (2016), pp.1343–68.

Das, Nandini, *Sir Thomas Roe: Eyewitness to a Changing World* (London, 2018) pp.1–20.

Doelman, James, '"A King of Thine Own Heart": The English Reception of King James VI and I's *Basilikon Doron*', *The Seventeenth Century* 9 (1994), pp.1–9.

Doran Susan, *From Tudor to Stuart: The Regime Change from Elizabeth I to James I* (Oxford, 2024).

Draper, J.W., 'Shakespeare and Muscovy', *The Slavonic and East European Review*, 33.80 (1954) pp.217–21.

Dunning, Chester S.L., 'James I, the Russia Company, and the Plan to Establish a Protectorate over North Russia', *Albion: A Quarterly Journal Concerned with British Studies*, 21.2 (1989), pp.206–26.

Dunning, Chester S.L., 'A Letter to James I Concerning the English Plan for Military Intervention in Russia', *The Slavonic and East European Review* 67.1 (1989), pp.94–108.

Dunning, Chester S.L., 'A Singular Affection for Russia: Why King James offered to intervene in the time of troubles', *Russian History*, 34.1 (2007) pp.277–302.

Dutton, Richard, 'Hamlet and Succession', in *Doubtful and Dangerous: The Question of Succession in Late Elizabethan England* (Manchester, 2014) pp.173–91.

Dutton, Richard (ed.), *Jacobean Civic Pageants* (Keele, 1995).

Farrington, Anthony, *Trading Places: the East India Company and Asia, 1600–1834* (London, 2002).

Fedorowicz, J.K., *England's Baltic Trade in the Early Seventeenth Century* (Cambridge, 1980).

Ferrier, R.W., 'An English View of Persian Trade in 1618: Reports from the Merchants Edward Pettus and Thomas Barker', *Journal of the Economic and Social History of the Orient* 19.2 (1976) pp.182–214.

Ferrier, R.W., 'The Armenians and the East India Company in Persia in the Seventeenth and Early Eighteenth Centuries', *The Economic History Review*, 26.1 (1973), pp.38–62.

Ferrier, R.W., 'The European Diplomacy of Shāh 'Abbās I and the First Persian Embassy to England', *Iran*, 11(1973) pp.75–92.

Ferrier, R.W. 'The Terms and Conditions under Which English Trade Was Transacted with Ṣafavid Persia', *Bulletin of the School of Oriental and African Studies, University of London*, 49.1 (1986) pp.48–66.

Field, Jemma, '"Orderinge Things Accordinge to his Majesties Comaundment": The Funeral of the Stuart Queen Consort Anna of Denmark', *Women's History Review* 30:5 (2021) pp.835–55.

Fincham, Kenneth, and Peter Lake, 'The Ecclesiastical Policy of King James I', *Journal of British Studies* 24 (1985) pp.169–207.

Foster, William, *England's Quest of Eastern Trade* (London, 1933).

Fraser, Sarah, *The Prince Who Would be King: The Life and Death of Henry Stuart* (London, 2017).

Gajda, Alexandra, 'Debating War and Peace in Late Elizabethan England', *The Historical Journal* 52 (2009) pp.851–78.

Gajda, Alexandra, 'War, Peace and Commerce and the Treaty of London (1604)', *Historical Research*, 96.274 (2023) pp.459–72.

Galloway, Bruce, *The Union of England and Scotland, 1603–1608* (Edinburgh, 1986).

Gardiner, Samuel R., *History of England from the Accession of James I to the Outbreak of the Civil War 1603–1642* (London, 1883).

Gaskill, Malcolm, *Between Two Worlds: How the English Became Americans* (Oxford, 2014).

Games, Alison, 'Violence on the Fringes: the Virginia (1622) and Amboyna (1623) Massacres', *History* (2014) pp.505–29.

Games, Alison, *The Web of Empire: English Cosmopolitans in an Age of Expansion, 1560–1660* (Oxford, 2008).

Goldring, Elizabeth, '"So iust a sorrowe so well expressed": Henry, Prince of Wales and the Art of Commemoration', in T. Wilks (ed.), *Prince Henry Revived: Image and Exemplarity in Early Modern England* (London, 2007) pp.280–300

Grosjean, Alexia, *An Unofficial Alliance: Scotland and Sweden 1569–1654* (Leiden, 2003).

Hatch, Charles E., 'Mulberry Trees and Silkworms: Sericulture in Early Virginia', *The Virginia Magazine of History and Biography* 65 (1957).

Hood, Gervase, 'A Netherlandic Triumphal Arch for James I', in Susan Roach (ed.), *Across the Narrow Seas: Studies in the History and Bibliography of Britan and the Low Countries.* Presented to Amma E.C. Simoni (London, 1991) pp.67–82.

Horning, Audrey, *Ireland in the Virginian Sea* (Chapel Hill, NC, 2013).

Howarth, David, *Adventurers: The Improbable Rise of the East India Company* (London, 2023).

Hunt, Alice, 'The Bright Star of the North: James I and his English Coronation', *Medieval English Theatre*, 38 (2016) pp.22–37.

Ickes, Charlotte, 'The Sartorial and the Skin: Portraits of Pocahontas and Allegories of English Empire', *American Art* 29.1 (2015), pp.82–105.

Ittersum, Martine Julia van, 'Debating Natural Law in the Banda Islands: A Case Study in Anglo-Dutch Imperial Competition in the East Indies, 1609–1621', *History of European Ideas*, 42:4 (2016) pp.459–501.

Jack, Sybil M., '"A Pattern for a King's Inauguration": The Coronation of James I in England', *Parergon*, 21 (2004) pp.67–91.

Jackson, Clare, *Devil-Land: England Under Siege, 1588–1688* (London, 2021).

Johnson, Robert C, 'The Lotteries of the Virginia Company, 1612–1621', *The Virginia Magazine of History and Biography*, 74.3 (1966) pp.259–92.

Keay, John, *The Honourable Company: A History of the English East India Company* (London, 1991).

Kishlansky, Mark, *A Monarchy Transformed: Britain 1603–1714* (London, 1996).

Kupperman, Karen Ordahl, 'The Founding Years of Virginia – and the United States', *The Virginia Magazine of History and Biography*, 104 (1996) pp.103–12

Kupperman, Karen Ordahl, *Roanoke: The Abandoned Colony*, 2nd ed. (Baltimore, MD, 2007)

Lake, Peter, 'The King (The Queen) and the Jesuit: James Stuart's True Law of Free Monarchies in Context/s', *Transactions of the Royal Historical Society* 14 (2004) pp.243–60.

Lee, M., *James I and Henri IV: An Essay in Foreign Policy, 1603–1610* (Urbana, IL, 1970).

Lee, Maurice, *Great Britain's Solomon: James VI and I in His Three Kingdoms* (Urbana, IL, 1990).

Lee Jr, Maurice, 'James VI's "Government of Scotland after 1603"', *The Scottish Historical Review*, 55 (1976) pp.41–53.

Levack, Brian P., *The Formation of the British State: England, Scotland, and the Union, 1603–1707*. (Oxford, 1987).

Levack, Brian P., 'Towards a More Perfect Union: England, Scotland, and the Constitution', in Barbara C. Malament (ed.) *After the Reformation: Essays in Honor of J.H. Hexter* (Philadelphia, PA, 1980).

Lindley, David, 'Campion's "Lord Hay's Masque" and Anglo-Scottish Union', *Huntington Library Quarterly*, 43.1 (Winter 1979) pp.1–11.

Lockhart, Paul Douglas, *Denmark, 1513–1660: The Rise and Decline of a Renaissance Monarchy* (Oxford, 2007).

Lockhart, Paul Douglas, 'Denmark and the Empire: A Reassessment of Danish Foreign Policy under King Christian IV', *Scandinavian Studies* 64.3 (Summer 1992) pp.390–416.

Lockyer, Roger, *Buckingham: The Life and Political Career of George Villiers, First Duke of Buckingham, 1592–1628* (London, 1981).

Lockyer, Roger, *James VI and I* (London, 1998).

Loomie, Albert J, 'King James I's Catholic Consort', *The Huntington Library Quarterly* 34 (1971) pp.303–16.

Loomie, Albert J., 'Philip III and the Stuart Succession in England, 1600–1603', *Revue belge de philologie et d'histoire* 43 (1965) pp.492–514.

Loth, Vincent C., 'Armed Incidents and Unpaid Bills: Anglo-Dutch Rivalry in the Banda Islands in the Seventeenth Century', *Modern Asian Studies* 29.4 (1995) pp.705–40.

Lubimenko, Inna, 'A Project for the Acquisition of Russia by James I', *The English Historical Review*, 29.114 (April 1914) pp.246–56.

MacLeod, Catherine (ed.), *The Lost Prince: The Life and Death of Henry Stuart* (London, 2012).

Malcolm, Noel, 'Hobbes, Sandys and the Virginia Company', *The Historical Journal* 24.2 (1981) pp.297–321.

Marsh, Ben, *Unravelled Dreams: Silk and the Atlantic World 1500–1840* (Cambridge, 2020).

Mason, Roger, 'Debating Britain in Seventeenth-Century Scotland: Multiple Monarchy and Scottish Sovereignty', *Journal of Scottish Historical Studies*, 35 (2015) pp.1–24.

Mason, Roger A., ed., *Scots and Britons: Scottish Political Thought and the Union of 1603* (Cambridge, 1994).

Massarella, Derek, 'James I and Japan', *Monumenta Nipponica* 38.4 (1983) pp.377–86.

Massarella, Derek, '"Ticklish Points": The English East India Company and Japan, 1621', *Journal of the Royal Asiatic Society* 11.1 (2001) pp.43–50.

Massarella, Derek, *A World Elsewhere: Europe's Encounter with Japan in the Sixteenth and Seventeenth Centuries* (London, 1990).

Meikle, Maureen M., 'A Meddlesome Princess: Anna of Denmark and Scottish Court Politics, 1589–1603', in Julian Goodare and Michael Lynch (eds.), *The Reign of James VI* (Edinburgh, 2008) pp.126–41.

Millstone, Noah, 'Sir Robert Cotton, Manuscript Pamphleteering, and the Making of Jacobean Kingship during the Short Peace, ca. 1609–1613', *Journal of British Studies* 62.1 (2023) pp.134–160.

Mishra, Rupali, *A Business of State: Commerce, Politics, and the Birth of the East India Company* (Cambridge, MA, 2018)

Mishra, Rupali, 'Diplomacy at the Edge: Split Interests in the Roe Embassy to the Mughal Court', *Journal of British Studies* 53.1 (2014) pp.5–28.

Murdoch, Steve, *Britain, Denmark-Norway and the House of Stuart, 1603–1660: A Diplomatic and Military Analysis* (East Linton, 2000).

Murdoch, Steve, 'Diplomacy in Transition: Stuart-British Diplomacy in Northern Europe, 1603–1618', in *Ships, Guns and Bibles in the North Sea and the Baltic States, c. 1350–c. 1700*, ed. Allan I. Macinnes, Thomas Riis and Frederik Pedersen (East Linton, 2000), pp.93–114.

Murdoch, Steve, 'James VI and the Formation of a Scottish-British Military Identity', in *Fighting for Identity: Scottish Military Experience, c. 1550–1900*, ed. Steve Murdoch and A. Mackillop (Leiden, 2002), pp.3–31.

Murdoch, Steve, 'Stolbovo in Perspective: Jacobean Diplomacy in the Baltic Region, 1589–1618', in *Sweden, Russia, and the 1617 Peace of Stolbovo*, ed. Arne Jonsson and Arseneii Vertushko-Kalevich (Turnhout, Belgium, 2023) pp.47–66.

Neill, Edward D., *History of the Virginia Company of London* (Albany, NY, 1869).

Newton, Diana, *The Making of the Jacobean Regime: James VI and I and the Government of England, 1603–1605* (Woodbridge, CT, 2005).

Nicholls, Mark, 'Strategy and Motivation in the Gunpowder Plot', *The Historical Journal* 50.4 (2007) pp.787–807.

Nicolson, Adam, *When God Spoke English: The Making of the King James Bible* (London, 2003).

Norbrook, David, '"The Masque of Truth ": Court Entertainments and International Protestant Politics in the Early Stuart Period', *Seventeenth Century* 1.2 (July 1986) pp.81–110.

O'Callaghan, Michelle, 'Performing Politics: The Circulation of the "Parliament Fart"', *Huntington Library Quarterly*, 69 (2006) pp.121–38.

Ogborn, Miles, *Global Lives: Britain and the World, 1550–1800* (Cambridge, 2008).

Ohlmeyer, Jane H., 'A Laboratory for Empire?: Early Modern Ireland and English Imperialism', in Kevin Kenny (ed.), *Ireland and the British Empire* (Oxford, 2004) pp.26–60.

Ohlmeyer, Jane H., 'Seventeenth Century Ireland and the New British and Atlantic Histories', *The American Historical Review*, 104 (1999) pp.446–62.

Pagnini, C., 'Henry Stuart, "The Rising Sun of England": The Creation of a Prince of Wales (June 1610)', *Drammaturgia*, 16 (2020) pp.261–69.

Parker, Geoffrey and Simon Adams (eds.) *The Thirty Years' War*, 2nd ed. (New York, 1997).

Parker, Geoffrey, (ed.), *The Thirty Years' War* (London, 1987).

Parry, Graham, *The Golden Age Restor'd: The Culture of the Stuart Court, 1603–42* (Cambridge, 1981).

Patterson, W.B., *James VI and I and the Reunion of Christendom* (Cambridge, 1997).

Peacock, John, 'Inigo Jones Catafalque for James I', *Architectural History* 25 (1982) pp.1–135.

Peck, Linda Levy, *Court Patronage and Corruption in Early Stuart England* (Cambridge, 1993).

Peck, Linda Levy, *Northampton: Patronage and Policy at the Court of James I* (London, 1982).

Peck, Linda Levy, ed., *The Mental World of the Jacobean Court* (Cambridge, 1991).

Phipps, Geraldine M., *Sir John Merrick, English Merchant-Diplomat in Seventeenth-Century Russia* (Newtonville, MA, 1983).

Pollnitz, Aysha, *Princely Education in Early Modern Britain* (Cambridge, 2015).

Pugh, T.B., 'A Portrait of Queen Anne of Denmark at Parham Park, Sussex', *The Seventeenth Century*, 8.2 (1993) pp.167–80.

Pursell, Brennan C, 'The End of the Spanish Match', *The Historical Journal* 45.4 (2002) pp.699–726.

Pursell, Brennan C , 'James I, Gondomar and the Dissolution of the Parliament of 1621', *History* 85 (2000) pp.428–45.

Pursell, Brennan C., 'War or Peace? Jacobean Politics and the Parliament of 1621', in *Parliament, Politics and Elections 1604–1648*, ed. Chris R. Kyle (Cambridge, 2001) pp.149–78.

Pursell, Brennan C., *The Winter King: Frederick V of the Palatinate and the Coming of the Thirty Years' War* (Aldershot, 2003).

Price, Polly, 'Natural Law and Birthright Citizenship in Calvin's Case (1608)', *Yale Journal of Law and the Humanities*, 9.1 (1997) pp.73–145.

Questier, Michael C., *Dynastic Politics and the British Reformations, 1558–1630* (Oxford, 2019).

Questier, Michael (ed.), *Stuart Dynastic Policy and Religious Politics 1621–1625* (Cambridge, 2009).

Quinn, David Beers, *Set Fair For Roanoke: Voyages and Colonies, 1584–1606* (London, 1985).

Rabb, Theodore K., 'Sir Edwin Sandys and the Parliament of 1604', *The American Historical Review* 69.3 (1964) pp.646–7.

Razzari, D., 'Through the Backdoor: An Overview of the English East India Company's Rise and Fall in Safavid Iran, 1616–40', *Iranian Studies* 52.3–4 (2019) pp.485–511.

Redworth, Glyn, 'Of Pimps and Princes: Three Unpublished Letters from James I and the Prince of Wales relating to the Spanish Match', *Historical Journal*, 37 (1994) pp.401–9.

Redworth, Glyn, *The Prince & the Infanta: The Cultural Politics of the Spanish Match* (London, 2004).

Rees, Graham, and Maria Wakely, *Publishing, Politics, and Culture: The King's Printers in the Reign of James VI and I* (Oxford, 2009).

Robertson, Karen, 'Pocahontas at the Masque', *Signs* 21.3 (Spring 1996) pp.551–83.

Roper, L.H., *Advancing Empire: English Interests and Overseas Expansion, 1613–1688* (Cambridge, 2017).

Ruigh, R.E., *The Parliament of 1624: Politics and Foreign Policy* (Cambridge, MA, 1971).

Russell, Conrad, *The Crisis of Parliaments: English History 1509–1660* (Oxford, 1971).

Russell, Conrad, 'The Foreign Policy Debate in the House of Commons in 1621', *Historical Journal*, 20 (1977) pp.289–309.

Russell, Conrad, *Parliaments and English Politics 1621–1629* (Oxford, 1982).

Rypins, Stanley, 'The Printing of "Basilikòn Dôron", 1603', *The Papers of the Bibliographical Society of America*, 64.4 (1970) pp.393–417.

Samson, Alexander (ed.), *The Spanish Match: Prince Charles's Journey to Madrid, 1623* (Aldershot, 2006).

Schneider, Christian, 'A Kingdom for a Catholic? Pope Clement VIII, King James VI/I, and the English Succession in International Diplomacy (1592–1605)', *The International History Review* 37.1 (2015) pp.119–41.

Screech, Timon, 'The English and the Control of Christianity in the Early Edo Period', *Japan Review* 24 (2012) pp.3–40.

Screech, Timon, *The Shogun's Silver Telescope: God, Art, and Money in the English Quest for Japan, 1600–1625* (Oxford, 2020).

Seton, Walter, 'The Early Years of Henry Frederick, Prince of Wales, and Charles, Duke of Albany [Charles I]', *Scottish Historical Review* 13.52 (1916) pp.366–79.

Shapiro, James, *1606: William Shakespeare and the Year of Lear* (London, 2015).

Sharpe, Kevin, *Image Wars: Promoting King and Commonwealths in England, 1603–1660* (London, 2010).

Sharpe, Kevin, ed., *Faction and Parliament: Essays on Early Stuart History* (London, 1978).

Siochrú, Micheál Ó, and Eamonn Ciardha, *The Plantation of Ulster: Ideology and Practice* (Manchester, 2012).

Slack, Paul, *The Invention of Improvement: Information and Material Progress in Seventeenth Century England* (Oxford, 2014).

Sommerville, J.P., *Jacobean Political Thought and the Controversy over the Oath of Allegiance* (Cambridge, 1981).

Sommerville, J.P., 'James I and the Divine Right of Kings: English Politics and Continental Theory', in *The Mental World of the Jacobean Court*, ed. Linda Levy Peck (Cambridge, 1991) pp.55–70.

Smart, Sara, and Mara R. Wade (eds.), *The Palatine Wedding of 1613: Protestant Alliance and Court Festival* (Wiesbaden, 2013).

Smith, Edmund, *Merchants: The Community That Shapes England's Trade and Empire, 1550–1650* (London, 2021).

Smuts, Malcolm, 'Cultural Diversity and Cultural Change at the Court of James I', in *The Mental World of the Jacobean Court*, ed. Linda Levy Peck (Cambridge, 1991) pp.99–112

Smuts, Malcolm, 'The Making of Rex Pacificus: James VI and I and the Problem of Peace in an Age of Religious War', in *Royal Subjects: Essays on the Writings of James VI and I*, ed. Daniel Fischlin and Mark Fortier, (Detroit, 2002) pp.371–87

Smuts, Malcolm R., *Political Culture, the State, and the Problem of Religious War in Britain and Ireland, 1578–1625* (Oxford, 2023).

Steinmann, Linda K., 'Shah 'Abbas and the Royal Silk Trade 1599–1629', *Bulletin (British Society for Middle Eastern Studies)* 14.1 (1987) pp.68–74

Stern, Philip J., *The Company-State: Corporate Sovereignty and the Early Modern Foundations of the British Empire in India* (Oxford, 2011).

Stewart, Alan, *The Cradle King: A Life of James VI & I* (London, 2003).

Strong, Roy, *Henry, Prince of Wales and England's Lost Renaissance* (London, 1986).

Stoye, John, *English Travellers Abroad, 1604–166: Their Influence on English Society and Politics* (London, 1989).

Sullivan, Mary, *Court Masques of James I: Their Influence on Shakespeare and the Public Theaters* (New York, 1913).

Taylor, Harland, 'Price Revolution or Price Revision? The English and Spanish Trade after 1604', *Renaissance and Modern Studies* 12 (1968) pp.5–32.

Thirsk, Joan, *Economic Policy and Projects: The Development of a Consumer Society in Early Modern England* (Oxford, 1978).

Thornton, John, 'The African Experience of the "20. and Odd Negroes" Arriving in Virginia in 1619', *The William and Mary Quarterly*, 55.3 (1998) pp.421–34.

Thrush, Andrew, 'The Personal Rule of James I, 1611–1620', in *Politics, Religion and Popularity in Early Stuart Britain: Essays in Honour of Conrad Russell*, ed. Thomas Cogswell, Richard Cust and Peter Lake, (Cambridge, 2002) pp.84–102.

Vaughan, Alden T., 'Blacks in Virginia: A Note on the First Decade', *The William and Mary Quarterly* 29.3 (1973) pp.469–78.

Veevers, David, *The Great Defiance: How the World Took On the British Empire* (London, 2004).

Wagner, Joseph, 'The First "British" Colony in the Americas: Inter-kingdom Cooperation and Stuart-British Ideology in the Colonisation of Newfoundland, 1616–1640', *Britain and the World* 15.1 (2002) pp.1–23.

Wagner, Joseph, 'The Scottish East India Company of 1617: Patronage, Commercial Rivalry, and the Union of the Crowns', *Journal of British Studies*, 59.3 (2020) pp.582–607.

Walne, Peter, 'The Collections for Henrico College, 1616–1618', *The Virginia Magazine of History and Biography*, 80.3 (1972) pp.259–66

Waurechen, Sarah, 'Imagined Polities, Failed Dreams, and the Beginnings of an Unacknowledged Britain: English Responses to James VI and I's Vision of Perfect Union', *Journal of British Studies* 52.3 (2013) pp.575–96.

White, Jason C., *Militant Protestantism and British Identity, 1603–1642* (Abingdon, 2015).

White, Jason C., 'Militant Protestants: British Identity in the Jacobean Period, 1603–1625', *History* 94.314 (2009) pp.154–75.

White, Stephen D., *Sir Edward Coke and 'The Grievances of the Commonwealth', 1621–1628* (Chapel Hill, NC, 1979).

Wilks, Timothy (ed.), *Prince Henry Revived: Image and Exemplarity in Early Modern England* (London, 2007).

Williams, Ethel Carleton, *Anne of Denmark: Wife of James VI of Scotland: James I of England* (London, 1970).

Williamson, J.W., *The Myth of the Conqueror Prince Henry Stuart: A Study of 17th Century Personation* (New York, 1978).

Willson, David Harris, *King James VI and I* (London, 1956).

Working, Lauren, 'Locating Colonization at the Jacobean Inns of Court', *The Historical Journal*, 61 (2018) pp.29–51.

Working, Lauren, *The Making of an Imperial Polity: Civility and America in the Jacobean Metropolis* (Cambridge, 2020).

Wormald, Jenny, 'Gunpowder, Treason, and Scots', *The Journal of British Studies* 24.2 (April 1985) pp.141–168.

Wormald, Jenny, 'James VI and I, Basilikon Doron and the Trew Law of Free Monarchies: The Scottish Context and the English Translation', in *The Mental World of the Jacobean Court*, ed. Linda Levy Peck (Cambridge, 1991) pp.36–54.

Wormald, Jenny, 'James VI, James I and the Identity of Britain', in Brendan Bradshaw and John Morrill (eds.), *The British Problem, c. 1534–1707: State Formation in the Atlantic Archipelago* (London, 1996), pp.148–71.

Wormald, Jenny, 'A Very British Problem: The Stuart Crown and the Plantation of Ulster', *History Ireland*, 17 (2009) pp.20–23.

Wright, Louis B., 'Henry Robarts: Patriotic Propagandist and Novelist', *Studies in Philology* 29 (1932) pp.176–99.

Wright, Louis B., 'Propaganda against James I's "Appeasement" of Spain', *The Huntington Library Quarterly* 6.2 (February 1943) pp.149–72.

Zaller, Robert, *The Parliament of 1621: A Study in Constitutional Conflict* (Berkeley, 1971)

Unpublished Secondary Sources

Adams, Simon, 'The Protestant Cause: Religious Alliance with the West European Calvinist Communities as a Political Issue in England, 1585–1630', unpublished DPhil dissertation, University of Oxford (1973)

Al-Qasimi, Sultan bin Muhammad, 'Power Struggles and Trade in the Gulf, 1620–1680', unpublished PhD thesis, University of Durham (1999)

Caldari, Valentina, 'The End of the Anglo-Spanish Match in Global Context, 1617–1624', unpublished PhD thesis, University of Kent (2015)

Calgano, Rebecca A., 'Publishing the Stuarts: Occasional Literature and Politics from 1603 to 1625', unpublished PhD thesis, University of Columbia (2011)

Cross, Robert, 'To Counterbalance the World: England, Spain, and Peace in the early Seventeenth Century', PhD, University of Princeton (2012)

Fry, Cynthia, 'Diplomacy and Deception: King James VI of Scotland's Foreign Relations with Europe (c.1584–1603)', unpublished PhD thesis, University of St Andrews (2014)

Juhala, Amy L., 'The Household and Court of King James VI', unpublished PhD thesis, University of Edinburgh (2000)

Wilks, Thomas, 'The Court Culture of Prince Henry and his Circle 1603–1613', unpublished DPhil dissertation, University of Oxford (1987)

INDEX

100 YEARS of PUBLISHING

—◇—

Harold K. Guinzburg and George S. Oppenheimer founded Viking in 1925 with the intention of publishing books "with some claim to permanent importance rather than ephemeral popular interest." After merging with B. W. Huebsch, a small publisher with a distinguished catalog, Viking enjoyed almost fifty years of literary and commercial success before merging with Penguin Books in 1975.

Now an imprint of Penguin Random House, Viking specializes in bringing extraordinary works of fiction and nonfiction to a vast readership. In 2025, we celebrate one hundred years of excellence in publishing. Our centennial colophon features the original logo for Viking, created by the renowned American illustrator Rockwell Kent: a Viking ship that evokes enterprise, adventure, and exploration, ideas that inspired the imprint's name at its founding and continue to inspire us.

—◇—

For more information on Viking's history, authors, and books, please visit penguin.com/viking.